JOURNEY

JOURNEY

Memoirs of an Air Force Chief of Staff

GENERAL (RET.) NORTY SCHWARTZ
Chief of Staff United States Air Force

and SUZIE SCHWARTZ

with RONALD LEVINSON

Foreword by LEON PANETTA
Former Secretary of Defense, Director of the CIA,
and White House Chief of Staff

Skyhorse Publishing

Skyhorse Publishing books may be purchased in bulk at special discounts for sales promotion, corporate gifts, fund-raising, or educational purposes. Special editions can also be created to specifications. For details, contact the Special Sales Department, Skyhorse Publishing, 307 West 36th Street, 11th Floor, New York, NY 10018 or info@skyhorsepublishing.com.

Skyhorse® and Skyhorse Publishing® are registered trademarks of Skyhorse Publishing, Inc.®, a Delaware corporation.

Visit our website at www.skyhorsepublishing.com.

10 9 8 7 6 5 4 3 2 1

Library of Congress Cataloging-in-Publication Data is available on file.

Cover design by Rain Saukas

ISBN: 978-1-5107-1033-7
Ebook ISBN: 978-1-5107-1034-4

Printed in the United States of America

Dedicated to Suzie, who made this journey possible,
and all those members of the Armed Forces and their families
with whom we had the extraordinary privilege to serve.

Feathers shall raise men even as they do birds towards heaven.
That is by letters written with their quills.

—LEONARDO DA VINCI

The men and women [of our Air Force] are a national asset, and together we will recommit ourselves to our core values and uphold the highest standards of excellence that have made our Air Force the best in the world. Our nation deserves nothing less. *We will be ready if called upon.*

—GENERAL NORTY SCHWARTZ
upon nomination for Chief of Staff
July 22, 2008

USAF Photo

CONTENTS

The greatest book has not been written, the fastest train has not been built, the greatest painting has not been dreamed. Go to, young man, go to.

—JACK McCALMONT
USAF Academy Class of 1973

ACKNOWLEDGMENTS

Suzie and I started this project with the thought that some of what happened to us might be of modest historical significance, but it is also a story of two American kids, one from Arkansas, one from New Jersey, drawn together not by common experience, family or faith, but by respect for one another and a shared appreciation for the nobility of public service. We hope that our story illuminates the possibilities that our country offers to those who aspire . . . and care.

We would never have completed the effort without the dogged assistance of coauthor Ron Levinson; and all those working behind the scenes, including our agent, Dan Strone, editors Chris Evans and Joe Craig, and editorial assistant Mike Campbell. Nor would we have the had success we enjoyed without wonderful friends and mentors: Gene Reinartz, Al and Barbara Navas, Mort Freedman, Al Peck, Alan Gropman, John Shaud, Dick and Annie Potter, Jim and Diane Hobson, Mike and Jane Ryan, Pete and Cindy Schoomaker, Dick and Mary Jo Myers, Pete and Lynne Pace, Mike and Victoria Carns, Joe and Dede Ralston, Don and Joyce Rumsfeld, Bob and Becky Gates, Leon and Sylvia Panetta, Mike and Gail Donley, Mike and Deborah Mullen, George and Sheila Casey, Gary and Ellen Roughead, Jim and Annette Conway, and John and Jan Ellsworth. And from my youth: Bob and Pam Munson, Steve and Leslie Lorenz, Frank and Nancy Klotz, Mike and Sandra Mosier, Skip and Joanne Sanders, Ron and Mary Scott, and Jim Green. To each of them, and so many others, Suzie and I express our admiration and gratitude.

The stories in this book reflect my best recollection of events. Some names, locations, occupations, physical properties, and identifying characteristics have been intentionally changed to protect the privacy of those depicted. Other alterations are unintentional, as memory fades.

Aristotle reminds us that "memory is the scribe of the soul," but the older I get, the more I realize that the ink is not indelible. I've done my best to relay events in a way that evokes the feeling and meaning of what was said and what occurred; in all instances, the essence of the dialogue and events described are as accurate as memory allows.

Shortly after I was sworn in as Chief, I celebrated Air Force Week with a speech at Bellevue University in Bellevue, Nebraska. The words I shared that day still resonate within me, cutting to the core of why I embarked on this journey and how much I believe that the future of our great nation depends on others being similarly inspired to do so. To those who have, and those who will, I dedicate this book.

We are going to need young men and women to continue to step forward and say "Send me"—and that applies to every branch of our armed forces. We need people who know that accountability, character, and leadership are the only answers for the demands that we face. We need people who know that the blessings we enjoy come at a price. There are, indeed, some things worth fighting for and they are well worth defending for those who will follow us. We need people who know that the future of a free people will be written by people who serve. And those with honor, integrity, and creativity will justify America's confidence in us. It all depends on what we do now . . . and in the days to come.

FOREWORD
by Leon Panetta

Norty is, I believe, one of the finest officers I've had the honor to work with. He came at a very critical time in the history of the Air Force, and he responded with incredible leadership in making the Air Force an essential, credible, and capable partner in our national defense.

As a young man, he understood the importance of hard work and dedication to his country, values that led to his decision to serve this nation in uniform. These values have guided him through a distinguished career in both the conventional and special operations communities.

As the 19th Air Force chief of staff, Norty has led the Air Force with tremendous judgment, vision, and honesty. Even though he was planning to retire after his time at TRANSCOM, when he was called upon to help the institution he loves, he accepted the mission. And he always has.

Norty led the Air Force during a period of intense operational demands and evolving strategic and fiscal challenges. He quickly moved to restore confidence in our nuclear enterprise—an absolutely vital component of our national security.

[He was at the helm for] the Libya operation, where the Air Force flew over eight thousand sorties—conducting airstrikes and providing ISR (Intelligence, Surveillance, and Reconnaissance) and air refueling capabilities to the NATO-led coalition. All of this helped rid the world of a brutal dictator.

In Afghanistan, the Air Force flew more than thirty-three thousand close air support sorties in 2011 alone, in addition to having thousands of airmen serving on the ground. As the ground infantrymen tell me, there is no more comforting sound than jets arriving overhead to help get them out of a jam. Norty worked tirelessly to ensure that those jets would be there.

Norty worked with his teammate, Mike Donley, to help the Air Force prepare for the future—a future that includes the security challenges like cyber, and opportunities to have to deal with fiscal constraints, and opportunities to open up the Air Force to all of those who want to serve their country.

He played a key role in helping craft our new defense strategy. He has put the Air Force on a stronger footing by streamlining the fleet and pushing ahead with key platforms for the future: the Joint Strike Fighter, the new tanker, a next-generation bomber, and new, more advanced remotely piloted aircraft (RPAs).

History will mark the great work that he did on the RPA program, and how he helped get more of this capability into the field. The United States is engaged in a global war on terror, and drone strikes are an effective tool to eliminate militants planning terror attacks on the U.S. I can personally tell you, from my capacity as Director of the CIA and as Secretary of Defense, how essential these operations are to the fight against terrorism.

Norty's decades in the special operations community all seemed to be leading up to May 2, 2011—the night of the bin Laden raid. We could not have done that raid were it not for the help of Norty's airmen. And more importantly, as CIA director, I can tell you that we would not have been able to decimate al-Qaeda's leadership were it not for the great work of those [RPA] pilots. And for that Norty deserves tremendous credit.

Perhaps most importantly, America's airmen and their families were never far from the minds of Norty and Suzie, who championed numerous support programs that have improved their quality of life.

General Norty Schwartz is a good man, a good friend, a dedicated officer, but more importantly, a great patriot who has truly done his best in protecting the United States of America.

PROLOGUE

It was like a scene out of a Tom Clancy thriller, but not anything I'd ever experienced in real life. I was one of a roomful of top-level generals attending our June 2008 Air Force Corona conference when, one by one, every Blackberry in the room sounded an alert—a true "WTF" moment. The SECDEF (secretary of defense) had just relieved both the secretary of the Air Force and its chief of staff. Six fully functional W-80 nuclear warheads had mistakenly been loaded in AGM-129 cruise missiles, mounted on a B-52H bomber, and flown across the United States. None of the pilots, flight crew, weapons handlers, or security personnel had any idea they were dealing with live nukes. The bottom line was that they had lost track of six nuclear weapons for thirty-six hours, which was absolutely unacceptable.

Just a few months earlier, four MK-12 forward section reentry vehicle assemblies, used on Minutemen ICBM (intercontinental ballistic missile) missiles, had been inadvertently shipped to Taiwan instead of battery packs that were to be used in Taiwan's fleet of UH-1 Huey helicopters. They were eventually recovered, but it revealed a serious problem with nuclear-related inventory management. In two prior assignments I had been heavily involved in our nuclear mission, where anything less than doing it right and doing it well is intolerable.

The outgoing Chief had also been at odds with Secretary Gates over warfighting expenditure priorities, refusing to back down on the need to spend more on the F-22 advanced fighter program, whereas Gates saw the future in expanding the role of remotely piloted aircraft (often referred to as "drones") and prevailing in the ongoing fights. The Air Force was struggling on many levels, and we all understood that *one of us in that room would be selected to replace the Chief and become the highest ranking officer in the Air Force*—a member of the Joint Chiefs of Staff and military advisor to President George W. Bush—charged with the challenge of turning things around.

I had a few ideas of who that might be, but Schwartz was not one of the names on my list. The paperwork for my retirement was already approved, and all eighteen prior chiefs had been either fighter or bomber pilots. I was neither.

The following day was my wedding anniversary, and Suzie and I celebrated with a special night out. Dinner was delicious, but "dessert" was unforgettable. It came in the form of a phone call from Admiral Mike Mullen, chairman of the Joint Chiefs of Staff on behalf of the secretary of defense.

"Norty, the president would like you to be the next chief of staff."

So much for those retirement papers.

But what an honor, not to mention opportunity. As the first chief of staff chosen from the special operations rather than the fighter/bomber community, my challenge would be to return vigor to all the processes and missions with which we had been entrusted. I'd have to institute rigorous accountability and refocus our priorities to prove ourselves completely worthy of America's trust. General Merrill "Tony" McPeak, one of the prior chiefs, said that "feigned indifference" is part of the job specification. If such be the case, then history will judge me harshly—I'm just not that good an actor. There was not an ounce of my being that felt indifferent about the trust and confidence the president showed in me by this appointment, nor about the overwhelming responsibility that I felt to use this opportunity to transform the recent fiascoes into significant, far-reaching enhancements that would benefit our Air Force—and our country—for many decades to come. I was inspired and ready to get to it!

Introduction

MY TWO MISTRESSES

I must admit that I, like others in our business, had two mistresses. One was Suzie, and one was the military mission. Often my attention to the latter poorly served the former, but in every instance, Suzie understood—sometimes grudgingly—the reason for my sense of mission.

I grew up without a mother at home, and my father was not always the most supportive of individuals. He meant well, but he had a difficult time expressing it. He was demanding and had high expectations in terms of performance in school, behavior, etc. There was never any doubt that if I failed to live up to his expectations, the consequences would not be pleasant. He was proud that I went to the Air Force Academy and ultimately did very well, but I can't recall a single time that he actually told me so. When I married "out of the faith," Dad seemed to take it as a personal affront. He refused to attend our wedding and wouldn't have much to do with Suzie. It was awkward and regrettable.

Suzie and I had been married almost twenty years when we decided that enough was enough. Dad was getting up there in years and we had just learned that I was being promoted to lieutenant (three-star) general. We drove from Washington to my hometown of Toms River, New Jersey, and headed for the house to give Dad the great news. We arrived to find him sitting in his old Barcalounger like he usually was (by now it was worn to bits) as if he hadn't moved an inch in twenty years. "Hey Dad, guess what? We're getting promoted to lieutenant general."

He leaned back, cranked his head and fired back, "You know, Nort, you are no Omar Bradley."

I didn't know quite what to say. "No shit, Dad," I finally answered. "Isn't it a great country?" I caught the tiniest hint of a smile on his face for about a millisecond and then it went away. No doubt he was proud, but he was manifestly unable to show it. By the time I became a four-star he had passed away.

But sometimes family dysfunction leads to unexpected outcomes—exciting uncharted paths—and that's exactly what happened in our case. The Air Force became my home; it gave me a sense of community and purpose and a sense of worth that might have come from family but didn't, because of circumstances.

This book is the account of my term as the wartime U.S. Air Force chief of staff under Presidents Bush and Obama, and the journey that led me to such a humbling honor.

Far more than that, it's a book about leadership, in which I'll share specific lessons and original insights that will broaden the management arsenal of any leader. Unlike the military memoirs and leadership guides we've seen so many times before, it's a story about breaking the mold, flying in uncharted airspace, and how I overcame my own personal deficits to achieve success.

It's a book about battles—from Iraq to the Pentagon, Afghanistan to Congress.

It's about pushing the limits—in an era of diminishing budgets and fewer resources, finding inventive new ways to fuel the furnace of innovation and supercharge the engine of inspiration.

It's about controversial new technologies that give us the decisive edge in highly contested environments and allow us to prevail in all domains; recapitalizing our aging fleets with satellites and aircraft; and building new capabilities in cyber warfare. Many believe that my greatest legacy will be the "drone" program. It's a contentious topic and I'll get into why I'm such a staunch advocate in spite of all the controversy.

Most importantly, it's about teamwork—teamwork in the workplace, and the unique partnership between Suzie and me. The reality is that I would not have been half as successful had it not been for Suzie's passion and her kicking me in the rear and nudging me on those many occasions when I was reluctant to act. Without her motivation, inspiration, and insights, I would never have made it to Chief. She and I are justifiably perceived as a team, and I don't believe that is the case to the same degree with my predecessors or successors.

Suzie also took important independent action that led to a cultural transition from the traditional military spouse to the modern one. She cornered Donald Rumsfeld at a party to share why she believed a recent policy change of his was "just plain stupid," and ambushed a three-star general on the Pentagon's Air Staff to persuade him to do something about the impractical and uncomfortable dress skirts female airmen were forced to wear. Early on we agreed that she could do whatever she wanted (without having to clear it through me) as long as it was for the betterment of the airmen, their families, and the Air Force—but not for us, and never personal. Outspoken, direct, and sometimes a bit loud, her style is unique and in direct contrast to my soft-spoken demeanor. Suzie stops at nothing to blast through the bureaucracy and defend what's right for the airmen and their families. She's a rock star, and this book is as much about her as it is about me. That's why many of our stories will be told from both of our perspectives. Suzie's will be indicated by *italics*, and she will have a dedicated chapter of her own.

I've never been a believer in either saying or doing something in the interest of political correctness, and I'm not about to do that now. When I first sat down to contemplate how I wanted to approach this book, I asked myself what I could do in order to impart the greatest value to the readers. The word that kept reoccurring was *candor*. As a young lieutenant colonel at the National War College I prepared a paper on how the armed forces as an institution has not been very good in holding ourselves accountable and policing ourselves. I named names (often of superior officers) without regard for the fallout or potential detriment to my career. I did what I thought was necessary to stimulate debate and effectuate change. That same directness will be evident throughout these pages, and that includes personal disclosures that might not present me in the most favorable light. For starters, I've never disclosed how I grew up without a family to speak of and how this affected the choices I made. But I will do so now, in hopes that such openness will shed light into who I am and hit home with many readers who are struggling to transcend dysfunctional family issues of their own.

I'm often asked whether I always had my sights set on Chief, and if so, what kind of master plan I used to realize this goal. While there is certainly a prescribed order of ascension in the aviation specialty, I think serendipity played as much a part of my success as anything else. Yet that serendipity allowed me to deviate from the norm and become an outsider who could chart his own course. This wasn't by design, but it's how it played out. Despite having proficiency, it's very difficult to be noticed if you continue to swim with the rest of the pack. In many ways, I was better accepted by the Army than I was by the Air Force because my credentials as a trusted special operator were recognized and appreciated by people of reputation in the Army. I was a known commodity by much of the Army leadership, but it sent up red flares in the minds of many Air Force peers and seniors.

My service in our Air Force was profoundly influenced by my five tours in the special operations community. We worked hard to develop the tactics, techniques, and intelligence capacities to be able to execute a Desert One–like mission successfully. It took thirty years to create the world's finest special operations capability—one that could actually take down bin Laden despite significant, unanticipated challenges. They were well trained enough, well equipped enough, and sufficiently resilient enough to adapt. How we got to that place is a phenomenal story of the evolution of U.S. special operations. I was part of that journey, and it serves as the backdrop for this book. Had I not experienced the intensity of the special operations mission, associated with an assortment of remarkable joint teammates, and earned a reputation as being a "SOF warrior," I would never have had the opportunity to lead in our Air Force.

Chapter One

WE DON'T CHEW GUM ON HOT MIC

JUNE 1965–DECEMBER 1977

June of 1965 was blistering hot in my home town of Toms River, New Jersey, yet long stretches of Old Freehold Road looked like they were covered with snow. With a temperature of ninety-three degrees, of course it wasn't snow. It was chicken feathers. Even at age fourteen, I saw those chicken feathers as a tremendous opportunity.

By the mid-1950s New Jersey had become the top egg-producing state in the country, with over twelve thousand family-owned egg farms producing more than 485 million eggs a year. Jewish immigrants from Russia, Poland, Germany, and elsewhere in Europe were able to escape anti-Semitism in their own towns and start a new life in America by building chicken farms. A $2,000 loan would finance five acres of land, a house, chicken coops, and enough chickens to turn a profit. Between the low cost of land and the nearby markets of Philadelphia and New York, many settled in the southeastern New Jersey town of Toms River.

School was out for the summer, and a new Stuart Whitman movie was about to open at the Community Theater, just a few blocks from my house. Saturday matinees had just been bumped to thirty-five cents—sodas another dime—but I sure did want to see that film. We were not a wealthy family, so the only way that I could see it was if somehow I could make the money myself.

I was confident that I'd find someone to hire me in a door-to-door canvass of the neighborhood, but I'd have to make a great first impression. I donned my nicest dress shirt and a fresh pair of cotton slacks—the ones usually reserved for the Sunday school classes I'd attended since first grade—and I hiked from farm to farm in search of work. The Robinsons, Spielers, Epsteins, Rosses, Zwickels—all very polite, but none in need of help. "You be sure to tell your dad hello

1

for us," they would say as I thanked them and turned away. Dad was highly respected in the Jewish community, a founding member of our synagogue and its third president. He was later president of the United Synagogues of America. They all knew Si Schwartz, and he was never shy about letting you know it.

I'd been at it all day (completely forgetting to break for lunch), and dinnertime was rapidly approaching. Showing up late for dinner—or late for anything at my house—was not an option, regardless of the veracity of the excuse. I knocked on the front door of the Rosenkrantz farmhouse, my throbbing feet threatening to pop the laces of my stiff dress oxfords. Job or no job, this would be my last house of the day. I knocked harder, then turned to leave. I was halfway down the gravel driveway when a heavily accented voice emanated from inside the garage. "Over here," called Mr. Rosenkrantz.

I headed toward the garage and approached the short, balding man hunched over his workbench. A wisp of thick gray smoke curled up from the pipe extending from the corner of his mouth. "Damn transistor," he muttered. Then he slammed the red paperback-sized radio into the sheet of Masonite that comprised the work surface, prompting the voice of Phil Rizzuto to blare from the tiny speaker. "Did you see that? Unbelievable!" bellowed the Yankee sportscaster.

"Sir, my name is Norty Schwartz, and I need a job," I said, for what seemed like the fiftieth time that day. Without answering, he took a deep puff, reached into a lime-green refrigerator perched adjacent to the workbench, and withdrew four eggs. He handed them to me.

"Now put them in order," he said, just as serious as if he'd instructed me to defuse a bomb. I wondered if this was some kind of joke, but I did as he asked—carefully laying them out, smallest to largest.

"Be here at six tomorrow morning," he said with a nod, concluding the strangest job interview I've ever had in my life. I had just been hired as an "egg sorter." For the next three months, I would make fifteen cents an hour sorting eggs by size: small, medium, large, and jumbo. Maybe it wasn't the most mentally challenging of careers, but at that moment I felt like I'd been drafted by the Dodgers.

There's a certain sense of pride that comes from a successful accomplishment realized by having given it your all. And it's infectious. The more I felt it, the more driven I became to do more, to *be* more. I had felt it eighteen months earlier when—shortly after my thirteenth birthday—I stepped up to the bimah and stood before the congregation of my synagogue, looked down at the ornate Hebrew passages handwritten on the Torah scroll before me, and began to chant the same passages that my ancestors had been reciting for thousands of years. That was the first time I'd "flown solo" in front of a large group. Well over a hundred congregants packed the seats of Congregation B'nai Israel, not to mention my friends and family that had joined to help celebrate my bar mitzvah—the traditional Jewish coming-of-age ritual—after which I would be considered an adult according to Jewish law. From that point forward I would be responsible for my own actions and held accountable for my own ethical and moral obligations.

Some older friends had confided in me how terrified they were standing up there, a few to the point of completely blanking out—the boxy abjad symbols totally unrecognizable to them. But I had this. I had studied hard for over three years and I knew my stuff. I lifted a few strands of *tzitzit* (knotted fringe) dangling from the four corners of my *tallis* (prayer shawl), kissed them, then touched them to the passage I was about to read. "Bar'chu es Adonai . . ." I began to chant, in a voice that was still changing. *Preparation begets confidence.* I knew it then, and I knew it twenty years later when I would proudly represent our country in Pentagon briefings broadcast live to worldwide audiences in the tens of millions.

While I might not have felt like an adult when the ceremony was completed, I did hold my head a little higher and I felt great about myself, and that was exactly how I felt when I ran home to tell Dad the great news about my new job at the Rosenkrantz farm.

I grew up without a mother at home, and my only female role models growing up were June Cleaver, Harriet Nelson, and a stern yet kind German martinet named Erna Melde. Between the long hours Dad put in at Charney's—his small office supply store—and the longer hours he spent on his philanthropic causes and synagogue business, he was seldom at home. It was really Erna who raised my older brother Joel and me. Erna cooked for us, she taught us how to tie our shoelaces, how to dress, how to keep our rooms, and how to behave at the table. She was organized and disciplined, and she expected us to act accordingly. In most cases, we did.

It was a good summer, representative of my formative years growing up in Toms River. In addition to sorting eggs, I mowed lawns, raked leaves, and pitched in to help Dad as a stock clerk at Charney's. If you ever need advice on which ribbon to choose for your Royal Aristocrat manual typewriter, I'm your go-to guy. (A standard half-inch black/red on a two-inch spool will fit the bill.) Working hard became the norm from as early as I can remember, but you're not going to hear me complain about it. I have always loved the sense of accomplishment that accompanies the broken sweat of a job well done. A solid work ethic ranks high on the list of my most cherished takeaways from Toms River.

I also got to see that new movie, *Those Magnificent Men in Their Flying Machines*. No wonder I had wanted to see it so badly. From an early age I was enamored with anything having to do with flying. I was glued to the TV when John Glenn became the first American to be launched into orbit, and every bit as fascinated with the first *Gemini* flight in March of 1965. Like almost every kid growing up during that time, I secretly fantasized about someday becoming an astronaut. Lakehurst Naval Air Station was only ten miles away and Dad would take us to the air shows there. Lakehurst was the center of early airship development for the United States. It housed many blimps before, during, and after World War II, but its biggest claim to fame took place on May 6, 1937, when thirty-six people died as the German airship *Hindenburg* burst into flames as it attempted to dock with its mooring mast.

I've always enjoyed sports, even though I consider myself to be a very average athlete. I'm not big, not fast, and my natural ability is average. Fortunately none of that mattered in the backyard of 42 Park Street, where Joel and I would hone our skills in impromptu games of wiffle ball—just the two of us, with that long, thin plastic bat—and my, how I could curve those pitches with the oblong holes cut out of that lightweight plastic wiffle ball.

I had always been a Dodger fan, but never more than that year. The Dodgers made it all the way to the World Series, and my idol—Sandy Koufax—was slated to pitch the opening game. But he had a problem. The game fell on October 6, which just happened to be the Jewish high holiday of Yom Kippur, a day on which Jews are forbidden to work. Koufax was not a particularly observant Jew, yet there was never a question in his mind that he would stick to his convictions and refrain from even attending the game, let alone pitching in it. The Dodgers lost that game, but they battled back to clinch the Series with Koufax taking the mound in three of the remaining six games, pitching a shutout in the deciding game seven, and being named the Series MVP. Many don't remember that it was Twins who lost that Series, far less that it went seven games. But very few baseball fans are unaware of the story of how Sandy Koufax refused to pitch on Yom Kippur. My idol made an indelible impression on fourteen-year-old me about holding true to one's convictions, and about doing what's right.

A few years later, I became president of our local chapter of United Synagogue Youth, a Jewish organization committed to learning, community service, and social interaction. While I am far from observant these days, I have no doubt that my value set and moral compass were deeply ingrained within me by my years of Sunday school study and active participation in USY. Jewish tradition teaches us to live our lives in keeping with a concept called *derech eretz*. It's so central to our foundation that it precedes the Torah. It's a roadmap that charts our path toward behaviors that are righteous and just. In a broad sense it's as simple as the Golden Rule, and it certainly transcends any particular organized religion. I think this had a lot to do with my decision to join the military, an institution that encourages its members to serve others selflessly and gives them a sense of community, purpose, and belonging to something larger than themselves. I needed this, and I believe it's central to why I felt so comfortable with the military culture from day one.

I played a little baseball in high school, but far more significant was my time on the Toms River football team. Believe me, this had nothing to do with my great talent—in fact, far more of my game time was spent warming the bench than it was on the field. But it didn't matter—I was still a Toms River Indian and I would give it 500 percent. I fought hard to get there (another battle with Dad, who felt that tackle football was too dangerous for me), and I savored every minute. Coach Ron Signorino had considerable influence over all of us in ways that weren't immediately obvious or in ways that really related to playing football. He drummed in the importance of discipline and preparation, and he wasn't just referring to football. He had standards he believed in—character building and so forth. He was an important influence in my early days, as are coaches in many sports for kids. He was my primary mentor in high school and played an important role in my becoming the man I am today.

I couldn't wait for Saturday late mornings. We would start with a bit of gamesmanship, waiting in our locker room until well after the visiting team was out on the field, then we would race out and wend our way through their stretches and warmup drills. Our mascot was a senior dressed as an Indian. Just before the game was about to begin, he would charge onto the field riding a horse and brandishing a spear, then head for the opposing team's bench and hurl the spear into the ground in front of them. The crowd would explode and it was game on!

1968 was a memorable year for the Toms River Indians,
in no small part due to coach and mentor Ron Signorino.
Schwartz personal collection

Coach Signorino positioned me as what he called "monster"—an outside linebacker, essentially. On one occasion during a pre-season game against Rancocas Valley High School, I attempted to tackle their oversized running back, and I bounced off him like a maroon-and-white pinball hitting a turbo bumper. It was Franco Harris, the number-one draft pick for the Pittsburgh Steelers, who would go on to become a Hall of Fame superstar that *The Sporting News* would list as number 83 of the 100 Greatest Football Players. (Coincidentally, my jersey number was 83 for the Indians—but that was the extent of the similarity.) "Nice hit," he told me after the play.

1968 was an outstanding year for the team. We went 9–0 and won the Shore Conference Class A title that year, with quarterbacks Drew Altans and Rip Scherer taking the snaps. Rip went on to coach for the Carolina Panthers and Cleveland Browns, and he's now the assistant athletic director for football at UCLA.

My question was what I was going to do with the rest of *my* life. Joel was already in college at Columbia University, so I had to either get a scholarship or go to work for two years, which we had planned to do. I met with my high school guidance counselor for some advice.

"Norty, have you considered Annapolis?" he asked, fully aware of my love for aviation. "Perhaps you can fly for the Navy, and it's a full scholarship." This was long before Tom Cruise became a Top Gun for the Navy, so it really wasn't something I had thought about. But I sure liked the thought of earning my flight wings. "For any of the service academies, besides the actual application you have to be nominated for the appointment," he continued. "This can be by your congressman, senator, the vice president, or even the president. But I have to tell you that it's very, very competitive, and the number of requests far out-number the available slots—so let's talk about how we can make this happen for you, Norty."

I left his office and kicked into high gear, ultimately scoring an appointment with Congressman William Cahill. But just as when I went door-to-door in search of employment as a young teen, I knew that I would have to impress the elder politician, who was serving his sixth term in Congress and running for governor of New Jersey (an election that he would win just a few months later).

It was always somewhat awkward when I asked my dad for anything, and this time was no different. He was thrilled with my decision to apply to Annap-olis, but to ask him to pay $99 for a kid's suit was pushing it—serious money in those days. It was late evening when I approached his Barcalounger and showed him the newspaper ad I had cut out. "Dad, we're talking about my entire future here, and this suit will really, really make a difference in that interview." He studied that ad like his life depended on it, then shocked the hell out of me.

"Norty, I couldn't agree with you more. Meet me there at noon tomorrow and let's have them fit you up. Wouldn't want you to meet the congressman with a baggy vest, now, would we?" I don't know whether that suit made any differ-ence with Congressman Cahill's decision, but it sure made me feel good during the interview. The congressman seemed particularly impressed that I played ball for Ron Signorino, which says a lot more about the coach's esteemed reputation than it does about me.

The good news is that I received his nomination. The bad news came in the form of a letter I received from the Admissions office: *After much consideration, we regret to inform you that we are unable to offer you admission to the United States Naval Academy. This year's application pool was especially . . .* Those few words came terrifyingly close to destroying any real hope I had of becoming a pilot . . . except for one remaining long shot. Despite not really knowing where Colorado was, much less Colorado Springs, I had also asked Congressman Cahill, very late in the game, for a nomination to the Air Force Academy.

One might assume that the story ends with him agreeing to that nomina-tion, and my subsequently getting accepted to Air Force, but that's not how it played out. The problem was that Cahill had already selected an athlete from an adjoining town to receive his nomination to the Air Force Academy. The best that he could offer me was "first alternate," which did me about as much good as if I'd come in a close second in a presidential election. I shored myself up to accept that fact that I just wasn't meant to fly—or for that matter even attend college at that time. I would work for a few years and see how the family finances were when Joel graduated from Columbia.

Then the phone rang. "Sir, this is Congressman Cahill's office calling. The congressman would like me to let you know that his primary candidate for the Air Force Academy was unable to pass the entrance physical, so he would like to extend the nomination to you." It turned out his original choice had a bad knee, which was bad enough to keep him from the Academy, but not bad enough to keep him from ultimately becoming a Division 2 All American. For me, it was a stroke of good fortune, and that was the beginning of a long career of service in the Air Force.

I have no idea whether I would have enjoyed the same success had I gone Navy, but I consider it an immense stroke of luck that I was rejected by Annapolis. It's the one event that set my entire Air Force journey in motion.

Throughout my career, the puzzle pieces seemed to fall into place, putting me at the right place at the right time. Call it luck, call it good fortune. Whatever it is, I learned never to disregard its significance.

★   ★   ★

On June 23, 1969, Joe Frazier TKOed Jerry Quarry in the eighth round to win the world heavyweight boxing title; Warren E. Burger was sworn in as U.S. Supreme Court chief justice by retiring Chief Justice Earl Warren; and I raised my right hand and took the Oath of Allegiance to support and defend the Constitution of the United States and to faithfully discharge my duties as a cadet in the United States Air Force Academy.

Less than twenty-four hours earlier, I had tossed my solitary suitcase into the trunk of Dad's well-traveled Dodge sedan, slid onto the passenger side of the long vinyl bench seat, and never looked back as Dad pulled away from the only house I had ever known. He and I didn't really speak much during the hour and a half drive through the lush, green pines and oaks lining the two-lane highway that cut through the peaceful New Jersey countryside, but my mind flashed back to the many heated discussions we'd had around the dinner table. Vietnam was a constant topic of conversation, and lively debates surrounding foreign affairs and national security were frequent.

U.S. combat deaths in Vietnam had topped the 33,629 men killed in the Korean War, and Walter Cronkite grimly shared the details of an encounter known as the Battle of Hamburger Hill. After U.S. forces took the hill, the U.S. commander had ordered them to abandon their positions, allowing the North Vietnamese army to move back in and recapture the hill, completely unopposed. Forty-six members of the 101st Airborne were killed and another four hundred wounded. Senator Edward Kennedy called it "senseless and irresponsible," and that was one point on which Dad, Joel, and I certainly agreed. We questioned whether we could ever really win the war with our military alone, and just what impact all the heavy bombing was having on our international perception.

Our family had misgivings about the conduct of the war, but never about those who fought. The same could not be said about so many others at the time. A hundred thousand anti-war demonstrators had marched on New York City. In October, the "Vietnam Moratorium" would find a million Americans participating in sit-ins and protest rallies across the United States. This was a far cry from the way Americans had banded together to support our soldiers during prior wars. That's how it was in August of 1942, when Dad walked into a Philadelphia recruiting station and enlisted in the U.S. Army. His military career was short-lived, but he did earn a battlefield commission as a second lieutenant. He respected those who put their lives on the line to safeguard our liberties, and he made sure that we knew the difference between having issues with the politicians who decided which causes warranted our nation's intervention and the brave warriors who'd be carrying out those orders.

With all of our discussions about the war, not once did we address the elephant in the room. The reality was that if all went well for me at the Academy, I'd emerge a second lieutenant in the U.S. Air Force and potentially be inserted directly into the eye of the storm. True, I had misgivings about the war itself, but there was never any question that my future would rest in success at the Academy and being afforded the opportunity to serve my country by earning one of the limited combat pilot slots. It would be a "show-me" scenario and I tried to steel myself for the challenge. Frankly, I was glad to be leaving Toms River and incredibly grateful for the opportunity. I would give it my best shot and never take it for granted.

Before I knew it we were on the Walt Whitman Bridge, crossing the Delaware River with the Philadelphia skyline coming into view beyond the tall green towers supporting the suspension cables. Dad followed the signs to the Philadelphia Airport and I could feel my adrenaline kick in—more excitement than nerves—as he pulled to a stop beneath the red and white TWA sign. He waved off the skycap and removed my bag from the trunk. "Just take it one day at a time and you'll do fine," he said, handing me the airline ticket.

"Thanks, Dad. Take care," I responded. Then we shook hands and went our separate ways. A few hours later I was enjoying the in-flight meal onboard a 727 en route to Denver, then I changed planes for the short skip to Colorado Springs, where I spent my very last night as a civilian watching TV in my tiny room at the Ponderosa Motor Inn with many other cadet candidates.

★ ★ ★

"From now on, you will not speak unless spoken to, and when you *do* speak, the only sound coming out of your mouth will be one of the seven basic responses: *'Yes, sir. No, sir. No excuse, sir. Sir, I do not know. Sir, I do not understand. Sir, may I ask a question? Sir, may I make a statement?'"* The tall, immaculately groomed upper-class cadet barked the instructions at the top of his lungs. His crisp blue officer's uniform commanded respect.

The Air Force bus chugging down Interior Drive toward the Academy was packed with a hodgepodge of cadets-to-be, some shell-shocked at the instantaneous transition from the genial host who had welcomed us on board from outside the bus. One wise-ass actually snickered—big mistake. The cadet officer got into his face, even though the words were meant for us all. *"If you choose mediocrity, do not insult the Long Blue Line by exiting this bus once we arrive. If you are not a person of absolute integrity, do not get off this bus. If you are not willing to sacrifice your life for your country, stay on this bus and we will gladly transport you off these grounds. If you accept 'just getting by' as your personal standard, do not, under any circumstances, get off this bus."* By this point he was at a fever pitch, veins bulging from his neck, his words literally spraying the wise-ass in the face. "But if you are ready to dedicate your life to something greater than us all, to selflessly develop yourself as a warrior and to fight for our great nation, then pick up your bags and GET OFF THIS BUS! But stick together, because you *absolutely . . . will not . . . successfully complete cadet training . . . on . . . your . . . own!"*

A handful of my fellow "basics" were already hunting for their ejection seat handles, but I was fired up. This was all that I had signed up for and more. *It had never been so clear to me that I had made the right decision.* Of the 1,406 cadets entering the Academy that day, only 60 percent of us would make it to graduation.

★ ★ ★

I arrived at the Academy upbeat and optimistic—some might even say naive or delusional—that the skepticism and rebelliousness of the sixties would be left behind once the bus passed through the main gate. The truth was that the institution I was about to enter—the Academy in the micro sense, but the entire U.S. Air Force (if not all of our military)—was in the midst of a metamorphosis of its own. Recent scandals had rocked the Academy. In 1965, 109 cadets were expelled in a cheating ring, another thirty-three in 1967, and a very small segment of our graduates believed the diplomas they would be awarded at graduation were in fact one-way tickets to a death sentence in Vietnam. I hadn't even completed my first week when the cadet wing commander stood up at noon mess and announced the death of Captain Gary Brunner, class of '66, whose C-130B had taken off from Tan Son Nhut, Vietnam, on a resupply mission to the Special Forces camp at Kontum when its port wing was hit by quad .50 caliber antiaircraft fire. His Herc spun to the ground from three thousand feet, killing the entire crew.

Whenever a graduate died in the line of duty, the name would be read in front of the entire cadet wing at lunch in Mitchell Hall. All three thousand cadets would stand and softly sing the third verse of the Air Force Song in tribute. By the time I graduated, there had been hundreds of such recitals. While each of us had nothing but respect for those who made the ultimate sacrifice, such was certainly not the case with everyone outside the military. Anti-war sentiment was far-reaching, and unlike the heroes' welcome rightfully showered upon returning World War II vets, it was not uncommon for Vietnam soldiers and airmen to be spat upon and insulted.

The good news was that the tide had begun to turn. A few years before my arrival, Colonel Robin Olds had taken over as commandant of cadets, entrusted with the daunting task of restoring morale. If anyone could do it, he could. The fighter pilot triple-ace was a maverick notorious for bucking the system—but an inspirational motivator and electrifying leader. Well known for his extravagant handlebar mustache that defied Air Force grooming regulations, he was bold, brash, flamboyant, yet always approachable—a leader the wing would instantly rally behind.

Not long after his arrival, the Air Force decided to honor those Academy graduates serving in Southeast Asia by placing a decommissioned F-105 on static display at the northeast corner of the Terrazzo, the pavilion in the cadet area. This was a very big deal, and the dedication ceremony would include a number of dignitaries, Air Force officials, and the entire cadet wing assembled in parade formation. The press was well represented to capture the speeches and festive celebration, which culminated in a low-altitude, high-speed flyover by four F-105s, known as "Thuds," in diamond formation. The cadets erupted in cheers, a perfect climax to a perfect day . . . until all hell broke loose.

The four Thuds looped around to make a second pass, this time approaching in single file from the east. The lead hit the burners and pulled away from the others, dropping down to about one hundred feet. As it silently sped by, a visible shock wave radiated from its nose. Then *boom!* First the deafening sound of the sonic boom. Then breaking glass from all directions. The entire glass façade of Vandenberg Hall shattered from the north. Ditto Mitchell Hall from the south. Shattered glass rained down from all directions. In less than five seconds, over three hundred windows had burst, and chaos ensued. Cadets broke formation and ran in all directions; dignitaries sought protection from the shower of shrapnel.

The cadet wing commander, Ralph "Ed" Eberhart, restored order while the injured were being treated. (Thirty-three years later, *General* Ed Eberhart would step up to the plate once again, this time as NORAD (North American Aerospace Defense Command) commander during 9/11. Twelve years after that, he would be the first to offer me new office space following my retirement.) The following day the front page of the *Chicago Tribune* read "SONIC BOOM INJURES 15 AT AIR ACADEMY." Coincidentally, that's the same day Commandant Olds was promoted to brigadier general.

General Olds was far from the only legendary role model at the Academy. In August of 1970, Lt. General Albert Patton "A. P." Clark became the Academy's sixth superintendent. The first uniformed U.S. pilot captured by the Germans in World War II, General Clark was instrumental in planning and implementing all the escape activity from Stalag Luft III, including the renowned "Great Escape" made famous in the Steve McQueen/James Garner movie of the same name.

Like so many of the great leaders I would encounter at the Academy, General Clark was a firm believer in discipline, rigorous training, and walking the walk according to the tenets of the Air Force core values.

From the moment we stepped onto that bus, those core values were drilled in to us. They would take their final form many years later:

Integrity First
Service Before Self
Excellence in All We Do

As a fourth-class cadet, these were themes for me to memorize. By the time I graduated, they had become central to my very foundation. They defined who I was, what I did, and how I did it. They made difficult choices easier for me and bolstered my sense of confidence and sense of pride. It felt good to look in the mirror and an honor to don the Air Force uniform.

If there's one skill that we'd become proficient at, it was marching. We'd march to meals, march to classes, and even march to the weekly religious services we were then required to attend. Our first march took place almost immediately after we stepped off the bus, when our ragged bunch of newbies (officially called "doolies"—from the Greek *duolos,* meaning slave, or servant) marched from the parking lot up "the Ramp" onto the Terrazzo, our first venture into the Academy proper. Prominently displayed on a stone arch above the ramp in two-feet tall, raised, aluminum letters, were the words "Bring Me Men"—a real sign of the times since there were no women cadets until Gerald Ford signed Public Law 94-106 on October 7, 1975, permitting women to enter the military academies. In truth, the words were part of the poem "The Coming American," written in 1894 by Sam Walter Foss.

Bring me men to match my mountains
Bring me men to match my plains
Men with empires in their purpose
And new eras in their brains

The words remained to mark the symbolic threshold between the old life and the new until Secretary James Roche and Chief of Staff General John P. Jumper called for their removal in response to a sexual assault scandal in 2003.

Unceremoniously taken down and tossed into the back of a four-wheel during the March spring break, they were replaced a year and a half later with the Air Force core values—a much more appropriate and inclusive reflection of all the institution stands for.

Symbols matter, but they are not necessarily meaningful in perpetuity.

★ ★ ★

The Academy was multidimensional in terms of athletics, academics, and military. On the athletic side, I wasn't really big or strong or quick enough to be an intercollegiate football player, so I had to consider the other options. Fencing, gymnastics, tennis, soccer, ice hockey . . . none felt right. It was during a meal at Mitchell Hall that one of the senior cadets noticed my particularly long reach and suggested that I pursue boxing. Tall, slender, and somewhat agile, it sounded like fun to me.

At that time the cadets boxed under Amateur Athletic Union rules, which were not so much about knocking out your opponent as they were about the number of effective punches thrown. This was more about the art of boxing. Strategy played a big part, as did technique to multiply the number of hits rather than the consequence of a hit. A jab was as important as a solid right hook. I very much enjoyed the plotting, developing a plan of attack, then efficiently executing that plan. In my mind, it was more akin to chess than a display of brute force, though I'm not sure my opponents agreed with that when my solid right cross smashed into their face.

If only I had honed these skills back in eighth grade, when a gang of bullies pummeled me in the gut, taking issue with the fact that a Jew would have the nerve to attend their intermediate school. It wasn't the first time I had to defend myself but it was not something I went out looking to do. What skills I had were largely defensive, both physically and diplomatically. I certainly wasn't afraid to strike back, but I did learn that in most cases violence should be held as a last resort. I developed an effective arsenal of tactics to avoid confrontation in the first place.

Perceptions of strength and purpose are a prerequisite in any successful negotiation.

★　★　★

Long before I was ever allowed to climb into the ring, I was introduced to an inanimate hundred-pound opponent chained to the ceiling—the "heavy bag." I strapped on a pair of thick maroon Tuf-wear gloves and laid into the five-foot, sand-filled leather cylinder, the same type later made famous by Stallone in *Rocky*. With every punch I gave it all I had. The harder I punched, the better I felt. Explosive "cracks" echoed off the bag with growing intensity. But my euphoria was short-lived and it didn't take long before I was drenched in perspiration and almost gasping for breath. So much for the great shape I thought I was in.

My instructor (the same senior cadet who had convinced me to pursue boxing in the first place) found humor in this, but it was nothing personal. Almost every novice pugilist had the misconception that boxing was all about power, trying to destroy the opponent with all your might. But it didn't take too long for me to learn that expending all you have without proper technique is a pretty good blueprint for ending up on the receiving end of a knockout.

"Let me show you how it's done," offered the instructor, whose interaction with the bag was a thing of beauty. Where I'd been standing flatfooted and focusing my blows on a single spot, he was in constant motion, dancing around the bag and firing blistering combinations of punches. They were sharp, crisp, and accurate. I had a lot to learn. But I was an eager student, and appreciative of his patience with my original ineptitude.

I caught on rather quickly. Snapping punches (allowing the punch to rebound back into position) came naturally to me, as did executing flowing combinations as I eyed the bag, always in motion, yet in such a way as to conserve my energy. "That's it, but don't jump around, Norty . . . stay balanced," he would warn. *Pop-pop-pop . . . pop pop.* So much more effective than just blindly flailing away.

What I didn't realize at the time was that I was really being taught valuable concepts that transcend the ring, strategic philosophies that apply to all aspects of the military, and certainly military aviation.

Brute force without a balanced, well-executed plan, including specific objectives, is a blueprint for disaster.

★　★　★

I'd see this over and over throughout my career, but there's no better example than March of 1999, when NATO green-lit Operation ALLIED FORCE, air strikes inside the former Yugoslavia. The airstrikes were intended to degrade the Serbian military structure led by Slobodan Milošević—troops Milošević was using to exterminate the Albanian civilian majority in Kosovo. I had just received my second star—promoted to major general and working as Air Force director of strategic planning at the Pentagon.

NATO's operation was orchestrated by its Supreme Allied Commander Europe, General Wesley Clark, who apparently believed that the most effective way to smash the enemy forces was to blindly swing a massive airborne hammer—kind of like my original attempt to destroy the punching bag with haphazard blows. Within a few days, the futility of this ploy escalated to the highest level of the Pentagon, the chairman of the Joint Chiefs of Staff. General Hugh Shelton's phone was ringing off the hook with calls from his counterparts in France, England, Germany, and Italy, plus the NATO air component commander in Europe—all expressing concern about Clark's seemingly arbitrary choice of targets and lack of focused battle plan. General Mike Ryan, Air Force chief of staff, had shared similar concerns with Shelton, who convened an immediate session with the Joint Staff to develop a central theme replete with specific categories of targets selected to address that theme. The initial intent would be to degrade Serbia's military capabilities and then, after that was successfully accomplished, their economy.

The Joint Staff came up with four categories of targets:

1. Military infrastructure
2. Economic targets
3. Belgrade bridges and power grid (psychological demoralizers)
4. Tank engine factory (employed 32,000 workers)

Chairman Shelton faxed the new plan to General Clark "for his consideration," and the following day, Clark presented "his" new strategic plan to the NATO partners. The fleet of F-15s, F-16s, F-117s, and all the support equipment and personnel that went with them would now be used in focused strikes carefully orchestrated to achieve a well-defined strategic objective. It was the difference between my randomly attempting to beat the crap out of the punching bag, and my instructor's planned and well-rehearsed combinations.

★   ★   ★

I boxed as a fourth-class cadet (freshman) and came back to coach the squadron team for my subsequent three years. I had a pretty good left jab, not much of a right hand, but it was good enough. I actually had skills I didn't realize, and I turned out to be a surprisingly good boxer.

I learned a lot from boxing, and those lessons were unlike any others taught during my four years. Everything in the cadet experience is about teamwork, camaraderie, and working as a unit. Even the solo flight experience is far from independent. Without the instructors, maintenance crews, meteorologists, and air traffic controllers, there would be no "solo" flight. But inside that ring you really are by yourself. You have to maintain your composure and compete with laser focus—great training for how to deal with being solo when under stress.

Boxing taught me valuable lessons in how to deal with being "in the ring" solo when under significant stress.

★   ★   ★

The Academy military component is structured in such a way as to mirror the organization of the entire Air Force. First-class cadet commanders command forty squadrons of approximately a hundred cadets each. Each of these commanders reports to four cadet group commanders who all report to a single cadet wing commander, who is in charge of the entire cadet wing. Supervising these cadets are Air Officers Commanding (AOCs), usually active duty majors located in each squadron and group. The AOCs serve as role models to the cadets and oversee all cadet activities. They are the front-line personifications of Air Force core values and the honor code. Their character is typically beyond reproach, and it is expected that we as cadets demonstrate that character within ourselves. At least, this is how it's supposed to work. The truth is that sometimes you learn from positive role models and sometimes you learn from those who are not so positive. I had instructors who were Silver Star recipients, another who went on to be chief of the Air Force. On the flip side are those who just make you scratch your head and wonder how in the world they ever got assigned to their positions of authority—let alone promoted in the first place.

Case in point was my AOC, a major who was in charge of all one hundred cadets in our squadron. Early on I sensed there was something off about this guy, and it turned out he had real problems telling the truth. He was a climber with career ambitions and would relate events in ways that were supportive of his own agenda rather than factual. The honor code is a vitally important component of the cadet environment, so it was less than ideal when the expectations we had for ourselves were not reflected by the officer who was supposed to be our role model. He was eventually busted, as most are. It wouldn't be the last time I would encounter superiors who had no business being in positions of authority, but instead of getting pissed off at them, I'd reflect back on this major and

Try to learn as much from negative role models as from positive ones.

★ ★ ★

I'm always amazed at the remorse they feel *after* the fact. But why do it in the first place? What's the lure? The temptation? It all goes back to Sunday school—Hebrew school—doing what's right—not fear of getting caught. I've found life to be a lot less complicated if one just follows the Golden Rule.

★ ★ ★

Fortunately these foul balls were rare exceptions at the Academy. In fact, I'm often asked what single factor sets the Air Force Academy apart from other top institutes of higher education, and what constitutes my most vivid memories. While it's pretty tough to top that first solo flight, even that doesn't compare to the awe of being taught by the very best of the best. Imagine learning how to bat from Babe Ruth, or how to putt from Arnold Palmer. That's the level of instructors they provided for us. Just meeting these guys was humbling; being given the opportunity to learn from them one-on-one, day in, day out, was inestimable. I mentioned how the Air Force core values are drummed into us from day one. These are the guys who personified those values, selfless heroes who inspired me each and every day. This, more than anything else, is what the Academy experience was all about for me. Living examples of what can be achieved through discipline, hard work, and focused determination accomplished within the framework of our core values.

Mike Dugan was an A-1 pilot who came out of Vietnam, a Silver Star recipient who went on to be chief of staff of the Air Force. He was one of my military training instructors, and a group AOC who had oversight of ten squadrons. Dugan flew more than three hundred combat missions during the Vietnam War, logging 4,500 flying hours. He was all business and spoke in short, clipped sentences. He only lasted seventy-nine days as CSAF before Dick Cheney—secretary of defense at the time—fired him for revealing our plans to take out Saddam Hussein. He was immensely proud of the Air Force, and perhaps Cheney believed he went overboard in communicating that enthusiasm to some journalists. But from our perspective, that fervor was inspiring. Hearing him share firsthand accounts of his missions kept us spellbound and eager to return for the next installment.

Ron Fogleman was a history instructor who also went on to be chief of staff of the Air Force.

Al Gropman was another history instructor, and he became a mentor of mine. Years later he was a colonel at the Pentagon and he brought me in to work for him in the shop that conceptualized Air Force thinking—a total 180 from the operational lane that I was accustomed to at the time. He saw something in me and stretched me outside of my comfort zone, which is fundamental if one wants to grow. It was fun.

John Guilmartin was an H-3 rescue pilot who had been awarded the Silver Star twice, and he was both a history instructor and a teacher down on the flight line. He was smart, courageous, and patient with me as a student. He was one of the reasons that I was inspired to move to special operations later on. He's another one whose candid disclosures kept us captivated. Like this one, in his own words, as he shares the experiences that led to his two Silver Stars:

The first was for getting a Thud [F-105] driver out of the mouth of Mu Gia Pass on 19 February '66. It was on what amounted to my aircraft commander upgrade pre-check. We were short of IPs [instructor pilots] and I was paired up with our strongest IP, Barry Kamhoot. We were crewed up together and switched seats for instructional rides in the pattern on alert at NKP [Nakhon Phanom Royal Thai Navy Base]. Our last alert tour before my (nominal) a/c check took us into Mu Gia Pass to pick up an F-105 driver who'd gotten stitched by a 57 mm and landed within a mile or so of the gun! It was a sporty proposition. When we finally got a firm set of coordinates on the survivor from Sandy Lead, it plotted out to within a mile and a half of a big-time 37 mm concentration. Barry was cool as a cucumber and didn't waste a second. The survivor, Bob Green, stretched his descent a few yards away from the worst of the enemy concentration thanks to two blown panels in his chute, and we had the best Sandy Lead in the business in Elmer Nelson. We were also, as Elmer emphasizes, VERY lucky.

The second was for digging an F-4 crew out of "Happy Valley," a delightful open spot on the Ho Chi Minh Trail between Ban Karai Pass and Tchepone. The back seater landed on the edge of the valley and was spotted by the bad guys. He ran for his life—literally—for fifty minutes . . . with a serious compression fracture (he had a Mae West chute malfunction). The front seater was easy, though we did have to snuggle down into the trees to get the penetrator to him. We put out all 250 feet of cable and had to thread the tail rotor down between two trees for the last ten feet. Knowing that the back seater was in trouble, I elected to stay low and assist in the search; it was a violation of one of the cardinal rules, but I felt the circumstances justified it . . . and they did. When we got to him, the patrol chasing him was only 75–100 yards behind him. They wounded my PJ [parajumper] on the way in and the flight mech deputized the recovered front seater as our door gunner and gave him the PJ's M-16! I have no conscious recollection of it, but he was blazing away while we picked up his back seater. As far as I know, I'm the only Jolly Green who had a lieutenant commander for a door gunner!

The more I heard stories like these, the more I was inspired to excel—personally and professionally—and the more I fell in love with flying. I was even more driven to earn my wings. Doing so became my primary focus.

Ultimately, it is purpose and mission that motivates in the armed forces and the private sector.

★ ★ ★

Before arriving at the Academy, you could count my in-flight experiences on one hand, and those would be limited to the economy cabin on TWA. That all changed with what they referred to as Operation STARDUST, our Basic Cadet

Orientation Flight—an hour-long joyride strapped inside the cockpit of a T-33A fighter jet.

A couple dozen of us enthusiastic Basics boarded an Air Force bus for the short ride to nearby "Pete Field" (designated Peterson Air Force Base on March 1, 1975), where we disembarked in front of a large white hangar. After watching a short 16 mm safety film, we were taken into a room that can best be compared to the men's department of a small department store. Garment racks lined two walls, but instead of suits and Levis, one rack was crammed with well-worn olive-green flight suits and black leather flight boots, the other aviation helmets and oxygen masks. A great deal of time was spent being fitted with the perfect helmet and oxygen mask. I was impressed by the professionalism of the airman carefully placing the mask over my nose and mouth. "Supplemental oxygen is required above 10,000 feet," he said as he adeptly adjusted it to ensure an airtight seal. "At 30,000 feet, without it you'd only have a minute or two before hypoxia would lead to loss of consciousness." That moment slammed home the life and death stakes of this profession.

Just like the business suit had instilled so much confidence for my interview with Congressman Cahill, once I zipped up the front of my flight suit I felt ten feet tall. At that point I couldn't tell you the difference between an altimeter and an airspeed indicator, but I sure did *feel* like a pilot. We were fitted with a mock parachute and hooked up to an egress simulator—a small crane where we learned how to safely execute an in-flight ejection and parachute descent—prerequisite training for the real chute/ejection seat to which I'd be harnessed. "In the unlikely event of a real ejection scenario, keep your chin down and elbows tucked into your sides," the instructor warned. "And keep your hands *away* from those yellow ejection handles unless you are directly commanded to raise them." No arm twisting needed to follow *that* advice.

Stepping out of the hangar and onto the pavement of an active flight line for the first time can best be described as sensory overload. The distinctive smell of jet fuel fills the air as tanker trucks disgorge their loads into perfectly aligned rows of fighter jets. Flight crews inspect their aircraft, Auxiliary Power Units wind up the turbines, tail pipes roar as fuel and exhaust gases ignite. My heart thumped in overload as I was led to Captain Reed Maxwell, the instructor pilot who would take me on this well-orchestrated motivational excursion. Was it just coincidence, or did all the IPs look just like Tom Cruise? Captain Maxwell stood next to the T-bird, busily perusing its maintenance papers as I approached, then saluted. He returned the salute, then glanced at the crystal-clear cerulean sky. "You ordered us some perfect conditions, Norty," he observed.

I accompanied the captain on a thorough preflight walk-around inspection of the aircraft. Low-mounted wings radiated straight off the fuselage just aft of the rear seat, each terminating in a distinctive wing-tip fuel tank. On both sides of the fuselage aft of the nose were C-shaped intakes to channel the air into the single extraordinarily *inefficient* Allison J33-A-35 turbojet engine. "We burn about the same amount of fuel on the ground as we do cruising at high altitude," he explained. "That means every minute we spend idling on the ground costs us seven miles in range—so the quicker we complete our checklist and get up, the better."

He pulled out an aviation map and previewed our route. "We'll be taking off to the north, then break to the west right here as we approach the Academy, which you'll see right beneath us. We'll continue our climbing left turn and head southwest toward Cripple Creek. That's where we'll go through the very same basic fighter maneuvers we're employing right now in Vietnam. I'll talk you through everything, but your main job is to sit back and enjoy." I assured him that I'd have no problem following that instruction.

"Ready to do it?" asked the crew chief, guiding me to the yellow ladder hooked beneath the open seven-foot glass canopy. The two-seat tandem cockpit had dual controls. I climbed into the back seat, which the chief lowered to accommodate my six-foot frame. "Wouldn't want your head poking a hole in the canopy," he said, then proceeded to strap me in and hook me up—lap belt, shoulder straps, parachute harness, oxygen mask, communications links—lots more that flew over my head at the time. "All good?" he asked before stepping back to allow Captain Maxwell access.

"All good," I said, nodding back. In truth, I felt awkward. I was surprised at how cramped it was. I had an unobstructed 360-degree view, but my legs wrapped around the stick in such a way that they barely cleared the rounded cutouts of the cockpit instrument panel. The left and right consoles hugged me on either side, and the airtight fit of the oxygen/communications mask would definitely take some getting used to.

"Once I remove these, the seats are hot," he warned, reminding me not to pull on the yellow ejection seat handles.

"Got it," I assured him as he proceeded to remove the red-bannered ground safety pins.

He slid back to descend the ladder, then, almost as an afterthought—certainly a tacit forewarning—he reached into his pants pocket and handed me an airsickness bag. "You won't need it," he said reassuringly. Even though I'd heard a number of stories to the contrary, about 90 percent of me believed him.

Captain Maxwell leaned in from the top of the ladder before taking his place in the seat directly in front of mine. "Once we're at altitude, I'll give you a chance to fly the airplane, so I want to review a few of the controls. What you have here are almost perfect duplicates of mine up front. This is the throttle, and that's the 'push to talk' radio button. You don't want to push it. You'll be on intercom hot mic to me the whole time, so whenever you talk I'll hear you without you having to press any buttons. And we always exercise what we call positive transfer of control. When I'm about to have you take over the controls, I'll say 'You have the airplane.' That's when you take over the controls and respond with 'I have the airplane.' The same applies when you turn it back over to me."

"Got it, sir," I responded. He went on to point out the other relevant controls: air speed, attitude, and rate of climb indicators; altimeter; accelerometer . . .

"I'll read the checklist out loud but there are over fifty settings for me to check even before we start the engine, so I won't have time to explain the details. Just soak in the experience."

"Looking forward to it, sir," I assured him.

I found it interesting that we began to taxi with the canopy still open; apparently the T-33 air conditioner is all but worthless at low power settings. Feeling the wind hit what little of my face was still exposed felt invigorating. "Keep your hands clear," cautioned Captain Maxwell as we approached the runway. A loud electric buzz emanated from the canopy's motor as he lowered the transparent enclosure and sealed it tight. "Canopy locked, flaps 75 percent, elevator trim tab neutral, oil pressure normal, oxygen normal . . . Here we go."

We were cleared for takeoff and he smoothly advanced the throttle to military power (100 percent). Strangely, I was not pinned to the back of my seat as I had expected. "Fifty knots, the rudders are now effective so I'm sliding my feet from the brakes onto the pedals . . . Ninety knots, I'm pulling back on the stick to raise the nose just a bit . . . 110 knots, I'm pulling it back to rotate . . . retracting the gear, gear up and locked . . . retracting the flaps." Captain Maxwell went above and beyond in talking me through everything. Our acceleration was gradual at first, but about ten seconds later it really kicked in. "How are you doing back there?"

I wisely censored the honest response of "F***ing awesome!" and instead replied "Fine, sir," in as cool a voice as I could muster.

I've found that the first time we do anything in life is generally the most memorable, but for an inexperienced neophyte like I certainly was at the time, the elation I felt rocketing skyward at 6,000 feet per minute was almost inexpressible. While gazing out the small window of a 727 was exciting, there was never any doubt that I was *being flown*—a passenger transported to my destination. The same can't be said about that first T-bird flight. With 360 degrees of unobstructed visibility afforded by the glass bubble encircling the cockpit, it literally felt like I was *flying*—much the same as Wart (young Arthur) described when he was turned into a bird in *The Once and Future King*.

We banked to the left and I had a magnificent view of the Academy complex beneath us. I could recognize the golf course, Falcon Stadium, and a few of the buildings, but it was impossible to see the markings on the Terrazzo defining where we had to march throughout the day, or for that matter *any* borders or boundaries on the ground. I understood why similar observations are often the first shared by astronauts when describing what it's like to orbit the Earth.

We leveled off at altitude and Captain Maxwell accelerated to just under 450 knots. "Here we go, Norty," he announced before commencing with the same tactical aerobatics used in combat dogfights. He pulled the nose up a bit, then smoothly drew the stick all the way to the right. We rotated a full 360 degrees along our longitudinal axis in my first aileron roll. It happened so quickly it was hard to believe that we were actually flying inverted, and I certainly wasn't feeling the crush of g-forces I'd anticipated. That was about to change.

"Don't forget to squeeze," the captain reminded me, referring to the Anti-G Straining Maneuver technique I had learned to mitigate the potential for grayout and loss of consciousness resulting from positive g's forcing blood from my brain to my lower extremities. The next thing I knew we were in a slight dive to pick up speed, then the stick came straight back into my stomach. Our nose arched skyward as I was slammed with almost 800 pounds of pressure—just under 4.5 g's smashing me into the seat. I strained hard by contracting the muscles in my legs and thighs, doing everything in my power to prevent the blood from draining from my brain. It took almost thirty seconds before we arced all the way around through the inverted position and returned back to straight and level flight; my first loop had just taken us through about 4,000 feet in altitude. While I didn't experience any gray-out, I was sweating up a storm from the anti-g straining exercises.

The next thirty minutes were consumed with a potpourri of exhilarating Basic Fighter Maneuvers (BFMs) that seemed to have us spinning and rotating in every conceivable direction: the Immelmann, Split-s, Cuban 8, High-g barrel roll—all well-rehearsed aerial dogfighting tactics that meant little to me at the time, but that I'd soon be executing on my own during undergraduate pilot training.

During debrief, Captain Maxwell shared that only a small percentage of those who aspire to become pilots actually earn their wings. "Don't believe it when you hear about 'natural born pilots,' Norty. There's no amount of innate aptitude that can replace focus and discipline. If you study hard enough and learn your craft that much harder than the next guy, you'll be amazed at how 'lucky' you'll get, and before you know it, you'll be up there at the controls on your own. This is probably the most competitive profession in the world, but if you want it bad enough, you can make it happen. You *will* make it happen."

Those words kept me going through the grueling physical, mental, and emotional rigors of basic cadet training inside the cadet area, and even more punishing when we marched to Jack's Valley, a 3,300-acre wooded training zone where we were pushed well beyond what we *thought* had been our physical limits. I was supercharged to do whatever it took to earn those pilot wings. I remember a distinct moment—right in the middle of Hell Week, in the midst of various "initiation rituals" that have long since been banned—that I stopped and looked out the window, and clear as day it hit me: *I really want to do this. I don't care what they throw at me or how bad things get; there is nothing that will stop me from achieving this goal.*

I sure hoped he spoke the truth about hard work and study compensating for less-than-stellar aptitude, because the first time I took the stick of my T-41 trainer was a real challenge for me. While Captain Maxwell flew that fighter as if it were his second skin, I had difficulty keeping the most basic single-engine prop plane in straight and level flight. A small wind gust had me overcompensating and setting my modified Cessna 172 rocking and rolling on all three axes, cutting through the Colorado sky like a hundred-mile-per-hour washer-tumbler swishing back and forth. It was disappointing for me to see that I was not a natural pilot. Sticking with it through my subsequent 26.5 hours of flight time required extra effort on my part, and a great deal of patience on the part of my instructors.

There are a number of things at which you might not necessarily be a natural. That's when you compensate with extra focus and discipline to gain those skills that will allow you to succeed. It's the old adage that hard work pays big dividends.

★　★　★

It would be easy to just leave it at that and I've heard a number of motivational speakers who do so. But the reality is that sometimes, in spite of prodigious effort, success just doesn't seem to be in the cards—when the cold, hard facts make it clear that this one is never going to land in your court. Let's face it, it doesn't matter how focused and disciplined I am, I'm about as likely to quarterback the Redskins as I am to dine with Julius Caesar. It would be disingenuous for me to say that we can do *anything* we want. So the question becomes, *does there ever come a point at which the smartest course of action is to just cut your losses and throw in the towel?* About midway through my fourth-class year I looked in the mirror and struggled with that same question.

To achieve my goal of becoming a pilot, it was imperative that I excel academically. I knew of no better fit than a degree in aeronautical engineering. On paper, this was an impeccable plan. The only problem was that in spite of round-the-clock study sessions and dogged determination, I couldn't generate anything better than a "C" on any of my assignments. The only aircraft that would get me into would be headed back to Toms River, one way. It was frustrating at best, and the thought of facing Dad with word that I had botched the opportunity was downright disheartening. Failure was not in his lexicon.

That's when Bob Munson stepped in. Bob was ultimately our class president—one of those guys whom everyone looked up to. He was—and is today—my very best friend. The hard science disciplines came easily to Bob—physics, math, chemistry. It's no surprise that he'd become a physician. Bob could probably set his watch by all the nights I'd drop by his room or desk—interrupting his own studies—completely flummoxed by some concept that was flying miles over my head. "They haven't given us enough information to calculate this one, right?" I'd lament, tossing the impossible assignment onto his desk. *Evaluate the derivative of x 3 + x 2 + 5x at x = –2,* he would read, probably wondering to himself how he could be best friends with someone who couldn't even grasp elementary equations such as these.

Then he'd patiently try to help me understand the concept so that I could figure it out myself. It was an uphill battle, and I never seemed to make it to the summit. So many nights I'd get so frustrated that I'd redirect our conversation to some world event that had just occurred, and I'd debate the implications of whatever happened with him. "Hey, Bob . . . Did you hear that Nassar just died? What do you know about this new guy, Sadat?" "Kent State? That's in Ohio, right?" "Nixon's right about this one . . . tipping our hand with a withdrawal deadline would kill any leverage we might have in any negotiations with North Vietnam." I found those topics far more stimulating than math or chemistry equations.

One night when I approached Bob with yet another math dilemma, he tossed aside the workbook and turned the tables with a question for me. "Schwartz, how long are you going to torture yourself like this? Besides your whining about anything that involves the left side of your brain, all I ever hear about is *Nixon did this,* or *the UN did that.* Get over to the faculty offices and migrate to one of the soft sciences: Poli Sci, IR, Home Economics, *anything* but Engineering."

It made perfect sense on so many levels, and I'm still baffled why I didn't think of it myself. Thanks to Bob's advice, I switched majors and ended up on the dean's list for academic excellence in every subsequent semester, graduating with a double major in political science and international affairs. But I learned a greater lesson that helped me deal with challenges in my commands all the way up to the Tank (the chairman of the Joint Chiefs' private conference room), as it helps me with today's challenges in the boardroom.

This was my attempt to be "studious" in our senior year at the Academy.
Schwartz personal collection.
Photo by Rick Douglas.

**Instead of throwing in the towel,
change the playing field and ADAPT.**

★ ★ ★

Volunteering came naturally to me and resulted in my serving in a number of cadet leadership positions. I became a squadron commander and wing operations and training officer—high-visibility positions in which I learned advanced leadership skills. I was having fun and building a reputation.

During the summer months I would occasionally visit Dad in New Jersey, but the truth is I didn't particularly characterize that as my home anymore; I found my time much better spent exploring the plethora of specialized training opportunities the Air Force offered.

In one case I took the basic underwater demolition course with the SEALS out in Coronado—my very first introduction to special operations. Even back then I had great respect for the special operators of all the services, whether SEALS, Special Forces, or Rangers. Talk about a sense of camaraderie and family—you'd be hard-pressed to top the dedication and commitment of the operators. In another I took the Army Basic Airborne Course (Jump School) at Fort Benning, Georgia, where I learned how to safely jump out of airplanes. I emerged a fully accredited paratrooper before starting my sophomore first semester.

In my final summer before senior year, I led the so-called K squadron, whose purpose was to help cadets who had trouble acclimating to the Academy way of life during basic training—perhaps attitude problems, or just not putting forth the effort required to succeed. Our job was to "retrain" them and hopefully get them back into the swing of things. Turning their lives around felt very rewarding, but I also learned early on that we weren't going to bend the rules for slackers. Our intent was not to make friends. Standards were high for a reason, and the last thing we

Winter Commander

Norton A. Schwartz

After leaving the Wing Staff, I served as the 34th Squadron Commander during the winter term. Leading one's peers at the wholesale level was an important lesson.
Schwartz personal collection

wanted was for those who failed to meet those standards to become Air Force officers. In those cases, we suggested that they just move on.

★ ★ ★

When I reflect back on my four years at the Academy, certain highlights come to mind:

- July 20, 1969, a few days shy of my first full month at the Academy. TVs were set up all over the Terrazzo-level meeting rooms, but not nearly enough to accommodate the two-thousand-plus cadets (not to mention instructors and staff) cramming to witness *Apollo 11* touching down on the surface of the moon. You could hear a pin drop until Neil Armstrong announced "Houston, Tranquility Base here. The Eagle has landed." Then a great cheer erupted as my brethren shared this historic event. Almost six hours later, Col. "Buzz" Aldrin became the second man to walk on the moon, and this cheer was even louder than the first. Aldrin was one of our own, having served as aide to the dean of faculty in the original Academy cadre in 1955 and 1956.
- Thursday night pep rallies and Saturday football games.
  - On October 18 of my first year, the Falcons beat Oregon 60–13 in a game known as the "Fog Bowl"—the fog so bad that we couldn't see the field from the stands.
  - November 1, 1969. We emerged the victors 13–6 over Army, perhaps inspired by the Army's antics the day before the game, when Army helicopters "strafed" our cadet area with twelve thousand leaflets— their own attempt at PSYOPS (Psychological Operations) that backfired on them.
  - October 16, 1971. Army tried again with four helicopters flown in from Fort Carson, but they were chased away by Air Force F-4s, with a 20–7 victory serving as perfect icing on the cake.
- Singing in the Academy Jewish choir.

The common thread is that each of these recollections can be traced directly back to that newfound sense of family, camaraderie, and bonding that the Air Force provides. This would continue to expand through the years, and still serves as a unique foundation for the magnificent and lasting friends we've made.

Can you spot the real fighter triple-ace amidst the four imposters? Skip Sanders,
Bob Frohlich, Bob Munson, and Ron Scott . . . and our first Commandant of Cadets,
Colonel Robin Olds, shortly before his arrival at the Academy.

USAF photo / Schwartz personal collection

I found cadet life supportive of my personal needs for routine and high expectations; throughout my life I'd been raised with both. It reinforced what I'd
been taught: that from challenges come opportunities. Napoleon once said that
"ability is of little account without opportunity." The key is being fully prepared
to take advantage of those opportunities. The playing field was one where just
being good enough didn't cut it. I pushed myself to the very limit of my ability.
The Academy pushed me harder—helped me to reach deep within to tap capabilities I didn't even know I had. It was the first time in my life that I felt a real
sense of family, and this would only grow through the years as the larger Air
Force became my family.

★ ★ ★

On June 6, 1973, I made my final march as a cadet. Along with 843 of my class-
mates, I marched into Falcon Stadium, took my seat, and listened to Senator
Barry Goldwater deliver our commencement address. I graduated with both academic and military honors for all eight semesters and ended up twenty-eighth
in our class of 844. It was a great experience that had a lot to do with building
my character, both shaping my values and amplifying those that I had gained
earlier. It also provided me with a potential career path that would be both
meaningful and fun. It was four years well spent.

You can tell a great deal about a military aircraft by its nickname. There's the Phantom. The Eagle. The Tomcat. The Hornet. Carefully chosen handles that strike fear in the enemy. Then there's the T-37. Some called her the Screaming Mimi, others the 6,000-pound dog whistle. Officially she was known as the Tweet—the very first jet that I trained on. With side-by-side seating like the T-41, there was no ladder for entry; we just popped open the canopy and, with one quick step into a small cutout rung in the side of the fuselage, climbed right in—kind of like mounting a horse. The high-pitched squeal of her twin J69 engines penetrated our earplugs like a dozen smoke detectors screaming in protest of a burning side of bacon.

Welcome to Del Rio, Texas, in 1973, one of the few places where you could find an Iranian, a Saudi, and a scrawny Jewish kid from Jersey munching on Whataburgers while quizzing each other on aircraft emergency procedures.

Hamid held up a flashcard that read ABORT.

"Throttles—idle. Wheel brakes—as required," I replied as I reached for some fries.

Del Rio was the home of Laughlin AFB, where I spent a year in undergraduate pilot training. Each day began with a briefing that would include an instructor's "Stand Up," where he would call upon students to stand up and recite—verbatim—procedures and protocols unique to whatever aircraft we were flying at the time. A correct answer to these "Boldface/Ops Limits" would be met with an almost imperceptible nod. Any deviation would elicit a simple, "Sit down," which was not indicative of the repercussions—sometimes a grounding from that day's flight activities.

Undergraduate pilot training was another rung on the ladder to earning our wings. Those who couldn't cut it would be eliminated from training; such ejections were not uncommon.

We had exchange programs with foreign governments. Regardless of background or nationality, we all bonded as a team and helped each other. I learned a valuable lesson way before it became politically correct, one that served me well years later when I'd be working hand in hand with foreign leaders and chiefs of defense from Turkey, Saudi Arabia, UAE, Korea, Japan, and scores of other countries.

Embrace diversity.

★ ★ ★

Mike Harmon, a fellow Academy grad, was my roommate. We helped each other out, we pushed each other. Mike was much more of a natural flyer, while I was much more an "understand and follow procedure" student. He counseled me on flying skill and I helped him on process and procedure; one couldn't ask for a better dynamic. We initially lived in the barracks together. About six months in, they allowed us to move off-base and we jumped at the opportunity. We moved into the King's Point apartment complex right around the time we progressed from the 37s to 38s, so it felt like a sense of freedom and cutting the cord on all fronts. This was literally the first time I had lived on my own, so that was an adventure in and of itself—my first opportunity "outside of the fence."

We started with academics, progressed to simulators, and finally got actual flight time. At first it's pretty basic: takeoffs and landings and learning how to be safe. How to communicate with air traffic control and so on. Then, ultimately, we flew solo. Up until then I only had three or four hours of flying solo in the T-41, so soloing the 37 was a major big deal—a substantial milestone for me, as it was later on in the T-38.

Schwartz personal collection

Following our solos, we started to do more advanced maneuvers like formations and aerobatics—those same BFMs I'd experienced in that first orientation flight. Only now—just like Captain Maxwell had predicted—I'd be the one at the controls, and I'd be doing them solo.

The 37 is a medium-performance airplane, with a ceiling of around 25,000 feet. The 38—at least in those days—was definitely considered a high-performance aircraft. Everything happens twice as fast in the 38, and it's not nearly as forgiving as the 37. She'll let you know in no uncertain terms if you've missed the mark. But you're rewarded big-time by that performance.

For me, I had to work to get the hang of both of these aircraft. I've seen some who are natural aviators and I envy them. They just look out of the aircraft and "feel" what to do, but it took quite some time for me to reach that point. Becoming proficient was a real challenge for me—but a fun one.

We had a good class that worked our asses off during the week, then on weekends we'd let off steam waterskiing on Lake Armistead, where the beer flowed quite freely. Work hard, play hard—that defined the year. You put it all together and it was a very good one.

It all culminated in graduation from pilot training. The ceremony was truly the highlight of the entire year. The graduation speaker was James Robinson "Robbie" Risner, who was a brigadier general at the time, a former Vietnam POW and double recipient of the Air Force Cross. The first was for extraordinary heroism in aerial combat, the second for extraordinary heroism and willpower in the face of the enemy during his time as a prisoner of war in North Vietnam. He endured seven years of torture and mistreatment in North Vietnamese captivity, three of which were spent in solitary confinement. To receive my wings and the class academic award from this great man is one of those life moments that I will never forget.

It must have felt incredible for a man of his stature to have such an indelible impact on so many young lives. Never in a million years would I have predicted that thirty-five years later, I would be the one standing at that podium, delivering the commencement address and pinning flight wings on more than thirty young pilots. But on April 24, 2009, that's exactly what happened. Del Rio had changed in those thirty-five years, but the small-town sense of community was still a major feature. That close-knit sense of camaraderie is unforgettable.

When I looked around the auditorium—standing in the exact spot that General Risner stood—a flood of memories came rushing back to me. I was hit by how very much more than flying I had picked up back then. I tried to put myself back in time—to the extent that I asked myself what I had learned over the course of the past thirty-five years that I really wish I'd had the benefit of knowing back then. This is what I came up with, the thoughts that I shared with the new graduate pilots:

I learned that your professionalism and reputation start at the beginning of your career—not when you move up in rank, but right at the very beginning.

I learned that you need to know your business, to be professional, and to understand the platforms which you operate.

I learned that you have to be good at what you do and always stay trustworthy.

If you're not trusted, you can't be effective. On the flip side, if you earn trust and credibility, then opportunities will undoubtedly come your way.

★　★　★

Thundering through Mach 2 she could track and engage enemy targets well beyond visual range, and when her twin GE J79 afterburners kicked in, she howled skyward with an astounding rate of climb that was almost unheard of at the time. As our principal interceptor, air superiority strike fighter, and re-connaissance platform, the F-4 Phantom held fifteen world records for in-flight performance, including those for both absolute altitude and absolute speed. Jam-packed with air-to-air missiles, air-to-ground missiles, and a vast array of bomb packages, the Phantom was our deadliest airborne threat, and like most of my graduating class, I was determined to score one of the few remaining F-4 pilot slots and exploit her immense capabilities to further our objectives in Southeast Asia.

But our participation in Vietnam was winding down, and the reality was that only a select few in my graduating class would receive assignments beyond our own borders. While I would work my buns off in whatever assignment I was given, I really did feel that I could contribute most in some kind of overseas deployment—and never having ventured beyond our own shores, I knew I'd have fun too.

Assignments were determined by a combination of officers' preferences, aircraft availability, and training evaluations. While nothing in the Air Force is guaranteed, between the objective part of my class standing (academic and flight performance evaluations) and the leadership assessments, I didn't find it an unreasonable hope that someday they'd be painting "Captain Norty Schwartz" on the polished titanium airframe beneath the canopy of my first advanced fighter jet.

I wasted no time in filling out the appropriate request forms, then anxiously awaited the good word. It was probably only a few weeks before the notice arrived from the assignment "drop," but it seemed like forever. I ripped open the envelope and saw that I had been slotted for a C-130 position in the Philippines.

If the Phantom was the Ferrari of our fleet, then the 130 "Hercules" might be seen as the Mack Truck. Big, loud, and rugged, the Herc's a noble, blue-collar, versatile machine that can take a beating. The high-winged, rear-ramp-loading four-engine aircraft are stable, light on the controls, and can take off and land almost anywhere that you can find a fairly flat three-thousand-foot-long stretch of land. You're not going to find a better workhorse. On more than one occasion I've lost engines mid-flight, and while these are not situations that I'd look forward to repeating, the decrease in performance was not profound, and I did feel comfortably in control of the aircraft at all times—without any doubt that we'd be able to land safely.

About a year after my arrival at Clark Air Base in the Philippines, the Israeli Air Force used four C-130s in the successful counterterrorist hostage rescue at Entebbe Airport in Uganda. The lead pilot was taught how to fly the C-130 by U.S. Air Force instructors at the same Little Rock AFB where I qualified in the aircraft. IAF Brigadier General Joshua Shani (a lieutenant colonel at the time) told how his takeoff from Sharm el-Sheikh, Egypt, was one of the heaviest in the history of this airplane, substantially exceeding the allowable maximum takeoff weight. Completely packed with the assault team, a Mercedes to be used in a ground deception, Land Rovers, and an additional paratrooper force, by the time he reached the end of the runway under maximum power, he was only two knots over stall speed when he had to lift off. Then, for the next 2,500 miles, he would lead the other three planes in formation under the radar, at about one hundred feet above the water for most of the trip, but occasionally dipping down further at places he deemed particularly dangerous—entirely in the dead of night and under strict radio silence.

Missions like these were exactly what I'd be trained for later on when I transitioned to the special operations side of the business. So when people ask me if I was disappointed when I read about the Herc assignment instead of the F-4, I tell them, "Not only no, but *hell no!*" I was elated to be going overseas.

I am by no means a natural pilot, and I probably would have made a fairly average fighter pilot. Sure, I would have tried hard—but to this day I still think I'm better suited for a crew airplane and there were none any finer than the Hercules.

The Dalai Lama said: "Sometimes not getting what you want is a wonderful stroke of luck."

★ ★ ★

It certainly was in my case. By the time I retired I had accumulated over 4,400 flight hours in a variety of aircraft, and in no small way that's due to a lesson I picked up early on from mentors like Mort Freedman, Al Navas, and Al Peck—legends who saw something special in me despite my many flaws—and maybe even from Dad, who had enough faith in me to spring $99 to buy my first three-piece suit so I could make a good impression in my Academy nomination interview.

There are a number of things that you might not necessarily be a natural at so you have to bear down and work that much harder than the next guy to gain skills that allow you to compete.

★ ★ ★

For the next five months I immersed myself in soaking in everything I could about the mighty bird during my C-130 initial pilot training at Little Rock AFB, then I was off to my first overseas assignment: Clark Air Force Base on Luzon Island, about forty miles northwest of Manila in the Philippines, one of our main support bases for sorties into and out of Vietnam. And the great adventure began.

Flying into Clark for the very first time, I was struck by how lush everything seemed to be, nothing like the gray, dreary shots I recalled from photographs. Sandwiched between Mount Pinatubo to the west and Mount Arayat to the east, the base was a booming metropolis of its own, at that time the largest U.S.

Air Force base in the world outside of the U.S. mainland. Later on I would get a chance to explore the dense jungle foliage, rice terraces, and thatched huts that made this island so unique—but for now my sights were focused on the ramp, which was bustling with all types of military planes, plus a few passenger charters courtesy of Trans International and World Airways. The bulk revolved around the 3rd Tactical Fighter Wing's fleet of Phantoms—F-4Es and F-4Gs—and its aggressor squadron's F-5Es. Up until now, Saigon had been relatively peaceful, but very few believed that calm would continue as the rapidly advancing communist forces made the fall of Saigon imminent. With it would come a massive explosion of evacuation missions. Clark's two parallel runways would barely be able to accommodate the steady stream of Hercs, along with C-141s and the massive C-5s, among the largest aircraft in the world.

With the war winding down, I suppose I wasn't expecting such frenetic activity; certainly nothing like the more routine pace that I'd experienced at both Laughlin and Little Rock—but no complaints—I loved every second of it.

My first two months were all about accumulating flight hours to get certified in theater. The idea was to get as much experience as possible, so my persistent requests to build hours were not only tolerated, they were encouraged. We flew regularly to Thailand, Korea, Japan, and of course all over the Philippines. Each one was more exciting than the last. These were tactical training missions designed to build proficiency in the special tactics we'd soon be using in combat. Before being cleared to fly actual combat missions, we had to demonstrate our piloting skills on a check flight. Mine took place on a sortie from Clark AFB in the Philippines to Utapao Air Base in Thailand, and while I wasn't nervous, the adrenaline certainly flowed, particularly with my examiner standing right behind me. I was enthusiastically chomping on a stick of Juicy Fruit as I pulled up the button for "Hot Mic," a standard procedure that kept the microphone live during takeoffs and landings. "Utapao tower, Sierra five-one-niner on final approach for runway one-eight, gear down," I reported, shortly before making a respectable landing and shutting down the engines.

I swiveled around to jump out of the seat when a big hand clamped down on my shoulder. It belonged to then Staff Sergeant Arne Suvatne, our well-seasoned loadmaster, who shared words of wisdom I will never forget: "Kid, we don't chew gum on hot mic." I suppose being forced to listen to my mastication was not a part of my flight crew's job description (or that of all the air traffic controllers on the net). Message received, and it was one of many that I would receive from NCOs (noncommissioned officers, staff sergeant through chief master sergeant), the real backbone of the Air Force.

It wasn't much later that I was on a flight with Chick Anderson, the flight engineer on the very first C-130 ten-thousand-pound M-121 "Earthquake" bomb drop in Vietnam. Chick was another one of the folks that saw something special in me and maintained an interest over the years. He ended up retiring as a chief master sergeant and was one of the guys who helped me learn the airplane, get a sense of what it meant to be a crew commander, and how to lead NCOs. "Always remember where you came from," he would tell me. Great advice that I would never forget.

The best NCOs have a knack for spotting promising young officers and whipping them into shape, sharing their own tough love to mold the leaders of tomorrow. Some young hotshots discard their counsel, brandishing the gold bars on their epaulets as if they trump twenty-plus years of hard-earned NCO battle scars. They become defensive and resist the advice. Few of these will make it past captain. I have always found it humbling that these seasoned professionals cared enough to take the extra time to share their personal insights with me. Particularly since my next mission would take me into the heart of Vietnam.

Good advice has no rank.

★ ★ ★

Captain Dave Antoon was one of our very best pilots, and I was fortunate to have him beside me one night in late April of 1975 when I was at the controls of his C-130 as it spiraled down over a hot war zone into Tan Son Nhut, South Vietnam. The Saigon airfield was crammed with thousands of South Vietnamese civilians awaiting our arrival so we could whisk them off to safety, only days before the airfield was bombed by VPAF pilots who had defected from the South—pretty exciting for my very first real-world mission.

Dave was an expert aviator—so accomplished that our squadron leadership had enough confidence in him to take this young second lieutenant along with him in-country on this challenging evacuation mission. This was his second of two tours spent in Southeast Asia flying C-130s, including those missions in Cambodia where our country denied its participation.

But now, South Vietnam's demise was imminent. For two years the North Vietnamese had been methodically moving masses of Soviet armored vehicles, artillery, and surface-to-air missiles into the South, setting the scene for the major offensive that was about to ignite. This time it would bring an end to South Vietnam. The U.S. Air Force had flown 5.25 million sorties over South Vietnam, North Vietnam, northern and southern Laos, and Cambodia, and had lost over 2,200 aircraft.

The initial discomfort I felt behind the yoke was a thing of the past. Sure, getting the hang of certain tactics was more challenging than others, but controlling the great behemoth was starting to become as much second nature to me as driving a car. It had better be. I had just been told that *I'd be the one at the controls flying us in.*

★ ★ ★

We suited up and reported in for our preflight briefs, where we learned the day's code words, radio frequencies, and the latest weather conditions. Intel briefed us on the security situation. North Vietnamese and Viet Cong forces now controlled over 60 percent of South Vietnam. Three NVA divisions were closing in on Saigon. There would be no time to refuel, and until we entered the relative safety of Tan Son Nhut's security perimeter, we would be prime targets for the Soviet-made SA-7 Grail shoulder-fired, heat-seeking antiaircraft missiles that played a vital role in neutralizing the South Vietnamese Air Force in the final days of the war. Small arms fire would be a serious threat under 4,500 feet; AAA (antiaircraft artillery) batteries extended our zone of vulnerability.

Even with the most thorough and accurate intel briefs, the reality was that we were flying into hot combat zones and at times it felt like our paint scheme was a giant iridescent bull's-eye rather than our camo green. Our "spiral down" approach pattern was designed to mitigate the threat.

Today's aircrews have the benefit of "smart" countermeasures systems— elaborate sensors tied into onboard radar and missile warning receivers—computers that instantly analyze antiaircraft threats and automatically dispense the appropriate infrared and radio-frequency countermeasures, plus jammers, chaff, and flares. At the press of a button, today's AC-130 SPECTRE gunship can become an airborne fireworks display, dispensing hundreds of flares that emit blinding effervescent trails from both sides and its belly, each a potential target intended to divert incoming missiles away from the aircraft. But in 1975, our onboard suite of countermeasures was decidedly less sophisticated. We would position a loadmaster by the parachute doors with a flare gun, on the lookout for incoming missiles. He would scan the ground and fire the flares toward the flash and trailing smoke trail of any SAMs (surface-to-air missiles) he spotted homing in on us, then radio the cockpit to "Break left" or "Break right," our cue to initiate a vigorous evasive maneuver by heavily banking at a sharp angle *away* from the flare (and terminal trajectory of the missile), while reducing speed so as to decrease the temperature signature of our engines and exhaust. In theory, the missile would be drawn to the two-thousand-plus degrees of the flare's burning magnesium instead of our airplane, but I have no idea if it would have worked or not. Thankfully we never had to employ that tactic.

★   ★   ★

We took off from Clark and crossed the South China Sea without incident, but that was only the beginning. I'd rehearsed the combat "spiral" tactic throughout my prior two months at Clark as I became certified to fly in theater, but despite our realistic simulators and training flights, there's no amount of simulation that can replicate actual battle conditions, where a miscue could earn one a posthumous ribbon instead of a reprimand.

You want to minimize your vulnerability going into an airfield when you're not quite sure what's happening outside the fence line, so the idea is to try to stay above 15,000 feet—above the effective range of AAA and SAMs—until you're well within the confines of the controlled ground area within the fence line. The "Random Steep" approach enables the aircraft to approach upwind at high altitude and high speed, then rapidly corkscrew down in up to a sixty-degree bank, bleeding off enough energy in the downwind break so the flaps and landing gear can be lowered for landing. Timing all this so as to end up properly aligned with the runway can be tricky, particularly when your heart is beating out of your flight suit thanks to the adrenaline rush that comes standard equipment on that initial combat sortie. At about fifty feet I pulled back on the power, executed the flare, and fifty-five tons of airplane gently kissed the runway without my having sheared off the landing gear. Dave gave a quick nod that signaled his satisfaction, but there'd be no time for attaboys. This would be a lightning-fast turnaround in which we'd keep the engines hot, combat load our precious cargo, and get the heck out of Dodge.

★ ★ ★

A standard airdrop mission meant sixty or so paratroopers packed into the back of a Herc. They sat on thick nylon cargo straps running the length of the plane, configured in the shape of a seat. Although no Barcaloungers, they weren't too uncomfortable. On these evac missions, we crammed up to three hundred refugees back there. There were no seats or benches, and no windows except for a few small portholes near the side parachute doors. These "first-class" accommodations consisted of metal pallets spread the length of the aircraft, and cumbersome cargo straps for securing passengers as if they were pallets of ammunition. Children were pinned against their parents and grandparents, some clinging to a single bag stuffed with whatever possessions they were able to throw together before escaping for their lives. A few wore their Sunday finest; many more sported well-worn, perspiration-soaked garments befitting the hot and humid climate. Little girls clutched their favorite dolls. One young, wide-eyed lad wore a Mickey Mouse T-shirt that read DISNEYLAND. THE HAPPIEST PLACE ON EARTH. His father spoke some English and thanked our loadmaster as he assisted them onto a floormat.

"Nắm chặt lấy các dây thừng, khi máy bay cất cánh thì sẽ bị dằn xóc rất mạnh," the staff sergeant warned the man. *Hold onto the strap. Once we take off it will get very bumpy.*

★ ★ ★

Inside the cockpit, we were still on high alert. "You have the airplane," Dave said as he turned over the controls to me to prepare for takeoff.

"I have the airplane," I responded, assuring positive control at all times, just as I had learned from Captain Maxwell during my very first T-bird indoctrination flight.

Once our tires cleared the pavement, I feathered the yoke to establish the six-degree pitch up that we'd need to clear the ground, then pulled back to generate an attitude that allowed us to maintain our initial climb speed. Dave retracted the landing gear and I pulled us into the tight forty-five-degree bank (the maximum allowed with fifty degrees of flaps engaged) that would safely spiral us up without leaving Tan Son Nhut's outer limits. We had made it out safely. But just a few days later, the crew of C-130 72-1297 from the 314th TAW wasn't as fortunate. Destroyed by rocket fire while on the ground at Tan Son Nhut, she became the final USAF C-130 lost in the war.

★ ★ ★

My next mission was somewhat similar, but this time would forgo the cover of darkness and fly in and out in broad daylight. Operation FREQUENT WIND (the evacuation of American civilians and at-risk South Vietnamese from Saigon during the final days of the war) was in full swing and time was not on our side. We spiraled down into Bien Hoa, a fighter/tactical airlift base slightly northeast of Tan Son Nhut in the northern part of Saigon. If anything, security at Bien Hoa was even worse than Tan Son Nhut. North Vietnamese forces had severed the roads around Saigon and they were about to begin shelling Bien Hoa. Once the town of Xuan Loc fell on April 23, 1975, Bien Hoa became indefensible. During our descent we could see the civilians attempting to flee the countryside and jam the main thoroughfares in their hasty mass exodus for the coast. Even that was nothing compared to what we saw at Bien Hoa—a beehive in which thousands of refugees were frantically trying to convince the authorities to grant them access to our planes so they could flee before the impending communist takeover.

Once again, we combat-loaded hundreds of refugees, packing them in and strapping them down as we raced to remove them from harm's way. It was well over a hundred degrees that day, with the harsh midday sun beating down on the olive-green fuselage, creating a blast-furnace effect inside—almost three hundred evacuees strapped together inside an airborne sauna—less than ideal conditions in which to experience our high-degree corkscrew ascent. When all was said and done, we made it out safely and without incident—one of the final aircraft to do so. I remained on high alert until we had cleared Vietnamese airspace and were well over the South China Sea on our six-hour flight to Guam. When "Red Crown" control bid us "Good Day" and indicated clear skies, I heaved a deep, cleansing breath of relief. Big mistake.

Flying into Tan San Nhut or Bien Hoa—or any combat zone—it's only natural that I'd be 100 percent focused and engaged. It's hard not to be, considering the firepower that was aimed in our direction. But over the course of the five- to six-hour flight to Guam, I tended to relax and let my guard down. It's not as if the fishing boats we were flying over at twenty-five thousand feet posed much of a threat, and our descent into Andersen would entail a standard landing pattern, unlike the dangerous spiral tactic we employed in combat. "Andersen tower, Juliet six-one-niner is with you at five thousand feet," Capt Antoon radioed in, after being instructed to switch to the tower's frequency.

"Roger, six-one-niner. Enter a left downwind for runway zero-six left at 1,600 feet," rattled off the controller, speaking at a mile a minute in attempt to service a cacophony of flights trying to cut in. With over 110,000 Vietnamese refugees transported to the United States through Guam, it's no wonder the frequency was jammed with landing and departing aircraft. The airfield was taxed well beyond its intended capacity.

"Left downwind for six left at 1,600 feet, Juliet six-one-niner," Dave confirmed.

All well and good. I was now under the purview of Andersen's air traffic controller and in just a few minutes we'd be touching down on Andersen's main runway. I continued to follow the controller's instructions until we had our gear down on short final approach for landing. It was then that I noticed a C-141 still occupying the same runway upon which we were about to land. "Juliet six-one-niner confirming runway zero-six left?" Dave questioned.

"Six-one-niner, go around! Go around!" responded the controller, clearly alarmed that he had cleared an aircraft to land on a runway that was already occupied. I jammed the throttles full forward and our nose pitched skyward. What had been a smooth descent rather quickly became an aggressive ascent, accompanied by g-forces that were foreign to the folks crammed in the back. Many tipped and convulsed all over each other. We brought the aircraft back around and this time we were able to land without incident, but it was really raw back there. Up front, we had the luxury of donning oxygen masks, but I didn't envy the crew who had to clean up that mess.

I learned a great lesson that day.

Never let your guard down, and expect the unexpected.

I learned that not a single mission was routine. I'd have to consciously psych myself up for every one. You'd think that nearly flying into a seventy-ton cargo jet would be enough for this to sink in. But it wasn't. It would come back to haunt me on more than one occasion.

★ ★ ★

These were exciting times for this young man, and by now it was clear to me that I wanted to devote my life to this profession. In the aviation field, the idea is to accelerate as rapidly as you can from a copilot to a pilot to an aircraft commander to an instructor to a flight examiner. There is a hierarchy in the flying game and you want to be recognized for both your competence and your leadership capacity, whether you fly in a single-seat airplane or multi-place airplane.

Every bit as important as your airmanship is your capacity to build teams. A solid, well-oiled team is the foundation of formation flying—a group of airplanes flying in perfect synchronicity, sometimes approaching the speed of sound with only a few feet separating your wing tip from that of your wingman's. The aircraft lead runs the show, and he damn well better know how to inspire trust in his team because everyone's life depends on it. Wingmen follow the lead almost without question, and they've got to inspire trust of their own by maintaining a constant awareness of the potential for a midair collision, and a situational awareness that keeps them at the ready to assume the lead if necessary.

So you want to accelerate, you want to accumulate hours, you want to build experience as rapidly as possible, and you want to move ahead in this incredibly competitive scenario. To break ahead of the pack would take more than just proficient flying skills—at this point almost all of us had those. I noticed that those who were less activist might not accelerate as quickly as those who were constantly volunteering for missions, so I volunteered for every flying opportunity on the planet. But so did almost everyone else.

The problem was that there were only so many missions to go around, and I was rapidly becoming restless. So if I wasn't flying, I'd volunteer for anything else that I could do—in many cases chores that others might choose to turn away from. It all goes back to that Toms River work ethic that was pounded into me by Dad and Erna. I tried to do the best I could no matter the job—to be the best officer I could be. The more that I took on, the more that earned me other opportunities along the way. Higher-ups were starting to notice me.

I had only been there for five months or so when it was announced that there would be a change in wing leadership. Colonel James "Bagger" Baginski would be replaced by his vice wing commander, Colonel Al Navas, in a change-of-command ceremony that would take place on August 1. Bagger had just received the Air Force Distinguished Service Medal for being "personally responsible for the administration and execution of the entire aerial resupply effort of Cambodia and the Air Force's support of the Saigon evacuation." He was well respected, well liked, and known for his ready smile and firm handshake. A founding member of Airlift Tanker Association and a fellow C-130 pilot with more than five thousand hours, he would go on to become a major general and driving force behind building our air mobility into the global force it is today. The ceremony would be no small affair. In fact, General Paul K. "P. K." Carlton would be flying in to officiate Colonel Navas's assumption of command.

While I certainly looked forward to attending the ceremony, I never thought that I'd be the one running it. But that's exactly how it played out. To this day I can't say who chose me for the assignment—maybe it was our squadron commander—but out of the entire wing, I was selected to plan and execute the entire event.

So here I am, a first lieutenant who's been on the base for only a few months, responsible for coordinating a multitude of base elements that I barely even knew existed: Protocol, Public Affairs, Security Police, Transportation, Civil Engineering, Communications—each would play a central role, and just one of them failing to perform could spell catastrophe for the entire event. Even the smallest detail would have to be anticipated and executed, and I'd have to contemplate all the "what-ifs" and build in plenty of backups.

Pieces of the puzzle would include invitations, venue preparation (podium, PA system and backup system, weights for the speeches, seating for the public and VIPs, signage, lawn mowed, flags secured and in place, flowers), live band, honor guard, security police, base entry for guests, transportation, escorts for Distinguished Visitors (DVs) (along with welcome packages), corsages for spouses, bouquet for Bagger's wife, media, agenda, scripts, rehearsals, writing and printing certificates of appreciation, troop formation and alignment . . . and this was just for the *ceremony*. Throw in the reception, and coordinating the *funding* for all this—without sacrificing any of my time in the cockpit—and you have an exciting growth opportunity and display of confidence by the boss, who never doubted that I could handle it. And it came off without a hitch.

I can't tell you how many of my peers came up to me in the days that followed and asked how I had pulled this off, as if I were the one cutting the grass and painting the bleachers. It all goes back to putting into practice everything we had just been taught back at the Academy: having a clear vision and inspiring others to help you achieve that vision. It's called leadership. Empowering those who would be executing the tasks, respecting their qualifications without micromanaging, and getting them excited about the important role they had in creating an unforgettable event for the boss(es).

I got an assignment that nobody really wanted. I took it on with enthusiasm and gratitude for the challenge. I worked my ass off and stretched myself to navigate totally uncharted waters and never stopped to question whether I could perform, even though it meant that this first lieutenant would be coordinating elements all the way up to the general officer level.

I worked hard on it and it turned out well and it earned me a bit of visibility both with Bagger and with the Navas family. I became known to them and respected by them. It was one of those serendipitous moments that I never could have planned or plotted, or even imagined, really.

That awareness turned out to be quite helpful both professionally and personally. I grew extremely close with both Barbara and Al Navas, to the point of them unofficially adopting me, and it was a wonderful thing. They invested in me. They took an interest and they paid attention and then, within the bounds of an elder and a junior, they coached me and they mentored me, and on more than one occasion they kicked me in the ass—which was well-deserved at the time.

Al offered me everything I always thought a father should, yet for whatever reason my own father was unable to provide. We continued to stay quite close with the Navases through the years and ultimately they stepped in to become my surrogate parents at my wedding. And it all started with my taking on a challenge that, frankly, nobody else wanted. That change-of-command ceremony became a key turning point in my life, professionally and personally. It allowed this young lieutenant to begin to separate from the pack a little, and that attention paid huge dividends many years later. This was the moment when people saw a breadth of possibilities in this young officer, who had reflected some good operational instincts and also some broader interests—that he might be valuable and worth investing in. They thought I had potential. And even more importantly than my superiors, my peers began to notice.

This is a very competitive business—some might even say cutthroat in certain regards—but this put me on the map in a very positive light. I did my best not to walk up anybody's back over the years. My hunch is that most people will tell you that was the case—that I never threw anybody under the bus, not because that was a politically correct thing to do but because that was just not my style, not how I was raised. Once again, it all goes back to character, values, and integrity. Forged in Toms River, reinforced in Colorado Springs.

I don't remember all the details of that day, but I do remember that I slept very well that night. Margaret Thatcher hit the nail on the head with this one:

Look at a day when you are supremely satisfied at the end. It's not a day when you lounge around doing nothing; it's when you've had everything to do and you've done it [well].

★ ★ ★

Even after the Academy, boxing remained a great source of exercise for me and I continued to follow the sport. In September of 1975 I was living in Chambers Hall, a high-rise BOQ (bachelor officers' quarters) on Clark Air Base in the Philippines. It had been a long day of flying and it was early evening when I noticed a group of officers gathered around the small black-and-white TV set in the squadron briefing room. I couldn't see the screen but I had no trouble hearing the distinctive voice booming from the speaker. "I'm gonna give him a real whoopin'! It'll be a killa and a thrilla and a chilla, when I get that gorilla in Manila," promised world heavyweight champion Muhammad Ali. The "gorilla" referred to archrival Joe Frazier, whom Ali was to battle for the heavyweight title in what would be one of the greatest boxing matches of all time—the "Thrilla in Manila."

Less than sixty miles northwest of the Araneta Coliseum in which the fight would take place, our squadron briefing room was standing room only. At 10:45 a.m., October 1, 1975, the bell signaled the start of round 1. Rather than his usual high-spirited dance around the ring, Ali marched flatfooted toward Frazier and unleashed a vicious series of combinations. The squadron erupted. When it was over, Ali raised his arms in victory, then collapsed onto the canvas. It was an inspiring match—so much so that I headed for the base gym, strapped on the gloves and gave the bag a whoopin' of my own.

★   ★   ★

My tour at Clark was successful in terms of flying airlift missions as a young aircraft commander, and I departed Luzon with a great sense of gratitude—thankful that I was given the opportunity to serve my country and emerge from combat safely—but even more grateful for those who paid the ultimate price in service to our great country.

In spite of the general antiaircraft threat over Vietnam, it would be dishonest to claim that I was ever actually fired upon while in the air, so I wouldn't want to misrepresent that. But our country needs people who perform challenging aviation tasks well and it was my great privilege to be on teams that fell into that category.

From Clark I went to Squadron Officers' School (SOS) and graduated number one in my class of five hundred—so I got to Little Rock with a bit of a reputation.

Chapter Two

I'LL NEVER BE
YOUR PUPPY DOG

DECEMBER 1977–JUNE 1989

From the moment I arrived back at Little Rock AFB in late 1977, I felt that all eyes were on me at the 61st Tactical Airlift Squadron: I was a young lead pilot—well qualified—and that top slot at SOS did not go unnoticed. Less than three years had passed since I'd left the base after my initial qualification training, during which I'd soaked in as much as I could from the finest C-130 flight instructors in the world. But now I'd be in the instructor's seat, honored to pass along whatever skills and insights I'd picked up overseas.

I consciously reflected back to those skills and examination techniques that worked best for me, and why I responded better to some examiners than others. One name that came to mind was Lieutenant Colonel John D. Butterfield, the DOV during the first half of my time at Clark. The DOV (Chief of Standardization and Evaluation) sits atop the pilot training hierarchy, a highly respected position of responsibility and leadership generally assigned to the wing's most proficient aviator. He or she ensures that standards are upheld and flight examiners are well trained and fully qualified. They oversee check flights and certifications, assess mission effectiveness and safety rates, and they're often among the first to recognize a young aviator's potential. I'd grown close to Colonel Butterfield; we worked well together and he was a big supporter. I was sorry to see him leave, but in many ways he was one of those I'd try to emulate.

So I joined 61st with a little bit of momentum. One of my first orders of business would be getting to know my new squadron commander; he'd be my boss, and more than just a little influential as to how successful the next few years might be. You can imagine my surprise when it turned out to be Colonel Butterfield—yet another example of how serendipity played such an important role in my success.

It turned out to be a superb squadron. I was surrounded by talented airmen; many of whom went on to be very successful, including several flag officers. Rich Mentemeyer became deputy commander of U.S. Southern Command; Chris Kelly earned three stars and became vice commander of Air Mobility Command; and Mike Moffitt went on to serve as director of logistics of Air Mobility Command. Somehow, the puzzle pieces continued to fall into place for me.

★ ★ ★

Many years before 9/11 made the word "terrorism" such a common part of our vocabulary, I was chosen to participate in an early certification exercise for the nascent counterterrorism capability that the Army was building. It was a classified project spearheaded by Colonel Bob Mountel of the 5th Special Forces Group, known as "Blue Light." We sent our three best crews to a location on the West Coast. Our job was to insert and subsequently recover Army Special Forces troops on tight drop and landing zones, always at night and with absolute minimum lighting.

While at Clark I had become certified in the special operations low-level mission area and carried that credential to Little Rock. It proved valuable since many of these flights were flown on a low-altitude flight course used to avoid enemy detection in clandestine settings or higher-threat environments. We'd sometimes use geographical features of the terrain as cover, by flying in, rather than over, valleys, ridges, and such. It allowed us to literally "fly under the radar."

Totally unbeknownst to me at the time, while Blue Light engaged in rigorous exercises to hone their new tradecraft, a second—and totally independent—counterterrorist unit was undergoing training of its own at a different location at Fort Bragg. Colonel Charlie Beckwith's organization would eventually be referred to as Delta Force. Both Blue Light and Delta would take time to come up to speed. Their missions were intense, as was the rapidly mounting rivalry between them.

Our military airlift piece of the puzzle was the same for both: to develop a reliable capability to deliver their teams to clandestine drop or landing zones anywhere in the world, in the black of night, utilizing little or no communication, with very little advance notice—and to safely get them home again. Major General "Bagger" Baginski, the outgoing wing commander at Clark for whom I coordinated the change-of-command ceremony, was deeply involved in this in his new capacity as deputy for operations, Military Airlift Command (MAC). New skills were being learned, new techniques and tactics developed. This was the embryonic stage of today's elite teams of operators under JSOC, the Joint Special Operations Command. What an honor it was to have played even a tiny part in its inception. It would not be the last.

★ ★ ★

One of my goals was to qualify in all of the special missions associated with the airlift business at the time, and I was fortunate enough to have achieved this—all with the exception of the ski-equipped variant that is used for snow and ice operations at the poles. Some of these include air-to-air refueling (AAR); AC-130 Spectre gunship; electronic warfare and electronic attack; airborne early warning and control; combat search and rescue; low-altitude parachute extraction system (LAPES); Fulton surface-to-air recovery system (STARS); and all manner of tactical airlift, including flares-ejecting night illumination devices.

The LAPES mission was a challenging one that we employed when supplies had to be delivered to areas in which neither landing nor high-altitude airdrops were options. The supplies were loaded into the cargo bay on special pallets that were connected to a cluster of large extraction parachutes. As we approached the desired drop point, we reduced airspeed and descended to an extremely low altitude—somewhere between five and ten feet off the ground. At that point, the rear cargo door was already lowered and the drogue chute released. Once that caught the wind, it would yank out the main extraction chutes, which in turn dragged the cargo out the door. Gravity took over and it would drop to the ground fairly gently. We'd ascend back to our cruising altitude and head back home. If you think this sounds easy, try maintaining stability just a few feet off the ground as the aircraft's center of gravity races from one end of the aircraft to the other.

Center of gravity is one of the primary factors we have to take into account in order to maintain that aircraft's stability. It's a state of balanced equilibrium that's achieved when the cargo is properly loaded. Can you imagine how that's disrupted when your cargo is a seventeen-ton Sheridan tank racing down the rails toward the open rear cargo door? As the weight moves back, it pulls the nose skyward, so we had to compensate with strong forward pressure on the yoke—perfectly coordinated with the tank's release. Then the instant the tank flew out that door, what had been an exceedingly tail-heavy airplane suddenly wanted to *drop* its nose and dive to the ground—our cue to immediately pull back the yoke from its nearly full-forward position, lest we slam into the ground. Picture two kids perfectly balanced on a see-saw at the playground. What would happen if one jumped off? If those kids had a combined weight of around thirty thousand pounds, you'd have a clear picture of one of the challenges a pilot is up against with the LAPES mission.

★ ★ ★

Out of hundreds of aviators, Major Al "Herc Driver" Peck was one-of-a-kind. Arguably the best C-130 pilot at "the Rock," he was the senior flight examiner and also my boss. During off hours we had grown quite close, to the point of his unofficially adopting me as a son. We were leading a large C-130 formation one evening on a nine-ship night instrument air drop mission, and I was being evaluated for my "Lead Formation" certification. Even though I was already a flight examiner myself (in fact, second only to Al at the time), it was obviously necessary that I pass this evaluation. But I choked.

For the LAPES mission, we descended to between five and ten feet off the ground, then the extraction chutes would drag our cargo out the rear door. If executed properly, the cargo would drop to the ground fairly gently. My crew never let me forget how I botched this up on my very first attempt! (USAF photo of LAPES drop during the Battle of Khe Sanh, Vietnam, 1968.)
Schwartz personal collection

As formation lead, it was my job to keep all nine airplanes in formation and ensure that our cargos were sequentially dropped at the right place and the right moment, in spite of the miserable weather conditions we were encountering. To do this, I was supposed to give the other planes a "one-minute notice," a "five-second notice," and a "drop now" electronic drop signal. Just as I was about to give the one-minute prompt, my radio barked with an important contact from air traffic control, warning me about other air traffic in the area. I responded, but in doing so missed my one-minute prompt. There was plenty of time for me to give the five-second and drop now notices, and of course I did that.

Those pilots who were supportive of their leader dropped their cargo as they were supposed to; others did not. But procedurally, I had goofed. Bear in mind that I was an instructor myself at this point, so I damn well should have performed better in spite of whatever conditions prompted the distraction. I had repeatedly reminded my students that we train hard so that we instinctively handle unforeseen challenges with precision. I had not done so.

So Al had this profound dilemma as to whether he should "bust" Schwartz or not. If he busted me, I would lose both my flight examiner and instructor credentials. It was painful for him to see me make that mistake, particularly considering the paternal relationship that we had developed. But it was all about upholding the standards; either one met the standard or they didn't. For the system to work, you can't favor one person over another.

In the end Al did something that I probably would not have done. He rationalized that the ATC radio distraction was a mitigating circumstance that contributed to my error, and he passed me with a verbal "caveat" that would not go into my record. If it had, most likely I would never have gotten into Special Ops, and probably would not have been able to progress to the level I've been honored to reach. There are a few great lessons here that have stuck with me for life:

While standards must be upheld, enforcement decisions have consequences and must be carefully and thoughtfully applied. Very little is black and white, and applying informed judgment is what's called for.

★ ★ ★

We rotated to Europe, where I flew missions every day. That much flying honed my skills to the highest proficiency level of my life. We were based at RAF Mildenhall, in Suffolk, England, from July 13 to September 13, 1978. We flew to France, Italy, Saudi Arabia, and a number of other Middle Eastern countries; we even flew some missions into Berlin. This was still the Cold War, so at that time we couldn't even talk about some of the tight places into which we flew.

For example, the Army had a facility perched high atop a seven-hundred-foot hill on the northernmost peninsula of the Turkish Black Sea, just over three hundred miles east of Istanbul, overlooking the ancient port of Sinop. Called Diogenes Station (or unofficially "the Hill"), its intelligence professionals monitored events and transmissions emanating from the Soviet Union, right across the Black Sea.

We utilized the Sinop Army Airfield (SAAF), about seven miles west of the Hill. Until this time, the bulk of the airfield's traffic consisted of U-6 Beavers and U-1 Otter aircraft that the Army affectionately referred to as "Esek Airlines." The newly constructed five-thousand-foot runway was a considerable improvement from the tiny east-west strip that it replaced. That first flight into Sinop is the only time I have ever seen a pristine piece of concrete like that with no tire markings at all.

We were really heavy that day, loaded to the max, and the crosswinds were treacherous. Add to that the blinding glare of the runway and you had a landing that was another real test of airmanship. We were far more fortunate than an Army twin-engine U-21F that had crashed just a few months earlier on a return flight from Istanbul, killing all five on board.

★ ★ ★

The Herc is a reliable workhorse, but it's a machine and as such, not infallible. We had a number of engine failures, not uncommon at the time. Most were single-engine failures that occurred in flight. But engine loss was not the only system failure that could prove catastrophic. You can read about these things and you can train for them in the simulator, but until you experience a dozen warning buzzers screaming in your ear while the plane begins to buffet on a real-world mission—and you know it's not a drill—you don't know for sure how you're going to handle the situation.

We departed Little Rock AFB and ascended to altitude without incident on a standard airdrop mission—if any mission is really "standard"—then set the autopilot on a direct vector to our drop zone in the Fort Campbell (Kentucky) Range Complex. It was a clear day and a smooth flight; in fact, our flight engineer had just made a comment to that effect. Suddenly about a dozen bright-red warning lights popped on, accompanied by the piercing *beep-beep-beep* of the audio warning systems. The plane began to rock back and forth—not like we had hit a pocket of turbulence, more like an uncomfortable, rhythmic shaking. All four syncrophasers had lost power (the syncrophaser ensures that the four propellers rotate at the same speed and in sync with each other), along with a dozen other systems—a significant electrical malfunction of some kind had occurred. The autopilot shut down, along with the compass and heading indicators. Both hydraulic suction boost pumps went dead, and the normally responsive control yoke took a great deal more energy to operate without the trim tabs. Correcting that one was easy; I flipped the switch to initiate the emergency backup and trim was restored. We all agreed that we had lost the essential AC electrical bus—but the question was why, and how did we get it back?

We'd been trained on a few procedures to restore the power, but none of them worked. About the only thing left was to throw out the book and think outside the box. Eventually we isolated the problem in a very unconventional way and repowered the bus. The process of safe isolation required extensive knowledge of the aircraft electrical system and how to sequence the disconnection and reconnection of the bus without permanently frying the circuits and adjacent electronics. Once restored, that allowed for a safe and ultimately uneventful return.

It was a hectic pace and I loved everything about it. I enjoyed the structure surrounding every mission: first starting with the crew rest, then mission briefs, flight plans, walk-arounds, preflight checks, and of course the unparalleled thrill of control guiding 150,000 pounds of aeronautical excellence through the clouds at 19,000 feet, knowing all the while that our mission—and our passengers who were the key elements of that mission—demanded that we perform reliably and with precision. Almost every day I learned something new, and met new members of my military family—comrades with the same sense of dedication and diligence in pursuit of our common objective. Life could not have been much better.

★ ★ ★

In the flying business we try our best to anticipate all eventualities and train for even the most obscure anomaly. Mishaps are painstakingly analyzed and often result in revised tactics and procedures. In developing a battle plan, commanders formalize myriad what-ifs via "branches and sequels"—contingency plans and subsequent operations based on anticipating an enemy's action or response. Despite these best efforts, it never fails that nature will come along and throw us a curve. In my case, how could I have anticipated that I was about to be struck by a bolt of lightning?

It appeared completely out of the blue in December of 1978. Her name was Suzie Ptak. At five feet six inches with azure eyes that were impossible to resist, she was a megavolt dynamo unlike anyone I had ever met, let alone dated. We were polar opposites, and had there been computer dating back then, I doubt if any website would have predicted success pairing this conservative Jewish man from Jersey with a popular Catholic schoolteacher from Arkansas. Bear in mind that I had not a single female role model growing up—no mom at home and few females at school—so I had a very idealistic vision of what a relationship should be, and no understanding of what constituted real-life male/female interaction other than what I saw on TV.

One Friday night after a long day of flying, I had taken Suzie out to dinner and I passed out on the sofa shortly after we returned to my apartment.

There are many sounds that we grew up with that today's generation will never experience: the rapid *clacks* of typewriter keys striking the paper, followed by the *ding* that signaled the end of each line, then the *zipppp* of the carriage being swung back into position; the *click-click-click* of a rotary phone dial returning to its starting position; and the booming crash of a brand-new Sony Trinitron TV picture tube imploding.

It was the latter that awakened me from my deep slumber on the sofa, preceded by a *SLAM! BANG!* Apparently men dozing off in the middle of dates was not something Suzie was accustomed to—and just to make sure that I fully grasped her dissatisfaction, she had stormed out and walked home, slamming my door so hard that it dislodged a large wall-hanging that smashed right into my new Sony. This confused me—it was not something I'd seen June Cleaver do when she was upset with Ward. Even Harriet Nelson seemed a bit more diplomatic when Ozzie didn't toe the line. But Suzie was patient with me and we were very good for each other; I knew she would draw the best out of me, and she has. She is independent, strong, very smart, and about the kindest person I have ever known.

Here's how it played out from Suzie's perspective, in her own words:

Suzie: *Before I ever met Norty, I stalked him. This was long before online Facebook stalking—it was good old American "sneak out at night, hide behind a tree" stalking. My girlfriend wanted to set me up with him so I had to check him out first, right? Well, he passed the test. From the start he was different than anyone I had ever met—opposite all the young guys I'd been dating. A serious, quiet, financially stable intellectual like Nort was uncharacteristic for me, but kindness trumps seriousness any day, and he was (and still is!) the kindest man I'd ever met. He sent a dozen roses after our first date. I still haven't figured that one out; it was the first and last time he sent roses in the forty years that I've known him.*

Now, getting back to that stalking: My good friend Angie had met Norty at a New Year's Eve party and they hit it off, at least to the extent that they exchanged numbers in hopes of getting together. Months went by before that actually happened, but when it did she could barely contain her enthusiasm . . . not because she had found the man of her dreams—more like she was certain that he was perfect for me!

"I'm coming right over," she bubbled on the phone the following evening after work. "I want to tell you all about him!"

"But I'm already in my pajamas," I told her, knowing that I'd have to be up at oh-dark-thirty to welcome my class of special education students at the Arnold Drive elementary school where I taught.

"Perfect, I'm on my way!" she fired back, with a quiver of Cupid's arrows deeply implanted in her imagination.

Bursting through my front door, she made a beeline for the thick Little Rock phone book I kept wedged in beside my tiny microwave.

"Let's see . . . Santiago, Saunders, Schultz . . ." she mumbled as she ripped through the pages to find his address. "Here it is, Schwartz . . . Nathan, Neil, Nelson, Norton . . . That must be him, Norton A. Schwartz." She was so proud of herself that she found him, and I'm like, C'mon, you've already got the man's phone number and you know his name—this is not exactly rocket science, here.

"Oh my God, Suzie. He lives right here in the McCain Park Apartments,

only two buildings over! Put on some shoes, we're going on a hike. He told me that he jogs twice every day, once at 5:00 a.m., then again at 7:00 every night. If you'd move a little faster than a turtle we should be able to sneak a peek when he gets home from his run tonight."

It was only 7:30, but with the short days of winter, the skies were already jet-black out there. I grabbed a flashlight and reverted back to my college hunting days—hunting for boys, that is. "But there is no way in heaven that I'm a match with anyone who gets up at 5:00 a.m.," I whined as we slipped out the door.

OK, so we found the right apartment. "Now what?" I asked, feeling like a fool standing outside a grown man's apartment—an Air Force officer's, no less— wearing pink wool pajamas with a huge Curious George printed on the front.

"Personally, I'm hiding in here," she said, climbing into a thicket of bushes immediately across the street from his front door. "But if you'd prefer to stay and introduce yourself, be my guest."

She nodded toward the roadway, where a tall, thin, very handsome man ran in our direction from about a quarter-mile away. Needless to say, I dove in beside her . . . but I came way too close to being busted. That man could run!

We dropped completely out of sight as he ran past, but it was pretty clear to Angie that I liked what I saw. I decided that maybe there were some things in life for which I'd get up at 5:00!

She waited until he was well inside his unit and we saw the lights turn on. Then she blurted out, "Why don't I invite him to be my date to Julie's wedding? That way he can see you all dressed up in your maid-of-honor dress, instead of the monkey suit you have on now. We could all go out for dinner after."

We could not have scripted this any better. She invited him and he accepted— very odd since he hates attending those kinds of things. Now that I think about it, I guess he really did like Angie!

So we went to the wedding and just as planned, she introduced us just after the ceremony, then started complaining how hungry she was. What's the poor guy going to say? Of course he had to take her somewhere to eat. So we got to his car, and ever the gentleman, he walked around and opened both passenger side doors—the front one for Angie, the back for me. "I'm fine here," she said with a devilish grin as she sped into the back seat, leaving me to sit beside him in the front. He drove us both home, first dropping off Angie, then me. Of course he walked me to my door, but there was not even an attempt at anything beyond a quick handshake.

"*By the way, you looked very nice tonight,*" *he said, then turned and walked away.*

I stood outside my door and watched him get inside his car and start the engine. He started to pull away, then stopped and stuck his head outside the open window and left me with these words: "But I think I prefer you in those fuzzy pink pajamas." What?? I wanted to bury my head in the sand.

We started dating on the weekends. Angie was out and I was in. I found it strange that we'd often have to stop at Albertson's on the way home from our dates. First it was for a pack of gum, then a loaf of bread, next a dozen eggs. I started to wonder if he had some kind of shopping fetish. Thing is, each time we'd stop to pick up whatever tiny thing he said he needed, we wound up leaving with an entire basket of groceries—for me! Later it hit me that this was his way to help me make ends meet by stocking up my fridge for the next week. I had never met anyone like him.

I was teaching school and he was flying. Fine at first, then more and more things starting popping up that really got me irritated. We would lock in a time for a Saturday night date, then on Friday he'd call to cancel. "I'm really sorry, but I've got to fly again this weekend," he'd say, having no clue how impolite it was on so many levels. Besides being irritated, I was also worried. I knew that most of his missions involved night flights and that scared me. Scared and irritated—not a great combination for young love. I suppose it wouldn't have been so bad if he made up for it with awesome dates, but the truth is that when we did finally get together, "Mr. Thrill Ride" was so exhausted, he had very little, if anything, left for me. That's how that whole TV thing came about—because he fell asleep in the middle of our date! While we were sitting there watching TV. I looked and he was out like a light. And that's when I lost it because I was thinking, "You are dating! This is not married people, this is dating and he's sleeping in the middle of our date!" So, yes. I slammed the door so hard that this stupid piece of scrap metal he had mounted on the wall completely broke loose and . . .

Norty: Not to interrupt, but what Suzie is calling a "stupid piece of scrap metal" was actually a fifteen-pound section of a LAPES (low-altitude parachute extraction system) pallet that was custom framed. You could only get it done like that at Clark Air Base in the Philippines.

Suzie: *Would you please describe it?*

Norty: It's a long, flat section of aluminum that's strong enough to support a tank . . .

Suzie: *Thank you, Mr. Webster. As I said, this big, heavy, stupid piece of scrap metal that only a bachelor would have framed fell off the wall and apparently smashed the TV. I did feel bad about that part, but it was probably improperly hung in the first place, and I did have to show him that I was mad. I'm very good at being mad. And making up, which he isn't. He hopes that by closing his eyes and ears that all the problems will just magically go away.*

Norty: Speaking of problems, I suppose now is as good a time as any for me to fess up with full disclosure about the "artwork." It's true that it's a piece of a LAPES pallet from my time at Clark. I've just never really divulged how that came to be.

We were on a training practice mission because there was a big inspection coming up and we were going to be the LAPES crew. We had to nail this thing. I was in the right seat and Major Wolf was in the left seat. It was the right-seat pilot's responsibility to release the chutes that pulled the load out of the airplane. For it to work, the key was to make the release at that very instant that the airplane bottomed out at five to ten feet above the ground. Well, I got a little overanxious and I let it go at about forty feet. At these speeds, the difference between forty feet and ten feet is probably two milliseconds, but it was premature and the outcome was not pretty. Instead of skidding upright onto the turf as if should have done, the load smashed into the ground and disintegrated into a thousand different pieces. The piece that I had hanging on the wall was the largest piece that remained of this thirty-six-foot piece of extruded aluminum. Following the flight, the crew somehow had it framed and presented it to me. Now that I think about it, having it meet its end by smashing into the TV set is an appropriate bookend to how it was "conceived" in the first place.

I may laugh about it now, but this was not a good situation. The squadron leadership could have taken me off the crew for that, and I'm sure they talked about it. Bottom line, they hung in there and believed that I would deliver the goods—and I did. We went out on that inspection and nailed it. More importantly, we continued to do so on real-world missions. I used that piece of "fine art" to remind myself that anyone can make a mistake, but *don't do it again.*

I never did.

Suzie: *So we dated through the summer—by then school was out and I had taken a summer job as a lifeguard at the base pool—and occasionally Norty would drop by to "say hi"—which really means check me out in my swimming suit . . .*

Norty: There is certainly merit to that observation.

Suzie: *It was during one of those pool visits when I had 90 percent of my attention focused on two little kids who had absolutely no business being in that pool alone— that Norty decided to share with me, in passing, that our relationship (if that's what you call it when two people are dating with no stated commitment of any kind) was about to be totally turned upside down. Months beforehand, apparently he had applied for a very special—very elite—assignment at the Pentagon. "I got it," he said. "And it looks like I'll be leaving for DC in a few weeks."*

So that was that: he moved out of his apartment and left town. We agreed to try the long-distance thing, which meant exactly one phone call each Sunday—no more, no less. Atomic clocks could be set by the exactness off those calls. We were still dating, I suppose, but there was no talk about any next step or anything beyond that. He got so focused on work that he probably never gave it a second thought, but for me, it was kind of sad. Well, real sad.

★ ★ ★

So often you'll hear those in the field talk about the pencil pushers in the Pentagon, as if a Pentagon assignment was akin to being banished to Siberia. But I loved working there. That "elite" program Suzie referenced was called the Air Staff Training program (ASTRA), a sort of internship for promising young officers. As a twenty-seven-year-old captain, I had an E-ring office and worked directly for Lt General Charles A. Gabriel, the Chief of Staff for Plans and Operations (then designated AF/XO). He would go on to become chief of staff of the Air Force. They were actually paying me to observe the inner workings of the U.S. military from the highest level, and what I learned was incalculable.

Earlier I mentioned how I don't consider myself to be a particularly pious Jew, yet so often events or situations take me back to earlier times and remind me how significant those core Judaic principles—and traditions—are to my foundation. My acceptance into the ASTRA program was one such experience.

Once a year we celebrate the eight-day festival of Passover, which commemorates the Jews' liberation from slavery in Egypt. We begin the observance with a Seder—a ritual feast where family and friends assemble to recount this ancient story from the book of Exodus. The Seder is so rich with symbols and customs, it's always been one of my favorite traditions.

As we close the front door following the prophet Elijah's symbolic visit, we enjoy our fourth cup of wine, then everyone at the table breaks out in song—multiple generations doing their best to stay on-key while belting out the fifteen stanzas of "Dayenu," the consummate Passover song. It's an upbeat, cheerful song about our gratitude for God's blessings. As specific blessings are recounted, we enthusiastically chime in with "Dayenu," a Hebrew word that translates to "It would have been enough." In this case, the theme reflects that while we are grateful for each of these blessings independently, our appreciation for them as a whole is multiplied exponentially.

The concept is one that has evolved to encompass secular experiences, and there's no better example than the gratitude I felt for my ASTRA selection. At this point in my career, almost any Pentagon position would have yielded growth opportunities for which I would have been extremely grateful. But to have an E-ring office and the chance to observe (and learn from) a three-star the likes of General Gabriel? Unimaginable. Was it really just fate that aligned my stars so perfectly that of all the young officers in the Air Force, I'd be the one chosen for such an opportunity?

While providence may have played a role, months later I learned that the real "man behind the curtain" was Colonel Al Navas, the wing commander at Clark for whom I orchestrated the change-of-command ceremony. It turned out that he and Jack Eddlemon, who, like Al Navas, was a respected colonel and in this case one of three Air Force Planners, lobbied on my behalf to get me the ASTRA executive assistant position in the front office. It's yet another example of why I am forever indebted to Al. Having the opportunity to work with him again was the icing on the cake, my own personal "dayenu moment."

Lt Gen Gabriel's deputy was Maj Gen Jerry O'Malley, a fellow cadet at West Point and subsequently Gabriel's vice commander at the Udorn Royal Thai

Air Force, Thailand, where each of them flew over a hundred F-4 combat missions. Later on, when Gabriel became Chief, O'Malley would once again serve as his vice.

These were two inspired leaders. It's one thing to be taught effective leadership techniques, quite another to be a fly on the wall and observe them firsthand in the day-to-day interactions of two of the top military leaders of the time—to see how they interacted with civilian seniors, how they interacted with peers and subordinates, how they prepared for meetings, and how they navigated the complex issues of the day. So many things about the man I am today can be traced back to the principles, communication techniques, and decision processes I gleaned from Generals Gabriel and O'Malley back in 1980.

This was a busy time in the AF/XO front office. Besides the usual suspects, anti-American sentiment in Iran was intensifying, with Ayatollah Khomeini's rhetoric against the "Great American Satan" garnering more and more support. On November 4, 1979—just a few weeks after my arrival at the Pentagon—the American Embassy in Tehran was overrun by a group of Iranian students who supported the Iranian Revolution, and fifty-two American diplomats and citizens were taken hostage. Diplomatic attempts to free the captives were proving fruitless; days stretched into weeks, then months.

Ted Koppel ticked off the days with late-night newscasts devoted entirely to the hostage crisis. Originally entitled *The Iran Crisis: America Held Hostage, Day XXX* (with "XXX" representing the number of days the hostages had been held), the show captured an enormous audience—so robust that ABC News president Roone Arledge believed it should become a permanent addition to the ABC late-night lineup, one that he felt would break *The Tonight Show's* longstanding late-night ratings dominance. He renamed the show *Nightline*, and it has remained on ABC's late-night schedule for the past thirty-six years, not to mention its franchised offspring sold to TV networks around the world. (ABC newsman Frank Reynolds hosted the original broadcast four days after the takeover. Koppel took over a few weeks later.)

While the hostage situation was certainly at the forefront of all of our minds, there were broader enterprise issues that occupied the bulk of our time in the AF/XO organization. Our fleet of aircraft was in the midst of an unprecedented expansion, with recent acquisitions including the F-15, F-16, and A-10. Various classified programs ushered in a new buzzword that foretold a technology that would change the face of air combat: *stealth*. Although the

A classic photo of the quintessential Air Force couple, Jerry and Diane O'Malley. Seen here with General Gabriel.
Personal collection of Sharon O'Malley Burg

public wouldn't be made aware of them for years, we were well into the development of the F-117 stealth fighter and B-2 stealth bomber (known at the time as the Advanced Strategic Penetrating Aircraft—ASPA). There could not have been a better team to handle these complex issues than Generals Gabriel and O'Malley.

General O'Malley was a charmer, a natural people person with one of the broadest professional networks I have ever seen. He was upbeat, completely transparent, and had a natural ability to spot one's strengths and zero in on them—disregarding potential deficits yet taking full advantage of the assets to build highly effective teams. It was very empowering, and naturally motivational. By the same token, he was keenly aware of his own strengths and shortfalls, and eager to surround himself with experts who knew more about certain areas than he knew himself.

Surround yourself with experts in those areas in which you are not so strong.

We grew quite close over the course of those six months, to the point of him unofficially adopting me. No matter how busy he was, he never missed an opportunity to pull me aside and share some personal insight that would serve as a growth opportunity for me. Questions were always encouraged, but he had no tolerance for subordinates wasting his time with requests for him to intercede on issues they were fully capable of handling themselves. He assigned the right people to tasks that suited them, and cut them loose to succeed. In most cases, they did. Observing his leadership style early on taught me that:

Micromanaging is for micro-minded managers.

It's a surefire formula for winning a few battles, but losing the war.

O'Malley made no bones about the fact that the bulk of his leadership philosophies were derived from Gabriel, just as so many of my own evolved from O'Malley's. His top three leadership philosophies championed:

- Integrity
- Job Expertise
- Sensitivity in Interactions with Others

I happened to be in his office when he became aware of an Inspector General (IG) investigation filed against a high-ranking Air Force officer. "What a goddamn waste!" he vented, tossing the file into his out-box. "Here's an excellent officer whose career will, most likely, be finished, because he was unable to keep his zipper zipped. There's a reason we say 'Integrity First,' and it starts with integrity to yourself. You've got to be able to look at yourself in the mirror every morning, and respect what you see. You've got to be honest to your boss, and honest with the people you have working for you."

"Seems to me that he violated all three, sir," I replied.

While my own interaction with O'Malley encompassed his time on the Air Staff, there was never any doubt that he was a pilot's pilot. Just after noon on March 21, 1968, he slid the throttles into "Max A/B" and departed Okinawa's Kadena Air Base on the first operational mission of the most advanced strategic reconnaissance aircraft in the world at the time, the then Top Secret SR-71 Blackbird. Reaching speeds over three times the speed of sound, he penetrated North Vietnamese (and other) airspace and recorded enemy missile sites, positions, and radar signals.

The Blackbird was one of over forty different aircraft models he had piloted. "You can't expect to lead your people if you don't thoroughly understand the platforms they are working with," he once told me, shortly before leaving the office to pilot his Air Force CT-39 (VIP transport jet) out of Andrews. He retained his flying aptitude even as a general officer, having received a unique authorization as the operations officer of the Air Force from General Gabriel that allowed him to perform "temporary operational flying" of up to twenty-four missions per year.

Those six months allowed me to witness the decision-making process as it applied to strategic issues that affected the entire Air Force, almost unheard of at the captain's level—but General O'Malley and Colonel Navas helped me to understand how those same processes can be effectively employed at all levels.

I remember vividly one Friday morning, about a month after I transferred over from the Airlift shop. Between studying for my master's degree and completely immersing myself in the new Ops and Plans position, it had been a particularly demanding week. By 7:00 a.m., many in the office were well into their second cup of coffee; we'd already been at it for hours. A voice called out from across the room.

"Hey, turn on the TV!" It was Colonel Lowell "Mac" McAdoo, General Gabriel's XO (executive officer), who had just received a notification over the phone. "President Carter's about to speak." It was April 25, 1980, 175 days into the hostage crisis.

General Gabriel stepped out of his inner office and joined us as we all gathered around the wall-mounted TV in the conference room. We fell silent as the picture faded in to a drawn and haggard-looking Jimmy Carter, seated at a barren wooden desk in front of a simple gold curtain flanked by the American and president's flags. He looked up from the small stack of papers before him, and began his solemn description of the calamity of Desert One:

> "Late yesterday, I cancelled a carefully planned operation which was underway in Iran to position our rescue team for later withdrawal of American hostages, who have been held captive there since November 4. Equipment failure in the rescue helicopters made it necessary to end the mission. As our team was withdrawing, after my order to do so, two of our American aircraft collided on the ground following a refueling operation in a remote desert location in Iran. . . . to my deep regret, eight of the crewmen of the two aircraft which collided were killed, and several other Americans were hurt in the accident."

Five of those whose lives were lost in Operation EAGLE CLAW (the aborted rescue attempt at "Desert One"—the code name for the salt flat rendezvous zone some two hundred miles southeast of Tehran) were Air Commandos from Hurlburt Field's 1st Special Operations Wing, 8th Special Operations Squadron—the very squadron I'd be joining upon leaving the Ops and Plans office.

Within months I'd be working side by side with the Eagle Claw participants, pioneers of our special operations forces who first employed many of the tactics and procedures still used today, including multi-aircraft air field seizure, clandestine insertion of small helicopters, blacked-out landings, landing on unprepared runways, and many others that remain classified to this day.

This was a fragile force and the mission was a failure. But it became known as the "most successful failed mission in history." Much of what was developed is still in use today, and it prompted a complete organizational restructuring of the United States special operations forces. Thirty years later, these legends would find redemption in the force that succeeded in taking down Usama Bin Laden (usually referred to as "UBL" in our intelligence reports). Even though they had faced significant mechanical challenges, weather challenges, and changes in environmental conditions, they were well trained enough, they were well equipped enough, and they were sufficiently resilient enough to adapt. It's a phenomenal tribute to the generation that said "never again."

Two days later, I spoke with Suzie. It felt particularly good to hear her voice that Sunday. We discussed the rescue mission, and while she had nothing but respect for all those involved, it served as yet another example of inherent dangers in any missions having anything to do with special operations.

"There is no way that I will ever agree to live a life of fear like that, so just put that wild idea out of your head," she snapped. "There are plenty of other flying opportunities for you, and as much as you drive me crazy, I'd very much appreciate your coming home to me after each flight."

It was at that point that I attempted a new communications tactic that worked fairly well: I let her vent, then completely changed the subject.

"How would you like to come out here and join me for the summer?"

That got her attention.

Suzie: *I agreed to fly out to Washington and stay with Norty for the summer, but my parents were less than thrilled about this. Sure, they liked him, but they knew that I was emotionally raw from having just lost two very close friends—one in a car accident, another on a night mission when his C-130 crashed into the side of the mountain . . . which was another reason that sometimes I got so scared whenever Norty went out on night flights.*

I assured my parents that I'd be in good hands with Norty, and they agreed that I could join him for the summer.

On the flight out, I was a mishmash of emotions—a little nervous, a little scared—but a lot excited. Having Norty show me all around Washington, hanging out with his friends and buddies from work . . . it would be fun!

Uh, maybe not so fun. Remember when I joked about not being a good match for someone who got up at 4:30 a.m.? Well, he got up at 4:00! He would take his run, shower, and head directly for the Pentagon, where they would typically keep him well past dinnertime every night.

He was also working on his master's degree, so when he did finally make it home he'd head straight for the books until bedtime. I probably got more time with him back home during our weekly calls!

Then it occurred to me: does this man not have any friends? Is he hiding me from them? Embarrassed about me? And why on earth would his bosses keep him there so late every night? Something was amiss.

I'd been there about six weeks or so when I learned that he hadn't even told anyone that I was in town! His bosses threw a fit because had they known, of course they would have sent him home early to spend some time with me. And why would he plan to spend the whole summer on his master's degree knowing that I was coming to town? Wouldn't you share that before I bought the ticket? I should have seen the pattern.

One day after work he did something that was so shocking, I almost fainted. He walked in the door, tossed his briefcase onto the sofa, and actually asked me out on a date.

"We've just been invited to next week's Friday Night Parade," he proclaimed, pretty proud of himself that he had actually planned such a special event.

A parade? Hmm . . . Well, it wasn't exactly dinner with the president, but beggars can't be choosers, and pretty much of anything would beat another Friday night at home watching Fantasy Island while he studied.

"By the way, I'll be wearing my summer whites," he added as he headed for the bedroom to change into his workout attire.

"Isn't that a little overkill?" I thought. Dress whites to a parade sounded like the equivalent of me wearing my prom gown to a ball game. But hey, any excuse to go out and buy a new dress, right?

Norty: Suzie wasn't the only one who took second notice of the call for summer whites. In fact, that's how we scored the invitation in the first place.

General Gabriel had recently been transferred to Europe and newly promoted *Lieutenant* General O'Malley had taken over Gabriel's position as AF/XO. Every year, the Marine Corps' deputy chief of staff for plans, policy and operations hosted a semiformal pre-party to accompany the Corps' storied "Silent Drill"—more commonly referred to as the "Friday Night Parade"—for his counterparts in all the services. Contrary to Suzie's preconception, this was no ordinary parade; in fact, it was more of a pageant than a parade.

I happened to be passing Mac McAdoo's desk shortly after the invitation arrived in the Pentagon interoffice messenger pouch. General O'Malley stood beside his XO's desk, shaking his head. He glanced up as I passed.

"Hey Norty, know anything about these new 'summer whites'? Who has white shoes and a white belt, anyway?"

"Lots of them over on the Navy side, sir," McAdoo sarcastically retorted.

"Great idea, Mac. Why don't you run on down the hall and borrow Admiral Hayward's for me," the general fired back, referring to the chief of naval operations.

"Sir, I'm happy to shoot over to the Navy Yard and purchase whatever you need," I volunteered. "I actually had one uniform custom-made before I left the Philippines, so I know exactly what to pick up."

"That'd be a big help, Norty. Thank you. Nice to hear a *constructive* idea around here for a change." He shot McAdoo a dirty look, but it was all in good fun. They had a mutual respect for one another and an excellent relationship.

I took down his sizes and turned to leave. It was only five miles from the Pentagon to the Washington Navy Yard, but by the time I caught buses (both ways) and did the shopping, I'd be lucky to make it back before day's end. I'm sure that Suzie would have preferred that I just headed straight home early, but to me, things like that always felt like I was cheating the government. I was honored to have been given such an opportunity, and I sure wasn't about to try to find excuses to shirk the responsibilities that came with that honor.

I was almost out the door when the general called back to me. "Norty, your girlfriend is still in town from Arkansas, right?"

"Indeed she is, sir. Suzie."

"Well, it'd be a shame to let your custom-made new uniform go to waste. Why don't you join us for this Friday night shindig? I'm sure Diane would love to meet Suzie. As would I."

I was floored. What an act of kindness, yet something so typical for General Jerry O'Malley. While I always knew the invitation was an act of benevolence on his part, I now realize that he also saw it as a valuable learning experience for this up-and-coming young officer. And indeed it was!

Suzie: *Date night finally arrived, and I remember being pretty terrified during that car ride over to the Marine Corps Barracks at 8th and I. I still didn't really know exactly what we were going to; all I knew was that the guest list pretty much consisted of a bunch of generals from all the service branches and all kinds of notables from Washington.*

I had never met a general in person, and the only thought that kept popping into my mind was my father's stern warning to me when I was a little girl. He was driving through the base and I was glued to the back window, soaking in all the sights and sounds that constituted the mini-city of an Air Force base. One spot really caught my attention, even though my father did his best to exit the area as quickly as possible. Unlike the cookie-cutter houses and offices we'd been driving past, this was a carefully coiffed street of stately homes on an isolated section of the base.

"That's called general's row," he declared. "If you ever go in there and you get in trouble, I am not bailing you out because you have absolutely no business going anywhere near that place!" I guess that made a pretty big impression on me since that was the dominant thought on my mind as I was about to enter a lion's den where apparently most everyone I'd encounter would have stars on their shoulders. I'd be surrounded by them.

Norty turned onto 8th Street and pulled up to a home adjacent to this three-story, two-hundred-year-old mansion, the Home of the Commandants. A row of marines stood at attention on the redbrick sidewalk immediately in front of a black wrought-iron and brick fence that encircled the compound.

Norty had barely eased the car to a stop before two young marines approached the vehicle. With a precision choreography so smoothly executed as to make it look effortless, one opened my car door while the other reached in to help me out of the car. Before I knew it, we were arm in arm and I was being escorted up the red carpet that covered the steps leading to the porch of the residence of Lt Gen O'Malley's Marine counterpart.

Just inside the door were our hosts, the three-star Marine general and his wife, who were about to welcome Norty and me to this storied Marine Corps event. Fortunately the noise level was fairly high so the general couldn't hear the rattle of my knees shaking against one another.

"Lovely to meet you," he said, warmly shaking my hand. "We're so glad you could come."

What struck me was his eye contact, which projected a sincerity that really made me believe that he meant it. Did it help to ease my state of terror? Hell no. I still felt like I was about to run the gauntlet.

I had never experienced anything like this in my life. The place was packed as we made our way past a plaque that acknowledged each of the Marine "Ops Dep" predecessors.

The main rooms were as you would expect, decorated with antiques, artwork, and Marine Corps memorabilia. We were promptly offered champagne, and boy did we feel out of place!

"Follow me," said Norty, taking my hand and deftly guiding me through the throng. I assumed he had spotted someone he knew, but no, he just kept right on walking.

"Here, this is much better," he said, having navigated our way to a remote corner of the house where we could safely hover unnoticed.

There were senators, congressmen, and who knows who else. Some of them must have been military intelligence because the instant we put our drinks down, some immaculately uniformed server would come and swoop it up, then someone else appeared with a tray of fresh ones.

What I knew about politics could probably fit inside one of those tiny canapés the servers kept bringing. But I recognized some faces from TV. This was 1980, so there were some pretty well-known senators at that time, like Strom Thurmond, Edmund Muskie, George McGovern, Bob Dole, Barry Goldwater, John Glenn, and a gentleman whose wife I would work with some thirty years later, Joe Biden.

Of course now I know that the thing to do would have been to fake it and mingle (which is what the rest of them were doing, I'm sure!), but at that time I was in perfect accord with Norty's solution—hiding in the corner.

Norty: But Diane O'Malley, God bless her, was worried about us. Throughout the event, this petite, wonderful lady would gracefully appear to check up on us and ask how we were doing. As if she weren't busy enough intermingling with her husband's peers and associates. I didn't even know her that well at the time. But she understood that we helped with the uniform, and that the general was thoughtful enough to have invited us.

Every time she came over, she would leave us with another intriguing bit of history about the house.

Diane O'Malley's charm, strength, and determined advocacy on behalf of military families caught Suzie's attention—a fine example of an involved, proactive military spouse. Seen here with Lt Gen Jerry O'Malley shortly after he took over as AF/XO.
O'Malley personal collection

We had no idea that thirty years later, we'd be back at this historic mansion, as husband and wife, and personal guests of our fellow Service Chief and his wife, Jim and Anette Conway. Schwartz personal collection

Suzie: *I watched her after she slipped away into the horde—totally at ease, comfortably breezing from this group to that. As I look back I realize that's what a good hostess does. But the art of "mingling" is one that's learned over time. Back then, I didn't have a clue—but I sure was in awe.*

We were led to the porch through double glass doors that were flanked by two large mullion windows. Marine guards snapped to attention under each as we stepped onto a small stoop with double side steps. "Captain and Mrs. Norton A. Schwartz," bellowed a third marine, so loud that I'm sure it rattled the White House china.

Well, they messed that one up, I laughed to myself, as we were led through a small garden to the parade ground. As soon as we were seated, Norty leaned over and whispered, "Did you tell them that?"

Where I would have just laughed it off and let it slide, he pressed—and how would I have known who to tell anyway? Knowing him as I do now, it was probably more about the information being factually incorrect than it was about feeling any embarrassment for people to think we were married. Because he's a very black-and-white kind of guy. But once the lights dimmed and the program began, he was over it and we had a wonderful evening.

The ceremony began with a concert by "The President's Own" United States Marine Band, followed by impressive precision marching, then powerful performances and demonstrations by the United States Marine Drum and Bugle Corps, the Marine Corps Color Guard, and the Marine Corps Silent Drill Platoon.

Norty: Never in a million years could I have imagined that exactly thirty years later, Suzie and I would be back at the Marine Barracks, but this time in the commandant's mansion, as guests of our fellow service chief and his wife, General Jim and Annette Conway. That, too, was a special evening—but it didn't compare to the overwhelming awe that this young captain and his soon-to-be fiancée experienced for the first time in the company of Washington's elite—thanks to the boundless thoughtfulness, generosity, and kindness bestowed on us by General Jerry and Diane O'Malley. O'Malley would go on to earn his fourth star and become vice chief of staff of the Air Force and commander, Pacific Air Forces.

Suzie and I thanked them profusely as we bid them goodnight on the steps of the Lt General's home, having just experienced the night of our lives with the finest boss—and mentor—one could ever imagine. If only we had known that in less than five years their lives would be cut short when the general's CT-39 Sabreliner would experience a mishap upon landing at the Wilkes-Barre Scranton International Airport, killing Jerry, Diane, and the three others onboard.

As Senator Barry Goldwater (chairman of the Senate Armed Services Committee at the time) pointed out on the floor of the Senate, "Jerry O'Malley was a true rising star in all the military. At fifty-three years of age and already a four-star general, I am certain, destined to command our Air Force and, one day, likely even to serve as chairman of the Joint Chiefs of Staff."

Following their parents' death, the Air Force and the O'Malley children established the General Jerome F. O'Malley and Diane O'Malley Award in memory of their parents. The award honors the Air Force wing commander and spouse team whose contributions to the nation, Air Force, and local community best exemplify the highest ideals and positive leadership of a military couple serving in a key Air Force position. I had the personal honor of bestowing this award in each of my four years as Chief, with the O'Malleys' daughter Sharon at my side to memorialize the legacy of her parents.

Jerry O'Malley sent me to Hurlburt and special operations. How different our course would have been without his intervention.

Suzie: *It turned out to be a pretty good summer. I entertained myself during the days, walked to Crystal City (Pentagon City Mall would have been much closer, but that wasn't built for another nine years), spent some time at the pool, and I even tried to cook—which for me was a major achievement.*

But as summer wound down and the daylight hours diminished, it was time to trade in my vacation gear for my gradebook and fly back home to begin preparation for the new school year.

Norty dropped me off at National Airport and we stumbled through some pretty uncomfortable goodbyes. "It was nice having you here," he said with a smile. "So we'll talk on Sunday?"

"You know where to find me," I quipped, feeling more than just a little uneasy.

Mom and Dad picked me up at the airport, and Dad had barely swung my overstuffed bag into the trunk before my mom—who doesn't know the meaning of the word "subtle"—excitedly blurted out, "So is anything going to happen?"

That was the million-dollar question, wasn't it? And it was one that swirled inside my head for the entire three-hour flight home. I took a deep breath, then shared my unfortunate conclusion. "No, Mom, I don't think so."

She didn't even try to mask her disappointment.

"I really love being around him, and you know full well how kind and wonderful he is . . . But his career is so important to him that I don't believe he sees me figuring into the mix."

"Did he tell you that?"

"It's what he didn't say that spoke volumes. Bottom line, I've already spent two years with him—not to mention lived with him for an entire summer—so if

he still doesn't have any desire to move forward, it's pretty obvious he never will. I think any more time with him would just be a waste."

Norty: Suzie didn't realize that since the moment she stepped onto that plane, I pondered the question endlessly: Was Suzie in fact the girl for all time? Evidently my anxiety was fairly obvious. At least Al Navas picked up on it. By midweek, he approached me.

"Got any plans for tomorrow night? Barbara's looking for a guinea pig to test out some new stuffed cabbage recipe. She cooks enough to feed a whole squadron, so I could sure use a wingman."

As was so often the case, Al seemed to know me better than I knew myself; I would welcome his shrewd advice (as well as Barbara's delicious meal). But the office was certainly not the venue for such a discussion. We were always meticulous in keeping our personal and professional interactions separate.

Al's living room—between dinner and Barbara's famous peach cobbler—would provide a more appropriate setting for our session.

"Do you love her?" Al asked, cutting to the chase with an intimate candor that I never really shared with my own dad.

"Yes . . . but we fight," I rationalized, exposing my complete lack of understanding of real-life male/female dynamics.

"Honey, do we ever fight?" he bellowed into the kitchen, where Barbara was finishing up with the dishes.

"Believe me, they fight!" quipped a voice from upstairs.

"Close your door and finish your homework, Kathy," the colonel hollered back to the nineteen-year-old. He turned back to me and lowered his voice. "Hell, Norty. Everybody fights. They just don't do it in public so you never see it. People disagree, so they argue; that's how they work things out. The last thing you want is somebody who holds everything in and doesn't feel safe enough to be honest with you!"

"Suzie certainly doesn't hold things in."

"Great! So don't let her get away. And don't let your dad or anybody else get in the way." He knew that this had been the case with a prior girlfriend.

Al had a natural ability to separate the wheat from the chaff and make complex issues crystal clear. He was firm, often blunt, but never judgmental. I felt safe in discussing *anything* with him, his sole motivation being my well-being.

Suzie:　*That Sunday at exactly 2:00 p.m., I answered the yellow phone hanging on Mom's kitchen wall midway through the first ring.*

"Hi Norty," I said, perhaps a little less enthusiastically than usual, having already decided that our situation wasn't going anywhere.

"I bought a diamond, so you need to go pick out a setting."

Those were his first words, and that was his proposal! Romance is not Norty's strong suit. That was Casanova's way of asking me to marry him—on the phone in my parents' kitchen. He couldn't even make an unscheduled call to pop the question. No, he had to wait until our weekly Sunday call. And that's the marriage proposal that will live for all eternity.

So I hung up the phone and joined my mom and dad on the back patio.

"Well, what did you guys talk about?" Mom probed.

"Nothing," I replied, much the same as I had responded when she asked me "What'd you learn at school today?" every day for twelve years of my life. I wasn't trying to keep it a secret from her; I think I was just a little underwhelmed by Norty's presentation—maybe even a little embarrassed. But in my heart, I was doing cartwheels. I completely believed in him, and I completely believed in us. And somehow I thought that my outgoing personality would complement his quietness. I believed that I would draw out the best in him, and he certainly filled in so many areas that were lacking in me.

Norty's time at the Pentagon was winding down, and now that the tour had ended, I looked forward to him resuming his piloting career on standard airlift missions out of Pope AFB. North Carolina would be a nice, calm environment in which to begin our married life.

Norty:　In my mind I was never trained to do simple logistics missions, as important as they may be. It was Special Ops that excited me and motivated me, even though at this point they were going through some tough times. The Cadillacs of the C-130 fleet were in the special operations wings, and those pilots were the cream of the crop.

I made it very clear to the personnel shop at MAC (I was still a Military Airlift Command asset) that my ambition was to migrate to special operations, which was under Tactical Airlift Command at the time. What I viewed as following my desired career path, they viewed as losing a high-time flight instructor and examiner. I had hit a roadblock and my only option was to escalate my case up the chain of command. My presentation to the Director of Personnel

(Bagger Baginski, by the way) would have to be persuasive. Fortunately, it was, and he finally relented.

But if I thought it was tough to convince the United States Air Force to allow me to transfer to Special Ops, I had neglected to anticipate the depth of resistance I was about to encounter with my fiery new fiancée. We had already discussed the issue many times, and she was never shy about making her position abundantly clear. While Suzie was entirely supportive of my Air Force career, the idea of my becoming enmeshed in the special operations community sent hackles up her spine. It was just too dangerous for her. She knew that it entailed flying low-level night missions in specially modified airplanes, and she had just lost a close friend when his C-130E (the same basic plane I would be flying) crashed into the side of a hill while practicing in a four-plane formation, one of eight fatalities on that warm September night. We were still in the shadow of the Desert One debacle, and it was not a good time for transferring to Special Ops.

So I had a choice to make: Did I go for the dream and accept the new assignment I had just been offered with the 8th Special Operations squadron in Florida, or respect my new fiancée's concerns and take the more mainstream position at Pope AFB in North Carolina?

Suzie was not happy when I called to inform her that I had made the decision and accepted the former. A selfish decision? Perhaps in that I knew that this road would lead to the most personal satisfaction. But from a broader perspective, I also understood that my opportunities to contribute would be maximized in the special operations community. The Air Force—and the United States—would get a bigger bang for their buck by assigning me to the highly specialized missions of which I was about to become a part.

Suzie: *I was livid and I had every right to be. First of all, Norty knew how much this kind of flying terrified me. I could not imagine any man intentionally making a choice that he knew would subject his wife-to-be to a life of abject terror. Even worse, why would he commit to this without talking to me first? Is that how this marriage was going to work? Shockingly, yes! At least for the first few years. That's how long it took him to grasp the concept of "consult" calls rather than "you're not going to like this but here's what I did" calls.*

I just didn't know how to respond to calls like this, so each time, I just said nothing.

Norty is not an apologizer or a let's-talk-about-this kind of a guy. He will sit there forever in silence and I couldn't imagine anything getting resolved that way.

But over time I learned that throwing the silent treatment right back in his face was the best way to be mad at him. As much as he liked to dole it out, he couldn't stand it when I was the one who closed up and didn't open my mouth. It became a great way to get his attention and get my point across when I became angry. Lord knows that in those early days the man was seldom at a loss for things that got me angry—like the time he bought our very first house.

Norty moved down to Hurlburt (just outside of Fort Walton Beach, Florida) about six months before the wedding. As much as I would have loved to join him, I was still teaching, so I had to stay home in Little Rock up to the very last minute. Once again, our interaction consisted entirely of weekly phone calls.

"How would you feel if I were to buy a house for us down here?" he asked in one of those calls, finally grasping the concept of what it meant to make decisions as a team. And how nice it would be to have him handle all that before I arrived.

"I'm going to make this so easy for you, Norty, because what I want is very simple. It doesn't have to be a mansion, but it should feel warm and welcoming . . . I'd like a big kitchen and a master bathroom with two sinks. That's all I ask. Everything else is up to you."

Within a month he had found the perfect home, closed the deal, and moved in all his belongings. He was much faster at buying houses than popping wedding proposals, although that Sunday he did make a different kind of proposal that I promptly accepted.

"Spring break's coming up, so why don't you drive down here for a few days so you can check out the house. I can't wait for you to see it."

I made it to Fort Walton Beach in a little over ten hours, wondering the entire time what the house was going to look like. Sure, Norty had described it, but I hadn't seen a single picture, and who knew if his captivating description bore the slightest similarity to reality.

I pulled up to the house to find Norty waiting for me, standing on the sidewalk with this little impish grin. I think my first reaction upon seeing the house was one of shock. It was cute as a button, right on the cul-de-sac of a perfectly groomed, safe neighborhood that was lined with actual palm trees. Before then, I had never even seen a palm tree. Norty hit it out of the ballpark with this one.

Ever the gentleman, he proudly opened the front door, then took a small step back for me to go in first. I was so excited! I stepped inside . . . and was totally horrified, struck by a monstrosity straight from the pages of Architectural Nausea. Okay, maybe I'm exaggerating—but it had flocked wallpaper! A thick, gold, velvet flock that looked like it had been imported from some New Orleans brothel. The carpet was brown and dingy, and the whole place felt so dark. As for my few requests, the kitchen was tiny and the master bath had only a single sink—a small one, at that. He obviously disregarded everything I asked for.

Norty: It was a first-generation solar home, which intrigued me.

Suzie: *We fixed it up a little so it was only semi-horrible, and it was the first street off the base, so Norty's commute to work couldn't be any shorter. Now that I think about it, that's probably the reason he ignored every one of my requests and bought it in the first place—to provide himself with as short a commute as possible!*

Norty: It was the only house I looked at. So, yes—that pretty much sealed the deal for me. I actually thought it was a decent home for $69,000, but it fell substantially short of Suzie's expectations and remains an issue to this day—over thirty years later.

We got married in a modest ceremony at the Little Rock Air Force Base Chapel on June 6, 1981. Guests came from all over the country. Of course Suzie's parents were there. You couldn't ask for finer people. Even at that early stage we had already become very close. They liked to say that I hung the moon. Suzie's younger sister Cindy and her husband Jim came in from Christiansburg, down by Virginia Tech. She was Suzie's matron of honor. And her brother Jeb made it in from Tyler, Texas. Of course Joel wouldn't miss the opportunity to see his younger brother tie the knot—perhaps because he couldn't believe it was really happening unless he saw it with his own eyes. His presence meant a great deal to me. Interestingly, my mom was there too, as fragile as she was with her illness; she still made the effort. It was a kind act of generosity on her part.

Significantly, my dad elected not to attend. In part, somehow he viewed it as a matter of principle. He did not approve of the marriage, and he did not approve of Suzie. Our different religious backgrounds were part of it (Suzie was raised as a Catholic), but it also appeared that for some unfathomable reason, he believed Suzie wasn't worthy. But he had no clue. He knew nothing about her and he had no desire to learn anything about her. It was also a political statement on his part; an affirmation that somehow the marriage didn't meet his expectations given his stature in the community. That really disappointed me. Until that point, I carried the hope in my heart that someday Suzie and Dad would hit it off. But his boycott of the wedding drove the nail into the coffin. It was irreconcilable after that.

Later on I did go to him and I chided, "Dad, get over it. We've been married for over ten years now so maybe it's time you get past it and *adapt!*"

I suppose he tried to do so at that point, but that attempt was marginal, at best.

It was an awkward time, an awkward situation. But I was surrounded by so much love that day, by so many wonderful, caring, loving friends and other family members who *wanted* to be there to celebrate our joy, and celebrate my remarkable, beautiful bride—I refused to let him win by ruining the best day of my life.

I think, in many ways, his absence heightened my appreciation of all those who did choose to attend. High atop the list were Al and Barbara Navas, who by this time had become my surrogate parents, and they considered me to be their fifth child.

They immediately hit it off with Suzie, and welcomed her as a member of their family, too. They were gifts from heaven, given by grace. Their presence was very meaningful to me, as I believe it was to them: to support the young lieutenant that they met and mentored and coached and invested in and hoped for success, and now to hope for success in marriage. They were flattered that they served that role and it was important to me that they did so.

Through the years, they continued to be there for me, attending almost every promotion ceremony and change of command you can think of. Whether I was taking Suzie's hand in marriage, assuming my first squadron command, or taking the oath as Chief of Staff of the Air Force—whichever of life's milestones I was experiencing at the time, the one constant was that I'd look out and see the pride radiating from Al's and Barbara's faces, and I would feel the warmth of their unconditional love blanketing me. It's a rare—if not totally unique— occurrence for a wing commander and his wife to literally assume the role of parents for one of their young second lieutenants, but that's what happened, and it was life-changing for me.

★ ★ ★

Suzie: *Let me put it another way: If it weren't for Colonel Navas's fatherly advice to Norty over thirty-five years ago, there might never have been a wedding. Most likely, to this day Norty would still be debating whether he should propose to me, because "we fight." And if there wouldn't have been a wedding, then I wouldn't have had the opportunity to test whether a white satin wedding gown can withstand Arkansas temperatures way hotter than the surface of the sun. Because that's how hot it was on our wedding day at the Little Rock AFB chapel.*

My dressing room was stifling, and the small tabletop electric fans did little more than blast the heat in our direction. This was 1981, not 1881. Had they not heard of air conditioning? By the time the music started and my three bridesmaids led me out of that inferno, we looked like four members of the U.S. Olympic swim team who had just climbed out of the pool after the 4 x 100 relay.

Dad and I stayed out of sight around the corner as the bridesmaids sauntered down the aisle, Dad looking surprisingly dapper girdled into his Air Force mess dress. Then the music transitioned to Wagner's classic "Bridal Chorus" (a.k.a. "Here Comes the Bride") and Dad took my arm to begin our stroll down the flower-draped center aisle of the chapel. I leaned over to him and whispered my final words as a single woman: "Dad, do you think they'll be able to see the sweat rolling down my back?"

"Honey, no one is going to see anything but how beautiful you look, you're fine," he kindly lied. But I'm sure that he was thankful not to have anyone behind us who might slip in the puddles of perspiration I was leaving in my wake.

Then I looked up and spotted Norty and his groomsmen (best man Bob Munson, Dave McClure, and Chris Lauderdale), immaculately decked out in their formal mess dress, looking like movie stars fresh off the cover of Esquire. *Had the Air Force trained them in some secret new technique to counteract the body's natural reaction to extreme heat? None of them showed the slightest signs of discomfort from the heat.*

It wasn't until well after the ceremony that the chaplain came up to me and apologized for not having repaired the broken air conditioner in the women's dressing room. Mine was the only room without it!

The ceremony itself was nondenominational—not really by design, but more because in those days no priest would perform the ceremony since Norty is Jewish, and we couldn't find a nearby rabbi to officiate because I'm Catholic. So I did miss the festivity of seeing a priest in all of his finery when I walked down the aisle, and I also missed having Norty smash the glass at the conclusion of the ceremony with everyone shouting "Mazel Tov!"

It was a very lovely ceremony and the reception at the officers' club served as my first opportunity to see that yes, the man really did have friends. By the way they swapped stories like a bunch of frat boys, they appeared to be a warm, close-knit group. In the course of the reception, I think at least twenty of them came up to me and declared, "You just married a future general." And remember, he was just a captain at this point.

My parents and the Navases instantly sparked with one another, laughing and carrying on like they were lifelong friends. This thrilled Norty and me to no end.

Norty and I actually slipped out early so that we could catch a few hours of sleep at a Little Rock hotel before awakening with the sun and departing for Florida. As we said our goodbyes and thanked everyone for coming, my mother— seldom one to be sentimental—pulled me aside for a private mother-daughter moment. This was so out of character, it truly touched my heart.

She took both my hands and looked me straight in the eyes. "Suzie, through the years, your dad and I have shared a lot of advice with you, but what I am about to say is more important than all of it put together . . ."

"Is this really my mother?" I thought, probably starting to tear up a little in anticipation of her benevolent guidance.

She nodded over toward Norty, who was sharing some final laughs with his posse. "That man is the best thing that's ever happened to you, so don't mess it up. If there's a problem, recognize that it's your fault, so suck it up and don't call me!"

Now that sounded more like Mom.

That night, as our heads hit the pillows, I reached over and extinguished the tiny lamp atop the nightstand by my side, then opened up to Norty with a full disclosure. "There's something you should know . . . I will never be your puppy dog."

"Understood," he acknowledged, with a firm, efficient brevity to which I'd already grown accustomed. As I lay there, I thought that perhaps that band of brothers were on to something—Norty certainly did sound like someone I could picture as a future general.

The drive to Hurlburt took about twelve hours, and by six o'clock the following morning, Norty was already at the office—happy as a clam embarking on his new career in Special Ops. What I felt, on the other hand, were emotions that I've shared through the years with spouse groups at bases all over the world. Those feelings are so common to newlywed military spouses, thrust into totally unfamiliar lifestyles, often in new and unfamiliar locales: I was in a house that I didn't buy, and didn't like. I was in a city that I didn't know, and I didn't know a soul. I had no car because we left mine back in Arkansas, and even if I did have a car, I really didn't have anywhere to go. I had no idea where he worked (other than "at Hurlburt"), and no clue how to get a hold of him.

For weeks, I spent every afternoon gazing out the picture window in the dining room, surrounded by the world's most hideous flocked wallpaper. I left my job, I left my friends, I left my car, and my life consisted of looking out that window and staring at the palm trees. And every day I would hark back to Mom's advice and just suck it all up and have a nice meal waiting for Norty when he got home. I would smile, I would laugh, but inside I kept asking myself, "What have I done?"

That self-pity lasted for a few weeks. Then I had an epiphany.

I was standing in the same dining room in front of the same window looking at the same palm trees, when suddenly a strange vision popped into my head. Instead of me standing there looking out, I saw a younger version of Diane O'Malley—the general's wife who was so kind to us at the Friday Night Parade. Here was someone who was polished, well respected, completely at ease in any situation, yet I could tell that she had a real strength about her. She was a woman with a purpose—not only the eyes and ears of her husband—but someone driven to further her own independent causes. She was the first military spouse that I could see myself emulating one day, particularly if those prognosticators were right about Norty becoming a general. It struck me that long before she was the general's wife, she, too, must have experienced the same frustration that I was feeling—Captain O'Malley's young bride, dropped off to fend for herself in completely unfamiliar waters. And how many other military spouses had the same experience?

That single realization that I was not alone was enough to break me out of my funk. And who said that being the perfect officer's wife precluded my making independent strides on my own? I was determined to do both.

Major General Dick Scholtes was the first commander of JSOC (Joint Special Operations Command), the Special Operations component that oversees top-tier special operations mission units. Driven by his passion and belief in the "mission," he retired from active service so he could candidly testify before Congress about the pressing need for a separate special operations command.

Then Senator William Cohen (later secretary of defense) described Scholtes's testimony as vital in the decision of Congress to create the United States Special Operations Command.

"General Scholtes has a reputation for integrity and principle. He would tell it like it was. That was important to the Armed Services Committee members," Cohen said. "The Pentagon was waging a frontal and rear assault in opposition to the creation of a special operations command. Without his testimony, US-SOCOM might not have happened, or we might have created a command with only two or three stars."

Many years earlier—in fact, not too long after Desert One in Tehran—General Scholtes spoke with us in the theater at Hurlburt Field (in the Florida panhandle, where Air Force Special Operations is based), offering these prophetic words about our embryonic special operations efforts: "What we have now is a diamond in the rough, y'all. And we are going to polish this diamond until it shines." And we did.

He was a source of inspiration for everything that followed; for me personally, his words were the fuel that lit the fire which continued to burn in me for the next thirty years.

★ ★ ★

Almost immediately after the failure of Operation EAGLE CLAW, all bets were off and the checkbooks were open. Finding a viable way to rescue the hostages and safely extract the rescue team became an urgent noncompete situation of the highest priority at the Pentagon. Under the name HONEY BADGER, the Joint Test Directorate worked to develop and validate a range of potential scenarios. High atop the list was a joint undertaking of the USAF, U.S. Navy, and Lockheed-Georgia designed to remedy the primary deficit of the previous attempt, the heavy-lift helicopter. Code-named CREDIBLE SPORT, the Top Secret mission was to create a large "Super STOL" (Short Takeoff and Landing) fixed-wing aircraft that was designed to perform some incredible feats of airmanship—an aircraft that required so little distance to generate lift, it was more akin to a helicopter than an airplane at the time. A highly modified C-130 was selected for the task, and three Talon crews were formed to fly it—one from the 1st SOS (Special Operations Squadron), one from the 7th SOS, and one from the 8th SOS, which was based at Hurlburt Field in the Florida panhandle, where much of the late-stage testing would take place. Additional flight-test crews were provided by Lockheed-Georgia, the company that would actually be making the modifications.

To achieve such a dramatic performance enhancement, aircraft modifications included the installation of thirty rockets in multiple sets: eight forward-pointed ASROC (antisubmarine rocket) motors mounted around the forward fuselage to stop the aircraft upon landing, eight downward-pointed Shrike rocket motors mounted on the fuselage above the wheel wells to brake its descent, eight MK-56 rocket motors (from the RIM-66 Standard missile) mounted on the lower rear fuselage pointing rearward for takeoff acceleration boost, two Shrike rocket motors mounted in pairs on wing pylons to correct yaw during takeoff transition, and two more ASROC motors mounted at the rear of the tail to prevent it from striking the ground from over-rotation. These rockets provided significant propulsion boost to accelerate takeoff, and radically slowed the plane on landing. Just watching a behemoth the size of a Herc perform with rocket assist was a sight to behold!

Other features included aerodynamic and control modifications to further assist with performance and in-flight refueling, sophisticated new electronics to bolster navigation and self-defense, and a tailhook for landing.

The rescue plan called for the modified Combat Talons to depart from the United States and fly directly to Iran by employing five in-flight refuelings, penetrating Iranian airspace at low altitude under the cover of darkness to evade Iranian air defenses. It would land on the grass field inside the Amjadien soccer stadium, located directly across the street from the American Embassy where the hostages were being held. The stadium had previously been designated the exfiltration point for the Delta Force and freed hostages in the original EAGLE CLAW rescue mission. The CREDIBLE SPORT was specifically designed to land inside the stadium, retrieve its priceless cargo, then subsequently take off, within a distance of about a hundred yards (approximately the length of the soccer field)—a far cry from the three-thousand-foot minimum required for standard variant C-130s at the time. The aircraft would then proceed directly to a recovery airfield positioned in the Arabian Gulf region. There has been much speculation that the tailhook was intended for landing on an aircraft carrier, but the truth is that it was augmentation for the airland mission in the soccer stadium. After testing, it would not likely have been used.

Three C-130H aircraft were sourced for the program, with two to be fully modified to the CREDIBLE SPORT configuration, and the third to be used for rocket testing and control modifications while the other two were being modified.

From the initial concept to partial modification of the first aircraft, CREDIBLE SPORT was flying three weeks after the program began. Within sixty days a fully modified aircraft had been delivered to the test crews. The first fully modified aircraft (tail number 74-1683) was delivered on October 17, and between October 19 and October 28, a number of flight tests were performed at Wagner Field (Auxiliary Airfield #1), an auxiliary airfield in the Eglin Air Force Base range complex, not far from Hurlburt in Florida—the same remote airfield used by Doolittle Raiders in preparation for their raid on Japan. One by one, systems and procedures were checked, tested, and retested. The results were outstanding. The one and only glitch (an aileron flutter problem caused by modified expanded ailerons) was corrected within two days. It was determined that the aircraft could be flown at eighty-five KIAS (Knots Indicated Air Speed) during final approach for landing, with an eight-degree glide slope—a vast improvement from the standard 130s. A final, full profile test was set for October 29.

On the morning of the twenty-ninth, adrenaline flowed like floodwater as the Lockheed flight-test crew strapped themselves into the cockpit of CREDIBLE SPORT aircraft 74-1683, fully cognizant of the fact that some seven thousand miles away, the fate of the hostages could very well hinge on the results of their tests. If all went well, they could become a significant part of military aviation history.

The commander engaged the throttle control levers and the four Allison turboprops roared to life, supplemented by the eight Mark 56 rocket engines igniting right on cue. The modified Talon lunged forward, and within the first ten feet of takeoff roll, the nose gear lifted six feet off the ground. One hundred and forty feet later, the 150,000-pound rescue craft was airborne. By the time it reached the length of a soccer field, it was thirty feet off the ground at an airspeed of 115 knots.

The takeoff was essentially flawless, setting a number of short takeoff records. If only such success had continued through the landing. The crew had to activate the manual input for the rocket firing sequence for landing, since the automatic sequence was not yet tested or validated. The first (upper) pair of forward-facing ASROC deceleration rockets successfully engaged; then the flight engineer mistakenly believed they had already touched down (his cue to fire the Shrikes), and he manually ignited the lower set of rockets. This premature ignition was catastrophic. Forward flight jolted to a halt, and the aircraft dropped to the runway like a seventy-five-ton brick, ripping off the right wing and bursting into flames.

Note the eight ASROC rockets extending from the front of the Credible Sport aircraft.

Mark 56 rocket motors point rearward at a forty-five-degree angle on each aft side.

 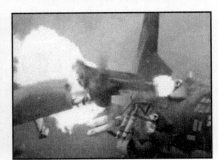

USAF photos

Thanks to the lightning-fast response of the emergency crews (who had the fire extinguished within eight seconds of the plane coming to a stop), the entire crew survived without injury. The same could not be said about the CREDIBLE SPORT rescue mission. Between an Algerian-brokered hostage release plan that was announced a few days later and Ronald Reagan's defeat of Jimmy Carter in the November presidential election, the program was terminated. On January 21, 1981, at the very moment that Ronald Reagan completed his inaugural address, the hostages were released into U.S. custody.

Many of the tactics and equipment developed under HONEY BADGER formed the foundation for modern-day U.S. special operations forces.

I arrived at Hurlburt for Talon School in November of 1980, right around the time that all this was playing out. But it was far from my focus at the time. I arrived as a reasonably well-qualified C-130 tactical pilot. I knew the airplane and basic airdrop tactics. Frankly, I was pretty confident that I would complete the process of picking up whatever enhancements were a part of the Combat Talon (MC-130E, special operations variant of the Herc) that we'd be flying. It took about ten seconds inside the cockpit to realize that mastering the intricacies of piloting the Combat Talon would require all of my attention and then some. Unlike the C-130E/Hs I'd flown previously, the CT was a specialized aircraft designed for our specialized mission: a low-visibility, long-range aircraft capable of worldwide low-level infiltration/exfiltration in denied airspace.

It took me weeks to fully adapt to the terrain-following/terrain-avoidance (TF/TA) radar that allowed us to fly as low as 250 feet above the ground—safely and for extended distances.

Later, I found the Fulton surface-to-air recovery system (STARS) equally as challenging. STARS is a tactic/technology that provides a means of retrieving personnel or equipment from the ground using an aircraft in flight. Picture a five-hundred-foot, high-strength, braided nylon lift line with a balloon in the sky at one end, and an individual or cargo harnessed to the line on the ground at the other. As retrieval pilot, our job was to fly the aircraft upwind directly toward the lift line, so that it was caught between two V-shaped arms of a yoke that extended from the nose of our plane, simultaneously snatching the individual from the ground and releasing the balloon. The crew in the back of our plane engaged a winch to reel in the "package," who at this point was being towed behind the plane at upwards of 150 KIAS. This is one of many tactics where failure was not an option.

Add in mastering day and night assault takeoffs and landings, airborne intercepts, and low-level evasive tactics—all utilizing the specialized TF/TA systems—and you have a demanding period of training that led to that all-important check flight.

From the first day that I arrived, the notable leadership and splendid squadron-mates of the 8th SOS were entirely supportive; they made me feel at home. That's not to say they didn't expect results. It was—and hopefully will always be—a business where performance trumps every other consideration. Lee Hess,

Schwartz personal collection

Tom Bradley, Ray Turczynski, Bob Meller, George Ferkes, Jerry Thigpen, Sam Galloway, Thom Beres, Bob Almanzar, Buff Underwood, Ray Doyle, and Taco Sanchez among many others—they had already stepped up to the plate and shone on multiple missions. A desire to prove myself worthy of their acceptance became my driving motivation.

By this time I had demonstrated a proficiency in all the requisite skills except two—NVG (night vision goggle) airland and aerial refueling. NVG usage in fixed-wing aircraft was still in its infancy, with blacked-out landing operations having recently been perfected during the preparation for the Desert One mission. Before this, Combat Talon crews required overt illumination to mark the runway during night flight operations—visible lights that could be readily seen by the flight crews, and by enemy forces. That all changed when Colonel Kyle (Desert One air mission commander) tasked the planners to develop a capability for the Talons to land without any visible lighting—none on the runway and none on the aircraft.

The only way to fulfill this order was by developing a means to safely employ the NVG technology in a fixed-wing environment. Arguably, doing so became the single most significant breakthrough for special operations aviation from this period.

Colonel (ret.) Jerry Thigpen, a fellow pilot in the 8th SOS, wrote an excellent book surrounding the history of the Combat Talon entitled *The Pretorian STARShip: The Untold Story of the Combat Talon*. In it, he shares how the first NVGs became such an indispensable part of our repertoire:

[On] 21 November 1979, [Bob] Brenci was in the squadron early, as were several crew members from the previous night's mission. Brenci was the chief pilot and assistant operations officer and was filling in for Lt Col Les Smith, who had been called away to Washington, DC, a few days earlier. Captain Thigpen, who had flown with Brenci as an instructor pilot on the flight the evening before, was also in the squadron. He was working behind the operations desk finalizing the following week's schedule when Brenci called him into his office and closed the door. Brenci had received a call from Smith in Washington directing him to begin preparations for conducting blacked-out NVG landings in the Combat Talon. The only unit in the 1st SOW [Special Operations Wing] that possessed the relatively rare NVG equipment was the 20th Special Operations Squadron, which was the rotary-wing (helicopter) unit assigned to the wing.

Brenci sent Thigpen to the 20th SOS to sign out ten PVS-5 NVGs so that the squadron could become familiar with their operation. Within the hour Thigpen had signed out the goggles and was back in the squadron. Two things impressed him regarding the transaction—first, his hand receipt totaled over $200,000 for the NVGs, a sizable sum for a captain to be responsible for, and second, the insistence by 20th SOS pilots who had said that fixed-wing aircraft could not be safely landed on NVGs due to the lack of depth perception and a limited field of view.

Several crew members, including Brenci and Thigpen, spent the afternoon familiarizing themselves with proper goggle operation. By utilizing a darkened room, basic functions of the NVGs, such as turning them on and off and focusing them both near and far, were reviewed. A night sortie was scheduled for the following Monday on TAB-6 (Biancur Field), one of the many local auxiliary airfields on the Eglin AFB range complex.

On Monday, 26 November 1979, the first NVG mission was flown by the 8th SOS. Combat Talon 64-0567 flew 4.6 hours, with Brenci, Major Meller, Major Uttaro, and Thigpen sharing pilot duties. Because there were no procedures written for airland NVG operations, the crew started its NVG work utilizing established airborne radar approach (ARA) procedures. Each ARA was flown utilizing heading and altitude calls provided by the left navigator. Meller and Brenci took turns in the left seat, and Uttaro and Thigpen swapped right-seat duties.

Partially because of the rotary-wing pilots' insistence that fixed-wing aircraft could not land on NVGs, the first several approaches were flown on "eyeballs" by the left-seat pilot. During the approach the right-seat pilot turned out all of his cockpit lights and focused his goggles on his instrument panel as the left-seat navigator called out headings and altitudes. The idea was to darken the cockpit enough to allow the left-seat pilot, the standing third (or safety) pilot, and the flight engineer to see outside the aircraft and not be blinded by the glare of lights coming from within the cockpit.

As the right-seat pilot flew the approach, the left-seat pilot and the safety pilot, utilizing their NVGs, assisted the navigators achieving alignment for each approach. In addition, the third pilot, standing behind the left pilot's seat, also backed up the flight engineer in such critical areas as landing gear and flap configuration. The right-seat pilot flew the aircraft down to ARA minimums, three hundred feet above the ground. When the left-seat pilot had the runway environment within view and the runway was confirmed by both the third pilot and the flight engineer, he took control of the aircraft from the right-seat pilot and landed the aircraft.

Without any lights on the runway or on the aircraft, landing the Combat Talon proved to be quite challenging. As soon as the aircraft touched down, the right-seat pilot focused his goggles outside the aircraft and assisted the left-seat pilot as the aircraft slowed to taxi speed. After several "bone-crushing" touchdowns, it was apparent that the left-seat pilot needed more help than his own eyes could give him. Depth-perception problems or not, the left-seat pilot actually had to land while wearing NVGs. From this first effort, the squadron made great strides in perfecting blacked-out NVG airland procedures. Within the next three weeks, NVG airland procedures were developed and refined, and those procedures formed the basis for a capability that would radically change Combat Talon airland tactics forever. When the first Combat Talon NVG landing was made, it had been 23 days since the 4 November 1979 takeover of the U.S. Embassy in Tehran.

The time had come for me to master my final hurdle before being assigned to a special operations flight crew: my NVG airland and aerial refueling check flight. It was not without incident.

These early PVS-5 model NVGs were less than ideal. They were heavy, had a limited field of view (akin to "tunnel vision") and very poor battery life. On the one hand, they provided poor light amplification; on the other, if you'd inadvertently look into a bright light you'd be temporarily blinded. Today's units have much higher acuity, longer lasting batteries, and much better amplification of available light. They swivel down from a hinge on the front of the helmet so they're much more comfortable to wear, and allow for viewing around the periphery of the tubes.

We began with our pre-engine start preflight check, with one significant addition: We put tape over the primary warning lights on the instrument panel so they couldn't impair the NVG performance. If you've seen the inside of a C-130 cockpit, there are a lot of lights and instruments. Taping them all would be no small undertaking. So in those days, it was hit and miss and we did our best, taping those that would have the greatest chance of illuminating during the flight. Today, there are totally compatible NVG cockpits or detailed taping instructions printed on a separate NVG preflight checklist, telling you exactly what to tape and how to tape it—but that certainly was not the case back then.

Once we got past that, we proceeded with the flight, including linking up with a tanker for midair refueling. By now I was comfortable with the Combat Talon, and fairly confident that my flight would receive a positive evaluation. My flight examiner, Jerry Uttaro, instructed me to turn the Herc around and head back to North Auxiliary Field in South Carolina.

Even with the poor acuity of the PVS-5s, I had no problem sighting the runway and lining up our nose for landing; besides a slight buffeting at about five hundred feet, the mild crosswinds presented no problems. Touchdown could not have been any smoother. I pulled the throttles toward me into the reverse thrust position when suddenly I was blinded by a bright flash directly in front of me. Coming from just above the airspeed indicator, it had to be one of the four nacelle overheat warning lights, signaling a serious overheat condition in the area around the engine compressor section. Since that condition so rarely comes up, we hadn't bothered to tape those lights. Every bit as pressing at that instant was the fact that I had just engaged the reverse thrust on seventy-five tons of momentum racing down an active runway, and the flash of the warning light had deactivated the NVGs. At moments like that, instinct kicks in—or maybe it's just repeated training that becomes reflex. Whatever it was, I knew that slowing down the plane and stopping with normal lighting was first priority, and we had to scramble to do so.

We returned the throttle levers to their idle position, switched on the overt taxi lights, removed the full-face goggles, slowed and stopped the aircraft, and departed the runway.

"You never do things the easy way, do you, Schwartz?" Uttaro said with a smile. It felt good to have that one behind me.

Thanks to the patience and aviation prowess of top instructor pilots like Bob Brenci, Jim Hobson, and Jerry Uttaro, I checked out and was ultimately assigned to Uttaro's flight crew by the early part of 1981; it was one of only five crews at the time. Along with Brenci, Jerry Uttaro was a veteran commander in both EAGLE CLAW and CREDIBLE SPORT, so I could not have been in better hands. Basic Combat Certification was a crucial step, a prerequisite to piloting special operations missions. But it wasn't enough. I wanted more.

In the flying business, you have the basic airplane capability and, for a small percentage of aircrew, advanced certifications called special qualifications. In the case of the C-130, these include unique ways to employ the weapon system, special operations low-level, low-altitude parachute extraction system, the flare mission, and other special tactics and maneuvers exclusive to the Special Ops trade. My goal was to become qualified in all of them. Once I achieved this goal (with the exception of "ski landings"), I became an even more valuable asset to the joint special operations community. No longer would my interaction be exclusive to the Air Force. The joint community encompasses Army, Navy, and the Marines as well as Air Force. Joint experience is an essential piece of a well-rounded officer's career portfolio, but in my case, the experience and visibility it provided me with my Army colleagues may have been the most significant factor in my progression to Chief.

For years I'd been focusing my sights on a career in Special Ops. I visualized countless scenarios: insertions and extractions in every conceivable configuration and environment, some friendly, others hostile, requiring specialized tactics to evade enemy antiaircraft fire and missiles; special operations low-level, with blacked-out aircraft and NVGs; HALO (High Altitude Low Opening), HAHO (High Altitude High Opening), and static-line airdrops; clandestine missions that hinged on deception. I anticipated (and experienced) each of these—with enthusiasm, I might add. But the opportunity that I was about to be assigned was something so extraordinary, it never crossed my mind that I'd be chosen to participate.

★ ★ ★

Sometimes when the boss calls you into his office and you have no idea why, even though you know you didn't do anything wrong, just a tiny part of you wonders if you screwed something up. That's how I felt when Lt Col Bob Brenci called me into his office in early summer of 1981.

"Norty," he began, after having me take a seat in the chair beside his desk, directly across from a wall jammed with framed photos documenting his esteemed career. "You've proven that you can fly the Combat Talon, now how would you like to help us design its replacement?"

"I'm not exactly sure what that means, sir, but it sure sounds like a worthwhile challenge."

He went on to explain. "I'm sure you're familiar with the CREDIBLE SPORT project that Jerry Uttaro and I were involved with last year. Well, TAC has assigned Jerry to lead a follow-on program that we're calling CREDIBLE SPORT II. This one's not about rescuing hostages like the first one. It's an effort to save funds and use the assets—and information—from the original CREDIBLE SPORT, to serve as a test bed for a new Combat Talon. It won't be using the rocket assists like the first CS project, but it will retain the other super STOL [short takeoff and landing] modifications. We'll be using the one remaining aircraft from CS I. We're designating it YMC-130. And I'd like you to work with Jerry on the project—serve as the project's second test pilot, and see what you and the team can come up with for the next-generation special operations aircraft."

When I walked out of his office, my head was spinning—for so many different reasons. First and foremost was excitement for the tremendous potential of being part of a challenge like this. Having the opportunity to work so closely with Jerry served to sweeten the pot. I made a beeline for his office to thank him for having such faith in me; certainly he played a key role in recommending me to Brenci.

They referred to the process as an Operational Utility Evaluation (OUE), and we were called the OUE team. Testing would be split into two phases, with the first to begin in late August of 1981, and continue until mid-November. In this phase we integrated minor alterations to improve aerodynamics and flight safety. Phase II involved modifications more specific to the needs of the new Combat Talon.

As Col Benci mentioned, by the time we received the test aircraft, the rocket motors had already been removed. But the other modifications were still very much intact. It truly was an ideal aircraft to work with since it already incorporated many of the subsystems, technologies, and concepts contemplated for Combat Talon II. These included integrated, self-contained navigation/precision approach avionics, aerodynamic STOL features, and advanced cockpit displays. It had double-slotted articulated (expanded) flaps, expanded structural surfaces that we called the horsal and dorsal fins mounted on the rear fuselage—these improved directional stability at slow speeds—and extended-chord fully powered aileron surfaces that were boosted to provide additional lateral control. Modifications also included a new radome, a FLIR (forward-looking infrared) turret with laser range system; an externally mounted refueling system to provide an in-flight refueling (IFR) capability; a Doppler radar tied in to the aircraft's inertial navigation system; a terrain-following/terrain-avoidance (TF/TA) radar to facilitate low-level flight; and a defensive electronic countermeasures (ECM) suite for added protection.

The guidance system—an important landing aid—was cutting edge at the time. This was also the very first usage of computer-aided visualization and sensor integration (both the pilot and navigator had CRT displays) that allowed us to operate the aircraft on internal guidance only; absolutely no external guidance was required. Integrating avionics to give the aircraft an autonomous landing capability was a totally unique concept at the time.

So I found myself deeply immersed in development of the next generation of fixed-wing special operations airlift, rather than flying actual tactical missions, and I was enjoying every minute of it. I spent a good deal of time in Atlanta at the Lockheed Marietta plant, both before Suzie and I got married and after. Not the ideal situation for a young newlywed couple, especially since these trips kept me out of town for weeks at a time. I was probably gone for at least nine of the first fifteen months of our marriage, and Suzie was not a particularly happy camper.

From time to time I would fly back for the weekend, but these would be spur of the moment trips without any advance notice—par for the course in the special operations field in the early '80s—not so much for a newlywed bride in an unfamiliar city without knowing another soul. Suzie had her own unique way of letting me know how she felt about it. Case in point: one Saturday morning when I stepped off the Republic Airlines DC-9 from Atlanta and approached a row of payphones at Fort Walton Beach's Okaloosa Regional Airport (now called Destin-Fort Walton Beach Airport). I inserted my dime and called home.

"Good news, Suz," I said enthusiastically. "I'm in town for the weekend, so could you please pick me up at the airport?"

"Excuse me, who is this? I don't recognize the voice," she fired back sarcastically.

I chuckled. "Message received. Now would you please come over and get me?"

"I suppose I could . . . but I won't. Until you find the common decency to give me some advance notice that you're coming in, you can find your own way home." Click. Fortunately, the taxi stand was only a few hundred feet away.

★ ★ ★

Uttaro and I spent months evaluating the CREDIBLE SPORT II aircraft and avionics performance. These included high- and low-level navigation, simulated aerial refueling (as helicopter tanker), airdrop, and night airland operations using NVG/blackout landing techniques.

In the twenty-five sorties and 60.5 flight hours that constituted Phase I, we found major design deficiencies in the airframe and in its avionics suite, and insufficient margins of safety required for peacetime operations. We also called for improved flight controls, the preparation of flight director/autopilot control laws, the installation of a stall warning system, improved stability augmentation, a better functioning radar system, improvements to the cockpit configuration, and proof testing of the STOL flaps. Once these issues were rectified by Lockheed, we transitioned to Phase II testing.

We finally flew the aircraft from Dobbins to Hurlburt so that we could run some tests in the Eglin Range Complex. It was parked on the ramp configured for slow-speed flight, so it looked demonstratively different from all the other C-130s lined up on either side of it. Picture a supercharged *Knight Rider* Mustang Shelby with hood scoop and high-performance rear racing wings parked amidst a row of standard equipped V6 GTs. I'd been passionately involved with this project for the past year or so, and in many respects I considered that aircraft to be my baby. For months I'd been telling Suzie about the added fins, extended flaps, FLIR turret, and such; I couldn't wait for her to come by to see them all for herself—to share my excitement.

To her credit, she arrived in under fifteen minutes. I was still near the CRED-IBLE SPORT aircraft when she arrived. I'll never forget how she had this big smile on her face as she approached me, looking all around at the various 130s so expectantly. "Which one is it?" she asked.

"You're joking, right?"

"Norty, if you got me out here for nothing . . . I thought you had this wonder-plane here."

She didn't notice the difference. To her, it looked just like all the other 130s. I was crushed.

Our next scheduled test flight was a night sortie to take place that Friday night. This was an overall evaluation of all the systems. We were flying in to Duke Field, not too far from Hurlburt, utilizing the autonomous landing system—the mechanism that allowed us to operate the aircraft independent from any external guidance. The FLIR sensors and associated apparatus automatically tracked our exact position, and exactly where we were supposed to be.

Being the mission commander, I was on PVS-5 NVGs in the left seat, looking outside as both a safety officer and ultimately to take the airplane for landing—but at that point I was allowing the right-seat pilot to take the plane in according to the internal navigation and guidance data he was receiving from the autonomous system. My reputation is that I'm a pretty quiet guy, and that's especially true when I'm in the cockpit. There's enough going on without idle chitchat providing distraction from the tasks at hand, so when I do say something, those around me know that it's of consequence.

As I gazed out the windshield through the blue-green cockpit lighting, I felt more and more uneasy. We were precisely following the guidance data, but to me it appeared that we were coming in well below a typical glide path. Apparently I mumbled to myself, "This doesn't look good." Immediately everyone perked up and sat up in their seats. I called for an immediate go-around, and it's a good thing that we did. Had we followed the computer's internal guidance data we would have landed in the trees, well short of the runway.

Later we learned one of the gimbals on the forward-looking infrared wasn't calibrated properly, so the data it was providing for guidance was inaccurate in terms of degrees from the waterline (symbol that indicates relative pitch and roll angles of the aircraft when compared to the horizon). That slight miscalibration would have landed us about a quarter mile short.

The lesson here is that good instincts in the special operations aircraft cockpit will always be essential to managing the inherent risks of and accomplishing that very demanding (and rewarding) special operations aviation mission.

The data from this flight would be added to the vast amount that we had already collected. Eventually, it would all be compiled for analysis and presented in the final OUE report, along with our recommendations.

The following night, we all got together for some beer to celebrate the birthday of one of our team members. I stood up and thanked everyone for their hard work and diligence, and they returned the favor by presenting me with a plaque. It was from the "Credible Sports," which was what we called ourselves. All it said, in big, bold engraved letters, was THIS DOESN'T LOOK GOOD. Their way of saying, "When Schwartz talks, we listen." The folks at Lockheed-Georgia corrected the calibration problem in such a way that it would never reoccur. We eventually perfected the autonomous landing technology, and it was an important contribution to the state of the art along the way.

In the fall of 1982, Jerry Uttaro was reassigned to the Pentagon and I was given the honor of taking over as the director of the OUE test team, with Sam Galloway, Chris Armstrong, Mike Dredla, Tom Daignault, Dee Newberry, Ken Bancroft, Dave Metherell, and others as teammates.

On one of our final test flights, we landed the airplane at Dobbins AFB in Atlanta right across the runway from the Lockheed plant. We were coming in at 140,000 pounds from fifty feet over the threshold with an approach speed of seventy-seven knots. Our landing roll was 991 feet. We were carrying about 11,000 inch-pounds of torque across all four engines. Performance like that was unheard of at the time. Those capabilities were only achievable because we created an aircraft that was aerodynamically unique.

The issue was that flying the airplane in that regime was well behind the power curve, so there was considerable risk involved. If you lost an engine, your margin of safety was substantially reduced. At those speeds, there came a point on approach where you were committed to land if you lost an engine, whether you wanted to or not. Losing an engine at seventy-seven knots is not going to have a happy ending. There were additional risks associated with some of the additional aerodynamic surfaces that the airplane had. These were flight safety issues which we considered an acceptable risk because of the urgency of certain high-value special operations missions—certainly not the case across the entire fleet.

In November 1982, we published the final OUE test report. The final report determined that the CREDIBLE SPORT II aircraft design, in its final configuration, was ready for production as the new Combat Talon II aircraft.

Unfortunately, Tactical Air Command disagreed. They determined it to be too expensive and perhaps not high enough utility to be employed or implemented on a fleet-wide basis.

While the model itself never went into production, elements of the YMC-130 we came up with led to the next generation of special operations fixed-wing airlift. The technology ultimately migrated into the newest version of the MC-130, the MC-130H—the first aircraft equipped with an autonomous landing system as "standard equipment." The integration between sensors, flight dynamics, and CRT visualization was an early forerunner of today's computerized cockpit display technology.

★ ★ ★

We left Hurlburt in July of '83, honored to have served alongside the real pioneers of the special operations profession. It was a wonderfully challenging period that provided me the first steps in building multiple decades-long relationships that paid huge dividends. We were a band of youngsters with a quiet determination—cutting our teeth together and growing up to be senior leaders in the armed forces of the United States. This was the period when Pete Schoomaker, subsequently a commander of Special Operations Command (SOCOM), then chief of staff of the Army; Doug Brown, also commander of Special Operations Command; Eric Olson on the SEAL side, commander of Naval Special Warfare Command (the Navy component of SOCOM) and later SOCOM; and myself all worked together, grew together, and dedicated our lives to help build the most capable special operations force in the world.

My service in our Air Force was profoundly influenced by my tours in the special operations community. Had I not experienced the intensity of the mission, associated with an array of remarkable joint teammates, and earned a reputation in the special operations community, I would never have had the opportunities to lead in our Air Force that I ultimately enjoyed.

For those interested in specifics, here are some details taken directly from our CREDIBLE SPORT II final OUE evaluation report. The entire OUE report is available online at www.nortyschwartz.com/credible_sport2.

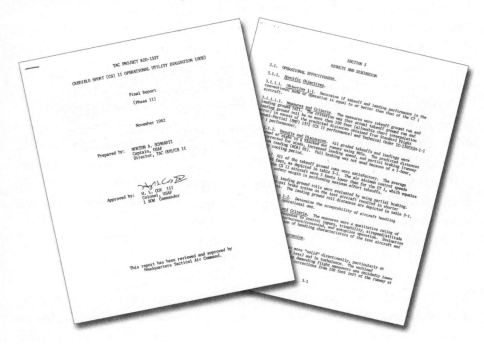

PURPOSE AND MAJOR OBJECTIVES. The purpose of the CS II OUE was to satisfy prototype test requirements of those CS systems/capabilities proposed for CT II. The major objectives were as follows:

a) Determine aircraft handling characteristics for operational use.

b) Determine mission requirements for enroute navigation.

c) Determine if CS II avionics meet mission requirements for approach accuracy.

d) Determine if instrument/avionics lighting is compatible with night/minimum light operation.

e) Determine if switchology/moding/panel configuration/displays are acceptable for operational use in normal and degraded operation.

f) Determine if representative missions can he effectively accomplished using the two-man navigator (nav)/electronic warfare officer (EWO) suite.

SIGNIFICANT RESULTS.

1. The CS aircraft was more "stable" directionally than the MC-130E, particularly at slower airspeeds (130 knots indicated airspeed [KIAS] and less) and in turbulence. Pilot comments emphasized that handling qualities were significantly better, overall, than the MC-130E. Pilot workload during demanding flight maneuvers was decidedly lower than for the MC-130E.

2. Average inertial navigation system (INS) accuracies were 1.95 nautical miles per hour (nm/hr) for all sorties (including overwater) in the Doppler/inertial mode, 1.23 nm/hr for overland sorties in the Doppler/inertial mode, and 1.35 nm/hr in the pure inertial mode. The independent Doppler provided 0.95 nm/hr accuracy. Although electromagnetic interference problems purportedly degraded INS performance, no consistently improved drift rates were achieved after a "fix" was installed. For example, a 0.77 nm/hr drift rate was experienced on 31 August. Additionally, use of the forward-looking infrared (FLIR) to update the navigation system during enroute operations was constrained by environmental conditions, limited field-of-view, and inability to properly cue the FLIR with the mapping radar.

3. Fourteen approaches were flown in the conventional, 100 percent flap assault configuration using 3.0 degree glide paths. Safe landings were performed during day and night/blackout conditions from all approaches flown in the inertial mode. Accuracies varied, as did the flyability of the computer-generated guidance, but overall results were favorable. However, all approaches performed in the Doppler/C-12 (noninertial) mode were unsafe in that the guidance, if followed, would have landed the aircraft well short of the runway. Data collected on the laser were invalid because of a protective cover inadvertently left installed on the laser receiver by factory technicians. Subsequent to the OUE, performance of the laser with the cover removed was impressive.

4. Cockpit/instrument lighting was adequate for test purposes, but workarounds were necessary. Several lights had to be taped and/or removed. The cathode ray tube (CRT) display created a hazard in that lowering the brightness for NVG compatibility caused the filtered FLIR video to disappear. In addition, a normal level of illumination was discernible from outside the aircraft—an undesirable characteristic in a combat environment.

5. The crew stations were functional, but deficiencies were identified which require additional design attention. These include inadequate CRT display flexibility, symbology, format, and video presentation. The computer display units (CDUs) were generally difficult to use, were programmed using different formats, and did not provide the operator with adequate feedback, control flexibility, equipment status monitoring, or access. The FLIR target tracking control (joystick) was poorly positioned on the navigator table, did not incorporate an integral "designate" function, and provided different radar and FLIR sensor slew rates. The Collins flight director did not incorporate a hearing pointer; displayed true rather than magnetic heading to the pilot; and did not provide automatic course intercept steering in the computer mode, adequate approach, or dedicated Doppler steering. Additionally, the attitude direction indicator (ADI) climb indexes were not NVG compatible, and airspeed indicators were poorly graduated and difficult to interpret.

6. The single navigator was able to perform all navigation tasks with minimum assistance—albeit with a high workload at times. Areas of unusually intense concentration/activity included system programming, enroute navigation updating, turnpoint procedures, and self-contained approach duties. The degree of task saturation experienced by the single navigator was directly related to the level of system degradation, inaccuracy of the inertial reference, and modest automation inherent in the CS II design.

MAJOR DEFICIENCIES. The overall CS II aircraft and avionics design represents a significant improvement over equipment now being used. However, five major deficiencies were identified.

a) Inertial navigation system inaccuracy.

b) Unreliability of noninertial approach modes.

c) Night lighting and CRT/NVG compatibility.

d) Man-machine interface/system automation.

e) Lack of internal software reasonableness testing to avoid unsafe flight conditions.

MAJOR CONCLUSIONS.

1. The handling characteristics of the test aircraft are superior to those of the MC-130E. A production aircraft equipped with CS flight control technology will perform the mission better and will enjoy improved margins of safety.

2. LN-15S navigation system accuracies are unacceptable while Dopper enroute accuracies are adequate.

3. Approach accuracies in the inertial and Doppler/inertial modes are acceptable. The Doppler/C-12 approach mode is unsafe.

4. The test aircraft CRT displays and formats are manageable and effective but only with extreme mental concentration. They are not adequate for prolonged safe and effective operation. Nevertheless, the FLIR video is a real asset during blackout operations.

5. The central avionics computer (CAC) CDU is completely unacceptable because of insufficient readout, display, and simultaneous operations capability.

6. The split configuration of the nav/weapon systems officer (WSO) station is not acceptable.

7. Processing of self-contained approach guidance by the Collins flight director yields unusable steering commands.

8. The software is immature and requires further development to improve operator interface, minimize aircrew workload, and achieve consistent patterns of mission reliability and performance.

9. Cockpit and avionics lighting is adequate for safe night operations but NVG compatibility enhancements are required to perform representative missions.

10. The two-man nav/EWO suite allows effective accomplishment of representative CT missions.

MAJOR RECOMMENDATIONS.

1. In addition to the CAC derived height-above-touchdown display at the navigator station, the current radar altitude must he displayed for qualitative assessment of CAC operation and flight safety. A barometric altimeter and radar altimeter should also be installed at the radio operator crew station. Additionally, a warning/caution annunciator, similar to the pilot's, is needed.

2. A truly multimode, high-resolution radar must he procured that is capable of simultaneous precision ground mapping and terrain following operations.

3. The software must incorporate internal self-test features which will alert the operator when reasonableness parameters are exceeded. An "above-glide-path" computation which exceeds current radar altitude, for example, should not go unnoticed by the aircrew.

4. A reliable airborne barometric calibration procedure must be incorporated in production software.

5. A reliable alternative to the inertial approach modes must be developed to allow for graceful system degradation.

6. An accurate and redundant INS must be provided. Consistent performance must be verified in the mission environment prior to production. Inadequate INS performance will incapacitate the CT II avionics architecture.

7. The navigation software must be optimized for the C-130 including automatic course intercept steering, automatic sequential steering, additional waypoint/target storage with elevation, and multiple offset aimpoint capability.

8. Design attention must he focused in the area of night lighting and NVG compatibility. Areas of greatest concern should he CRT design and cockpit/instrument light/annunciation control.

9. System and procedural changes must be made to alleviate navigator workload "crunchpoints." The objective should be to minimize/consolidate the number of steps and separate switches/keyboard operations needed to program, select update modes, and manage the avionics system. Additionally, a detailed procedural/task analysis must be conducted to identify nav/WSO tasks that may be shared.

10. CS flight control technology should be pursued for incorporation in the production aircraft.

11. Computer control must be optimized for simultaneous operations and provide annunciation of system moding, function, and system status for all crewmembers.

12. A FLIR video recorder should be installed for mission reconstruction, evaluation, and intelligence collection.

Once we completed the CREDIBLE SPORT project, I enthusiastically stepped back into the hectic pace of one of five crew commanders of the 8th SOS. Real-world missions were supplemented with exercises that honed established tactics and procedures, and experimented with new ones. An embryonic special operations aviation force was beginning to mature. Here are a few key operations and exercises that contributed to that growth:

Operation Night March was an around-the-world mission intended to perfect our skills at moving aircraft in a very low-visibility fashion, completely "off the radar" so to speak. It's a strategy that's as vital today as it was back then. Recently we've used it moving aircraft to Korea and the Middle East.

It involved a single airplane that I piloted, and it did not go well. Coincidentally, I was flying Combat Talon 64-0567, the very aircraft flown by Colonel Brenci, Major Meller, Major Uttaro, and Captain Thigpen on November 26, 1979, the very first mission to utilize NVGs.

This was an important mission that commanded the very best crew: There was no more proficient loadmaster than Taco Sanchez. If there was any question about that (which there wasn't), it would have been put to rest on April 24, 1980, when Taco was loadmaster on "Dragon 1," Combat Talon 64-0565, the lead plane into Iran on Operation EAGLE CLAW. Lt Col Bob Brenci piloted that flight. On that afternoon, before commander Colonel Charlie Beckwith stepped onboard, Taco had already coordinated a load that took every square inch of the cargo compartment. He'd loaded fifty-six operators, twelve Rangers (for roadblocks), two Iranian generals (advisors), six Iranian truck drivers, seven Farsi-speaking American drivers, John Carney and his CCT (Combat Control Team), aviation mission commander Colonel James Kyle, and 1st SOW deputy commander, Colonel Thomas J. Wicker. And they were in addition to the vehicles and equipment that previously had been packed inside. There was the gun-jeep for the roadblock team, a portable TACAN to be used to help the helicopters find the LZ, three motorcycles to be used by the rangers to provide mobility for the roadblock force, and two by Carney's team to mark a second parallel runway. Two large sheets of aluminum planking were loaded in, just in case the aircraft became mired in the desert sand.

Along with Sanchez, Dee Newberry would also be a vital member of our crew as flight engineer. Dee had also been a part of Desert One, going in on Jerry Uttaro's "Republic 6" aircraft.

Our objective was to make the trip in one single "invisible" hop from the Philippines to South Sudan, where we would perform a tactical airdrop insertion and then continue, undetected, direct to Mogadishu. It did not take long for the problems to rear their ugly head.

Equipment breakdown caused a navigation failure over the ocean. Under normal circumstances, this was something we could work around. Any deviations from our intended route would be covered by the extra fuel we'd take on during our IFR. But when we arrived at what we believed to be our intended rendezvous point—no tanker. By that point we were running low on fuel, and black ops radio silence complicated our attempts to rendezvous.

Eventually we did land in Mogadishu, only to find that our reception party (combined Central Command and intelligence personnel) had dropped the ball with inadequate homework, leaving us to fly into a shitstorm. They were supposed to have coordinated in detail with the host government or air force, but to my knowledge, this never happened. That left me to face penetrating questions from the host government air traffic control—unanticipated questions that were a challenge for me to manage. The more I spoke, the worse it became. Mogadishu authorities were not buying my story. Tensions escalated.

The senior representative from the host civil aviation authority grilled us in detail about how we had conducted our flight inbound to Mogadishu. It was unexpected, a serious challenge to our "story," and clearly implied the potential for mission compromise. The official could have demanded we depart, or asked to inspect and impound our aircraft—a sovereign U.S. asset—or he could have delayed our departure until we brought in diplomatic intervention.

Ultimately, a Sudanese Air Force officer interceded. His intentions were honorable, but now this had blown up and become an international incident. So much for keeping it "close-hold."

I learned more on that op than I could pick up in four years at Harvard.

Never assume the other guys aren't as smart as you are.

The Somalian supervisor who busted us *was*. When he crunched the numbers from my story, he realized that they didn't add up.

I am not a very good liar.

I would have to train myself to be far more convincing when delivering my stories, and the stories themselves would have to be more refined. Up 'til now this had never been an issue. I never *had* to lie. At home, at school, during sports competitions, at Sunday school—from as early as I can remember—fabrications were not only forbidden, but perpetrating them would reap unpleasant consequences: a firm swat on the backside from Erna, or a stinging crack of the belt from Dad. But when dealing with operations that required realistic explanations, lives literally depended on the plausibility and believability of my charade.

I'd have to be a much more convincing actor than I was when I played Mr. Spock at the Clark Air Base annual Winter Gala.

Prepare, prepare, then prepare some more.

I'm no good at winging it, and I'd have to war-game potential scenarios and what-ifs, whether the situation entailed operations, congressional testimonies, or even press conferences.

Effective litigators never ask a question without being fully primed for whatever response an opposing witness tenders. They've done the legwork and crafted detailed matrices (whether on paper or in their minds) anticipating every possible reply, and they're ready to fire back with a totally convincing argument no matter what they encounter. I could never again let myself be caught with my pants down, no matter how much time and energy it would take me to become fully prepared.

Ocean Venture 81: We on-loaded a Combat Rubber Raiding Craft, or Zodiac, and a U.S. Navy SEAL team at Norfolk, Virginia, and a second Combat Talon did the same at Pope AFB, North Carolina. After completing our IFRs en route to the exercise zone in the Caribbean, we successfully air-dropped our loads over the DZ near Vieques Island. We then air-landed additional personnel and equipment at Roosevelt Roads AB, Puerto Rico.

Marvel Exodus: a large-scale exercise in which the 1st SOW deployed three MC-130Es, two AC-130Hs, six HH-53Hs, and 271 aircrew and support personnel. Mission included fuel blivets and heavy equipment airdrops, airfield seizures with U.S. Army Rangers, IFR, HALO (High Altitude Low Opening) airdrops, static-line personnel airdrops, and NVG airland operations.

On November 30, 1981, I was alongside commander Jerry Uttaro, piloting one of two MC-130Es that departed Hurlburt Field en route to **Bright Star 82**, which was to take place in Sudan. Eighth SOS squadron commander Bob Brenci commanded another Talon, with Lt Col Jim Hobson (who would replace Brenci as squadron commander seven months later) as his first pilot. While Brenci and Hobson utilized three IFRs and twenty-seven hours' flying time to fly a nonstop, long-range infiltration mission into Wadi Seidna, Sudan, Uttaro and I utilized one IFR that took us to Lajes Field, Azores, where we spent the night before flying on to Sudan the next day. The exercise itself provided outstanding desert training in low-level terrain-following and extremely low-altitude operations, combined with NVG blacked-out landings. By the time we arrived back at Hurlburt on December 14, the two Talons had logged fifty-four sorties and 201 flight hours during our fifteen-day deployment—a rather typical OPTEMPO (operating tempo) as we dedicated ourselves to perfecting our skills.

Under ideal conditions, we had sufficient time to fully prepare for upcoming operations. Such was not the case with **Vagabond Warrior**, a no-notice exercise orchestrated by the newly formed JSOC (Joint Special Operations Command) at Fort Bragg, North Carolina. On the morning of January 28, 1982, we received an alert order, followed by a deployment order, which came in a little before midnight. On January 30, we departed Hurlburt Field en route to Barking Sands, Hawaii, along with forty-eight other officers and 117 enlisted personnel, a second Combat Talon, two AC-130H gunships, and two MH-53H Pave Low helicopters. After two IFRs during our seventeen-hour flight, we arrived at Barking Sands on the 31st, fully prepared to commence with the mission.

Ocean Venture 82 took place from April 26 to May 17, 1982, in the Caribbean. We flew twelve sorties out of Hurlburt Field under the operational control of the Air Force Forces Joint Unconventional Warfare Task Force Atlantic (AFFOR-JUWTFA), with missions that included infiltrations, resupply, exfiltrations, and a photoreconnaissance mission. In total, we devoted 32.9 flying hours to the exercise.

Roughen Turf: Operating out of Pope AFB, we began with a fuel blivets and heavy equipment drop, then spent the next several days on precision airborne radar approaches and NVG blacked-out landings, followed by rapid on-load and off-load procedures with U.S. Army Rangers. Finally, during the night of November 9, 1982, we conducted a full dress rehearsal, including NVG blacked-out landings, rapid on-load and off-load, and an airfield seizure operation. The actual mission was flown the following night, with exercise participants that included three Combat Talons, Delta Force, and Army Rangers.

There's one other position that I had always aspired to achieve, and my goal was to realize this triumph at some point during my time at Hurlburt. Each squadron has a standardization shop that bears the responsibility of ensuring that all the other pilots in the organization are maintaining standards and requisite levels of proficiency. Being Chief of Standardization and Evaluation in a flying squadron is as good as it gets for a young field grade officer. You're picked by the squadron commander based on knowledge of the missions, proficiency in the aircraft, recognized competence among the members of the squadron, and ability to not only fly the airplane but to manage the administrative operation associated with the standardization process. Jim Hobson was the commander at the that time and he took the risk of assigning me to the position. Hobson was both a gifted aviator and an inspiring leader, and I shall always be grateful to him for having such faith in me—at this point, and down the road when our paths would continue to cross. Hopefully I served him well.

Many years later I returned to Hurlburt for a memorial service commemorating the thirty-fifth anniversary of Operation EAGLE CLAW and the unveiling of the Combat Talon Memorial at the Hurlburt Field Air Park. I rose and paid tribute to those lost at Desert One, sharing thoughts and feelings that had solidified after thirty-nine years of service—reflections that germinated during that first tour with the 8th SOS:

> Special operations is a complicated, hazardous, risk-filled business. We ask Talon crews to execute this difficult and stressful mission, to devote themselves to a tradition of selflessness, mutual trust, precision, and reliability in all of their mission activity. So often, Talon crews did this not out of misplaced courage or vanity, but because *success in the business depends on the heart as much as it does the head.* This memorial compels us to remember to recommit ourselves to the fire that drives us and that which drove those no longer able to be with us now.

We sold the house and left Hurlburt in July of 1983, but not before Suzie made it a point to give Colonel Hobson one final message.

We got a nice early start since we had packed up most of the car the night before. I was somewhat dejected—certainly looking forward to our next challenge, but less than overjoyed to be leaving the mission—and colleagues—that had become such a valued part of our lives. Suzie, on the other hand, looked as though she had just won the $100 million Powerball. She was overjoyed that we were leaving this risky mission (and the flocked wallpaper) behind us. Before we hit the road, we made one final stop at the squadron headquarters. Suzie went inside with me.

"Sir, I couldn't leave without thanking you, once again, for all you've done for us. You have no idea how much we appreciate it. It's been a real honor."

Lt Col Hobson stood from behind his desk and smiled warmly as he approached and shook my hand. "It's in your blood now, Norty. You'll be back . . ."

Before he had a chance to continue, Suzie interrupted. "That's what you think, sir. You'll never see us again!" She gave him a quick hug and grabbed my arm. "Come on, Norty. Unless you want to be smack in the middle of rush hour traffic, gotta go!" I was mortified as she headed for the door with me in tow. "See ya, sir," she added as we flew out the door.

★   ★   ★

Moving on to the Armed Forces Staff College in Norfolk, Virginia, was quite a change from the adrenaline rush that surrounds a mission-oriented special operations aviation wing. We lived right on campus, across the street from now-retired two-star Nick and Mary Ann Williams. The coursework was valuable, but even more so was the networking and teamwork that crossed service boundaries; this was a joint school, so it was a continuation of my orientation into the joint world—again, this was relatively new at the time.

About halfway into the six-month course, I was in the kitchen with Suzie when our conversation was interrupted by a deep voice emanating from the TV. "We interrupt our regularly scheduled program to bring you an NBC News special report . . ." It was Tuesday, October 25, 1983.

We turned to the TV just as the screen cut to Tom Brokaw; the graphic insert above his shoulder read *GRENADA INVASION.* "Here is the latest situation as we now know it on the island of Grenada, which is a tiny island in the southern Caribbean—it has been invaded by a multinational force, as it's being described; the bulk of that force is American troops. . . . Grenada is an island-country that is now in the control of a Marxist military counsel after its Marxist military prime minister was executed in a coup just last week. There have been reports of casualties both from the Pentagon, and from Cuba . . . Chris Wallace reports from the White House."

"Tom, we're told that the invading aircraft were met with antiaircraft fire as they approached the Point Salines airport at the southern tip of the island."

My stomach tightened and my pulse accelerated.

Suzie turned back to me and verbalized the question that was echoing in my mind. "Think it was the 8th?" she asked, referring, of course, to the 8th SOS that we had recently left. I shrugged my shoulders because officially I had no idea. But in my gut I had a strong feeling that it was "my guys." It was exactly the type of mission for which we had been training. In fact, one of the very last exercises before I left (UNIVERSAL TREK 83) entailed long-range insertions to the Caribbean region, and long-range exfils from Puerto Rico to Pope AFB, North Carolina.

I picked up the phone and called Gary Weikel, a renowned Pave Low helicopter instructor pilot who would go on to command the 20th SOS. Gary was currently working at the Pentagon, and he unofficially confirmed my suspicion. Five Combat Talons from the 8th were at the very tip of the spear, with Jim Hobson and his Foxtrot 35 crew leading the airfield seizure at the Point Salines airport and rescue of Americans.

While on the one hand I was thrilled when I heard the news (and above all grateful that they made it back safely), at the same time full disclosure prompts a confession that I don't necessary feel great about: Besides the sense of pride that I felt knowing that the unit accomplished the mission in the exemplary manner you would hope they would have, I also felt a sense of disappointment that I was not a part of it. After pouring my heart and soul into training for this very type of endeavor, the timing was such that I missed the window by just a few months, and it hurt. Who knew if there would be other opportunities? Either way, it sure would have been a privilege to have been a part of this one.

Jim Hobson's calm under fire and decisive maneuvers were credited with saving the aircraft and the lives of all those onboard. It earned him the coveted Mackey Award for the most meritorious flight of 1983. It was well deserved and they could not have made a more appropriate selection. This became abundantly clear once I learned the details of how it all played out.

Originally intended to be a night airland mission, a volatile situation on the ground warranted a last-minute change to a combat-airdrop. With weather a real threat and daylight rapidly approaching, Hobson was to combat-drop the headquarters/command and control element of the 1st Ranger Battalion onto the Point Salines airport to kick off the invasion. In an effort to minimize the AAA threat to the aircraft and Ranger vulnerability to ground fire during their descent, the Ranger battalion commander informed Hobson that he wanted to jump from an altitude of five hundred feet, rather than the pre-determined one thousand feet. Wearing PVS-5 NVGs to enhance visibility, the flight crew spotted the airfield from about six miles out and began preparations for the drop. Suddenly, they were blinded by a burst of bright light, similar to how I'd been blinded by the nacelle overheat warning light on my NVG check flight. In this case, the source of the illumination was many times brighter: the aircraft had been targeted by a huge searchlight from the ground, its powerful swath of light clearly painting the Talon against the night sky. Just as the rangers began to jump, an intense barrage of antiaircraft fire erupted from multiple locations on the airport grounds, unleashing thousands of tracer rounds in Hobson's direction; miraculously missing the aircraft and the rangers, some of whom were still exiting the plane. The fusillade was so extreme that Hobson instructed the rest of his formation to terminate their approach, even though he had no choice but to maintain his course directly toward the source of the attack until the last jumper had cleared the jump door. Any deviation would have most likely landed the jumpers in the treacherous waters on either side of the airport runway. At the instant the final jumper was clear, he pushed the yoke full forward and put the aircraft into an extreme dive while banking sharply to the south away from the AAA.

It's no wonder that Jim would go on to become a major general and the third commander of the Air Force Special Operations Command.

★ ★ ★

I received word that we'd be heading back to the Pentagon, where I was to be an action officer in the Plans Directorate. To accompany the new position, on my very last day in Norfolk I learned that we had made the list for promotion to lieutenant colonel.

It felt good to be back in DC. So good, in fact, that we decided to lay down some roots, so we bought our second house. It was a townhouse, a beautiful end unit in the Concord Park neighborhood of Oakton, Virginia. It was a bit of a stretch for us at the time, but we ended up keeping it for over twenty-five years, so that stretch paid off many times over in the long run. What's more, it serves as proof that I am at least somewhat trainable: This time there was no way that I'd even consider buying anything without the benefit of Suzie's keen analysis and full approval at every step along the way.

It also felt good to be back at the Pentagon. Walking up the stairs toward the Second Corridor entrance I was upbeat, as I always am when embarking on new challenges like this one, where I was assigned to the special plans office of the Air Force Plans Directorate. I'd miss seeing Jerry O'Malley's smiling face every day, but I knew that he and Diane were enjoying their time at Hickam Air Force Base in Hawaii, where he was commander in chief of the Pacific Air Forces. General Gabriel was not only still in the building, but he was now Chief of Staff of the Air Force.

I didn't know much about my new boss, the two-star director of plans in the office of the deputy chief of staff, plans and operations, but I had heard that he was a good man from whom I'd learn a great deal. I was not disappointed.

Major General John A. Shaud is a brilliant man, with a PhD from Ohio State. A few years later he would conduct my pinning to lieutenant colonel. There were seven people pinning that day, so between the friends and families and coworkers, the old auditorium in the Pentagon was packed. This was not the kind of thing where General Shaud did a group pinning—quite the contrary. He went from person to person and extolled the virtues of what made each one so worthy of the promotion—going through specific assignments and regaling us with personal anecdotes. He did the entire ceremony without a single note. To this day, I've never seen anything like it.

One of my first projects took me right back to Operation NIGHT MARCH, that challenging "off the radar" flight in which we were damn near busted in Mogadishu. Movement of aircraft is no small endeavor, and the Air Force needed to establish a special program that had the organic capacity to successfully do this kind of work routinely and on a full-time basis. My assignment was to make that happen, and we accomplished it. It's a branch of a larger organization within the Air Force that does lots of different things, but it was the right fit for this type of work. And it still exists today. They maintain the very specialized expertise, the contacts, and the tradecraft—all inhouse. If a combatant command has a plan that requires movement of assets, these are the folks that help design the mission and then orchestrate that support. In the NIGHT MARCH exercise, I had found it challenging to move one single C-130. This branch routinely moves many assets—all via methodology we helped to develop.

Much of the rest of what I did in the plans office involved activities that to this day remain classified.

Subsequently I went to the Strategy Division, a growth opportunity that pushed me well outside my operational comfort zone and stretched me into a more conceptual kind of work.

I was tasked to clarify the Air Force role in a new organization known as the Center for Low Intensity Conflict (CLIC)—and then somehow get the Air Force establishment behind it so we could get it manned and off the ground. It was a real-life master's course in maneuvering big-picture concepts through the bureaucracy.

You have to have an idea that has traction and relevance, and you have to present that idea in a visual manner that people can clearly see will provide a productive, useful outcome.

While it made great sense to me, we encountered resistance from decision makers who were committed to other Air Force disciplines. They saw it as more of a distraction than a core mission. The fighter community and big war crowd were *not* on board, so somehow we had to convince the leadership at Tactical Air Command.

You have to develop champions for this kind of effort, and we did that.

General John Shaud was an ardent advocate and clearly instrumental, as was my direct boss, Colonel John Sullivan, and Colonel Alan Gropman, the deputy director—the same Al Gropman who had mentored me as a history instructor back at the Academy. He had a natural feel for emerging trends and understood the bureaucratic requirement to demonstrate competence in this area. He was also the one who hired me into this, knowing that it would be one that stretched me outside my operational lane into more conceptual work.

In this case, we required flag officer support. We had to bring the leadership at the Pentagon aboard, and also had to bring the leadership at Tactical Air Command aboard.

★ ★ ★

Suzie clarifies: *Not to interrupt, but Norty is being very kind and beating around the bush—maybe even to the point of being politically correct. He's a very positive man and it's very rare that you'll ever hear him talk "anti" anything— particularly when dealing with issues involving the Air Force. The fact is that especially at this time—the mid-1980s—the Air Force had a very "fighter/ bomber"-centric culture. By its very nature, low-intensity conflict didn't focus exclusively on fighters or bombers; it was focused on special operations. So it took away from the status the Air Force felt—and, frankly, had—at the time. They didn't like that, and this is what Norty was up against.*

He plays it down, but he had a tremendous challenge in convincing these people to come on board—a huge fight. You can't look at it through today's paradigm because today's special operations are revered and respected. That was far from the case back then. So today's operators (and the funding that allows them to excel) are reaping the benefits of those early- to mid-'80s bureaucratic battles like these. And Norty was just a major at this point—laboring to persuade the generals who were running the fighter and bomber communities.

Norty continues: I agree with that. I remember General Shaud contacting General Chuck Horner (who at that time was the Tactical Air Command Deputy Chief of Staff for Plans) on this, and asking him to fly from Tactical Air Command headquarters at Langley for a one-on-one briefing with me at the Pentagon—and bear in mind that he's a two-star and at this point I'm still a major. He was a little skeptical about attending, but to his credit, he made the trip. I knew going in that he'd be against the idea—coming at it from the fighter culture/mentality that Suzie referenced. I knew that it would be a profound effort to swim upstream and try to convince these powerful people that this was worth doing. But I had a good presentation package and I had been interacting with senior officers for so long that when the briefing room door swung open and the general stepped inside, nerves were never a factor. I knew that he would never become an enthusiastic supporter, but it was essential that by the time he walked out that door, I felt confident that he wouldn't submarine the effort. That's exactly how it played out.

★   ★   ★

The idea sometimes is not to hit a grand slam, but just not to ground out.

He was patient and listened to everything I had to say. Then he asked some questions about the resources that would be involved. How much money were we talking about? And how many people?

This was a joint endeavor between the Army and Air Force, and I was the action officer on the Air Force side. My counterpart on the Army staff was Andy Krepinevich, a brilliant staffer with a PhD. He and I were partners on this, working hand in hand at the Pentagon. We learned to trust one another and we remain good friends to this day.

We both understood that resources are precious, so we tried to size it in a way that wouldn't create unnecessary friction. Lean and mean.

You have to scope your idea in a way that people can tolerate—a way that is affordable in terms of both manpower and dollars.

In the end, we persuaded Chief of Staff Larry Welch that the Air Force needed a presence in this area. It created a generation of youngsters who understood counterinsurgency and capacity building, and it brought back some of the skill sets that we had in the Air Commandos of the Vietnam era.

★ ★ ★

Initiative 17 was a controversial initiative that I, along with others in the Pentagon's Plans Directorate, was tasked to implement. Based on the flawed assumption that rotary aviation was not something the Air Force should perform, it called for the transfer of all of the Air Force special operations forces helicopters to the Army, leaving the Air Force with only a handful of helicopters devoted to ICBM site support and search and rescue operations.

It was an agreed-upon initiative. Irrespective of my personal assessment that it never should have been signed, as one of the project's action officers, the task came to me, among others, to orchestrate its implementation.

It was one of the "31 initiatives" that General Wickham from the Army (John A. Wickham Jr., U.S. Army Chief of Staff from 1983 to 1987) and General Gabriel from the Air Force (Air Force Chief of Staff from 1982 to 1986) had agreed to in a memorandum of agreement signed on May 22, 1984. The overall intent was to provide for "the fielding of the most affordable and effective airland combat forces" by instituting an unprecedented level of cooperation between the two services, an early attempt to reap the benefits of what we now refer to as joint operations.

The process exposed me to the dark side of the building, where guerrilla operations occurred in terms of disregarding the chain of command in efforts to derail the initiative. The way it unfolded was ugly, with others inside and outside of my group—enlisting the support of people on Capitol Hill and elsewhere in Washington.

The truth is that I was against it as much as others on the team who engaged in these tactics, but I was never comfortable using disloyal maneuvers to dislodge it. Both the Army and the Air Force Chiefs of Staff had agreed to it, and signed that agreement. I felt that my responsibility was to make my arguments in as compelling a manner as I could, and I did my very best to highlight the risks associated with pursuing the initiative, but where I differed with others working the project, I never felt like I should operate outside natural boundaries and go around the Chiefs' backs—or my boss, for that matter.

Bear in mind that much of my team was comprised of the original operators, the Old School whose lives were 100 percent tied to those helicopters. With the choppers gone, where would they go, and what would they do? But more than this, I believe they were driven by a passion for the mission and a conviction that Army aviation (at the time) wasn't up to performing the mission of long-range clandestine penetration of denied airspace, and I couldn't argue with them on that.

A part of the job is to be a champion for your mission because this is a competitive marketplace, and missions rise and fall based on how effectively people advocate for and represent their capabilities.

I worked my ass off to champion my position, but I refused to go back-channel and usurp my boss. I didn't do it then, and I didn't do it twenty-five years later when, as Chief of Staff, I was at odds with the SECDEF over the number of F-22s the Air Force needed (see chapter 6). Throughout my career I respected my chain of command.

It was one of those lessons of bureaucratic competition that I observed and had mixed feelings about. Sure, I was happy with the outcome: the initiative died. But does the end justify the means? I don't think so. Usurping one's boss and the chain of command? I just wasn't comfortable with being disloyal, I guess.

★ ★ ★

Suzie: *These guys still had the Air Commandos spirit of "find a way, any way."
Most of them retired as colonels, very lovely officers but it was different for Nort in
that Nort was still going to be a part of the big Air Force and the Air Commandos
were totally—their heart, their soul, their being—was Air Commando exclusively.
They were going to protect that at all costs. They respected Nort—and Nort respected
them—because he always would choose the right thing. In their hearts, they knew
that even if he had been there with them, he still wouldn't have gone along with
it because he's straight and narrow and he never varies.*

Norty: In the end they went around the backs of the chiefs of the two services
and succeeded in making sure that this transfer never occurred. They did it of-
fline, behind the scenes, in a way that happens all the time in Washington where
people work back channels. Before you know it, you're sweeping up the ashes
of what used to be the initiative. In this case, most of those who pulled this off
never got caught. They got promoted and became damn good colonels. But one
individual, Lieutenant Colonel T. J. Doherty, took the heat for the whole group.
He got caught and he got fired. He had enjoyed a successful career as an MC-
130 pilot, ops director, and commander. And he ended up being relieved for
going to the mat and doing whatever it took to ensure that the Air Force did not
relinquish a vital special operations asset, our entire rotary-wing aircraft operation. Post Air Force, he went on to fly for TWA and American for over fourteen
years, but he went out with the satisfaction of knowing that he had won—for
himself, and for the entire special operations community.

★ ★ ★

In hindsight, looking back through the eyes of a four-star general, I see things
a little differently. The way it played out had consequences in ways majors and
lieutenant colonels don't appreciate. It set a bad example that soured a generation of conventional Air Force leadership on the special operations community.

On the flip side, I go back to Jerry O'Malley as an example of the appropriate way to handle these things. As early as 1980, O'Malley was an ardent proponent of forming a Space Command, both within the Air Force and ultimately at
the unified command level. This was no small endeavor, and his first step would

be to get the Air Force Council on board—a feat that many deemed impossible. The Council is composed of a small group of three-stars who control the purse strings, making high-level resource allocation recommendations to the Chief and secretary.

Through persistent and impassioned advocacy, O'Malley was successful in convincing the group that the concept was worthwhile . . . to the tune of a $7 billion increase in the budget. Exhilarated by the Council's official support, O'Malley met with the Chief, General Lew Allen, and laid it all out in a carefully conceived, eloquent presentation. While agreeing that a Space Command was ultimately warranted, General Allen believed that the idea was premature and would create a distraction resulting in a loss of capability. He would not support the plan.

Unsurprisingly to anyone who knew Jerry O'Malley, he persisted. He tried new approaches and new lines of logic, but he never went behind the boss's back. He never used the guerrilla tactics I had just witnessed. That was not a part of Jerry O'Malley's toolkit.

It took a few years, but finally, when O'Malley became the four-star Vice Chief of Staff of the Air Force, General Allen relented and agreed to support the endeavor—but that's a testament to Jerry O'Malley's unrelenting persistence, untarnished reputation, and inspired knack for coming up with innovative new perspectives to frame a challenge. In this case, just a few months prior to General Allen's retirement, O'Malley convinced him that the Air Force would be best served by rolling out the new Space Command under the leadership and guidance of a scientist with a broad space background who was well respected by the teams that would have to be brought on board—and there was nobody who exemplified these qualities more than General Allen.

It's another great example of the impact Jerry O'Malley had on me, in this case demonstrating firsthand that you'll win a lot more battles with an aggressive, persistent, imaginative, and well-executed plan of attack than you will by just flailing away below the belt.

I would not have participated in the back-channel activity. But I probably would not have reported it, either, since I wasn't their supervisor. Had I been in the supervisory position in that office, I would have been compelled to "break their legs." This is one of those complex things involving relativism and your values. It's a hard call, but upon reflection I don't think I would have done that to them, because I understood why they were doing it. I understood their passion.

But what it was really about was the culture. The rotary-wing culture and special operations in the Air Force was a very influential group. It elevated the state of play in the fixed-wing community. This was a bunch of guys who were close to their ground-force counterparts (Special Forces, Delta, SEALs, Rangers) who were in the fight all the time, in tight spaces, who carried their weapons with them. They actually knew how to shoot. These were the storm troopers of the Air Force special operations community. It was a tragic thing to lose that part of the culture. What they fought for was right; but how they did it I couldn't quite get my head around.

They were secretly referred to as the "SOF Mafia"—most came from the 1st SOW: Lt Col Lee Hess, Lt Col T. J. Doherty, Maj Gary Weikel, Maj Greg Colvin, and Maj Gary Heckman. These were the ones who made contact with Congressman Dan Daniel from Virginia, and Ted Lunger, one of his aides. It ended up playing out in the Readiness Subcommittee of the House Armed Services Committee, and supported by Congressman Earl Hutto. Before the chiefs knew what hit them, suddenly the "31 initiatives" had to reprint their title page to read the "30 initiatives."

★ ★ ★

There are certain indelible milestones in an officer's career, and the same is true for any profession. A baseball player's first hit, then his first home run. A salesman joining the Million Dollar Club, or a surgeon's first operation. For Air Force officers, taking the flag to assume one's first squadron command is one such milestone.

It was spring of 1986 and the cherry blossoms lining the Tidal Basin and the Jefferson Memorial had just reached peak bloom. I had just returned to the office when the phone rang. It was always good to hear from Colonel Gropman. "Norty, I'm sorry to have to break this to you . . ." he began, then paused before delivering the "bad news." " . . . but I'm calling so that I can be the very first one to be speaking to the new *squadron commander* of the Thirty-Sixth Tactical Airlift Squadron at McChord!" That's how I heard about it, and it's a moment I will never forget. I couldn't wait to share the exciting news with Suzie and embark upon the next leg of our great adventure.

★ ★ ★

Suzie describes how that played out: *When someone outside the service hears about a military transfer, I think they often just automatically assume you leave the office on Friday, then Monday morning bright and early, you show up at the new assignment, bright-eyed and bushy-tailed, ready to dive into the new job. Hello? What about the house that has to be packed up, and everything you own moved across the country, and then unpacked, and setting everything up to start your life all over again? And by the way, we did this twenty times over the course of our career!*

When we received word that Norty was going to be a squadron commander up in Washington State, you did not see me doing cartwheels in celebration. I was not happy to be moving to Seattle, and I was far too young to be a squadron commander's wife. But I sucked it up and went for it, thrilled to pieces that we each had to drive our own car twenty-eight hundred miles from one side of the country to the other.

We loaded up the cars, said goodbye to our beautiful townhouse, and crammed ourselves in beside the boxes jammed inside our respective vehicles. I lowered the window and called over to Norty, "You take off and I'm right behind you."

"Why don't you pull out and I'll follow you?" he called back.

That man knows me all too well. He figured that by being behind me for the whole trip, there was no way that I would chicken out, turn around, and head back to DC. Good call.

This was not one of those trips where you arrived and thought, "Wow, that drive flew by in a heartbeat." We drove . . . and drove . . . and drove . . . with the highlight being the diversity of beautifully decorated public restrooms I'd experience on our frequent comfort stops. When we finally got to the Montana line, I felt a big knot in my stomach. Montana was the ugliest state I'd ever seen in my life. I kept thinking, "Oh, my gosh, I sure hope Washington is better than this." It had to be, right? I can't tell you how many friends raved about the spectacular Mount Rainier. Well, guess again. The entire eastern part of the state is just one big desert. "This is not good," I thought. Or maybe I even said it aloud, I don't remember since I was so distraught at the time.

We arrived in May, so naturally I arrived in my summer clothes. It was so cold and so cloudy I came this close to freezing to death. Until that moment, I had never understood the concept of people wearing summer sweaters, but then I got it. We were about to move into the summer sweater capital of the world.

In spite of all my whining, the squadron was lovely, and the splendor of Rainier had not been exaggerated. I had a Spouses Organization that was really chugging along and they did great things. The only problem was the age thing. Norty was so young to be a squadron commander, which meant that at thirty years old, I was way too young to be a commander's wife. I wanted to be one of the girls, like I always had been. At first it wasn't easy for me to accept the reality that those days were over, and that wasn't who I was going to be. I could no longer hang with the people who had two-year-olds and the three-year-olds. I became so bored that I decided to get a job. That's when all the trouble began, and that silly little food and beverage job at the Tacoma Dome Hotel almost cost Norty his career.

I was smart enough to know that some people were not thrilled about working spouses, particularly when that spouse was the commander's wife. So I was quite adept at keeping it a secret . . . for a whopping month or two. Then one Friday night we were at the club, standing around swapping stories with a group from Norty's squadron—Norty had slipped away to get me another drink—and without thinking I blurted out, "You will not believe what happened to me at work today!" It was like the old E. F. Hutton commercials when suddenly the room becomes perfectly silent and heads swing around to look at you—that's how I felt. As soon as I said the words I knew I was in trouble.

I waited until we got home to drop the bombshell. "Honey, we're in big, big trouble," I told Norty, devastated that I had made such a blunder. "Hmmm" was all he said; apparently he thought I had blown it way out of proportion.

Norty: Suzie's instinct was correct. By Monday word had spread that Suzie was employed, and this did not sit well with my superiors at the base. Colonel Chuck Niggemeyer was the designated messenger. "It's simply not a good idea for a squadron commander's wife to work," he warned. "Either she gives up the job, or we may have to find another squadron commander."

"I'll talk to Suzie," I promised. "But if she wants to work, she's going to work and you'll have to look for another commander." At the same time, Suzie was having lunch with Niggemeyer's wife, who was hitting her with the same reproach.

Suzie: *She got right to the point and she just asked, "Is your job worth risking your husband's career?"*

I explained how our situation was different than most. "I understand that it's frowned upon for us to work, but Norty and I don't have any children. My job is way less time consuming than the other squadron commanders' spouses who have kids. They run them to soccer, then piano lessons and PTA . . . They look like little Energizer bunnies and they don't get to clock out at five o'clock every day; they never get to clock out. I have way more free time, even with the job." I felt I was pretty convincing, but I might as well had been talking to a mannequin. "If I hadn't spilled the beans, you wouldn't even know about my job because our squadron is running great! We have evening functions, and weekends. In the six months we've been here I have not missed one event. Who do you think it is that's cheering so loud at our volleyball matches? And basketball? And you name it. You could not ask for a more smoothly run organization."

She smiled as if we were best friends but I could tell that she was fuming inside. "I am trying my best to help you, Suzie, and the only reason I'm even telling you this is because I like you. But you are going to have to think very seriously about quitting because that's the unwritten rule." Logic clearly meant nothing to this woman, and I just didn't know what more to say to her. I was upset, but more than that I felt really sad. It wasn't until later on that I learned that she was doing what her husband was asking her to do. And he was just relaying the message of his boss, Colonel Ed Tenoso, the wing commander (who ultimately retired as a lieutenant general).

When I told Norty all about the lunch that night, he shared how he'd been hit with the same admonitions by Colonel Niggemeyer. And I was so proud of Norty because he told him right there that he wasn't even going to mention it to me since I could do whatever I wanted to. I couldn't believe that he would say that but I was blown away.

Later that night I phoned my mom to tell her all about it. I was still hurting inside and I knew that she would make me feel better. "What's the matter with you, Suzie?" she bellowed into the phone. "I can't believe you're doing anything to risk Norty's career!" Surprisingly, we did not have to call tech services for a new handset after I slammed it down and hung up on Mom. I did not speak to her for several months.

Norty: To Suzie's credit, she took all this as a personal challenge to her womanhood and an opportunity to demonstrate to everybody (including the youngsters in the squadron) what was possible for a modern military spouse. I was not replaced, and Suzie spent the bulk of her time shuttling back and forth between the base and the hotel on I-5. She busted her butt the entire two years and did spectacularly well. She didn't miss a single base function—not a change of command, not a ball game, not an awards ceremony. And she entertained like crazy in this marvelous house overlooking the Sound. She outperformed everyone's wildest expectations, and in many ways I believe we became the model for the modern military leadership team. Word spread, and slowly we started to see this same thing happen at other bases. The Air Force culture evolved, and today's commanders' spouses are afforded a lot more opportunities, due in no small part to Suzie's courage and chutzpah.

★   ★   ★

The Thirty-Sixth was the only C-130 squadron in the Air Force with a nuclear mission. It's called PNAF—"Primary Nuclear Airlift Force"—and it is an incredibly demanding mission in which we safeguarded and transported nuclear materials and components. Everyone involved required a special certification, and they would have to go through an intense background check called the PRP, Personal Reliability Program. They were thoroughly investigated as to their health (both physical and psychological) and other areas to ensure that they were suited to play a role in this arduous mission. We spent a great deal of time on this, and it paid off in the long run. What a great place to earn my spurs. All that goes into this is daunting, with every step coming under enormous scrutiny from the wing, the Air Force higher-ups, and even from the DoD. Having been promoted early, I was young to be assigned to such a prestigious command, and there were those who had issues with that. Not so Lieutenant Colonel Otto Dobias. Otto was one of the "goats," probably twenty years older than I was, and he was chief of the PNAF mission. He was the consummate professional and we came to respect one another early on. The fact that I was twenty years younger wasn't an issue for him. Otto was incredibly competent in this discipline and he ran that whole business for the squadron and did it extremely well. Our success had a hell of a lot less to do with me than it had to do with Otto.

Competence comes in all kinds and sizes of packages—young and old, heavy and light, and black and white.

Had I dismissed Otto as an old fart, I would have been so much poorer. Had Otto dismissed me as a young pup, we would have had a much less successful unit. But as it turned out, we both acted professionally and instinctively in a way that created a partnership that really was a wonderful thing to behold. This early experience with the nuclear mission would be put to good use down the road, when the secretary of defense looked to me and Air Force Secretary Mike Donley to get this mission back on track. Because of my time with Otto and PNAF, I understood the mandate for precision and the whys and hows of the very demanding inspection regimen.

In addition to PNAF, we were the active logistics airlift element in support of our embassies in Central and South America, and we did a lot of classified missions in conjunction with the intelligence community. One of my favorites entailed flying into Tegucigalpa, the capital of Honduras. It's no surprise that the History Channel ranks Toncontín Airport as the second most dangerous in the world, with one of the world's most difficult approaches. Sitting in a bowl completely surrounded by mountains, its exceptionally short runway and unpredictably strong wind gusts make it a fun place to fly into and a great place to send young pilots to grow. I remember one landing where we were committed to the descent profile when a truck darted across the highway at the near end of the runway, not appearing in the visual cross-check until a go-around was impractical. We had no choice but to continue our landing, albeit farther down the runway than is normal for that short a runway. Suffice it to say their air traffic control environment was not quite up to FAA standards. No comment about their driving "skills."

In 1987, the squadron was announced for closure, so the whole process of managing the psychology of a flying squadron that's going out of business was a very good experience. Once that's announced, the big questions are how do you manage this? How do you keep people thinking about flying airplanes rather than being distracted by the fact that they will soon be forced to move, and perhaps forced into other types of jobs? A key part of that process was meeting with them, one-on-one, and asking them, "What's your preference? What can we prevail on the Air Force to do for you?" We worked very hard to ensure that people landed in good places and that they could continue their careers. It played out that we did not end up closing at that time, but we certainly didn't know that it would play out that way.

This was written up as a case study somewhere, and the takeaway was that both Suzie and I really took care of our people. We worked very hard at it, and it seemed to be greatly appreciated.

One thing that helped was a rather unique idea that we came up with; it turned out to be a real morale booster. It took place at the end of May 1988, and I called it the 19-ship. It's a concept that met with a lot of resistance from the wing, but one that was well worth the battle to pull it off. A typical C-130 formation has nine airplanes, at the most. You just don't fly more than that all at once . . . especially from one squadron. Well, I had the idea of getting every pilot that we had, and every airplane that we owned, and flying them all together, end to end, in one massive trail formation. Nineteen airplanes launched in quick succession, flying a route around the state of Washington, including adjacent to the Needle in Seattle. Out of deference to our chief of standardization, I gave him the lead aircraft and I took the number two. But it was quite a sight, a memorable stamp on an equally memorable first command.

The last goodbye

Geff Hinds/The News Tribune

McChord Air Force Base said goodbye to the 36th Tactical Air Squadron Monday. As onlookers waved, the squadron's 14 C-130 Hercules airplanes made one last pass on the taxiway before taking off in formation. The Pentagon is deactivating the squadron to save money. The squadron's members are being assigned to other bases. Story, B1.

That's Suzie standing on the right on the infield. Schwartz personal collection

★ ★ ★

Suzie: *For some dumb reason, this wing had three squadron changes of command within about a week of each other. The 4th and 8th C-141 commanders were swapping out a week before Norty and I were leaving, and the pair shared the same change-of-command ceremony, which Norty and I attended.*

At almost 170 feet long with a maximum takeoff weight of over 170 tons, the 141 is one big jet airlifter. You cannot imagine what it sounded like—let

alone felt like—when two of them did a low-pass flyover in formation at that change-of-command ceremony. We felt it in our teeth, in our bones. Suddenly the bright daylight dissolved to dark shadows as the lumbering gray birds obstructed the sunlight and the thunderous rumble played havoc with our eardrums. It was impressive. Exciting. Terrifying for the toddler who erupted in hysterical sobs. The poor kid was almost as upset as Colonel Ed Tenoso—he was one unhappy wing commander. Tenoso is the one who hinted that Norty might be fired if I didn't quit my job at the hotel, and now, two years later, he was still finding issues to get upset about.

Norty had just congratulated the two outgoing commanders and we had finally made it over to the cake line, when Col Tenoso came huffing over. I had a feeling he wanted something other than an end piece with extra icing.

"Sorry, Suzie, I need to have a word with Norty," he grumbled, then pulled him aside. "Next week, there will not be any more of this BS flyby stuff," he warned Norty, except he didn't use the letters "BS." "You're going to do things by the book or I swear there will be hell to pay. Do you understand me, Norty?"

I was standing there looking at this and thinking, "You are an Air Force colonel in charge of an entire wing . . . don't you have better things to do than turning bright red and giving yourself a stroke because a couple of flight crews think enough of their bosses that they want to pay homage to them when they leave?"

Well, Norty being Norty, he of course called the pilot who was scheduled to fly at Norty's event the following week (who also happened to be chief of standardization) and he did his best to try to put the fear of God into him.

"Charlie, don't fool around with me on this one," he sternly cautioned. "The colonel was dead serious so do this by the book and maintain regulation altitude."

The following week the bleachers were packed with VIPs and all eyes were searching skyward to see the C-130 flying high overhead to pay tribute to Norty's time in command . . . but there was no plane. Safety is one thing, but completely forgoing any kind of flyby was disappointing for everyone . . . except for Ed Tenoso, I would imagine. Suddenly the ground trembled with the roar of four turboprop engines as the C-130 barely cleared the tree line at the end of McChord's long parade field, its rumbling sound waves reverberating off the nearby headquarters building. It soared over our heads so low that we all instinctively ducked.

"Yes!" I screamed, along with a fist pump, unable to contain my excitement. How cool! Colonel Tenoso was standing directly in front of me. He turned around and shook his head. "Suzie, to the very end."

Chapter Three

COLONELS NORMALLY DO BETTER THAN THIS

JULY 1989–MAY 1995

Committed to her career path at the Hyatt, Suzie chose not to join me for my next assignment to Special Operations Command Europe (SOCEUR), but that didn't stop her from picking up the phone and reaching out to me around 3:00 a.m. local time on my very first night in Stuttgart. "The car won't work," she vented, as if I had some four-thousand-mile screwdriver to make the repair. *We just had it inspected last week,* I thought. "There is the tiniest possibility that I filled the diesel engine with *regular* gas," she finally admitted. Whoops.

My two years in Europe took me deeper into the special operations community as chief of staff for the Special Operations Joint Task Force as well as the chief of the plans directorate (J-5) of the permanent Special Operations Command, Europe; yet I was heading even farther afield from the traditional Air Force career path.

Brigadier General Dick Potter was one of the original deputies in Charlie Beckwith's new unit, and when he took me under his wing and invested in me during the buildup to the Gulf War, it opened doors with other Army leaders that would never have been opened without it. It gave me instant credibility. But Potter was an *Army* general. I can't tell you how many times he'd shake his finger at me and say, "Schwartz, don't give me that Air Force shit!" but the truth is I learned so much from him in terms of operating, he may very well have been the key person in my entire career. How ironic it is that I would become the highest ranking *Air Force* officer when the bulk of my mentors were Army.

Potter was quite a remarkable man, older than any other brigadiers in the Army, with battle wounds that corroborated the depth of his combat experience—far more Special Forces experience than anyone I'd ever met. He was almost larger than life; tough as nails and at times difficult to please, but once you earned his trust, you could not find anyone more loyal. When Potter said, "Why don't you think about Schwartz for this one?" it was not a trivial thing in the joint world. It opened doors with other Army leaders that would never have been opened without him. In many ways, he and his wife Annie fulfilled a similar role to Al and Barbara Navas. Annie knew that I was flying solo over there, and she took great care of me.

In January of 1991, SOCEUR deployed to Incirlik, Turkey, in essence becoming the northern front for Operations DESERT SHIELD/DESERT STORM. We had the responsibility for rescues of downed pilots in the northern half of Iraq. SOCEUR is responsible to the United States European Command (EUCOM), one of the nine unified commands. With headquarters at Patch Barracks in Stuttgart, Germany, our area of responsibility then encompassed fifty-one countries and territories and over twenty-one million square miles; including Europe, Russia, Greenland, most of Africa (Central Command [CENTCOM] covers the rest) and then a part of the Middle East (Israel, Syria, Lebanon, and Turkey). The commander of EUCOM (General Jack Galvin at the time) is also the NATO Supreme Allied Commander Europe (SACEUR).

With war imminent, one of our first orders of business was to establish a base further downrange toward Iraq for helicopter operations, both for search and rescue and for reconnaissance insertions. But Turkish nerves were on edge. They were not about to let the coalition or the Americans just march in and take over their entire country. Their anxiety made our task—locking in a place where our Paves (MH-53 and MH-60 helicopters) could operate—more difficult. We tried to go to Diyarbakir, one of the largest cities in Southeast Turkey, but Diyarbakir is a metropolitan area and the Turks were not comfortable with that. So we ended up at a place called Batman. It was a Turkish Air Force base, which we essentially took over. Our communications went in, field billeting went in, intel and logistics went in; it was a well-coordinated relocation that resulted in Batman becoming the forward operating location for the Special Operations task force.

What started as a rugged, muddy piece of land became a well-equipped, efficient U.S. military operating base. It was fun to watch it come together. This was done largely by Air Force teams, who, some would argue, don't know how to handle field conditions. Well, these were as tough field conditions as one could imagine, and they delivered magnificently.

By establishing Batman as the forward operating location, we were able to cover quite a significant part of the north of Iraq, where fighter jets might go down or ground forces might become isolated. In every case, there were significant efforts expended to bring Americans home. Unfortunately, there were times when those efforts were not successful—like the following one, where the decision was made to transit both Syrian and Iraqi airspace.

No matter how many times we rehearsed for these rescue missions (and we rehearsed for them a lot), they always seemed to be accompanied by a sense of tension. This night's felt even worse than usual, and each of us in the Incirlik Joint Operations Center felt it. If I'd known then what I found out after the fact, there wouldn't have been any tension because I'd have done everything in my power to have the mission aborted. But I'll get into all that later on.

Seated directly to my left was Army Colonel Ken Getty, the J-3. He'd be calling the shots. As his senior airman on the staff, my job was to offer whatever advice I could, but let there be no mistake about it—these were Ken's calls. That is, if there were any calls to be made; by the time you got to this point, it was pretty much up to the folks at the 352nd wing—the Pave Low helicopter and tanker teams. They're the ones who'd be flying halfway across Iraq in hopes that they wouldn't meet the same fate as Col Dave Eberly, the Fourth TFW director of operations, and Major Tom Griffith, whose F-15E was hit by radar-controlled AAA just as they were about to release their bombs over suspected Scud missile sites.

The three nights since the F-15 had gone down seemed like an eternity, but there was one thing after another that precluded an immediate rescue effort:

- We believed that they'd been evading for three days, but there were no confirmed reports that they were still alive. It was a combination of unconfirmed reports that eventually prompted the mission's green light.
- The pilots were equipped with the older PRC-90 survival radios—poor range and incredible susceptibility to enemy interception and, even worse, almost magnet-like vulnerability to enemy DF (direction finding), allowing the enemy to use the transmission itself to home in on the downed pilots' location.
- Those few unconfirmed reports of contact were not accompanied by bona fide authentications. Without such authentication, who's to say that they were even really our pilots?

- There were three conflicting reports of their location, all three were in extremely high-threat areas—and all three were almost right in the midpoint of Iraq, just north of Baghdad, making it up for grabs whether the mission would be best served by our handling it, or having the CENTCOM teams attempt the rescue from the south.

- For us, the safest route would take us over sovereign Syrian airspace, but despite attempts to secure Syrian approval, none had come through. This is where I was of help in securing MajGen Tony Zinni's approval to proceed even without Syrian approval. (Ultimately, Syrian approval did come through—once our planes were in the air.)

- A Bedouin showed up at the American Embassy to report that he had located the pilots, and claimed to have one of their "blood chits" to prove it. (A blood chit is a notice, usually written in multiple languages, carried by military personnel that identifies the force to which the bearer belongs as friendly, and requests that they be rendered every assistance. These notices are often carried by pilots flying over enemy territory to be used in the event the pilot is shot down.) The time delay clarified his refusal to divulge either their location or present the chit—until after the embassy officials bought the man a new truck. Not surprisingly, it turned out to be a fabricated ploy.

The two Paves took off on their mission, not so much concerned about the Syrian overflight as they were about the conflicting positions and lack of isolated personnel information on the pilots. All they had was their call sign, "Corvette 03."

They flew south toward Al-Qaim for two hours at about one hundred feet above the ground, having some difficulty navigating the blacked-out aircraft with the NVGs. They arrived right on time, feeling relieved that a fighter would be just ahead of them to serve as OSC—on-scene commander—to contact and authenticate the survivors so that the Paves could be in and out as quickly as possible. The fighter never showed up. Another was to have provided a diversionary covering air strike, but it was late and short. The Pave's ROE (rules of engagement) did not allow them to commit to the threat area unless they had established positive communication with the survivors, which had so far not occurred. Still, they remained in the area and attempted to make radio contact on numerous different frequencies. After the third or fourth transmission, they noticed that they *were* receiving responses, just not the ones they anticipated.

Each press of the transmit button would solicit AAA bursts in their direction. The Iraqis were homing in on the signals for targeting purposes. There's a reason the MH-53s are called "Jolly Green Giants"—they present a *significant* target. That was their cue to return to base.

Unfortunately, despite valiant efforts on the part of all those involved, that endeavor was successful only as a learning tool. Lessons were learned, and hopefully miscues would not be repeated in the future. The next day, Iraqi television depicted the two pilots being paraded around by Iraqi soldiers. Captured, they were now prisoners of war. Colonel Eberly was the senior ranking allied POW during the Gulf War. He and Major Griffith were repatriated on March 5, 1991.

★ ★ ★

In March we returned to Stuttgart, unaware that the wrath of Saddam Hussein would result in a catastrophic refugee crisis that would prompt our return to Turkey just a few weeks later.

Believing that the war had decimated Saddam's military, the Iraqi Kurds had revolted against the dictator. Big mistake. After quashing a Muslim revolt in the south, Saddam turned his attention to the north. His troops soon overwhelmed the Kurdish Peshmerga fighters; then, on March 31, 1991 he bombarded the final Kurdish stronghold of Zakho with artillery fire and strafing by helicopter gunships. That night, amid rumors of an imminent chemical attack, the Kurds began a massive exodus in what they believed to be a last-ditch effort to survive. Their only hope was to seek refuge in the harsh mountains that lined the Iraq/Turkey border. Two million people tried to flee, most of them Kurds.

Led by Army Lt General John Shalikashvili, Operation PROVIDE COMFORT was our humanitarian mission to aid these Kurdish refugees. Air Force Maj Gen James Jamerson was his number two, and BG Potter was brought back on board to lead a joint special operations task force to support the operation. At first known as Joint Task Force Express Care, it was redesignated Joint Task Force Alpha (JTF-A) on April 17. Once again, I had the honor of working closely with Potter. The ground element of the task force was the 1st Battalion, 10th SFG (A) (Special Forces Group), supported by the USAF 39th SOW and the helicopters of the 24th MEU (SOC) Forward.

Potter's first order of business was to get up into the mountains to assess the situation. We climbed into an MH-53 and braced ourselves as the Jolly Green lifted off and banked steeply to the southeast, slowly gaining altitude as we headed for ill-conceived camps. In his storied career, General Potter had seen it all—but even he was shocked by the level of devastation. Crammed into forty-three separate "camps" along the frigid mountainside were over 750,000 refugees, dying at the rate of over a thousand each day—from starvation, exposure, and disease. It was classified as a "medical apocalypse," and all this was occurring in some of the most inaccessible and unforgiving terrain in the world.

Upon our return, Potter briefed General Jamerson on the dire situation. (It would be another week before Shali would arrive to take over the command.) Jamerson would coordinate with Maj Gen Hobson, our air component commander, on allocation of resources, deconfliction of air activity, and use of common assets, along with the other component commanders, to begin the enormous humanitarian endeavor.

Typical of General Jamerson's "can-do" attitude, his only question to Potter was "How can I help you?"

"Sir, I came here with [commanding Colonel] Bill Tangney and the 1st Battalion/10th Special Forces Group, but as good as that battalion is, after what I saw out there today we're going to need the entire 10th Group [two additional battalions]. Do I have your authorization to bring them in?"

"Absolutely," replied the two-star commander.

The additional battalions began to arrive by the end of the week. Military experts agree that this single decision saved tens of thousands of lives.

The talent associated with Provide Comfort is not sufficiently appreciated. Maj Gen Jim Jamerson (USAF) was General Shalikashvili's number two, and BGen Tony Zinni (USMC) would go on to become Commander in Chief (CINC) of CENTCOM. Both stand at Incirlik Air Base, Adana, Turkey.
Personal collection of MajGen Tony Zinni

Within a few days the humanitarian relief airdrops began. On April 8, six C-130s took off from Incirlik and delivered twenty-seven tons of food (MREs) and supplies to try to sustain these concentrations of displaced Kurds.

I was with Potter when that first flight of 130s made the drops. As the pallets drifted to the ground beneath the green G-12 canopies, I felt a sense of great relief. General Potter, however, appeared disturbed. He gazed at the airdrop, then turned to me, as if some solution just came to him.

"Norty, go find me a place to do wholesale and retail in Turkey."

"Say again, sir. That one flew right over my head," I told him.

"I want you to find a place that I can take humanitarian supplies, store them, then distribute them efficiently. I'm talking about a big place." He looked back at the throngs of refugees, now clawing over one another to grab whatever provisions they could scrounge. "Airdrop's just not going to cut it here."

Back at Incirlik, I pulled out a map and surveyed potential locations. I needed to find a place that was on flat land and close to the Turkey–Iraq border. It had to be large enough to support helicopter operations, and it had to have sufficient infrastructure that we could put together an efficient distribution operation—trucks for delivering the wholesale supplies, which we would repackage and take into the mountains to resupply and sustain the refugee concentrations.

We found a nice, modern Hajj location slightly south of Silopi, a small, quiet farming village in Turkey's Hakkari Province. Located only about eight miles northwest of the Habur Turkey–Iraq border crossing, the location seemed ideal. Two teammates and I went down to scope it out.

In the middle of our survey, an older, official-looking Turkish gentleman arrived and subsequently introduced himself as the governor of the province. I hoped that his presence might actually streamline our endeavors to secure the approvals we'd need to take over the facility. I explained what we had in mind, but he was not interested in our turning that place into a military facility.

"It's impossible," he kept repeating.

After almost an hour of our attempted "negotiation," it was obvious that this guy was not going to relent. *But do not worry*, he assured me—he had an even better place in mind.

We followed him on a short ride to what turned out to be an old Turkish tank battalion headquarters several miles north of our original site. The governor pulled to a stop beside the old headquarters building. Stepping out from his car, he signaled for us to do the same, all the while beaming with pride as if he'd just taken me to the Taj Mahal. Either this guy was the P. T. Barnum of Sirnak Province or he was flat-out blind, but this place was an armpit. Old and in complete disrepair, it was a far cry from what we had hoped to present to General Potter. But time was of the essence and it was ours for the taking, so we said fine.

A few days later, a convoy of vehicles and equipment departed Incirlik for Silopi. They arrived around noon on April 15. More than two hundred airmen from the 564th Civil Engineer Squadron (Ramstein, Germany) and the Thirty-Sixth Civil Engineer Squadron (Bitburg, Germany) began construction. They turned that battalion headquarters into a huge, modern, Amazon-like warehouse. There were tent cities and there were helicopter landing pads. They even dug a four-hundred-foot well to enrich the water supply.

What started as an old, decrepit former Turkish Army tank base was transformed into the core platform for the relief effort. Within weeks the base held more than three thousand military and civilian workers. Over six hundred tons of supplies were transferred at Silopi each day. The sprawling base soon extended several miles along both sides of the road.

I will never forget the look on Potter's face the first time he saw it. It was a great tribute to his vision and to the can-do attitude of the SOF people that were there. Personally, I can't overemphasize the sense of satisfaction I felt to have played even such a small role in a pursuit that saved thousands of lives.

The talent that was associated with the PROVIDE COMFORT mission was unbelievable, and it's not something that's sufficiently appreciated. There were at least a half dozen officers across all the service branches who grew up out of PROVIDE COMFORT and went on to become four-stars. That's a rather staggering statistic. Shalikashvili was the three-star who followed Colin Powell as chairman. Tony Zinni was the one-star deputy who became commander in chief (CINC) of CENTCOM. John Abizaid was the battalion commander of the 3rd Battalion, 325th Airborne, and he also went on to lead CENTCOM, following Tommy Franks. Col Jim Jones was the commanding officer of the 24th Marine Expeditionary Unit (24th MEU), and he became SACEUR (Supreme Allied Commander Europe). Finally, Potter's eager young J-5 would eventually become USAF Chief of Staff.

From April to June 1991, seventeen thousand tons of supplies were delivered to the camps. What had been mass chaos was structured and finely tuned.

Honored to be pinned to colonel in the middle of the Gulf War by two venerated generals:
Maj Gen Jim Jamerson and BG Dick Potter. Incirlik AFB, Turkey. February 1991.
Schwartz personal collection

My concentration in special operations was serving me well, taking me back to Hurlburt, where I was assigned deputy commander for operations. But first, after having been away for so long, it was time to surprise Suzie and celebrate my return by pampering her for a few days at the Ritz.

★　★　★

Suzie:　*Excuse me, "Mr. Revise History doesn't know the meaning of the word romance." Who is it that was working at the Reston Hyatt and was able to get us a special rate at the Ritz?*

Norty:　Suzie is absolutely correct. By this point she had developed an impressive slate of accomplishments in the food and beverage division of the Hyatt, and was highly regarded by her boss and peers, so much so that her boss had made the offer to contact some friends at the Ritz to get us that special rate. I believe the reason my memory temporarily faltered on that was because it was such a special time, I would have gladly paid full retail rack rate for the room.

Suzie: *Impressive save.*

Norty: Thank you, I thought so. To continue, it's about a fourteen-hour drive from Washington to Fort Walton Beach, Florida, and it served as a wonderful opportunity for the two of us to catch up. We had just passed through the toll booth on the Richmond-Petersburg Turnpike (the tolls would not be eliminated until the following year, 1992) when I shared my enthusiasm about the new assignment. "My expanded level of responsibility now includes all the flying squadrons—fixed-wing, helicopters, you name it. Obviously I'll still be working closely with the 8th, but now we're adding the 9th, 15th, 16th, 20th, and 55th squadrons to the mix." Suzie listened patiently, but I could tell there was something else on her mind.

Unlike so many of those cross-country trips where it seemed like we'd been driving forever, before I knew it we were crossing the Florida state line.

"We're on the home stretch now," I said, glancing out the window at the lush Florida oaks that I'd flown over so many times. Suddenly Suzie started sobbing. Being somewhat of a quick study, by this point in my life I'd gained at least a modicum of understanding of what might be going through a female's thoughts at times like these—at least *this* female.

"You're not staying, are you?" I asked, although it was really more of a statement than a question.

"It's not that I don't want to be with you; I do," she said between the sniffles. "I've just worked so hard to get to where I'm at, and if I move right now I'd be leaving them in a horrible bind. That's not fair to anybody. I will be coming, just give me a few months to wrap things up."

With all the focus I'd been giving to my career, it was certainly a reasonable request. She stayed for a few days, then caught a flight back home. She would have the opportunity to manage the transition from her career as I embarked on my new adventure at the base.

★ ★ ★

In the aftermath of DESERT SHIELD and DESERT STORM, the demands were high and Hurlburt was growing. Simple tasks we'd taken for granted for so long (like finding a parking space) were not so simple anymore. Congress was well aware of the force multiplier Special Ops brought to the table, and we were rewarded with newer and more resources. On June 29, 1991, about a month before my arrival, the first MC-130H Combat Talon II airplane was delivered to Hurlburt. When I arrived in August, it was midway through intensive acceptance testing—four months in which we tried to get any deficits to appear. Better to recognize them at that point—and *fix* them—than to have some glitch in the new automated control system present an erroneous reading when we were flying blacked-out one hundred feet over the ocean on a real-world mission.

The new Combat Talon IIs had entirely NVG-compatible cockpits and cargo compartments, eliminating the need to reduce the ambient light level and tape illuminated cockpit instruments. Each crew station had two video displays with keyboards that were used to control radios and navigation systems. The vast improvements from its predecessor allowed us to more efficiently penetrate hostile airspace with low visibility, at night and at very low altitudes; they also enhanced our capability to successfully infiltrate into sometimes politically denied, sensitive areas to resupply and/or exfiltrate special operations forces and equipment, while detecting and avoiding both radar and infrared- or radar-guided antiaircraft threats.

On October 17, 1991, we came to the conclusion that everything was in order and official flight operations were ready to begin. The milestone was celebrated by a grand acceptance ceremony thrown by AFSOC.

★　★　★

I'm a big believer in doing everything in my power to get to know my team, and that includes the crews that fly the aircraft under my command. They are the ones who are closer to our partners (Special Forces, Army Rangers, Navy SEALS, etc.) than anybody else in our organization. I also wanted to fully understand the demands of the aircraft and the demands placed on the kids who operated them. General O'Malley's wise counsel came to mind: *You can't expect to lead your people if you don't thoroughly understand their platforms.* The only way to do that is to fly with them in the seat. It's the reason I learned to pilot all the aircraft, both fixed-wing and rotary (helicopters). When I became the Wing Director of Operations at Hurlburt, I flew the gunships and the tankers, and I even learned to fly the helos. Rotary-wing aviation is much different than large aircraft operations. Like the fighter business, it's a more three-dimensional sort of flying game.

I flew with top pilots from both our 60 (MH-60 Pave Hawk) and 53 (MH-53 Pave Low) squadrons. I found the 60 easier to fly; it's a sports car as compared to the larger, bulkier Paves, which were real workhorses. Just trying to stay in one place while hovering was a real challenge for me in either of them.

Get to know your team hands-on.

The MH-60 Pave Hawk felt more like a sports car compared the the Pave Low, a real workhorse.
USAF photo

General Charlie Holland was a tough but fair boss when he was wing commander at Hurlburt. He would go on to become deputy commander of JSOC and commander in chief of SO-COM. Having piloted over one hundred combat missions in Vietnam, it wasn't surprising that he would personally jump into the fray when he walked in to find two airmen duking it out in a command facility at Fort Campbell.

Huffing and puffing in his Air Force flight uniform, the brigadier general did what he could to separate the two combatants before they injured each other. That's when I stepped in. I tapped the general on the shoulder, and when he spun around, I smashed a cream pie into his face. The packed room erupted in laughter and applause, and everyone belted out a chorus of "Happy Birthday." Orchestrating the whole thing was my way of showing respect

Piloting the MH-53 Pave Low was a real challenge for me, but it was the only true "penetrator" among all helicopters then in service.
US Navy photo by PO2 George R. Kusner

for another accomplished leader, and making sure the boss would have a special birthday he would never forget.

Don't take yourself—or the job
—too seriously.

The airmen don't even seem to notice my somewhat unorthodox headgear. Christmas Day visit to the missileers of our Air Force at FE Warren AFB.
Schwartz personal collection

Suzie: *It took me six months to be in a position to leave my job in Washington to join Norty in Florida, but when I finally did pull up chocks to make the trip, I couldn't wait to see what he had done with our new house. I opened up the door and damn near slammed into a stack of boxes he had crammed inside. In the six months he had lived there he had only unpacked some clothing and two items— the microwave and the TV. "Welcome, honey," he said, smiling, oblivious to the fact that he had hardly done anything in half a year.*

In October of '92, I was deployed back to the Middle East as the commander of the Special Operations Task Force in Kuwait. Fundamentally the mission was to provide combat rescue support for Operation SOUTHERN WATCH. As commander, I had a secondary responsibility as the mayor of Kuwait International

Airport. Bear in mind that Kuwait was still recovering from the war at this point, so we weren't exactly looking like JFK. There were probably more construction vehicles on those runways than there were aircraft.

Not long after my arrival, I received word that the Task Force Kuwait commander would be returning into Kuwait International. As "mayor," it was expected that I'd be there to meet his aircraft and officially welcome him back. In this case, I was especially looking forward to meeting him.

I suppose most professions have some name attached to them that really grabs your attention. If I'd ever meet someone named Heineken, it'd be hard to resist asking the obvious, "Any relation?" Most likely I'd have the same reaction if I'd meet a reporter named Cronkite, or a ball player named Musial. In the Army, this was one of those names: Brigadier General John Nelson Abrams. And in his case, he was one of "the" Abrams. He was one of three brothers who were Army general officers, and his father was General Creighton Abrams Jr., well known for commanding all military operations in Vietnam, and then going on to become chief of staff of the Army. General Patton (another one of "those" names) once said of him: "I'm supposed to be the best tank commander in the Army, but I have one peer—Abe Abrams. He's the world champion." Have you ever heard of the M1 Abrams tank? Same Abrams—it was named for Creighton.

At exactly 2:40 that afternoon, the tower contacted me with the heads up that his helo was within range, and I raced down the stairs and headed to the tarmac. When the helo touched down and the side door popped open, the first thing he saw was Colonel Norty Schwartz, standing at attention with a crisp salute. He stepped onto the pavement and returned the salute. I had heard about his swagger and he didn't disappoint. With a ruddy complexion and sandy blond hair that perfectly blended in to the barren desert surrounding, his stocky frame amply filled out his green jumpsuit.

I smiled as he approached and tried my best to make him feel welcome. "General Abrams," I said, "that's a mighty fine-looking flight suit you got on there!"

He tightened up and stared at me like I had just insulted his grandma. "Colonel, this ain't no flight suit. These are tanker overalls!"

Clearly I had picked the wrong guy to be offending on any issues surrounding tanks. So here I wanted to make such a great first impression, but the way he was standing there looking at me and shaking his head, I'm sure that he must have been wondering how this Air Force officer ever made it past first lieutenant. He started to walk away, then turned back toward me. "Incidentally, Colonel. When was the last time you were aboard an MA1A Abrams tank?"

"Well sir, regretfully I have never been."

"Well, you get your ass out here at two o'clock and there will be a helo right here to pick you up and you're going to have an experience this afternoon."

At exactly two o'clock, as ordered, that's exactly where my ass was. I climbed into the Blackhawk and was flown directly to the Udairi range, an immense complex somewhat similar to our own Army National Training Center at Fort Irwin. Ten minutes later, there they were—a perfectly aligned row of Abrams tanks. One impressive sight. Five minutes later, I climbed inside. With the deep growl of the Honeywell turbine engine, we lurched forward. What had to have been only twenty-five or thirty mph over the dirt and sand felt like we were going sixty. That's when the real fun began. Even with the earplugs and the thick composite armor, you certainly feel the power when that 120 mm shell explodes out the main gun. It was some experience.

I returned to the airport and of course the first thing I did was find General Abrams and thank him. Turns out he's a very cool guy who was just poking—a little bit of healthy interservice rivalry. Before I left, I assured him of one thing: "Sir, I will never again misidentify tanker overalls."

Three nights later, I happened to be with him as we were launching planes for one of our joint exercises when I got the call. There had been a mishap. I was briefed on what had occurred and immediately decided what had to be done.

"Colonel, is everything OK?" the general asked.

"No sir, it is not," I said in a massive understatement. "We've had a serious mishap back in the States and they'd like for me to come back. I will have a substitute here in forty-eight hours. Will you allow me to head back, sir?"

"Of course," he replied without a second thought. I hopped on a military aircraft and immediately flew back.

This was a bad one. An Air Force MH-60G Pave Hawk went down in poor weather. It was the last in a four-helicopter formation that was carrying Army and Air Force special operations troops from Hill AFB in Ogden, Utah, to the Army's Dugway Proving Ground, eighty-five miles west of Salt Lake City. The helicopter hit the water at 150 mph and exploded on impact just off the tip of Antelope Island in the Great Salt Lake. Three crew members and nine passengers died immediately. The only survivor was the pilot, Air Force Maj Stephan J.

Laushine. Somehow he was ejected from the aircraft, then rescued by three Army Rangers who paddled inflatable kayaks on choppy water and through the flames. The squadron commander of the 55th Squadron was in the right seat and two Ranger battalion commanders were also on the aircraft and perished.

So there were three battalion-level commanders that we lost on the same airplane—two-thirds of the leadership of the Ranger regiment were wiped out in an instant. And so, naturally, Suzie and I were off to multiple funerals. We took care of that and dealt with the other fatalities. It was a particularly painful thing; you work hard to bounce back from something like that.

The interesting thing is what happened to Maj Laushine. As you can well imagine, he went through quite a struggle, but he wanted to get back in the pilot's seat and fly again. Much to the credit of Charlie Holland and others who completely supported his return, he not only battled back, but he ended up getting promoted to lieutenant colonel and being the mission commander on two harrowing yet successful rescues. He received the Distinguished Flying Cross for the first one, where he and his MH-53M Pave Low led another MH-53M and an MH-60G Pave Hawk deep into Serbian territory to rescue the pilot of F-117 stealth fighter Vega 31.

The second was the rescue of Hammer 34, an F-16 pilot who was shot down by a Serbian SA-3 surface-to-air missile about forty miles southwest of Belgrade. The rescue choppers engaged their countermeasure to narrowly evade two SA-6 radar-guided missiles and an SA-9 infrared-guided missile—plus substantial antiaircraft fire and small arms fire. In no small part due to the fortitude and determination of Lt Col Laushine—and all the others who risked their own lives to make the rescue—General David Goldfein is now the Chief of Staff of the Air Force. Dave (a.k.a. "Hammer 34") is the pilot they rescued that night.

This was one of those wonderful moments of redemption where Lt Col Laushine hit the lowest of the lows—then struggled through the pain and the anguish and the doubts and came back to triumph, saving other lives as well as his own.

By the way, years later, when I was back in Washington as a one-star, General Mike Ryan called upon me to brief at Army TRADOC (Training and Doctrine Command) in Hampton, Virginia, in what turned out to be kind of a star chamber. There must have been at least twenty four-stars present. When it was my turn to speak, I stepped up and scanned the impressive group of flag officers—some familiar, others I was seeing for the first time. Sitting in the front row, directly in front of where I stood to speak, was none other than General John Abrams, who is now a four-star, and is in fact TRADOC commander. He was not wearing his tanker overalls this time. I did begin by deviating from my prepared presentation and told the story about how I had misidentified his tanker overalls as a flight suit. It was a nice icebreaker and they all had a good laugh.

★ ★ ★

In the fall of 1991, lean times and decreased funding prompted General Merrill McPeak, then Air Force Chief of Staff, to devise some means to increase efficiencies during a time when international tensions demanded increased warfighting capability. In layman's terms, it was kind of like challenging the chairman of Coca Cola to come up with a way to make twice as much Coke for half the cost. What McPeak came up with was called the Objective Wing concept. In essence, it changed the base command structure from a "Wing Commander/ Base Commander" system to a single wing commander ("one base-one boss") with multiple groups under his or her command. Bottom line, at the end of the day, I became what was known as the First Special Operations Group commander.

Another one of McPeak's brainstorms took place about five months after my departure. For some reason he decided that no two wings could have the same numerical designation. At the time, in addition to our designation as the First Special Operations Wing, there was the First Fighter Wing at Langley AFB, Virginia. To meet the Chief's new edict, one of us would have to be redesignated. Guess who drew the short straw? On October 1, 1993, the 1st SOW was changed to the 16th SOW. You can't imagine the fury that prompted among the Air Commando veterans of World War II and Vietnam. McPeak had his way during his tenure, but thirteen years later, on November 16, 2006, the wing reverted back to its original designation as the 1st SOW.

★ ★ ★

I had completed my "brigade level" command and flying supervisory opportunities and had already established credibility as a Washington bureaucratic operator. So we came back to Washington and I became the Deputy Director of Operations for the Air Force, working for Brig Gen Hal Hornburg. I learned so much about how to deal with controversial issues, which was priceless prep for the future. It seemed that every day presented another firestorm that had to be extinguished.

Efforts to retire the iconic SR-71 reconnaissance aircraft were extremely controversial and required some deft handling of congressional preferences—a great object lesson on how to deal with alumni and congressional interests, along with operational considerations. This was an ongoing issue that had been playing out for years through multiple administrations. The West Virginia delegation was not supportive of the retirement plan, so a great deal of my time was spent interacting with Senator Byrd's staff. I gained an appreciation for the role of the Congress and staffs in pursuing controversial force structure changes, and learned how best to approach members and staffs on such initiatives—all valuable skills for later on, when as four-star general, I'd be the one in the hot seat being grilled by both Senate and House Armed Services Committees on so many contentious issues of the day.

Efforts to retire the iconic SR-71 reconnaissance aircraft were extremely controversial and required some deft handling of congressional preferences.
USAF photo

While some contend it's best to passionately state your case, I've been more successful by being direct, persuasive, and *dispassionate*.

★ ★ ★

When Suzie stares me down and says "You're acting just like McPeak," I know that I've done something really dumb and probably acted very unreasonably with her. She's referring to General Merrill McPeak, the Chief of Staff who "had me for lunch" one day because he didn't like the data I presented to him, even though it was 100 percent accurate and given to protect him before he unwittingly reported the wrong numbers to Congress.

There was an effort underway to reduce the B-52 bomber presence at Minot AFB (thirteen miles north of Minot, North Dakota) and relocate them to Barksdale AFB in Louisiana. The Chief was about to go over and discuss the relocation with the North Dakota delegation, since their constituency could be impacted by the move. Understandably, for a meeting at this level, he wanted to be fully prepared and armed with all the appropriate backup data.

The problem was that somehow my three-star boss at the time, Buster Glosson, had sent a note to the Chief with some inaccurate data. We learned about this just as he was about to depart for the Hill. The worst thing would have been for him to have made this elaborate presentation based on faulty information. At some point it would have come back to haunt him and he would have looked foolish. Bear in mind that I was just a colonel at this point, so under normal circumstances it would have fallen to Bill Jones in our office to meet with the Chief and set the record straight, since Bill was the two-star Director of Forces. But Bill was out of the office at the time, so it became my task to meet with the impatient general and gently explain how the information that he had received wasn't quite right, but that I had brought the correct info to set the record straight. And of course I wanted to do it without throwing General Glosson under the bus. I double-checked to make sure that what I had was the latest info, then headed down the Arnold Hallway to share those two small yet consequential inaccuracies.

Entering the door beside the gold plaque that read CHIEF OF STAFF OF THE AIR FORCE, I stepped into General McPeak's outer office and checked in with his executive assistant, fully expecting to take a seat and wait for him, as had been the case with all of our prior interactions. Instead, I was briskly told, "Please, go right in, they're all waiting for you."

All? I wondered.

I stepped inside and all eyes swung in my direction.

"Well?" barked the Chief.

"Sir, it has come to our attention that some of the . . ."

"You're wasting my time, get with it and just tell me what you've got!" he demanded.

I succinctly explained the inconsistencies, and frankly thought that would be it. Now that he had the correct data, he could head to the Hill and make his case. The reality was that very little was straightforward with General McPeak, and he was not happy with the way this meeting was unfolding.

"Colonel . . . this is a complete disaster!" He grudgingly reached for his little black book and began flipping through the pages. "We are going to go over every tail number of every B-52 in our inventory and you are going to tell me where *you think* they are based."

And that's exactly what I did, one by one, every tail number of every one of the eighty-plus B-52s in the Air Force inventory. I opened my own notebook and began: "64-026 . . . Barksdale. On alert . . . 64-044 . . ."

"No, wait," he interrupted, then proceeded to rattle off some challenge as to how I was so certain that the aircraft wasn't actually in maintenance or somewhere else at the time. Considering the fact that I had already given him the corrected data in the first five minutes, I thought it was all a tremendous waste of his time.

We had probably gotten 90 percent through the list when he slammed his black book onto the coffee table in front of him. "Colonels normally do better than this," he grumbled, shaking his head and thumbing through some charts and spreadsheets.

I did my best to maintain my composure but it was not easy. I walked out of that meeting confident that I'd be fired as soon as my boss caught wind of it.

I wasn't fired, but I vowed that no matter how high a rank I achieved, I would strive to be demanding but not demeaning.

Suzie: *He was not a nice person.*

Norty: He was prickly.

Suzie: *Always. And that became our thing. Whenever Norty really pissed me off, the worst insult I could ever say to him was, "You're acting like just McPeak." Then he knew that whatever he did was really bad.*

Norty: It's true. Whenever I heard that, I understood that I had crossed the line. But that experience was one of those object lessons that you remember vividly and that affects the way you perform.

**Always treat people with dignity and respect,
and don't shoot the messenger.**

Chapter Four

YOU'RE NO OMAR BRADLEY

JUNE 1995–SEPTEMBER 2000

The last time Suzie had seen General Hobson (by then the two-star head of Air Force Special Operations Command) was when I wrapped up my time at Hurlburt as a major. "You'll never see us here again," she had told the commander, elated to be moving on and leaving Special Ops (and its inherent dangers) behind. But times had changed and hopes were high that I would be promoted to brigadier general, making me eligible to command that same wing.

General Hobson happened to be speaking at an Air Force birthday event we attended in Washington. He spoke about the state of Air Force special operations, which certainly captured my attention. Suzie, however, seemed restless—kind of like a top fuel dragster revving its engine at the starting line. It's not going anywhere quite yet, but when the light turns green, 10,000 horsepower of raw power will leave you in its dust.

Somewhere between the general's "Thank you for having me" and the first applause, Suzie had made it up to the front, waiting to corner him as he stepped off the dais. "Please, please, please, please can we come back to Hurlburt and live on the Sound in the house right next to you?" Suzie pleaded with him. I was totally mortified; she was basically begging him to assign me as his wing commander. He just smiled at her and remained silent, but to this day he razzes me about it. Independent of her pleas (I think), I did get the promotion and the wing commander assignment, and it was one of the real highlights of our career.

By this time we had made many moves, but this one back to Florida was the first time we drove down together. "General Norty Schwartz . . . Has a nice ring to it, don't you think?" Suzie asked rhetorically. The truth is that wing commander is something we had always aspired to do together; it was yet another shared dream coming to fruition. We lived in the wing commander's home on Hume Drive, right next to Jim and Diane Hobson, who occupied the AFSOC commander's house.

So there I was, an Air Force brigadier general select, about to take over an Air Force wing. It turned out to be yet another example of how very much my career was influenced by the Army, and in particular by highly respected soldiers who were pioneers of the special operations community.

General Wayne Downing was known as the "father of the modern Rangers," and he's certainly a member of that short list who paved the way. At the time, General Downing was commander of U.S. Special Operations Command (SOCOM). We had known each other since he was *Colonel* Downing, actually, when he was the first director of the SOCOM Washington office and its predecessor at the Pentagon from 1987 to 1988. No doubt he had heard about me from Potter, and he tried to hire me from the Air Staff to go downstairs and work for him. We had a lengthy interview that couldn't have gone any better. But once again fate stepped in, and just when I was about to accept his offer, I received word of the flying command opportunity at McChord AFB in Washington State, and there was no way that I could pass that up—which he certainly understood.

Later on he became more familiar with me during the time that I was the operations group commander, because he was the JSOC commander then, and we had a fair amount of interaction on ops and mission related issues. In fact, I'm sure that he had to sign off on me coming to Hurlburt as the wing commander.

I was honored to have him attend my change-of-command ceremony. He approached me at the Friday morning reception just as Suzie had handed me a piece of cake. He was smiling as he offered me congratulations, but it was one of those smiles where I could tell that something was bothering him.

He glanced down at the silver eagle rank insignia on my epaulet, and asked, "When are you going to pin on?" He was curious as to when I would actually begin wearing my general officer star.

"Well sir, you know, General Fogleman is not too keen on frocking." Frocking is a U.S. military term for a commissioned officer selected for promotion wearing the insignia of the higher grade before the official date of promotion (the "date of rank"). In this case, General Downing felt it was appropriate that as wing commander I wear the star, since I had already been approved and listed on the promotions list. General Ron Fogleman, Air Force Chief of Staff, did not agree with that logic. Since my formal date of rank for brigadier general was not until January 1, he felt it appropriate that I continue to wear the colonel rank until then.

"Okay, I'll call Ron," Downing said, true to his reputation of never letting the bureaucracy get in his way when it was impeding a cause in which he believed.

Apparently he did call the Chief, because I got a call from Hobson that Tuesday. He said, "We are going to frock you on Thursday."

Suzie was in the car with me at the time. "You're not going to believe this but they're going to frock me," I told her.

"As well they should! It'll be fun to have the family back down here again. Let me look at our calendar and pick a good date, maybe the middle of next month?"

"You don't understand. They're talking about Thursday, the day after tomorrow!"

We had just enough time to order another cake, but that was about it. The family had just come down for the change of command, so very few of them made it back for the promotion ceremony. Suzie was disappointed; she felt that it was somewhat anticlimactic with all the rushing, felt that I deserved more since becoming a general is such a significant milestone. But I thought General Hobson did a wonderful job with the pinning, out on a little patio in the rear of the Hurlburt club. And you won't hear me complain about the way it all played out—getting frocked was extremely rare, and to have a man of General Downing's stature step up for me like that—it's humbling. And General Downing prevailed. It's an Army thing. Downing wanted to have the airmen at SOW at an equal level with others in the Special Ops community. It was about stature. He didn't want to have me wait because people would get used to me as a colonel—he wanted this to happen quickly. In fact, I think he was a tinge miffed that it didn't happen at the change of command.

It goes back to what I've been saying about the support I've always had from the Army. It's also a prime example of how leaders lead. Downing looked at the big picture, supported his people, and wasn't afraid to go to the top or cross service lines to do so.

We continued to interact over the years even after he retired, and certainly maintained a relationship. When he passed away, Doug Brown (subsequent commander of SOCOM) and I were the only two four-stars at his funeral in Peoria. It was more than appropriate to render those honors.

★　★　★

I've always been big on total transparency; it's the example I would set from day one. That started with a welcome letter I distributed to everyone in the wing. It listed what I liked, what I believed in, what I expected, and what I didn't like. No surprises, just setting everyone up for success. It empowered them while showing them that we're a team, we're all in this together. It's the same basic list I used when I was squadron commander, and would use when I was Chief. I picked these up from leaders whom I greatly admire, and my hope was that they'd be as worthwhile to others as they had been to me. In any event, they were the framework for the culture under which I would operate the wing.

It's always better to be explicit about one's expectations.

DEPARTMENT OF THE AIR FORCE
HEADQUARTERS 16th SPECIAL OPERATIONS WING (AFSOC)

2 Jun 95

Proud Men and Women of the 16th Special Operations Wing

    It is an extraordinary privilege for Suzie and me to join you as your new first family. It is a very rare thing to get to do something like this. We are grateful for the opportunity and truly look forward to rejoining one of the world's foremost special operations teams—from the clinic to the backshop, from the dining facilities to the flightline, officers, NCOs, and civilians alike. While Suzie and I have been here before and many of you know us well, I thought I would use this letter as a way to get reacquainted and lay out, as clearly as I can, what I think matters.

    The 16th Special Operations Wing is unique—the premier special operations wing in the Air Force. The capability we offer the nation's leadership <u>is</u> important. Together, with our joint team mates, we have to perform superbly when called upon, whether repatriating Americans held hostage, conducting classic special operations in combat as we have four times in the last decade, performing humanitarian missions, or assisting developing nations. Everyone in our wing contributes—no one should measure their worth by their proximity to the flightline. Together, we will serve our leadership and the American taxpayer well, efficiently, and if need be, with courage, precision and reliability.

    What do I believe in? Here's a short list:

- A day's work for a day's pay
- High standards and self discipline
- Action: making things happen
- Merit as the only basis for judging people
- Being candid: telling it like it is
- Zero tolerance for discriminatory practices of any kind
- Rewarding excellence and holding leaders accountable for their actions
- Giving more than you take
- Delivering what you promise
- Taking care of people in all its forms: quality of life, performance reports, awards, work environment, dignity and respect, etc.
- Personal responsibility and leading from the front

Any Time . . . Any Place

What I don't like:

- Chronic complainers: those who have little interest in being part of the solution

- The status quo

- Those who don't stand up for what they believe and aren't proud of what they do

- Those who don't make their best effort to fulfill obligations to family, unit, and profession

- Those who don't share a commitment to airpower and the special operations discipline, regardless of individual AFSC

- Substance abusers

- Questionable loyalty or integrity

- Thinking I don't want to hear bad news or a different point of view (remember, bad news never gets better with time)

For as long as I can remember the 16 SOW has been a winning team—at the point of the Air Force spear. Over the past 15 years, no Air Force wing has sustained more combat casualties. We'll no doubt be called on again. As we prepare for that moment, let's do it with enthusiasm, quiet professionalism, and an abiding respect for one another and our joint team-mates. My promise is: I'll lead from the front; I'll work hard every day and strive to maintain the same high standards as each of you; and along the way, we'll have fun too!

NORTON A. SCHWARTZ, Colonel, USAF
Commander

2

Wing command was every bit as much of an opportunity for Suzie as it was for me, and by opportunity I mean opportunity to *contribute,* and *teach,* and *mentor,* and *effectuate important change.* She hit the gate running and still hasn't stopped. I don't think it's an exaggeration when I say that she did more good at that base than all the prior spouses combined.

HURRICANE OPAL

Suzie: *Far more than missions occupied Nort's time commanding the 16th Special Operations Wing at Hurlburt in Florida. Hurricane Opal was a Category 4 hurricane headed directly for the base in October 1995. While nearby Eglin AFB was evacuating all their fighter aircraft, Nort was getting resistance from some Air Force higher-ups about the need to evacuate his fleet; he was justifiably apprehensive about them being destroyed by the rapidly approaching 150 mph winds. My concern was how the twenty-two-foot storm surge would impact a row of eight houses that faced south directly on the water, especially since ours was one of them. For days I told Nort those houses had to be boarded up, and he kept assuring me that it was going to happen just as soon as he got the airplanes taken care of. I finally exploded. "I've been asking you for three days and frankly, I don't give a shit about your goddamn airplanes! I want the houses boarded up. It's our house, our friends' houses!" He finally had it taken care of, with alarmingly little time to spare.*

Norty stayed behind, but my getting out of that base so that we could hunker down somewhere safe was no small endeavor. I don't know who came up with the idea that there's some calm before the storm but it sure didn't apply to this one. By the time I stopped to pick up my friend Sally and her three-year-old son Ben, I felt like Dorothy in The Wizard of Oz. It was 7:00 a.m. and the sky was getting darker by the minute. Although nowhere near the 145 mph wind gusts that would eventually pound the base, the winds had already kicked up enough to impede our attempts to get Sally's critical possessions from her house to my Volvo. Let me rephrase that—to get Sally's crap into my car. While I had filled the trunk with blankets, pillows, paper towels, wet wipes, food, water, and such, Sally was trying to load up the car with armloads of papers. Not to mention the fact that she was doing this at a snail's pace as though we had months to spare. This was an urgent situation! "Sally! Storm! Hurricane! If you're coming with me, get in now because I'm outta here!"

The truth is that we were too late. With an estimated hundred thousand people trying to evacuate from the Gulf Coast, our attempts to make it to a shelter ahead of the storm were a joke. Traffic was beyond bumper-to-bumper, and once we did get halfway up to the Alabama border, we were told that the bridge was out in Alabama, so they turned us all around. We were still in our car when the storm hit, forced to pull to the side of the road on some bridge over a swamp. Unless you've experienced a hurricane firsthand, there's no way to imagine the enormous destructive power it breeds. We spent seven hours in that car, but we made it alive and unharmed. Others were not as fortunate.

It was days later before we finally made it back to the base and were recognized by the young airman at the back gate. "Ma'am, I'm so sorry about your house," he said. I took it in stride, thanked him, and drove toward the inevitable. Whatever it is, it is. Sally, on the other hand, panicked. "Oh my God, Suzie . . . What are we going to find? What are we going to do?" she whined.

Once we navigated the obstacle course of downed trees, power lines, and other debris and made it over to the house, it turned out that the young man had mistaken our house for General Hobson's. Ours was saved, but his was in ruins with his belongings strewn across his front lawn, one of fourteen homes we lost to that storm. Diane Hobson took it very well, but the general took it really hard. Who could blame him? All of his memorabilia had been destroyed. Irreplaceable, priceless pieces. It was devastating.

I kicked into gear and put together sort of a "Crisis Action Team" for spouses. We couldn't do too much the first day since we were all without power, but a few of them came over and accompanied me to the commissary so that we could gather some supplies.

We arrived to find that they were also without power. Even so, they were kind enough to give us bread and peanut butter, which we took back to my place. We made peanut butter and jelly sandwiches and distributed them to the homes.

Each morning our little spouse network expanded, finally getting to the point where I would have them assemble on our front lawn at 7:00 a.m. and I would dispatch them to different homes to provide help.

Once the power got restored, we went around with trash bags and picked up people's laundry. These were big lawn bags, far too heavy for me to carry once they were filled with clothing. But the neighborhood kids stepped in and helped me drag all these huge trash bags back to my house. They would unload them onto my back yard and we would start by hosing everything off because the whole lot was covered in muck; looking at them you'd think they were ruined, but we were able to save most of them. Once they were in a condition where they could be laundered, we'd stuff them into my washer, which was running almost twenty-four hours a day for the first three or four days. Those home units were not designed for that; I was concerned we might blow out the motor or something. So I said to Nort, "Could we get a washer set up in the marina parking lot?" Next thing I know, they showed up out there with a row of washers and dryers.

"Thank you so much, that's great," I told him. "But so many folks are working on their homes during the daylight hours and they need to do the laundry at night. Think we can get some lighting out there?"

Ask and you shall receive. That evening, our entire "mobile laundry facility" was bathed in a bright blanket of light, thanks to rows of emergency lights and generators set up by the facilities folks.

The Hobsons' place was still a disaster and far from habitable, but I knew that they came by every day to check on things. First thing every morning, I would wake up, make a fresh pot of coffee, then take it over to their place and leave it on the counter (which was still filthy and disgusting) along with some muffins or sweet rolls. I would run in early and get out before they saw me.

One morning I overslept, having worked the "night shift" on the laundry detail. By the time I made the coffee and prepared the tray, I didn't even have time to get dressed if I were to make the run before they arrived. I threw a robe over my PJs and hustled over there, quietly padded up to the back door, and snuck a glance. I was safe, the kitchen was still empty! I slipped in, quickly deposited the goodies onto the counter, and turned to leave.

"Honey, call the police, we have an intruder," boomed a voice from the next room. I spun around and nearly jumped out of my skin, I was so startled! Apparently the Hobsons arrived early and were already working in the back of the house.

"And all dressed up, too," the general said with a chuckle.

"Says the man with forty-eight golf shirts," I shot back at him. "I should know, because I just washed and folded them all last night. Who has forty-eight golf shirts? Arnold Palmer couldn't play that much golf!"

"I had a feeling you were the invisible daily welcome wagon. Thank you for that."

"Don't thank me. It wasn't for you, it was for her," I said, shooting Diane a quick wink. "Now if you'll excuse me, I have to get back and make sure that I

didn't leave any golf shirts in the dryer."

"Thank you, Suzie," Diane added as I bolted out the door to give them their privacy.

The good news is that we did end up with a thirty-seven-foot sailboat in our backyard. The bad news is it wasn't ours. (That's really Norty's line, but I temporarily borrowed it from him.) It had broken loose from its moorings a few miles up the coast. As the water subsided, it came to rest about three feet down from what used to be my vegetable garden, and it planted its centerboard more firmly than the sword in the stone; that thing wasn't going anywhere.

The following morning we're all out there with a bunch of workers who've begun their recovery efforts. Suddenly in the middle of it all—and to us this felt as surreal as it must sound now—this little rubber dinghy putted up the Sound, and pulled up to the seawall right behind all the activity that was going on. The "captain" of the dinghy stepped out and tied the boat off, and then approached Norty and me. Not to be judgmental, but the guy had a week-old beard and it looked like he hadn't been anywhere near a working shower in a week. Of course we were both wondering, "Who is this guy?" He pointed to the sailboat in the middle of the yard and said, "That's my boat. Think it's safe here?"

Norty and I both broke out laughing, because of course we had seriously escalated security to prevent any looting, and as he asked the question there were uniformed Air Force security forces all over the place on their four-wheelers.

"Trust me, it's not going anywhere," Norty assured him. He thanked us, turned around and putted away in his dinghy. I suppose the moral of the story is "You can't judge a book by its cover."

When he returned to arrange for the removal of his vessel he looked a lot more presentable. "Dan Gralnick," he offered while shaking hands with Norty, then handed him his business card. "Sincerely sorry about the inconvenience." Glancing at the card, Norty was surprised to see that this was Doctor Daniel Gralnick, a prominent Fort Walton Beach cardiologist. The sailboat was an ocean-going vessel that had taken him around the world.

A few weeks later, a towing company showed up with a crane and two eighteen-wheeler flatbeds. They picked the thing up, put it on the flatbeds, and towed it away.

We worked our asses off to recover that base, and while I took the lead in caring for the affected families, Nort's recovering the mission capability of that special operations base was one of those real tests of his leadership. I'm still in *awe of how he consistently pulls this off with total calm and focus. We got a lot of positive press on this one, with one reporter branding me "The quarterback of Hume Drive." I still kind of like that one . . . except we don't live on Hume Drive anymore.*

★   ★   ★

A few months later, General Fogelman (Chief of Staff) came by for a visit. Fogelman was not a man to mince words. He had barely stepped into my car when he caught me off guard.

"How does it feel to be the commander of the suicide capital of the Air Force?" he asked, referencing a problem of which I was very much aware; the night of my very first day in command an airman went out into the woods and shot himself. Basically, the Chief was saying, "Schwartz, you've got a serious problem here. Get your arms around it."

"Sir, point well taken," I responded. "Let me assure you that we are on top of it." I went on to explain that we had already implemented a number of changes, including an intervention campaign that suggested not allowing a wing teammate to spiral down. *If you note someone who's troubled, intervene. Act, don't wait.* We also tried to minimize the stigma associated with it. Going to see a mental health professional was not something special operators particularly aspired to do.

In addition to the steps that had already been taken, we certainly knew that the chief of staff expected even more progress, so we did our best in that regard. I shared his comment with my leadership team.

"The Chief has this perception and we obviously are concerned about this anyway, but we need to redouble our efforts to try to again reduce the incidence of suicide."

We put our heads together on the medical side, on the supervision side, and on the family support side.

But the truth was that expectations in this wing were high. This was not a good place for people who didn't carry their weight, and frankly that was not something I was going to change. This was a demanding operational environment and if people were not up to it, we would find a way for them to serve elsewhere in a productive way and continue their service. But we had to balance stress management aspect, with the fact that we were a very significant mission intent on carrying on the "never again" determination that was born from Desert One. This was a continuation of that process and if this mission was not for them, no harm no foul.

We did have to change that perception that going in for help would be a career-ender. We wanted them to know that once they recovered they would be welcomed back as full members of our team. There was a perception that going in for help—seeing a psychiatrist if necessary—would prompt a mark against them, and that's not true. This was not a nuclear mission where it would be, where they would lose their access for a period of time. There was management's discretion and we did our best to exercise prudential discretion. And the rates did come down.

This theme stayed with me. Till the very end I was haunted by Fogelman's words, "How does it feel to be the suicide capital of the Air Force?" Fifteen years later, when I was Chief, I spoke about it to the airmen at Little Rock AFB:

> Reach out to chaplains, supervisors or medical professionals if you're feeling stressed or under duress. We don't want anyone at Little Rock [AFB] to be affected by the phenomenon of suicide, because this is a family business. Make it your personal mission to make sure the airman to your left and the airman to your right is still here tomorrow.

THE LAST FEND

Earlier I spoke about the Fulton surface-to-air recovery system—or STARS system—that we used on certain specialized missions. It's the same one that's depicted in the classic final scene in *Thunderball* where a B-17 swoops overhead to snatch 007 (Sean Connery) and his femme fatale from a dinghy off the coast of Florida.

The very last time it was employed was in 1997, and as wing commander I was given the honor of piloting the aircraft that would execute the intricate maneuver during a special "farewell" ceremony. The crowd looked skyward to see Brigadier General Schwartz execute this perfect piloting maneuver. I lined up the nose of my C-130 so that its "whiskers" would perfectly intercept the lift line that dangled from the very last lift balloon in existence. The photographers snapped away as *I missed the target (we called that "fending") and destroyed the device*—easily the most embarrassing moment of my entire life.

I stepped off the plane and was assaulted with the expected friendly razzing, but on the inside, I felt more than a tinge of disappointment. We were all hoping for a successful intercept, closing this chapter of special operations history in a positive way. Suzie felt the disappointment both for her "boy" and the emotion of the moment for the Fulton community. Twenty-plus years of capability retiring to memories and the history books. Bittersweet.

★ ★ ★

In May 1997 as I prepared to transition from my first command as a general officer to new experiences at SOCPAC (Special Operations Command, Pacific) in Hawaii, I reflected back to my conversation with General Downing at our change-of-command ceremony. I recalled that after he stepped away I had challenged myself to leave the wing a better place than when we got there. Looking back, I believe that Suzie and I met that challenge. We successfully fostered a real sense of family, crisper management, and a better bench of talent. We hired and trained the best maintainers and support people as well as the best operators. Everybody contributed, and everybody mattered.

One thing that Suzie and I observed through the years was how you get a feeling about an organization the moment you arrive; it's a sixth sense that you develop. The longer I served, the stronger that instinct became. By the time I became Chief, it was pretty infallible.

Before I left Hurlburt, we hosted a glorious celebration of the fiftieth anniversary of the Air Force at the Air Park. The Air Park is a wonderful museum where over twenty historic old airplanes now live. From UH-1s to E-model Talons, Pave Lows to AC-130 Spectre gunships—they're all on display along with monuments and a Walk of Fame for Medal of Honor recipients. It's magnificent. Along with local dignitaries and alumni, General Fogleman came down for the event. This time when I greeted him, he responded differently than his prior rejoinder about our suicide rate.

He returned my salute, then shook my hand and nodded. "Good to see you, Norty." He didn't say much, but his look spoke volumes; it reflected that sixth sense that I referenced. He approved of what he saw. It was a good wing.

★ ★ ★

Admiral Joe Prueher was a highly decorated Navy combat pilot and my boss when I became commander of SOCPAC, Special Operations Command, Hawaii. We had a tremendous expanse of partners and territory to be concerned about. Our area of responsibility covered thirty-six countries spread over half the world. While I was being briefed by ADM Prueher, Suzie toured the island, after which she met Prueher and provided him with a brief of her own. "You know, Admiral, I just toured Pearl Harbor, and it's not exactly up to Air Force standards. Maybe you want to look into that?"

He smiled warmly and replied, "Pleasure meeting you, too, Suzie." It's not surprising that such a diplomat would go on to become U.S. Ambassador to China.

My dance card was full over the next sixteen months as I commanded Navy SEALS, Army Special Forces, and Air Force special operators in volatile hotspots throughout the Pacific theater. This was another one of those situations where due to the nature of how special operations assignments are set up, I was technically responsible to two bosses. Being attached to the Pacific Command, from day to day I'd be responsible to Prueher. In the big picture, being a representative of special operations, my second boss was General Hugh Shelton, commander in chief of USSOCOM at the time. Shelton is another one with ties to the community from early on. He was a member of the Project Delta team back in Vietnam, a Special Forces detachment that became the most decorated single unit in the Vietnam War—one that was integral in setting the standards for the operators who came after them.

Before I flew to Hawaii, I paid an office visit to General Shelton back in Tampa. The six-foot five-inch commander leaned in toward me and looked me squarely in the eyes. "Norty, if you only remember one thing, it's this," he began, about to share insight gleaned from over three decades in uniform. "Get into the back pocket of the J-3 [operations officer]. Show him what you're made of and how you can make his life easier. Earn his trust."

That one piece of advice made it well worth the trip, and it was something that I've never forgotten. His logic was that you want to have that officer's full confidence so that if something went down, he'd instantly turn to you to apply your capability to the problem. These things played out so fast, if you hadn't already earned that confidence before the execute order came in, chances were you'd missed the boat. Serendipitously, this played out within the first few weeks of my arrival.

Instability in Cambodia caused real concern about the safety of Americans, prompting President Clinton to authorize the 1st Battalion, 1st Special Forces Group's deployment from Okinawa to Thailand for a potential evacuation. Orchestrating JTF BEVEL EDGE was a big deal—the proposed rescue of a thousand American citizens trapped in Phnom Penh, Cambodia, by a possible civil war.

Deploying forces included three MC-130Hs, three MC-130Ps, three MH-53Js, and 340 personnel, plus a support fleet of C-5, C-17, C-141, and KC-135 aircraft. This earned me the respect of Admiral Prueher and, just as General Shelton had predicted, it also set up a valuable relationship with Joe Mobley, the J-3—one that served us well for the rest of my command. We acted expeditiously, we reported and stayed connected in a professional way that demonstrated a level of competence. From then on Joe had confidence that we could do what we said we could do.

Joe Mobley was quite a guy—an exemplary officer and an excellent operations officer. Just to give you an idea of his strength of will, for 1,724 days, Joe was a prisoner of war in Hanoi. He'd been flying as a bombardier-navigator when his A6A Intruder was hit at low altitude by AAA over North Vietnam. He bailed out, but suffered a severe broken leg in the shoot down. He was captured, tied—standing—to a pillar in spite of the fracture, then beaten, interrogated, displayed for public humiliation, and forced to dodge bricks and bamboo sticks hurled at him for over eight hours. When he was finally thrown into a cell, he had to set his own leg. He spent months in solitary confinement, then endured intermittent torture for the duration of his five years of imprisonment. Earning the respect of a man like this meant a great deal to me.

★ ★ ★

This was a period of engagement, and much of my time was spent reaching out to other countries, including Thailand (where I parachuted with the Thais during Exercise Cobra Gold), Indonesia, Sri Lanka, Korea, and Japan. I even traveled to Beijing to improve relations between our countries. Typically, I met with my special operations counterpart, and almost always the ambassador and country team. In addition to receiving written advance briefs, we would almost always have face-to-face intelligence briefings in which they would review pertinent American policy, especially objectives that the command leadership hoped that I would achieve.

Another role that I played was the deputy of the Combined Unconventional Warfare Task Force in Korea under Korean Lieutenant General Oh Chang Hwan. General Oh was quite unpredictable, and that scared the hell out of my real boss, U.S. Army General John Tilelli, who had me "unofficially monitoring" General Oh just to make sure he didn't get overly anxious and initiate some precipitous actions of which Tilelli would not approve.

OCTOBER 1998–JANUARY 2000

In 1970, Chuck Wald was a wide receiver at North Dakota State University—a pretty good one, in fact, so good that he got drafted by the Atlanta Falcons. But instead of playing football, he chose ROTC and went to Vietnam as a forward air controller—then went on to direct the aerial raid on Qaddafi's compound in Tripoli in 1986. He then flew bombing runs in F-16s over Bosnia. Chuck is the one whom I had just replaced in what turned out to be an important job in the strategic planning directorate for the Air Staff. The official title was director of strategic planning.

My boss was Lieutenant General Roger Dekok, a good man and an exceptional boss. Roger, who has since passed away, was the XP—deputy chief of staff for plans and programs. Very smart and kept me on my toes. Almost all of his career was spent somehow connected to the space program—aerospace surveillance, space systems planning, special White House assignments on security, and defense issues relating to the space program. The way he approached things gave me a fresh perspective. I liked that. We were located on the fifth floor of the Pentagon. It was one of those offices where the instant you walked in, you felt a kind of vibrant energy. Roger had a lot to do with that.

There were two major accomplishments during that period. The first was developing a new Air Force tagline. Sounds easy, right? Well, guess again. I gained a healthy respect for the challenges that ad agency execs must face every day. But in our case, there was no agency. Besides some outside help for focus groups and such, it was all done in-house. Our task was to create a line that generated an instant vision of who we were and what we did, while at the same time inspiring, exciting, and, in an ideal world, instilling a sense of fear (or at the very least, healthy respect) in the minds of our enemies. What we ended up with was *Global Vigilance, Reach, and Power.*

Coming up with the line was the first step. Getting buy-in from the highest levels of the Air Force was every bit as important, and it was no walk in the park. We presented the slogan, argued its merits, then engaged in healthy debate, over and over, with various decision makers—all leading up to our final presentation to the Corona group, the four-stars and senior civilians of the Air Force. At the time, General Ryan was the Chief of Staff, and Whit Peters was the secretary. They ultimately agreed to the slogan. That was almost twenty years ago, and it's still used today—it's one of the first things you're exposed to on the Air Force website, recruiting posters, command briefs, you name it.

The second major project was the creation of a document we called *America's Air Force Vision 2020.* It defined our Air Force vision—showing where we were headed and where we expected to be by the year 2020. What a challenge, but what great fun! On the one hand I felt a little like some sci-fi writer—lots of emphasis on space, comprehensive intelligence capabilities, and surveillance capabilities. Not too much cyber at that point, but even at that early stage, it was starting to creep into the dialogue. But unlike a science fiction writer, these predictions had to be grounded in reality and extrapolated from then current data—what we believed to be a realistic depiction of where we would be twenty years out.

We broke it down into six areas:

The Foundation: Our people and our values
The Domain: Aerospace
The Method: Expeditionary Aerospace Force
The Building Blocks: Our Core Competencies
The Approach: Innovation and Adaptation
The Commitment: Keeping the Trust

The entire document is available online at www.nortyschwartz.com/vision2020.

Here are a few pages:

The DOMAIN Aerospace

We are an integrated aerospace force. Our domain stretches from the earth's surface to the outer reaches of space in a seamless operational medium. We operate aircraft and spacecraft optimized for their environments, but the art of commanding aerospace power lies in integrating systems to produce the exact effects the nation needs. To meet this need, we've modified our command organizations to take full advantage of air, space and information expertise. We have implemented an Aerospace Basic Course that ensures newly commissioned officers understand the breadth and value of the different components of aerospace power. Our Space Warfare Center now emphasizes how to leverage the combination of space and atmospheric capabilities, and we've added space training to the air combat training at our Weapons School. Our information capabilities support operations across the entire aerospace domain. And we're putting air, space and information operators into all our key commands and training courses, focusing on expanding and cross-flowing knowledge to maximize effectiveness.

We will continue integrating air, space and information operations, while leveraging the strengths of each. Our airmen will think in terms of controlling and exploiting the full aerospace continuum on a regional and global scale to achieve effects both on earth and in flight regimes beyond the horizon. We will strengthen the ability of our commanders to command and control aerospace forces. Their Aerospace Operations Centers will be able to gather and fuse the full range of information, from national to tactical, in real-time, and to rapidly convert that information to knowledge and understanding—to assure decision dominance over adversaries.

To employ these aerospace capabilities effectively, we'll continue to develop commanders who think in terms of exploiting the whole aerospace continuum—leaders able to employ forces that produce the desired effects, regardless of where platforms reside, fly, or orbit. These leaders with experience and cross-competence in the increasingly complex range of military disciplines will lead aerospace and joint forces to victory for the nation.

Operation ALLIED FORCE demonstrated the power of aerospace integration. During combat operations over Serbia, space sensors identified time-critical targets, allowing airborne surveillance platforms to pinpoint exact target locations. The Aerospace Operations Center then rapidly directed strike aircraft to engage and destroy those targets. Tomorrow's fully-integrated aerospace force will realize even greater potential.

The FOUNDATION
Our People & Our Values

We are America's Airmen. We are warriors...we will fight and win wherever our nation needs us. The aerospace realm is our domain, and we are vigilant in our commitment to defend, control and use it in our nation's interest. We are leaders...we live our core values. We are a Total Force—Active, Guard, Reserve, and Civilian—seamless in providing aerospace power.

We do not operate alone. Our efforts are made possible by the great support of many. Our families, our retirees, the employers of our Guardsmen and Reservists, our industry partners, and the communities in which we live and work enable us to carry out our mission.

And we are partners in the Joint Team...we project aerospace power anywhere in the world, and operate in concert with America's land and sea forces, and with our allies. Wherever we serve, whatever we do, we are America's Airmen.

We will recruit, train and retain America's best young men and women to provide Global Vigilance, Reach and Power to our nation in the 21st Century. We will command and lead effectively at all levels—with decisiveness and concern for our people. We'll provide an environment that encourages all our people to achieve personal and professional excellence, taking pride in being part of the aerospace force that's respected the world over.

We will size, shape and operate the force to meet the needs of the nation. We must also manage the effects of tempo on our people. This is particularly important for those elements of the force currently in short supply, but in high demand. And we'll continue leading the way in leveraging the strengths of all our components to optimize Total Force effectiveness in peace as well as war.

America's Airmen will be smart, sharp and tough. We'll provide them with the education, equipment and training to perform at their best. And we will demonstrate commitment to our people and to their families, providing quality of life that lives up to their trust. Our Air Force will be worthy of the great men and women who join us.

The foundation of the force is our people... We will remain worthy of America's best.

★   ★   ★

A goal of many flag officers is to someday get that fourth star and be assigned to command one of the nine Unified Combatant Commands. These are joint commands that include forces from every service branch. SOCOM (Special Operations Command) is one of them, and it shouldn't be a surprise to hear that my ultimate goal was to lead that organization—down the road, of course, if it were to happen at all.

From early on I'd been interacting with the Special Ops community, and I earned a solid reputation as someone who would get the job done and someone who could be trusted. From Dick Scholtes, Carl Stiner, and Gary Luck in the early days, through Wayne Downing, Pete Schoomaker, Charlie Holland, Doug Brown, Eric Olson, Dell Dailey, Stan McChrystal, and others, I got to know the various commanders very well. I worked well with them and I became a part of the network. From the time I was a captain through my wing command, either I was a direct participant or I had people in my direct line of supervision who were part of their teams.

This was particularly true in the case of JSOC (Joint Special Operations Command), due to the nature of its structure. The logic was that the folks of the U.S.-based force weren't necessarily quite as knowledgeable about theater matters as would be the theater command. And so the arrangement of having the JSOC two-star (now three-star) serve as a PACOM (United States Pacific Command) joint task force commander with a theater representative (SOCPAC) as his deputy was a perfect mix. It was something that made the theater commander—in the case of PACOM, Admiral Prueher—comfortable. It was a good way to promote cohesion and cooperation. And it's a good example of how Pete Schoomaker and I intersected and stayed close with one another.

It had barely been a year since I pinned on my two stars, and almost all of that time had been spent on developing our new Air Force slogan and the *Air Force Vision 2020* document. In fact, I had just presented General DeKok with the final draft when I got the call.

"Norty, Pete Schoomaker here. Am I really going to have to look at that ugly face of yours again?" I smiled and wondered what he had in mind.

"I don't know about that, sir. Why don't you tell me?"

"Just saw the new promotion announcement and under 'three-stars' there's a 'Norton A. Schwartz.' Know anything about that?"

"You have got to be kidding me," I sputtered, completely flummoxed and caught off guard—*not* something I was expecting.

"Who jumps from two stars to three in *under two years?*" he asked.

Then it occurred to me: *why is Pete the one making this call?* He answered that question before I had the chance to ask: "Time to call Suzie and have her start packing those bags. You're coming to Tampa to be my deputy!"

★ ★ ★

Deputy Commander of Special Operations Command—a perfect fit on so many levels. It placed me in prime position to take over SOCOM when Pete retired. But beyond that, the assignment itself was a dream come true; I'd be working hand in hand with the legends of U.S. special operations—many of whom had been captains in the Desert One era. Pete was commander, Doug Brown was commanding JSOC, and Eric Olson led Naval Special Warfare Command.

By this point I had attended my share of promotion ceremonies, both as promotee and as the one doing the pinning. While the size of the audience and hoopla may grow in proportion to the level of rank, the basic protocol surrounding the event had always been consistent. Nobody was more on top of this than Suzie, who was—and still is—an event planner extraordinaire. She was well into the planning long before we left Washington, as I found out one evening in the fall of 1999.

I walked in from work to find Suzie at the dinner table, deeply enmeshed in calculations of some kind. The table was littered with index cards, directories, and lists she had consolidated from past events. Everything except for the steaks she had promised.

"Dinner looks delicious," I said with a smirk, wondering which of her many projects had so captured her focus this time.

"Thank you, I've been cooking all day," she quipped while still scribbling onto her yellow legal pad. "And don't bother taking off your coat, we're going out." How could she have seen that I'd already begun to do so? "So I've been

A glimpse of a too serious new teenager attaining a religious milestone, my bar mitzvah.
Schwartz personal collection

My father did not want me to play . . . I'm glad he conceded against his better judgment.
Schwartz personal collection

Me, Skip Sanders, Bob Munson, Mike Mosier, and Bill Chambers "relaxing" at the Air Force Academy.
Schwartz personal collection

This was an exerpt my dad saved . . . he was quietly proud.
Schwartz personal collection

NORTON A. SCHWARTZ

Cadet **NORMAN A. SCHWARTZ**, son of Simon Schwartz, 42 Park St., Toms River, has been named to the Superintendent's List at the U.S. Air Force Academy.

1972-1973 Wing Staffs

F
a
l
l

(Left to right):
George Rampulla
Dewitt Searles III
Ronald Moran
Dana R. Ideen
William Wilson Jr.
Norton Schwartz
Kenneth Womack
James Smith
Alfred Guardino
William Palles
Philip Walker
Kurt Conklin

I served as Wing Operations Officer for the Fall term of our senior year.
Kees Rietsema was the Cadet Wing Commander.
Schwartz personal collection

Captain Bob Woods, our Air Officer Commanding, swearing me in as a 2nd Lieutenant in our nation's Air Force. Bob ultimately retired as a Brig Gen.
Schwartz personal collection

My father and me during graduation week. How 'bout that sport coat!
Schwartz personal collection

In the days before settling down, I was an active sport parachutist. Here with friend John Butterfield at the Hartwood, VA, drop zone.
Schwartz personal collection

Suzie and I are married on June 6, 1981 with my surrogate parents, Al and Barbara Navas.
Schwartz personal collection

Mike Gecan, Dick Schmidt, and Merrill Yeary comprised the cockpit element of the "All Lt Crew."
Schwartz personal collection

Colonel Al Navas assumes command of the 374th Tactical Airlift Wing from General Carlton, then Commander of Military Airlift Command. Colonel Baginski observes at right.
USAF photo by TSGT Charles L. Huck Jr.

Suzie and I return to Hurlburt Field to assume command of the 16th Special Operations Wing . . . no better job in our Air Force.
Schwartz personal collection

Suzie and me in the late '80s.
Schwartz personal collection

On the patio of the Hurlburt Field Officers Club, I am promoted to Brigadier General by Maj Gen Jim Hobson. General Wayne Downing, responsible for that outcome, observes in the background.
Schwartz personal collection

The classic picture of BG Dick Potter, USA, leading the way in rescuing displaced Kurds during Operation Provide Comfort in the mountains of northern Iraq. Note the expanse of refugees in the background.
Schwartz personal collection

What a privilege it was to lead the 16th SOW, pictured here in front of an MC-130E, Combat Talon, special operations aircraft.
USAF photo

Chief of Staff Ron Fogelman pulled no punches when he showed up to ask me how it felt for me to lead the "suicide capital of the Air Force." Hurlburt Field, 1997.
Schwartz personal collection

One of many exercises in Korea . . . taking a fitness break supporting Ulchi Focus Lens outside Seoul.
Schwartz personal collection

Chairman of the Joint Chiefs, General Dick Myers and Suzie pin the fourth star in the Pentagon Hall of Heroes.
DoD photo by Darrell Hudson

Although I had the honor of attending the Combatant Commanders' White House conference as Director of the Joint Staff, this was the first time Suzie and I were invited to stay for dinner with the president. January 3, 2006, Commander, U.S. Transportation Command.
Official White House photo

Between the Joint Chiefs and Combatant Commanders, there were 68 "stars" joining (*l to r*) Deputy Secretary of Defense Gordon England, Vice President Dick Cheney, President Bush, and Secretary of Defense Bob Gates at the January 2007 White House conference.
Official White House photo by Shealah Craighead

Now as Chief of Staff of the Air Force, Suzie and I joined the Obamas for our last visit to the White House in May 2012.
Official White House photo by Lawrence Jackson

Visiting with our dear friend General George Casey, Commander of ISAF, during his 30-month tour in Baghdad.
Schwartz personal collection

Suzie was the last spouse to visit Afghanistan in April 2008 as the security situation then became more challenging.
USAF photo by MSgt Demetrius Lester

One of the responsibilities of the Transportation Command leadership was to cultivate relationships with those international partners who provided access to their port facilities, in this case Kuwait.
Schwartz personal collection

Suzie met with Afghan women from many fields of endeavor at some risk to their personal safety. *USAF photo by MSgt Demetrius Lester*

Secretary of the Air Force Mike Donley formally passes the flag to me upon assuming the role as Chief of Staff of the USAF. It was a beautiful and warm day on the Ceremonial Lawn at Bolling AFB, DC. *USAF photo by Scott M. Ash*

What a special day . . . and was it ever cold . . . celebrating the inauguration of the new president.
Schwartz personal collection

Gen George Casey, now Chief of Staff of the U.S. Army, me, and our staffs engaging in essential staff talks in Feb., 2009. This was not a photo op, but a forum for real work on issues of mutual warfighting concern.
USA photo

Admiral Gary Roughead, the Chief of Naval Operations, and I worked together to produce the Air-Sea Battle concept. It was a signature piece of work for both of our Services.
USAF photo by Scott Ash

The first time Suzie met Secretary Rumsfeld she was not shy about expressing her displeasure about some of his policies. He took it all in stride; in fact, telling her that she reminded him a lot of his wife. They met many times through the years.
Schwartz personal collection

President Obama holds a briefing on Afghanistan with the Joint Chiefs of Staff in the Situation Room at the White House on October 30, 2009. It was a somber meeting as he went around the table asking each of us for our candid opinion on troop strength. *Official White House photo by Pete Souza*

This was the final meeting to address the approach for reforming the "Don't Ask, Don't Tell" policy. *Official White House photo*

A 2010 meeting with President Obama in the Cabinet Room where I addressed nuclear preparedness. *Official White House photo by Pete Souza*

I had the extraordinary honor to award the Air Force Cross and Purple Heart to Staff Sergeant Zach Rhyner at Pope AFB near Fort Bragg, NC. Zach earned yet another Purple Heart during a subsequent tour of duty and he medically retired Aug. 21, 2015.
USAF photo

Military service is a team sport. Families support the service of their loved ones in so many ways. Here I shook hands with Jesse Bramblett at Little Rock AFB, AR. He and his mom experienced a tornado that damaged their home while Staff Sergeant Bramblett was deployed to Iraq. Suzie and I check on the family and the progress of repairs.
USAF photo by Airman 1st Class Rusty Frank

All of us stand on the shoulders of predecessors. General Lew Allen was the Chief of Staff of the Air Force during my first tour in Pentagon in 1980. Here I do my best, as a successor, to acknowledge and comfort his spouse on his passing at Arlington National Cemetary.
USAF photo by Senior Airman Marleah Miller

Nothing is as difficult as providing honors and comfort to the family of the fallen at a military funeral at Arlington National Cemetary. Here is a young man who will have only memories of his fallen father.
USAF photo

A solemn duty is to welcome the fallen home at Dover AFB, MD. On this night in Oct. 2009, the President, the Attorney General, and I welcome home eighteen U.S. casualties of war in Afghanistan.
Official White House photo by Pete Souza

One of the controversial matters the Joint Chiefs dealt with in 2010 was the potential repeal of the "Don't Ask, Don't Tell" policy. In addition to meetings at the White House, the Chiefs also testified before Congress. The final hearing with with the Senate Armed Services Committee in December, 2010. *USAF photo by Scott M. Ash*

Not my strong suit, but an essential part of the job was keeping the American people and the media well informed. Pentagon Press Room, January 2012. *DoD photo By Glenn Fawcett*

There are many hearings on Capitol Hill where a Service Chief must make his or her case for the needs of the Service. In this case, it was the House Armed Services Committee. Note then Maj Gen Lori Robinson over my right shoulder. She is now four-star General Robinson, Commander of U.S. Northern Command, the first female officer to command a major Unified Combatant Command in the history of the United States Armed Forces. *USAF photo by Jim Varhegyi*

Suzie and I shared the holidays with our Airmen. Here we celebrate the holidays with those on duty protecting our intercontinental ballistic missiles at F. E. Warren AFB, WY. *USAF Photo*

Spouse Clubs around the Air Force support all manner of worthy projects, including scholarships and sponsorships through their fund-raising activities. *Schwartz personal collection*

Suzie is always warm, friendly, and engaging. *USAF photo by Airman 1st Class Cory D. Payne*

Suzie cuts the ribbon for a renovated playground, reflecting her focus on the quality of our support to Air Force families.
USAF photo by Roland Balik

Preparing military members and spouses for leadership roles they may assume is an important responsibility. Suzie participated in many seminars for prospective Wing Commander spouses at Maxwell AFB, AL. *USAF photo by Wendy Simonds*

While I don't consider myself to be a particularly pious Jew, so often events or situations take me back to earlier times and remind me how significant those core Judaic principles—and traditions—are to my foundation. Here I light the menorah in the Hall of Heroes, at a Chanukah reception at the Pentagon.
Schwartz personal collection

A grand Air Force tradition is the "fini-flight." On July 12, 2012, I flew my last flight in MC-130E tail number 64-0568. It's an airplane I had flown extensively over the years and it was soon to be retired to the "Boneyard" in Arizona . . . somewhat like me. *USAF photo by TSgt Samuel King Jr.*

Nothing can surpass the joy of sharing that final flight with my girl, who had so much to do with making it all possible. The champagne tasted just fine too. *USAF photo by SSgt David Salanitri*

It doesn't get any better. *USAF photo by SSgt John Bainter*

My last day and final departure from the Pentagon after nearly forty years of service. I was surprised how emotional it turned out to be. When I saw Suzie at the bottom of the staircase at the River Entrance, I just lost it. *USAF photo by MSgt Cecilio Ricardo*

Neither one of us left anything in the gas tank. Mike Donley, Secretary of the Air Force, recognizes Suzie for her incredible dedication and service.
USAF photo by Scott M. Ash

Not to be outdone, Secretary of Defense Leon Panetta recognizes Suzie at the retirement ceremony as well. She was and remains a role model for military spouses everywhere. In retirement, she continues to mentor in the CAPSTONE course for new flag officer spouses.
USAF photo by Michael J. Pausic

Air House is the residence of the Air Force Chief of Staff at Ft. Myer, VA. It is one of seven homes on the hill at Ft. Myer, situated between the homes of the Vice Chairman and Chairman of the Joint Chiefs of Staff.
USAF photo

In retirement, I work for a well-regarded Washington nonprofit, Business Executives for National Security. In that capacity, I testified before the Senate Armed Services Committee in Dec. 2015 without the pressure routinely experienced on active duty.

going over the guest list for your pinning ceremony. Invitations should really go out by next week. Have you given any thought to who you'd like to do the pinning?"

"You know, having an Air Force special operator get his third star is not insignificant. Obviously it's a very big deal for us, but I'm talking about for the whole AFSOC family we've grown up with. I thought it would be fitting to have them enjoy the moment right along with us. Why don't we have it at Hurlburt? And there's nobody I'd be more honored to have officiate than . . ."

"General Hobson," Suzie interrupted. "I wish I'd thought of that," she said with a devilish smirk. Then she tossed me a prototype invitation that she'd drafted earlier that day. It read:

> *The Commander of the Twenty-third Air Force*
> *requests the pleasure of your company at a*
> *Promotion Ceremony*
> *In honor of*
> *Lieutenant General Norton A. Schwartz*
> *on January 12, 2000,*
> *at 9 o'clock*
> *Hurlburt Field, Florida*

General Hobson could not have been more appreciative when he accepted our invitation to conduct the pinning. Suzie worked her butt off to lock in all the arrangements. She coordinated the date with General Hobson's office as well as that of AFSOC commander Lt Gen Maxwell C. "Clay" Bailey, then ordered and subsequently sent out all the invitations. It promised to be a memorable event. Her taking care of everything so superbly allowed me to concentrate on wrapping things up at the Pentagon, which at this level meant a personal exit interview with the Chief, Mike Ryan.

It was a rather informal meeting in General Ryan's office, with the two of us sitting at the round table where he conducted many of his meetings. Like most of these exit interviews, this one was rather straightforward . . . until he began to wrap it up.

"So, who's going to do the pinning?" he asked.

"Well, General Ryan, I had asked Jim Hobson to do it. And we were thinking about doing it at Hurlburt."

He looked at me and he said, "Norty, the chief of staff has first dibs on three-star pinnings." I must have blanched because I should have been smart enough to know that, but I wasn't. It created rather an awkward moment. "No, I'm going to do the pinning," he stated calmly, as if that had been the case all along. "When did you say it's going to be?" he asked as he stood and walked over to the appointment book he kept next to the phone atop his immense desk. I told him the date and he scrawled it into the book.

"You know, I'm already locked in to fly to Europe that day—and there's no way that I can push that trip . . ."

Phew, dodged that bullet, I thought.

"Here's what I'm going to do . . . We are going to stop at Hurlburt en route to Europe and I'm going to do the pinning. Got it?"

"Got it, sir," I assured him.

I could not get home fast enough to give Suzie the news or to let Clay Bailey know what had occurred. "Holy crap, did I screw this up!" I blurted out to her.

I called Hobson to explain what had happened, then Clay Bailey, since this was playing out on his station. And Suzie, bless her, took care of everything else—as usual.

★ ★ ★

Suzie and I finished packing and were fully prepared to bid farewell to DC's frigid sub-zero January mornings. I looked around and gave the place one final survey.

"Looks good to me, let's hit the road," Suzie declared, anxious to be welcomed by the ninety-degree heat wave that had just hit Tampa.

"Hang on just a sec, I think we missed something."

Sticking out from behind the stairwell was a long, well-worn rod of some kind. I picked it up and smiled. Not much use for a snow shovel where we were headed.

"Give it to me," Suzie demanded, grabbing it and ferrying it out to a substantial stack of overstuffed boxes beside the driveway. "Might as well let someone get good use out of it." She tossed it on top, just beside a handwritten sign that read To BE PICKED UP BY GOODWILL.

★ ★ ★

Once the big day arrived, all had been forgotten and it was a glorious moment inside the big hanger at Hurlburt. The crowd was even larger than we had expected, and General Ryan did a wonderful job. Mrs. Ryan was there, too. Sharing the moment with our family in the community was one of the smartest decisions we ever made. By the time the last piece of cake was finished and the cleanup crew stepped in, General Ryan was well on his way to Europe and we were headed to Tampa to get to work.

We passed through the Bayshore gate at MacDill and were escorted to what we expected to be our home for the next two years—perhaps five if I were to be promoted and take over as commander after Pete retired in two years. It was a gorgeous house near the water at 2132 Staff Circle, surrounded by palm trees in a picture-perfect postcard setting. CENTCOM Commander in Chief General Tony Zinni's house was directly across the driveway, and General Schoomaker's was on the Bayshore end of the block, directly facing the bay.

Working with Pete did not disappoint. While he enjoyed staying actively involved in operations, his guidance was for me to focus on the budget side (resources and acquisition) as well as issues of staff performance. At this time Doug Brown was JSOC commander, so remarkably, you had this group of captains from the Desert One era now positioned as the senior leadership of the special operations community. As it turned out, I had a natural proclivity for budgeting issues, so it all worked out quite nicely.

The SEALS had long been expressing the need for a self-contained, stealthy submersible with which they could conduct long-range insertions of special operations forces on sensitive missions—an entirely enclosed mini-sub, as it were. For years they'd had "open" mini-subs of the wet variety, but, being "open," the combat swimmers' long exposure to cold water during the transit period impeded combat readiness upon their arrival. An enclosed environment would also allow for an enhanced underwater navigational capability, something that was lacking in the open SDVs (SEAL delivery vehicles). Ultimately, Northrup Grumman was contracted to develop and deliver the Advanced SEAL Delivery System, or ASDS.

The sixty-five-foot, sixty-ton mini-sub was built to accommodate the SEALs, including two operators. It would ride piggyback on much larger attack submarines until its release for independent propulsion to the insertion point.

When I stepped in, it was beset with problems. It was intended to be a type of stealth vehicle, but the propellers generated so much noise that the chances of any surreptitious approach would be highly unlikely. If that weren't bad enough, there were severe deficiencies in the silver-zinc batteries that caused them to deplete far more quickly than required for the mission.

I spent a fair amount of time trying to right that project. For starters, was it something that we still believed was needed? If so, were there realistic—and affordable—ways to correct its many deficiencies?

In my opinion, Northrup Grumman really was not a submersible builder, so they had a steep learning curve to even operate effectively in this field. The time delays were unacceptable and cost overruns approached epic proportions. The original projection called for six subs at a total cost of $527 million, with the first delivery to take place in 2000. By the time they delivered the first sub in 2003, costs had spiraled to a staggering $885 million. Three years later that would jump to almost $2 billion.

The good news is that ultimately they were able to come up with a material that obviated the propeller noise problem. The same could not be said for the battery issue. After many years, the endurance and heat management issues still precluded its ability to operate effectively in the field. Ultimately, this led to the program's demise.

In November of 2008, while the unit was being recharged at its Pearl City home port, the batteries started sparking and the vehicle became engulfed in flames. By the end of the day, the repair estimate came to $237 million. Eight months later, SOCOM came to the conclusion that the deficiencies were so severe that it was not worth investing additional resources. The project died.

On the personnel side, there were concerns from both DoD and the media that we had not worked diligently enough to have a sufficiently diverse team. At the time, the major concern was African Americans, and later women. Pete agreed, and our challenge was to work with the service components to energize their efforts to assess a more diverse cadre of operators. This had the attention of the vice chairman, General Joe Ralston, who challenged USSOCOM to be more creative and effective in recruiting and retention efforts.

General Schoomaker convened the leadership of the community to make diversity a priority. "It's time to recognize that effectively connecting with foreign audiences increasingly requires a broader array of experiences, backgrounds, and language skills," he asserted to the leaders of the respective components, both joint and service specific (Army, Navy, Air Force). He scanned the assemblage, which at the time consisted entirely of white males. "Look around you and tell me that we don't have a problem with diversity."

It was a good beginning. We then set about invigorating the recruiting and retention efforts to make minority outreach and recruiting—and career path management for SOF operators—a commander priority. These efforts continue with the SEALS and pilots in particular.

Chapter Five

THEY MUST HAVE
THE WRONG SCHWARTZ

SEPTEMBER *2000–AUGUST 2008*

Eight months later the temperature was in the nineties when the phone rang. I picked up and heard, "Hold for the Chief of Staff of the Air Force," followed by the voice of General Mike Ryan. "Norty, pack your bags. Charlie Holland's getting SOCOM and you'll be moving to Alaska for the Stevens' account." The "Stevens' account" referred to a "three-hatted" command based in Anchorage, Alaska. I was being reassigned to take over the Alaskan Command, the regional NORAD command, and the 11th Air Force.

I thanked him, disconnected, and called downstairs to Suzie. "The Chief called and he said we're going to Alaska."

Suzie yelled back up, "They must have the wrong Schwartz!"

Sure wish we'd have kept that snow shovel, I thought.

I glanced outside as a gust of wind caught the palm trees lining our street. They all swayed in unison, as if to mock the irony of the call.

Later that week Suzie bumped into Pete Schoomaker loading up his truck in the back alleyway behind our houses, and she had tears in her eyes. "I don't want to go to Alaska, there's no special operations there. I love everything about this life here."

Schoomaker said to her, "Suzie, the reality is you are never coming back. The Air Force has bigger plans for Norty but they will no longer involve special operations." She felt like a piece of her heart had just been removed. I tend to be more staid, but Suzie took it very personally—not just for herself, but for me, because she knew my entire professional life had in one way or another been connected to special operations. These were our people, our family. I felt disappointed, too, but by this time I had long since learned to get beyond it. I recognize it, accept it, and quickly move on. Her emotions won't allow her to do that. It's another reason why we're so good for one another. Looking back, I now realize that this wasn't just Pete's spin on how my career would play out. He'd been privy to inside conversations and meetings where these things are discussed—and determined, for that matter. This was not merely speculation on his part—it was inside information. But of course we didn't know that at the time.

★ ★ ★

I had been assured that Alaska was a prestige assignment and everyone who had gone before me went on to get their fourth star. Somewhat to our surprise, it turned out to be one of our favorite assignments, but simultaneously overseeing *three commands* was no small task. Between Alaskan Command, Alaskan North American Aerospace Defense Command Region, and 11th Air Force at Elmendorf, I had my hands full.

★ ★ ★

9/11/2001: While the world is well aware of the two planes that crashed into the World Trade Center and the third into the Pentagon, most have never heard of Korean Air Flight 85, a 747 with over two hundred passengers onboard en route to Anchorage. I had just put eight fighter jets on high alert when I got word that KAL 85 had reported being hijacked, and when asked to confirm, they did so by transmitting the international hijack transponder code.

We scrambled two armed F-15s to intercept them, then established direct radio contact with the pilots to confirm our rules of engagement. "Recognize this voice," I commanded, "and know that this is the only voice that can give you authority to engage the target and shoot it down. Do you copy?" In the event it became necessary for them to fire their missiles to destroy the 747 packed with innocent civilians, I wanted that responsibility to be 100 percent on my head, not theirs. The airplane was headed in my direction, and ultimately running low on fuel.

After directing an intentionally circuitous routing, I picked up the phone and called my counterpart from the Canadian NORAD region, Lieutenant General Angus Watt, who would go on to become the Canadian chief of air staff (now president and CEO of the Canadian Air Transport Security Authority, similar to our TSA).

"Angus, I need to take KAL 85 into Whitehorse."

"You want to do *what*? That's a potential hijack and you want to bring it here?"

"Here's the deal," I said. "I'm becoming skeptical about the hijack element, but either way, they don't have enough fuel to make it back to Anchorage or Fairbanks after our attempt to redirect the aircraft to Yakutat in southeast Alaska. Whitehorse is a right place and with your permission we will provide a fighter escort for it all the way to touchdown."

He knew that this was the real deal and that we needed his help. And of course the Canadians were tremendously supportive of diverting aircraft from U.S. airspace.

"Stand by, I've got to go upstairs with this. I'll get back to you," he said before disconnecting. My assumption was that he had to get ministry approval, if not even higher. He did get right back to me, and agreed to allow the plane into Whitehorse—as long as we provided the escort and maintained control in Canadian airspace.

The fighters stuck with it right up to the moment when the wheels safely touched down onto the runway, then they engaged full throttle and made steep climbing turns to the west. The Royal Canadian mounted police surrounded the airplane and the crew was taken off. They confirmed that it was not, in fact, a hijack, but rather a mistaken signal.

Had the crew not adhered to the air traffic control instructions as precisely as they had, it might have turned out differently. I was fully prepared to shoot the airplane down; I was not going to have a repetition of what happened on the East Coast. And we had authorization to make that call. Ed Eberhart, commander of NORAD, had communicated to me that we had authority to declare targets hostile and engage them according to the standing rules of engagement, and so we proceeded according to that guidance. But he did accompany the authorization with the admonition not to be precipitous. Those words still ring in my ear. Very crisp, very clear. "Don't be precipitous," he warned.

The takeaway is that we performed professionally, dispassionately, and with diligence, and it turned out that our restraint was justified.

In the weeks that followed, it was clear that life around that base would never be the same. Secure phones showed up in places where there had never been secure phones before. Secure VTCs (video teleconferences) became daily events. There were new protocols for how to handle potential hijacked airplanes and how to avoid creating debris over populated areas—lots of procedures came into being that had not existed prior to 9/11. It was an exciting thing to be a part of, and those procedures are still practiced today.

★   ★   ★

It took seven high-level interviews for Donald Rumsfeld to approve me as the J-3 (director for operations) on the chairman's Joint Staff at the Pentagon. Two months later, he was so upset with me I was certain I'd be fired.

The Joint Chiefs of Staff (JCS) is a body of senior uniformed leaders in the Department of Defense who advise the president, the secretary of defense, and the National Security Council on military matters. The chairman of the Joint Chiefs of Staff (CJCS) serves as principal military advisor to the president and SECDEF. To understand how the chairman is able to ensure the personnel readiness, policy, planning, and training of an organization consisting of over two million men and women (2017 = 1,281,900 active duty, 801,200 reserve) with an annual budget of $600 billion (FY 2015 = $597 billion), it's helpful to understand the basic structure of the Joint Chiefs.

Under the chairman are the vice chairman (VCJCS) and four service chiefs (each a four-star flag officer), who represent the various military branches, and the chief of the National Guard Bureau:

Service Chiefs
Chief of Staff of the United States Air Force
Chief of Staff of the United States Army
Chief of Naval Operations
Commandant of the Marine Corps
Chief of the National Guard Bureau

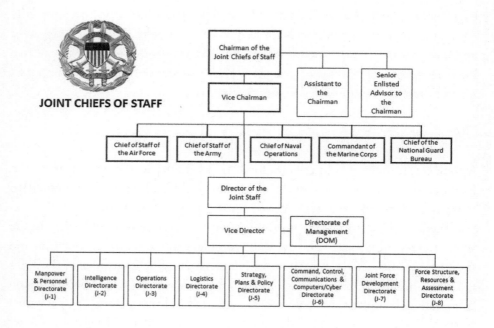

JOINT CHIEFS OF STAFF

J-1	Personnel and Manpower
J-2	Intelligence
J-3	Operations
J-4	Logistics
J-5	Strategic Plans and Policy
J-6	Command, Control, Communications and Computers/Cyber
J-7	Operational Plans and Joint Force Development
J-8	Force Structure, Resources, and Assessment

Assisting the chairman and vice chairman is the Joint Staff, about a thousand exceptional officers and civilians from the Air Force, Army, Navy, and Marines—many of whom have advanced degrees from top universities. The director of the Joint Staff (DJS), a three-star flag officer, manages the Joint Staff much like the chief of staff of any organization.

The J-3 (director for operations) assists the chairman as principal advisor to the president and SECDEF in the area of current operations and plans. As the senior officer of the Operations Directorate and member of the Joint Staff, the J-3 works very closely with the Joint Chiefs. Supervising over three hundred employees at the Pentagon and providing guidance to combatant commanders on every U.S. military operation anywhere in the world, it's often considered the most important—and demanding—three-star staff job in the military.

Suzie and I had thoroughly enjoyed our two years in Alaska—surprisingly so, in fact. I'd been told that we would be leaving and coming back to Washington, and the scuttlebutt was that I was about to be assigned to the top Air Force operations position, the AF/XO (now called A-3). If those rumors were true, that would place me on the Air Staff as one of the senior leaders of the Air Force, reporting directly to the chief of staff—General John Jumper at the time. A fighter pilot and past commander of Air Combat Command, Jumper also served as senior military assistant to two secretaries of defense. Working so closely with him would be a tremendous learning opportunity for me.

It was sweltering hot on a bright summer day when General Jumper called me at Elmendorf AFB to officially advise me of the new position. (In Anchorage, Alaska, that meant it was in the midfifties.)

"Norty, looks like you're coming back to the building," he said. "They want you to fly out and interview with the boss."

"Sir, if I'm not mistaken, you're the boss," I said, not really following where he was going with this.

"Not if you ask my wife, I'm not. Secretary Rumsfeld has requested a meeting."

Now this was making even less sense. "Sir, if I may ask . . . since when does the SECDEF get so involved with Air Force staff selections?"

"Norty, you're not under consideration for the Air Staff; you've got quite the constituency of advocates who believe you would make an outstanding J-3. Myself included, by the way."

I did not see this coming, and getting that job would be a game changer. It meant bypassing the Air Force operations position and working directly for the chairman on the Joint Staff. That is, if the interview with Rumsfeld went well. While I certainly had great respect for the man, from what I'd heard, that meeting could be a real challenge.

I immediately began prepping for the interview, as best I could. I reviewed Rumsfeld's history and considered what I had heard of his agenda, as well as the demands of the J-3 job. I researched reports, books, and articles to see what others had to say about him, reviewed *Congressional Record* and C-Span videos to glean insight from his testimonies, and read as many press clippings as I could secure: *Washington Post, Wall Street Journal, Military Times*, and the *New York Times*, in which Elaine Sciolino and Eric Schmitt had written a thorough overview just prior to him assuming the office in 2001: Eagle Scout . . . NROTC at Princeton where he was captain of his football and wrestling teams . . . political science degree . . . naval aviator . . . young congressman from Illinois . . . early proponent of all-volunteer military . . . served as Ford's chief of staff and subsequently secretary of defense—the youngest to have held that office . . . fought hard for increased military spending (including development of cruise missile and B-1 bomber) . . . ultra-organized . . . politically adept . . . master bureaucrat . . . CEO of two Fortune 500 companies . . . philosophy on the military: "'You can be provocative by being belligerent, and you can also be provocative by being too weak and thereby enticing others into adventures they would otherwise avoid" . . . structured workplace culture . . . highly disciplined, no excuses—I liked that . . . takes the Boy Scout motto "Be prepared" to the extreme—if you're not, watch out. Finally, I picked up—and thoroughly enjoyed—*Rumsfeld's Rules*, a witty and poignant collection of reflections and quotations he had consolidated over the past forty years. A few samples:

- Don't be a bottleneck. If a matter is not a decision for the president or you, delegate it. Force responsibility down and out. Find problem areas, add structure, and delegate. The pressure is to do the reverse. Resist it.
- "First law of holes: If you get in one, stop digging."
- "History marches to the drum of a clear idea." (W. H. Auden)
- When cutting staff at the Pentagon, don't eliminate the thin layer that assures civilian control.
- "If you get the objectives right, a lieutenant can write the strategy." (General George Marshall)
- [As secretary of defense . . .] Reserve the right to get into anything and exercise it. Make your deputies and staff realize that, although many responsibilities are delegated, no one should be surprised when the Secretary engages on an important issue.

I called vice chairman Pete Pace for pre-interview pointers. Pete had served as J-3 under General Hugh Shelton (my old boss when Shelton commanded SO-COM), and would go on to become the first chairman from the Marine Corps. Loyal, smart, and seldom seen without a smile, Pete is one of those guys who it's impossible not to like. He has always made the time to share his keen perceptions with me—guidance that has consistently steered me in the right direction. We spoke for over an hour about what it takes to meet the demands of the J-3 position without allowing it—or the bureaucracy of the building—to eat away at you to the point of diminishing your effectiveness and taking a toll on you personally.

"Just relax, and don't be too intimidated by him," he counseled. "Good luck, Norty."

"Thank you, sir. I'll let you know how it goes."

I then called Lieutenant General Greg Newbold, then the serving J-3. Greg had held the position since October 2000, which put him smack in the center of the 9/11 storm. You'd never guess from Greg's slight build that he was the tough Marine infantry commander who led the first boatload into Mogadishu in 1992, then went on to command the 1st Marine Division. I'd heard that there had been friction between the three-star and the SECDEF, but those were mostly just rumors until Greg went public with an op-ed in *Time* a few years after his retirement, followed up in even greater detail by David Margolick's "Night of the Generals" piece in *Vanity Fair.*

"It was not a secret that Rumsfeld and I were not on our respective Christmas-card lists," Greg shared with Margolick. The article continues:

> . . . the secretary of defense once abused him so badly that he was moved to complain to Rumsfeld's senior military assistant, Admiral Edmund Giambastiani. If Rumsfeld ever so disrespected him again, Newbold said, he would "put his stars on the table"—that is, resign. "And Admiral Giambastiani said, 'Oh, Greg, you know, it's too bad, but that's the way he deals with people, and he doesn't mean anything by it. It's just his style.' And [Newbold] said, 'It isn't with me. You make sure he knows it.'"

In the course of our phone call, Greg was candid about the demands of the position; his deep, distinctive, baritone voice familiar to many from his Pentagon press briefings, yet another task that's often undertaken by the J-3. He concluded with a perspective not unlike the one Giambastiani had shared with him: "Just relax and don't let him get to you. It's just his style and he pretty much treats everyone that way."

Somewhere between Pete's "don't be too intimidated by him" and Newbold's "he pretty much treats everyone like that," I started to wonder whether prudence dictated that I wear body armor to the interview, rather than the customary dress blues.

I arrived in Washington a day early, which allowed for some final preparation and a good night's rest in the DV (distinguished visitor) quarters at Fort Myer, just north of the Pentagon. For some reason I had the misconception that the interview day would consist of a vigorous early morning run followed by a light breakfast, then a short drive to the Pentagon for my interview with Secretary Rumsfeld. Not even close. Turned out to be more of a forced march. Seven sequential interviews with seven different "screeners" in seven different offices. Had I known that I'd be hustling through the 17.5 miles of corridors from one meeting to the next, I might have forgone that morning run.

First up was Ken Krieg, executive secretary of the Senior Executive Council. Until I read the plaque affixed to Ken's door, I had made it through almost thirty years of military service without even knowing that we had a Senior Executive Council. That would also be the last time I heard of it. Ken was one of Rumsfeld's special advisors and a trusted member of his inner circle. Not long after our meeting, he'd be promoted to undersecretary for acquisition, technology, and logistics where he oversaw every DoD purchase from $6 billion aircraft carriers to Wrigley's for the vending machines. Good man, good interview. We spent about an hour together—all the while Krieg was taking copious notes—then he stood, shook hands, and informed me that I was to meet with Ray DuBois, another special advisor to the secretary, with an even longer title—two of them, in fact. Besides his responsibilities as director of administration and management and principal staff assistant for manpower, real estate, and organizational planning, Ray was concurrently director of Washington Headquarters Services—commonly referred to as the "Mayor of the Pentagon"—no small task as he directly managed twenty-five hundred employees and a $1.3 billion budget. Ray would go on to become undersecretary of the Army. Like Ken in the prior interview, after every one of my responses, Ray would pause and scribble something onto his notepad. I didn't think too much about it at first, but as the day progressed, I noticed that almost everyone I met with had the same ritual. I'd say something and they'd write it down. Strange.

The interviews continued as I was led from one civilian advisor to another, then finally taken in for a short visit with Deputy Secretary of Defense Paul Wolfowitz. Surely this would be my final stop before being escorted to the secretary's office, just a stone's throw down the third floor E-ring corridor.

Wolfowitz had been undersecretary of defense for policy under George H. W. Bush during the 1991 Persian Gulf War, after which he made no secret of his belief that Saddam could have been eliminated had it not been for a premature ceasefire. This became a recurring theme that escalated in the days immediately following 9/11, when he, along with Secretary Rumsfeld and Vice President Cheney, advocated regime change in Iraq. Hugh Shelton was chairman at the time. In his own autobiography, *Without Hesitation: The Odyssey of an American Warrior*, Shelton details how this unfolded in a series of high-level meetings between September 12 and September 15, 2001. There were two White House meetings on September 12, the first of which took place in the Cabinet Room. General Shelton describes what transpired behind closed doors, as President Bush was briefed on all that was known about the attacks:

> Needless to say it was a very somber meeting—probably about as serious a meeting as I've ever seen. Andy Card was present, as was the Secretary of the Treasury, the Attorney General, Scooter Libby, Condoleezza [Rice] and her deputy, Steve Hadley, and many more. . . . I was at the far end of the long table, immediately to the left of the vice president, who had the president on his right side, next to Colin Powell [secretary of state at the time]. . . .
>
> First, George Tenet [director of Central Intelligence, CIA] said that everything clearly pointed to al Qaeda. . . . Bob Mueller [director of FBI] shared that 100 percent of what he had pointed to UBL [Usama bin Laden]. [We went around the room and at some point] Rumsfeld and Wolfowitz started pushing hard to attack Iraq. In their minds, this disaster could be turned around into an ideal opportunity to end the problems we were having with Saddam.

By the time I walked into deputy's office in August of 2002, the president's sights were focusing in on Iraq. Operation SOUTHERN WATCH—the military response to violations of the southern Iraqi no-fly zones—was long underway;

from June until the war began in March of 2003, we flew 21,736 sorties over southern Iraq, attacking just under 350 targets. James Baker (secretary of state under Bush 41) had just written an op-ed in the *New York Times* in which he outlined what he believed would be required to institute a regime change in Iraq, including the following on the issue of troop strength:

> The only realistic way to effect regime change in Iraq is through the application of military force, including sufficient ground troops to occupy the country (including Baghdad), depose the current leadership and install a successor government. Anyone who thinks we can effect regime change in Iraq with anything less than this is simply not realistic. It cannot be done on the cheap. It will require substantial forces and substantial time to put those forces in place to move. We had over 500,000 Americans, and more soldiers from our many allies, for the Persian Gulf war.

Wolfowitz would publicly reject this advice, instead advocating much smaller numbers both for the war itself and the subsequent occupation of the country. In February 2003, General Eric Shinseki estimated that "several hundred thousand soldiers" would most likely be required for the postwar occupation. Wolfowitz challenged that estimate in his testimony before the House Budget Committee, when he countered that fewer than 100,000 troops would be required. It wouldn't be long before Congress would draw me into this contentious issue of troop strength. How it played out nearly derailed my confirmation as chief of the Air Force. More on that to come.

My meeting with Deputy SECDEF Wolfowitz was short and cordial. In no time I was finally heading down the hall toward the distinctive blue flag and wall-mounted seal that identified the entrance to suite 3E880; the brass plaque affixed to the ornate wooden entry door read DONALD H. RUMSFELD. SECRETARY OF DEFENSE.

I approached the nearest of four desks, each of which was occupied by a thoroughly engrossed assistant who brought order to the horde of calls, correspondence, and every sort of administrative task that ended up in the highest office of the Department of Defense. I smiled at the smartly dressed woman seated behind the desk as she concluded a phone call on one of the two sophisticated phone devices immediately beside her oversized computer monitor.

"Good afternoon, Lt General Schwartz to see Secretary Rumsfeld," I said.

She looked up and returned the smile with the confident demeanor of a protective gatekeeper who took seriously her responsibility of insulating the boss from those who inappropriately tried to gain access, either on the phone or in person. Considering the heightened security surrounding the building after 9/11, the "crashers" were predominantly pre-credentialed regulars who felt entitled to forgo the appointment process and "drop by" for a quick tête-à-tête: legislators, lobbyists, defense contractors, and of course the press. But they were no match for Arlene Nestel, who always had the boss's back. It was really no different than the corporate world, where she served the same function for Rumsfeld in Chicago before accompanying him to Washington when he took the job as the leader of the Department of Defense and principal defense policy advisor to the president.

"Good to see you, sir," she began. "But I'm afraid the secretary didn't make it in today. He's still recovering from some minor surgery on his thumb he had earlier in the week."

I thought: *After flying over four thousand miles (including connections) and enduring a half a dozen pre-meetings, he's not even going to meet with me?*

"But he does very much look forward to seeing you today," she said, obviously having picked up on my disappointment. "We'll have a car drive you to his home so that you two can have some private time without all the interruptions that seem to pop up around here." She then glanced over my shoulder. "But first, I believe the admiral would like to spend a few minutes with you. General, have you met Vice Admiral Giambastiani, the secretary's senior military assistant?"

Wearing bright Navy summer whites, Ed Giambastiani's gold wire-rimmed glasses projected an intellectual aptitude that would continue to be reinforced the more I got to know him. At fifty-four, he was still in excellent shape; his thinning hair had not yet begun to display the strands of gray that would appear in just a few years, once he became vice chairman and head of the Pentagon's powerful Joint Requirements Oversight Council, a vital link in the process of deciding which new weapons programs would go forward. "Good to see you, Norty," he said with a broad smile and firm handshake that were naturally welcoming. "Come on in and let's see if we can solve the problems of the world."

"I look forward to that," I replied, following him into a small conference room within the SECDEF's suite of offices. We didn't know each other well at this point, but I'd always found his background in submarine warfare to be impressive, likewise his keen grasp of military budgets and programs.

"Have a seat and make yourself comfortable," he said, gesturing to one of six thick brown leather chairs surrounding a well-polished mahogany table. It was barren, except for a single unopened bottle of water next to a yellow pad and pencil at the spot that he had indicated. Unlike the day's prior sessions which entailed exclusively verbal interplay, once I took a seat the admiral—still standing—presented me with a challenge:

"It's 2:10 a.m. and you are now the J-3. You've been asleep for hours when you're jarred awake by the bedside red switch phone. Get used to it—an uninterrupted night of sleep is *not* a perk that comes with this job. It's the NMCC DDO [National Military Command Center Deputy Director of Operations] advising you that there has just been a confirmed UBL sighting in the Kunar province of Afghanistan. So what I want you to do now is prepare a briefing sheet for the secretary, along with your recommendations on potential courses of action." He paused and just stared at me for a beat. "Any questions?"

"None, sir. Got it," I snapped back.

With a quick nod of approval he headed for the door, then turned back toward me. "I'll be back in thirty minutes. Good luck."

It struck me that not even a year had passed since the acrid smoke of 9/11 filled the very suite in which I sat, a fact that somehow made my assignment feel more like a premonition than a fictional exercise. It was a realistic scenario that could very well fall under my watch if I were to get the J-3 position. Glancing down at the blank pad of paper, I knew that as fast as those thirty minutes would fly by in this exercise, a real-world situation would require far swifter action. I took a deep breath and let history be my guide—roughing out various options based on responses that had been utilized in the past:

- Cruise missiles—They'd been used by President Clinton following the 1998 U.S. embassy bombings in Tanzania and Kenya, and it was realistic to assume that we had platforms in place from which a similar strike could be launched today. (As J-3, I'd be well aware of such positioning.)
- Predator strike—Although still in their embryonic stage, unmanned aerial vehicles (UAVs) were already an option to consider. In his autobiography, George Tenet shared how the CIA believed they had spotted UBL on a Predator trial run in September 2000, but that was *before* the devices were armed, so they were forced to go the cruise missile route. By the time the missiles arrived on target, bin Laden had departed and once again slipped

off the grid. Just a few months earlier, the Air Force had been given direction to explore the possibility of arming the aircraft (under its BIG SAFARI program). Wings were reinforced to handle the added load of munitions, and laser designators were installed to maximize targeting capability. Systems were refined as testing ensued near Indian Springs, Nevada. Once perfected, the armed Predator was given the new designation of MQ-1A. Even before 9/11, Hellfire missile simulated attacks were conducted on an approximate replica of UBL's complex in Tarnak, Afghanistan, that was built on one of the Air Force Nevada test sites. But it wasn't until early October 2001 that the United States received host nation approval to fly armed Predators. On October 7, 2001, such flights began.

I refined these options and included a few more—spending the bulk of my limited time compacting the data to a concise format that I believed would best serve the SECDEF's need to make an immediate, informed decision.

I wouldn't be surprised if it was thirty minutes to the second when I heard the admiral's voice in the doorway. "How are you coming, Norty?" he asked.

"You tell me, sir," I said as I stood and presented him with the brief that I'd prepared—about three pages handwritten on the yellow legal pad. "I'm hoping this would serve the SECDEF well."

"I'll be surprised if it doesn't," he replied even before looking at the brief. "Are you ready to meet the boss?" he asked, my cue to follow him down the stairway immediately outside the suite and out through the River Entrance, where a black SUV was waiting to transport me to Secretary Rumsfeld's residence.

Greek for "beautiful view," the Kalorama neighborhood of Washington, DC, is one of the wealthiest residential communities in the United States. William Howard Taft, Woodrow Wilson, Warren Harding, Herbert Hoover, and Franklin D. Roosevelt all lived there before or after their time at 1600 Pennsylvania Avenue; on January 20, 2017, while Donald Trump was being sworn in as our forty-fifth president, a fleet of moving vans was transporting the Obama family possessions from the White House to their new home within its borders—ironically, just a block away from where Ivanka Trump and Jared Kushner had recently moved in. I was finally about to meet with Donald Rumsfeld at his home on Kalorama Road.

"It's just up ahead, sir," said the government driver who was shuttling me from the Pentagon to the interview. We passed a stately beige edifice on my right—the red, white, blue, white, red horizontal stripes on its flag identifying it as the Royal Thai Embassy—then made a slight jog onto Kalorama Road. While I naturally had assumed the secretary would live in an impressive residence (after all, he'd run three major corporations in the private sector), the expansive estate that we approached was beyond my wildest expectation. A chateau in the Tudor Revival style, I'd later learn that its 27,000 square feet of living space had nineteen bedrooms and twelve bathrooms. I'd also learn that it was *not* the Rumsfeld abode. "That's actually the French ambassador's home," the driver clarified with a hint of a grin. "The secretary's home is right across the street." He pulled into the driveway of the federal style brownstone, parked, and walked around to open my door. Over five thousand square feet with seven bedrooms and six and a half baths, the home was impressive nonetheless.

Following another interview with LTG John Craddock (who was interviewing for the position of senior military advisor to the SECDEF, which he ultimately got), I was led to a spacious garden room at the rear of the home. Bright and airy, it was an enclosed patio of sorts, with white lattice walls, a vermilion sofa, distressed antique tables, and a pair of white ceiling fans that kept the room comfortable in spite of the harsh summer sunlight that reflected off the swimming pool and into the makeshift study.

The secretary rose as I entered the room; at five feet seven inches tall, he was shorter than he came across on TV, yet certainly every bit as imposing. With a squint of his eyes and a warm smile, he simultaneously extended his right hand to shake mine while raising his left, which was heavily bandaged. "Serves me right for too much hitchhiking during my younger days," he deadpanned, with the same sarcastic wit we'd witness in the coming four years. "Good to meet you, General."

"A real pleasure, sir," I replied.

He gestured toward the red sofa where I sat across from him for the next hour, talking about my background, Special Ops, and 9/11. It was an informal, comfortable exchange, with his only apparent "reference material" being a single manila file folder that he retrieved from his desktop. Scanning the dozen or so pages, he gave a slight nod and mumbled, half to himself and half to me, "Tough game today but it appears you slammed it out of the ballpark." It suddenly struck me that all the writing that took place in each of the day's meetings was actually contemporaneous notes for the SECDEF's review prior to my meeting with him. I felt it went fairly well, and I certainly did not experience any of the tension I'd heard so much about.

Later I would find out that Ron Keys—another Air Force three-star who was in Europe at the time—was also in prime contention for the J-3 position. Ultimately, it played out that Ron became the XO of the Air Force and I ended up with the incredible honor—and responsibility—of the J-3 slot.

Suzie and I headed back to Washington in early October 2002, and thus began the busiest and most demanding two years of my career—of my life. Those two years would be the only time in my life, since I was eighteen years old, that daily runs would not be a routine part of my early-morning ritual. They were sorely missed, but on many days there was just no time. I would awaken at 3:30 a.m., be in my second-floor, D-ring Pentagon office not later than 5:30 a.m., work nonstop for the next fifteen hours or so, then hop into my car for the twenty-minute drive back to our home at 64 Westover Avenue SW, Bolling AFB, where I'd join Suzie for a quick dinner and be in bed by 9:00 p.m.

The saving grace was the extraordinary group of officers with whom I worked. Dick Myers was the chairman and Pete Pace was his vice. I worked extensively with Pete, and he coached me along the way. Being a former J-3 himself, he was fine-tuned to my challenges and I sought out his counsel frequently. John Abizaid was the director of the Joint Staff for the first few months until George Casey (eventually Army chief of staff) moved across the table from his J-5 (strategy, plans and policy) slot to become director. Hoss Cartwright was the J-8 (force structure, resources, and assessment). Air Force Maj Gen Glen Shaffer was the J-2 (intelligence) initially and then Army MG Ron Burgess stepped in. BG Stan McChrystal was my vice—he'd already been there for a few months when I arrived, and he would move on to become Commanding General of JSOC in September 2003. Former Secretary of Defense Bob Gates called Stan "perhaps the finest warrior and leader of men in combat I have ever met," and he certainly served me well as my vice. The truth is that I was grateful to work side by side with all these exceptional officers from across the service branches. It's a good thing, since I'd see far more of them than I saw of Suzie. But she understood the mission, and as difficult as it must have been for her, she never uttered a single complaint. Coincidentally, about a month after we arrived, Ron and Valerie Keys moved into the general officer quarters immediately next to ours—affording us the opportunity to have frequent talks and family gatherings on the patio.

By the time I arrived in October of 2002, the preparations for war were already well underway. There'd be no time for me to come up to speed with this job; I'd have to dive in head first. Boxes would be left unpacked, pictures unhung. In my first few weeks:

- CENTCOM was in the midst of a war game for the demise of the Iraqi regime.
- Fourteen hundred U.S. Special Operations troops, along with personnel from Jordan, Oman, Kuwait, and Great Britain, were in Jordan honing their skills in EXERCISE EARLY VICTOR '02.
- While the hunt for UBL (that's how we in the DoD commonly referred to Osama bin Laden) was in full force, other al-Qaeda operatives gained prominence and demanded our attention and resources. Al-Jazeera broadcast an audiotape from al-Qaeda's Ayman al-Zawahiri in which he claimed responsibility for the April synagogue bombing on Djerba Island, Tunisia, as well as the May 11 suicide car bombing in Karachi.
- The chairman (General Myers) issued the planning order for air and ground operations from Turkey.
- Two Kuwaiti gunmen (trained by al-Qaeda in Afghanistan) opened fire on U.S. Marines during maneuvers on Kuwait's Falaika Island. One marine was killed and another wounded before fellow marines leveled both attackers.
- Both the House and Senate approved resolutions authorizing President Bush to take military action against Iraq.

Force planning was largely led by CENTCOM and its commander, General Tommy Franks, but a good deal of work on that front was also taking place in the Pentagon. On October 31, 2002, General Franks published (within the Pentagon) OPLAN 1003V, the (then classified) battle plan for the invasion of Iraq. Carefully conceived and comprehensively charting fresh approaches to a large-scale, major theater war plan that had been on the shelf since 1998, the plan still required much work to be done before the president would deem it worthy of sending hundreds of thousands of our sons and daughters into harm's way. That was J-3 business, and the bulk of my time was spent in the ramp-up to the war, hashing out the battle plan with my counterpart at CENTCOM, Air Force Major General Gene Renuart. (Gene would go on to earn his fourth star and command NORAD and USNORTHCOM.) Finalizing the forces required to execute that plan was a major focus, but not my exclusive one. Afghanistan continued to percolate, and that was within my purview; I also had responsibility for the nuclear deterrent, security for domestic airspace, and every current U.S. military operation/mission anywhere in the world.

One of those functions entailed my presenting the SECDEF (Rumsfeld at this time) with every set of deployment orders or execute orders that required his signature. It's important to understand that the chairman doesn't own forces and cannot deploy a single troop overseas in his own name. Every order to transfer forces and change command relationships must be signed by the secretary of defense. It's the very essence of civilian control of the military, and yet another precious doctrine conceived by our founding fathers that makes this country great.

The mechanism we used to obtain the secretary's authorization for these actions was a Friday afternoon meeting where the J-3 would walk the orders upstairs to the secretary's office and secure the SECDEF's signature on a written authorization called a deployment order (DEPORD), which would then be issued by the chairman. The process usually began weeks—if not months— earlier as the highly skilled action officers would interface with the service branches to identify force sourcing, deployment timetables, geographics, rules of engagement, and a multitude of other details that would be folded into the order. As J-3, I would have the staff consolidate this material into a big black notebook we called the Secretary of Defense Operations Book, or simply "the Book" for short. Once approved, we would copy the contents and assemble about a dozen identical black three-ring binders for distribution to all those in attendance at the meeting—the goal being to thoroughly brief the SECDEF on the requested orders and walk out the door with his signature for delivery to the chairman, who had already signed the orders prior to our presentation. It was my responsibility, or my vice's in my absence, to talk through the purpose, who was involved, why it was the right thing to do, whether the White House had indicated approval, State Department position, and other pieces of information we deemed instrumental in helping the secretary gain a full understanding of what he was being asked to sign. The request could just have easily been for a two-person detachment as it was for a twenty-thousand troop combat division. Regardless of the size, location, purpose, or command authority, there was one fact that was indisputable: attempting to present to Rumsfeld (on this or any presentation) without a total understanding of every aspect of the matter at hand was akin to a 35,000-foot HALO (High Altitude Low Opening) jump, without the benefit of a parachute. There were typically many questions, scrutiny of every detail, and questioning of long-standing assumptions and strategies. It was never dull, seldom what I would call fun, but always intellectually stimulating. In looking back, I believe it was a process that worked. While not necessarily an approach that I would use, it did keep us on our toes and ensured that we did everything in our power to afford our brave warriors every possible opportunity to succeed.

There are few places that I find more beautiful than Washington, DC, in winter, when the freshly fallen snow blankets the similarly toned monuments and landmarks. On the other hand, there are days like this particular Friday afternoon in December 2002. The record-breaking bitter cold had been supplanted by a warming trend—not warm enough to want to spend any time outside, but just enough to turn the snow into slush, and ensure that the steadily falling rain wouldn't turn to ice until the temps dropped back down after dark—right around the time I'd be ready to drive home. This was one dreary gray day that I was glad to be spending inside, using my brief break for lunch as an opportunity to take one final pass at the Book before presenting to the secretary that afternoon.

I didn't know it at the time, but while I was munching on my turkey sandwich at my desk, the secretary was downtown with a National Guard audience when someone stood up and essentially said that one of his units had received only five days' notice for a mobilization to the Middle East. Can you imagine? Only five days to handle all your personal affairs at home, with your wife or husband, with your kids. Many of these men and women would be deployed for over eight months at a time, so arrangements had to be made. Who's going to pay the bills? Prepare and file the tax returns? Set contingencies in place in case the worst were to occur? These are America's finest heading off to war. The reality was that some would never come back, and those arrangements would have to be made up front. Five days for all this? Clearly unacceptable. When Rumsfeld found out about it, he was not pleased.

By the time he made it back to the Pentagon, we had already assembled in his conference room. I was seated directly adjacent to the head of the table where Rumsfeld would sit, since I'd be doing the presenting that day. Immediately across from me was the chairman, and Pete Pace to my right two removed.

Those present varied from week to week, but this day's included the usual suspects: Paul Wolfowitz, DSD (deputy secretary of defense); Stan McChrystal, my vice; Doug Feith, the newly appointed undersecretary of defense for policy; Stephen Cambone, later the first undersecretary of defense for intelligence; Jim Haynes, general counsel; John Craddock, who had recently taken over for Ed Giambastiani as secretary of defense military advisor (SDMA); and finally Jack Keane, vice chief of staff of the Army. Stan was filling me in on a call he had just received when the door burst open and a red-faced Rumsfeld made a beeline to his seat and engaged.

"Five days' notice?!" he barked in a raised voice. "What did you know about this? How could this possibly happen?" While the words were directed at me, there was little doubt that the communication was intended for the others as well, through me. I just happened to be the lightning rod of the moment. "You alerted a Guard unit to mobilize to Iraq with just five days' notice?!" Someone else at the table began to speak, but he was drowned out by the secretary slamming his fist onto the table and continuing to gesture. "This is a steam-driven industrial age process. A steam-driven industrial age process!" He was beside himself. "This is nonsense. Totally unacceptable!"

Chairman Myers tried to explain. "You're right that five days is unacceptable, but this is an anomaly and in no way representative . . ."

Rumsfeld spun around to the chairman and banged his fist again. "Steam-driven industrial age!"

General Pace spoke up. "What the chairman is trying to say is that this was a deviation . . ."

"You say it's a deviation, I say it's systemic!"

What he failed to realize was that we presented the orders to him in a timely way. Once he signed those orders, we immediately turned them over to the appropriate service branch for implementation. In this case, the DEPORD was the trigger for the National Guard mobilization, but the process of orchestrating the deployment was an Army function, entirely independent from the Joint Staff.

There was no dispute that the Army had to improve its process. And later on I'd work closely with all the branches to facilitate that improvement, but at that moment, the Army wasn't the target of Secretary Rumsfeld's displeasure—I was.

I shot a glance across the table at Jack Keane, hoping that the four-star vice chief of staff of the Army would step up and take responsibility—or at the very least say something to deflect some of the heat. But the truth is, as much as I respect Jack, I observed him silently thumbing through the thick black binder, as if doing his best to become invisible. In his defense, he was not alone. With the exception of Dick Myers and Pete Pace, the rest of the esteemed assemblage was doing their best to blend into the woodwork. It was not an unwise approach; this was not the time to argue the issue. Would the chief of the Army, Ric Shinseki, have spoken up had he been there? He had never been shy about speaking his mind to the boss on other issues. But getting a word in edgewise when someone is this agitated? Almost impossible.

I drove home that night with the realization that my time as J-3 had ended, and I wondered if I'd bear the distinction of serving the shortest term in history. If the fates were kind, it was possible that I'd be transferred to another position—that is, if there were any three-star assignments in need of filling. More likely, I'd be thanked for my thirty years of service, and forced to retire—and at the worst possible time. We were on the brink of war and I passionately believed that I had more to contribute. On the flip side, it sure would be nice to get to spend time with Suzie again. I pulled into the garage and thought about how to break the news.

"How can he fire you for something that's not even your doing?" Suzie demanded, more miffed about "her boy" being disrespected than upset that my career might have just ended.

"Because he really doesn't even know me, yet," I explained. "I've only been there for a few months and it's conceivable that at the moment he sees my greatest value to him is the example my firing would be to the rest of the staff."

"But there's nobody more loyal than you, or smarter!" Suzie declared, so distraught that I halfway thought she might jump into her car and confront Rumsfeld directly.

"Unfortunately, this occurred before any trusting relationship had the opportunity to mature."

"When do you think you'll hear?" she asked, barely completing the question before the ring of the kitchen phone seemed to provide the answer to her question.

"So who do you think drew the short straw, General Pace or General Myers?" I asked, trying to defuse the tension.

"Does it matter?" Suzie sarcastically retorted as I picked up the handset to learn my fate.

It was the chairman. "You are very lucky," he began. "Pete intervened with the boss after everyone else left the room. Good thing you had the Marines on your side."

"He's been in my shoes, so he understands," I said. "But that doesn't diminish my gratitude. And that goes for you, too, sir. I'm sure that you had some say in it, as well. So I thank you."

"Yes!" exclaimed Suzie, as she enthusiastically pumped her fist.

"Please tell the cheerleader beside you that you're far from out of the woods. In fact, you've been banished to the penalty box. You are still persona non grata in the eyes of the secretary—at least for now."

"But what about running the Book?" I asked, fully understanding that it was an important—yet very time-consuming—task for the J-3. The last thing I wanted to do was shirk my responsibility and let down the team.

"No longer a part of your job description. In the morning I'll tell George that he's to take it over. I'm sure that he'll be thrilled," he deadpanned.

He was referring to General George Casey, who at the time was director of the Joint Staff. For a J-3 to lose access like that, not to mention having this key function taken away from him, was unprecedented—and frankly, somewhat humiliating. But as bad as it was for me, I think it was even worse for George. As DJS during the ramp-up to the war, the last thing he had time for was to take on my chore. And he hated it.

For the next three weeks, every time he would see me, he'd shoot me a dirty look. I felt awful. My guess is that at some point he went to the chairman and said, "This is nonsense. This is Norty's work, and that whole business about the mobilization glitch wasn't his doing, anyway. You've got to talk to the SECDEF and tell him that enough is enough. He's more than made his point. But now we've got to get back down to business."

By then, the secretary had calmed down and it all returned back to normal. I was back on the team. But none of us would ever forget what became known as the "PNG Event," the time that I became persona non grata.

Over time, I believe that trusting relationship with Rummy developed, and I think he would tell you today that perhaps in some ways I wasn't his cup of tea, but that I was always a trustworthy, good, hardworking, dependable officer. Was it a cakewalk? No. But I believe that I served him well.

KOREA

Leave it to the North Koreans to throw a wrench into the Schwartz family holiday festivities. Envision the glittering Disneyland Christmas parade on steroids, and you're still not coming close to the magical transformation that takes place at our house every year, thanks to the unbridled imagination of my wife. She spends months designing, unpacking, assembling, wiring and erecting boxes of Christmas treasures she has accumulated from all over the world. While the exterior would be the envy of Chevy Chase in *National Lampoon's Christmas Vacation*, it's the wonderland she creates inside that prompts jaws to drop and even the most acerbic of scrooges to exult in holiday cheer.

It had only been a few months since the Defense Information Systems Agency team had come by to install a "red switch" phone—the NSA-approved encryption devices that would allow me to conduct classified communications through the Top Secret / SCI level with the Pentagon, any of our unified commands, bases, or other similarly connected facilities around the world. Located upstairs in my office adjacent to the bedroom, I didn't have to go too far to receive the time-sensitive notifications that would invariably deny the luxury of an uninterrupted night's sleep over the next two years. That's the phone whose distinctive tone I heard while lying on my back and attempting to erect Suzie's world-famous "upside down Christmas tree." I untangled myself and made it upstairs to the phone before its fourth ring.

"This is General Schwartz," I said, a little out of breath.

"Sir, this is ADDO Colonel Latimer at the NMCC. I'm calling to advise you that the Yongbyon nuclear reactor has just gone hot."

I resisted the temptation to respond with, "Bah, humbug!" and instead merely thanked him and wished him a happy holiday.

The Yongbyon Nuclear Scientific Research Center was North Korea's main nuclear facility, and the reactor was its central element. Located a little over fifty-five miles north of Pyongyang, the center contained a short-term spent fuel storage facility and a fuel reprocessing facility that recovered uranium and plutonium from spent fuel. The plant had been inactive since 1994, when it was shut down in accordance with the U.S.-North Korea "Agreed Framework," a nonbinding political commitment that was intended to replace North Korea's nuclear power plant program with more nuclear proliferation–resistant light-water reactor power plants. The agreement had been troubled from the start, but it completely broke down in late 2002. The fact that the reactor had just been reactivated had very significant implications.

I made the appropriate notifications and a sequence of intelligence-oriented efforts were initiated. Reconnaissance assets were positioned to provide the best possible insight into what had taken place. That raw data was analyzed and became the focus of countless meetings and discussions that consumed the next few weeks—meetings with scientists, engineers, military strategists, and all manner of intelligence experts and specialists—the very top minds joining forces to provide answers that would help us determine the severity of the threat.

The conclusion was chilling: not only had the production cycle begun, but estimates were that as soon as it reached its full capacity, the plant could produce six kilograms of plutonium a year, enough to make two nuclear bombs.

The North Koreans expressed outrage at our contention that the plant was being used to produce weapons-grade material. "Its sole function is to produce electricity to power and heat our city," they declared to the International Atomic Energy Agency. That was about as believable as the time I struck out Musial, Maris, and Mantle—in order, with nine straight hundred-mile-per-hour fastballs.

Two years later, they recanted their assertion, instead rationalizing that a bona fide nuclear deterrent was essential for their own self-defense. "The Democratic People's Republic of Korea is compelled to bolster its nuclear weapons arsenal in order to protect the ideology, system, freedom, and democracy chosen by the people," their foreign ministry announced.

Around 9:45 p.m. on October 9, 2006, Secretary of State Condoleezza Rice's evening was interrupted by an alert from the U.S. Embassy in Beijing. Within minutes, she personally relayed the urgent message to National Security Advisor Stephen Hadley, who instantly conveyed its contents to President Bush. The Chinese had tipped us off that the North Koreans were moments away from conducting their first nuclear test—the culmination of many years of planning, research, development, and financial investment. No sooner did Hadley disconnect from the president than the United States Geological Survey detected a tremor of 4.2 magnitude on the Korean Peninsula. An explosion had taken place in the North Hamgyong Province, once and for all eliminating any doubt about their intentions all along.

Since that time, the threat has intensified significantly. By September 2016, North Korea had successfully conducted four more nuclear tests, all at the Punggye-ri Nuclear Test Site about sixty miles from their border with China, with each one increasing in explosive yield. From a yield of just under one kiloton in 2006, the 2016 blast approached twenty kilotons, generating shock waves equivalent to a magnitude 5.3 earthquake. It's highly unlikely that they'll be stopping there.

In April 2017, the *New York Times* ran an article titled "North Korea May Be Preparing Its 6th Nuclear Test." As I read about recent indications that a sixth test might be imminent, I couldn't help but flash back to the call I'd received about the Yongbyon activation. It also brought to mind a colonel I had worked with at the Pentagon. At the time, I was Chief of Staff and he was chief of the Air Force Senate Liaison office. Today he's a three-star and back at the Pentagon—which is why he came to mind. As the current director for operations (J-3), John Dolan might very well have been the one to receive the NMCC alert of the incident that prompted that *Times* article. In late March 2017, satellite imagery revealed noteworthy anomalies at the Punggye-ri testing site: expanded spoil pile (rocky debris) excavated from one of the underground detonation tunnels, uncharacteristic auto and rail activity, a large gathering of people assembling at the main administrative building, plus various classified signs—more than enough to catch our attention and raise the red flag.

In June 2017 testimony before the House Armed Services Committee, Secretary of Defense Jim Mattis categorized the North Korean nuclear bomb and missile programs as the "most urgent" threat(s) to national security. "The regime's nuclear weapons program is a clear and present danger to all, and the regime's provocative actions, manifestly illegal under international law, have not abated despite United Nations' censure and sanctions," he said.

Retired Air Force General Michael Hayden, the former director of both the CIA and the NSA, injects an even more ominous prediction: "I really do think it is very likely that by the end of Mr. Trump's first term, the North Koreans will be able to reach Seattle with a nuclear weapon onboard an indigenously produced intercontinental ballistic missile."

The current DIA director, Lt. Gen. Vincent Stewart, concurs, reporting to Congress that if left unchecked, North Korea is on an inevitable path to obtaining a nuclear-armed missile capable of striking the United States mainland.

Regardless of whether North Korea will ever succeed in their goal of fielding a fleet of ICBMs, there's no dispute that it is South Korea that faces the most imminent danger from North Korea's burgeoning ballistic missile arsenal. Prior to leaving office, President Obama struck an agreement with the then current South Korean leader to deploy the THAAD (Terminal High Altitude Area Defense) antiballistic missile system to enhance the existing missile defense. Designed to intercept and destroy incoming missiles from the North, each system consists of six truck-mounted launchers (each capable of firing eight interceptor missiles), a fire control and communications unit, and an AN/TPY-2 radar.

On April 25, 2017, six oversized trailers lumbered up the winding mountain road that terminated at the entrance to the Lotte Skyhill Country Club in the southeastern county of Seongiu, South Korea. At over 2,200 feet above sea level, its eighteen-hole, par seventy-two championship golf course provided a spectacular view of the cottages and sprawling melon farms below, and an ideal location for the country's first battery of THAAD missile launchers. Cutting sharply off the access road and onto the fairway, South Korea's first THAAD antiballistic missile system had arrived at its destination.

TROOP STRENGTH TESTIMONY

"General Schwartz, thank you for coming to this closed hearing of the Senate Armed Service Committee. It's nice to have the benefit of your experience in the profound issues of interest to this committee, and we are honored to have a man of your experience and integrity working with us . . ."

It was late February 2003, and Chairman John Warner could not have been more affable in welcoming me. I had been up there to meet with staffers, members, and for hearings, but this was the first time as the J-3 that I'd been sworn in and questioned in a formal congressional hearing. There would be many more. Most would take place in one of the huge caucus rooms located in the various House or Senate office buildings. These are the ones often seen on TV, with the long row of senators or congressmen gazing down at the witness from a raised wooden dais, as the witness stares back from a small table bearing only a microphone, a glass of water, and an identifying name placard. Add in the visitors and throngs of reporters packed in behind the witness, plus the pit jammed with photographers kneeling out of view in front, and it made for a fairly intimidating setting—at least that's how I found it for my first few testimonies.

But this was a classified hearing, so it took place in one of the smaller, secure committee rooms inside the Russell Senate Office Building. The purpose of this one was for the senators to gain a better understanding of just exactly where we stood on the matter of troop strength for the potential conflict in Iraq, which by this time had grown into a contentious topic. It was one on which I felt intimately well-versed.

Besides the many months spent in close interaction with Gene Renuart on behalf of CENTCOM, I had been interacting with Doug Feith (undersecretary of defense for policy) and Ryan Crocker (then interim chargé d'affaires to the new government of Afghanistan)—a world class diplomat—on matters related to a potential Iraq mission. Feith was very hands-on during the entire process, which was fine by me, but didn't go over too well with General Tommy Franks (CENTCOM commander), who called him "the dumbest fucking guy on the planet." Rumsfeld, however, held Feith in high regard, referring to him as "one of the most brilliant individuals in government, just a rare talent." Same man, viewed entirely differently by two strong leaders thrown together to take our great nation to war: one a civilian corporate head who believed that less is more—new approaches, more efficiencies, transformation to take us into the future and give us a decisive advantage today; the other a battle-hardened, hardcore Army infantry officer who rose to the top with a belief that there's strength in numbers—overwhelming the enemy with a decisive force advantage in terms of decidedly more well-trained warfighters armed with lots of effective weapons and equipment. Both were well-intentioned; both adamantly believed that they knew best. Observing how these two strong leaders battled through their differences—and in fact working with Gene to capitalize on the strengths of *both* positions—gave me new tools that I'd find indispensable in years to come as my level of responsibility increased.

I felt well prepared as I entered Room SR-222 of the Russell Senate Office Building for that Armed Services Committee session. It was a far more intimate setting than the massive caucus rooms. SR-222, just like the almost identical

SR-232a and SR-236, had the senators seated along the outside of tables that had been configured in the shape of a hollowed-out rectangle. Perched beneath a pair of stunning crystal chandeliers, the tables had room to accommodate six senators along the two long sides of the arrangement, and I was to take a seat in one of two black leather chairs on the short side at the north end of the room. Directly across from me were Chairman John Warner and Senator Carl Levin, at that time the ranking member. Immediately behind them was an enormous gold-framed mirror that tended to make the room look much larger than it really was. Set atop an imposing marble fireplace mantel, the mirror served to frame the two senators in a way that seemed to give them an air of royalty. Truly an interesting design.

I took my seat, had a quick sip of water, and made note of the wooden "push to talk" box from which the microphone extended. I felt appreciative of Chairman Warner's kind introduction. On the cusp of his twenty-sixth year in the Senate, the five-term Republican senator from Virginia was one of few veterans to have served in two branches of the military—first as a seventeen-year-old sailor in World War II, then subsequently as a marine in Korea. By the time he was first elected in 1978, he had already served as both the secretary of the Navy and sixth husband to actress Elizabeth Taylor. As would always be the case for our many interactions over the following nine years, between his thick silver mane and his hand-made double-breasted black suit, he exuded a distinguished and elegant presence completely befitting the upper chamber of Congress.

"Thank you, sir," I responded. "Rest assured that I will do everything in my power to live up to your kind words."

It didn't take long before the pleasantries gave way to an intense grilling as they sought to pin me down for my personal estimate of the number of combat troops that would be required in Iraq. It was Senator Levin (six-term Democrat from Michigan) who first posed the question. This was just one day after General Shinseki had testified that he believed "a couple hundred thousand" troops would be necessary to secure and keep the peace in a post-hostility Iraq. As for the estimates for force strength during the combat phase, they had not yet been finalized. In fact, they were all over the place—anywhere from 150,000 to 550,000. So the truth was that I had no accurate idea. In addition—and this has never been released to the public until now—just a few hours earlier in our morning meeting, Secretary Rumsfeld had issued explicit guidance to avoid such speculation. I answered Levin's question per the boss's guidelines: honest, yet delicately phrased.

"Senator, the plans are far from firm," I said. "So because of that, I prefer not to speculate."

He tilted his head down and hunched over a bit, gazing at me over the top of his wire-rimmed reading glasses, which seemed to be permanently affixed to the tip of his nose. He pushed—still respectful, but clearly not thrilled with my response. "General, I understand. So then just give us a range . . . it doesn't have to be an exact number."

"Sir, it would be inappropriate for me to speculate," I explained, hoping that he would understand and just leave it at that. But instead, the back and forth continued. He was getting agitated. Then others tried to get me to commit. I held firm. What started as uncomfortable became awkward, and finally quite tense. I had just started giving these testimonies and already it appeared that I was not satisfactorily providing them with the information they desired. They were displeased with me and I felt that I had let them down and lost a no-win situation. In the weeks and months to come, the matter seemed to fade from the radar screen as other more pressing issues demanded their attention. I thought I'd heard the last of it, but years later it would resurface with a vengeance, not only catching me completely off guard, but almost derailing my entire career.

What I failed to mention at the time, due to Rumsfeld's explicit guidance, was that we had put together a range of options depending on how the plan unfolded. It could have been as few as 150,000 or as many as 550,000. It was all clearly delineated in a then secret graphic (which the Joint Staff subsequently had declassified) unofficially referred to as the "green mountain chart." It summarized what the force buildup would look like in terms of personnel, with different options represented in the form of off-ramps predicated on our level of success at the time. In the case of maximum success, we'd be able to use an off-ramp that indicated a lower troop level than would be required in the event that our efforts were not sufficiently successful at that point. Greater success allowed for less commitment of personnel. The debate continued well into early 2003.

With each subsequent testimony I'd become more at ease. Good thing, because soon they'd be occurring at least every few weeks—sometimes before the

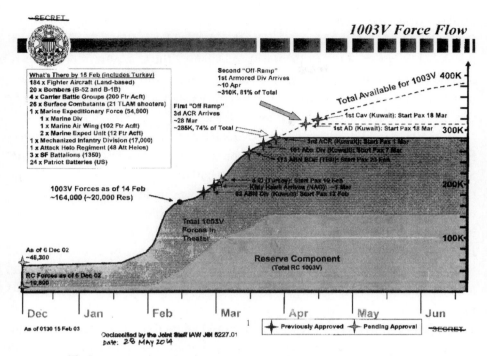

The "green mountain chart" summarized force buildup, including off-ramps based on various levels of success.

House, sometimes the Senate. Both needed to be kept fully abreast of the latest combat operations and other military-related issues that would pop up.

WAR COUNCIL

Once we actually "crossed the line" on March 19, 2003, what had been a nonstop marathon suddenly became a year-long sprint. IRAQI FREEDOM was in full force and demanded even more of our attention than did its buildup, and that was in addition to the ongoing requirements of Afghanistan and every other crisis that erupted anywhere in the world. Secretary Rumsfeld was working six days a week, and the rest of us were working seven.

Every morning at exactly 7:00 a.m., I'd leave my office and make the short walk to the E-ring, then bound up the stairs and down a small corridor across the hall from the SECDEF's office. This is where I'd enter the Executive Support Center, a little-known highly secured facility that contained the "OSD

Cables" area—the secretary's communications link to the military's NMCC (National Military Command Center), the White House Situation Room, and the global footprint of the Department of Defense. The Cables staff of nineteen operate twenty-four hours a day, seven days a week, maintaining direct communications with all key members of the secretary's staff, the Joint Chiefs of Staff, the Executive Secretariat, and the State Department.

By 7:05 a.m. I'd be inside the secretary's Secure Video Teleconference Room, most likely visiting with the other attendees as they filtered in for the SECDEF's daily War Council. It was a relatively small group, considering the magnitude of the discussions. The conference table seated about twelve, with five on a side, Secretary Rumsfeld at the head, and usually Paul Wolfowitz straddling the corner between Rumsfeld and Doug Feith. Immediately to Doug's right was Steve Cambone (then newly nominated undersecretary for intelligence), followed by Ric Shinseki (Army chief of staff) and Vern Clark (chief of naval operations). Opposite Doug (to Rumsfeld's left) was the chairman, then Pete Pace (vice chairman), George Casey (then director of the Joint Staff), John Jumper (Air Force Chief of Staff) and Mike Hagee (commandant of the Marine Corps). Stan McChrystal and I would usually sit along the wall just behind Generals Myers and Pace. On some days Vice President Cheney made an appearance via video conference. He'd be patched in to the huge wall-sized video on the far side of the room opposite Rumsfeld, often in a split screen including General Tommy Franks from CENTCOM's forward headquarters at Camp As Sayliyah in Doha, Qatar, and Lt Gen Michael "Rifle" DeLong (CENTCOM deputy commander) from the CENTCOM secure VTC facility in Tampa.

Just to the left of the huge screen was an American flag—a constant reminder of why we were all there—and immediately above it were four red LED digital clocks, respectively labeled Zulu, Local, Kabul, and Baghdad. Once the "Local" clock clicked over to 0710, Rumsfeld would burst through one of the thick steel doors that sealed the room and take his place at the table's head. The meetings were brisk and to the point, and there was no time for chitchat. To his credit, the last thing he wanted was "yes-men." Debate was encouraged, but arguments were expected to be impeccably well thought out and backed up with thoroughly documented research. Citing precedent as one's rationale was a surefire way to incur the boss's ire. It's not that he wanted change for the sake of change, but I do believe he felt that there was almost always a better way. The weak need not apply.

Still on the way to his seat, he'd zip up the black collared vest he so often wore over his shirt and tie and utter a terse "Good morning, everybody," as he glanced my way. "Norty, what do you have for us?" Generally, I'd be the first up with an ops/intel update, followed by an abbreviated report from theater, then inputs from JCS and OSD principals.

Day number one—D-Day—was electric. We had unleashed a barrage of forty Tomahawk cruise missiles from four ships and two submarines, and an initial air strike led by two F-117s targeting Iraqi leadership just outside of Baghdad. F/A-18 Hornets launched from the USS *Constellation* struck targets around Basra. A second wave of aircraft took off from the USS *Abraham Lincoln* and other platforms in the Persian Gulf, safely returning after successfully completing their bombing runs.

Coincidentally, on the same day, we also launched Operation VALIANT STRIKE against the Taliban and al-Qaeda in the Sami Ghar Mountains east of Kandahar in Afghanistan. As a result of intelligence gleaned from interrogations of Khalid Shaikh Mohammed (who was captured in Pakistan just a few days earlier) and other al-Qaeda operatives, a combined force of around six hundred special operators and conventional troops zeroed in on targets where they confiscated weapons and rooted out al-Qaeda and Taliban forces.

While I won't go so far as to say that the mood in the room was euphoric, I would categorize it as more than cautiously optimistic.

In contrast to the elation we felt the first day, day number four (March 24) felt more like a swift kick to the gut. Three entirely unrelated operations had gone afoul—and it was my responsibility to report the grim details.

Thirty-three AH-64D Apache helicopters of the Army V Corps, 11th Attack Helicopter Regiment had taken off on a late-night mission to attack and destroy a battery of T-72 tanks and artillery of the elite Medina division of the Iraqi Republican Guard; our belief was that doing so would clear the way for the 3rd Infantry Division's advance into the suburbs of Karbala.

Approaching the target area, they came under heavy antiaircraft and artillery fire—not entirely unanticipated—but then, taking them completely off guard, there was an eruption of small arm and RPG (rocket-propelled grenade) fire from the surrounding residential areas. Bombardment was hurled at them from every direction. One chopper was hit, then another, and a third. Within minutes, every single Apache incurred some level of battle damage—one so severe that it was unable to remain airborne. While the other aircraft limped back to base, the two pilots of the downed Apache were on the run, doing their best to escape and evade. Their aircraft became the focal point of live news interruptions beamed across Iraq by its state-run TV network. Not long after, the broadcasts were picked up by CNN. The chopper was surrounded by mobs of joyful Iraqis, two of whom danced with Kalashnikov rifles waving over their heads, two more brandishing our soldiers' helmets.

It wasn't much later that the disabled AH-64D burst into flames and was for all intents and purposes demolished—along with it all the classified equipment it held within. A demolition like that was a textbook example of what's supposed to happen when a target is struck by one of our long-range ATAC-MS (Army Tactical Missile System) missiles. Our successful launch of that missile was about the only part of that sequence that one might categorize as a "success."

Like the helo that was plucked from the sky, so too were our hopes that the pilots could escape their pursuers. It didn't take long for Iraqi TV to cut in with yet another breaking news event: The two Army aviators had been captured. Now prisoners of war, they were paraded on Iraqi TV, a clear violation of the Geneva Convention. Contemptible? Of course. But not particularly surprising since playing by the rules had never been a part of Saddam's modus operandi.

In the days to come, there'd be hearty debate as to whether the Apaches should be used for deep penetration and attack missions such as this, without the benefit of fixed-wing escorts flying overhead or preparatory artillery to provide cover and reduce their vulnerability. We did end up pulling back on that particular tactic, but even today, you can still hear the issue hotly debated.

The whole thing was widely covered by CNN, who had a reporter embedded with the command and control helicopter. That piece of the pie prompted stimulating discussion surrounding First Amendment challenges. Reporters were allowed to be embedded only after they had signed off on stringent rules governing what they could and could not divulge—for instance, anything related to tactics or locations was strictly forbidden. The last thing we needed was for this to become a source of intel for the enemy, so anything that came close to jeopardizing the safety of our troops would be dealt with harshly. To their credit, I'm not aware of any instances where the embeds violated these guidelines. But we did end up with certain situations where worldwide television audiences were viewing events in near real time, sometimes even before our own intel officers had secured the information. It paved the way for a whole new way of newscasting.

Upon completion of my briefing, there was extensive discussion about how and why the attack unfolded the way it had. The Army wasn't happy with me for reporting the event in the first place and the Air Force wasn't happy with me for not exposing all the disappointing details.

I've generally found that when two sides of an argument are mad at you, you're probably doing or reporting the right thing.

My second report of the day involved an A-10 mission gone wrong. It occurred at a bridge in the western Iraqi town of Rutba, not far from the Syrian border. The objective was to destroy the bridge. Once the bridge was identified, the pilot made the appropriate passes to ensure that the target was clear, then he flipped the master switch to ARM, rotated the knob to designate the appropriate missile pylon, carefully lined up the bridge in the head-up display, and finally squeezed the consent switch on the control stick, prompting the missiles' solid propellant to ignite and begin its seven-second journey to the bridge, leaving a long trail of smoke in its wake. About a second after ignition, a small bus came into view as it turned onto the bridge and began to cross it, stopping at the very instant the missile made contact. In a massive fireball, five Syrian civilians were killed and at least another ten seriously wounded.

I completed the report and the room fell silent. There were no excuses, and no rationalizations. I waited an extra moment before continuing with my next report.

My final report focused on a devastating friendly fire incident that resulted in the deaths of at least ten marines. In the midst of a brutal battle on the ground, two A-10s from the Pennsylvania Air National Guard spotted what they believed to be enemy vehicles near a bridge just outside of the southern Iraq city of Nasiriyah. Following protocol, they established radio contact with the battalion's forward air controller to confirm that the targets were, in fact, the enemy. Unaware that U.S. Marines had made it that far north (in this case to gain control of the critical bridge), the Bravo Company controller cleared the pair of attack aircraft to take out the "enemy" vehicles, which turned out to be our own amphibious assault vehicles of Charlie Company. For fifteen minutes, the two Warthogs circled the bridge and unleashed an overwhelming salvo of 30 mm Gatling gun fire, precision bombs, and ultimately Maverick missiles. Multiple passes, devastating consequences. Before the A-10 pilots were finally commanded to cease fire, at least ten United States Marines had been killed.

The following day, President Bush showed up at the Pentagon to attend the secretary's morning meeting. Make no mistake about it: he was intimately involved every day, with Generals Myers and Pace delivering personal updates in the Oval Office or by VTC at least daily, and frequently two times a day. But his coming to the Pentagon gave him a chance to delve into greater detail and deliberate with the Joint Chiefs, and every bit as important, it gave him an opportunity to "rally the troops" and make it crystal clear that he was 100 percent with us. As the photographers left the room (being a SCIF, a Sensitive Compartmented Information Facility, only two were allowed in to snap a few shots for dissemination to all the media outlets), I could see the president glance at the red OBSERVE COMSEC sign beside the heavy door as it was sealed, then he turned and looked each one of us in the eye and delivered what appeared to be totally off-the-cuff remarks about the pride he felt for the men and women of our armed forces, giving of themselves in the interest of protecting our liberty. What began as a "good old boy" country chat soon transitioned to an eloquent discourse on our great country and those who fight to protect her. There was not a soul in the room who did not feel the sincerity of the president's inspirational charge.

Once the war started, the White House kept us busy working closely with the National Security Staff on efforts to identify WMD, secure conventional munitions (leading to another Senate testimony that would come back to bite me in the butt), and get a biometric capability established in Iraq. I worked closely with Condi Rice and Fran Townsend on all these fronts. Fran and I established a particularly close relationship, and we're still friends today. She served as the president's top advisor on counterterrorism, so the two of us worked hand in hand on counterterror issues related to the pursuit of bin Laden and other high-value targets.

Two other areas are worthy of mention, and these are both examples of how Major General Stan McChrystal (Vice J-3, my deputy) stepped up to the plate and took over for me in areas in which I had little time to service myself.

In the case of the war, it quickly got to the point where we felt that daily face-to-face congressional briefings were in order as well as daily media presentations, something that to my knowledge had never been done before. But it's a great indication of the lengths to which we went in order to build a strong, collaborative relationship with our legislative colleagues—one of complete cooperation and transparency. This is one of so many areas in which I found Stan to be worth his weight in gold. Six days a week, he would head over to the Hill to brief Congress on the real-time operational details of the war. The briefings would be hosted by the respective Armed Services committees, but any member with the appropriate level of clearance was welcome to attend. (The information we shared required a Top Secret clearance.) Stan, along with Ambassador Ryan Crocker and Colonel William Caniano, an Army intelligence officer on the Joint Staff, would first head to the Capitol for the Senate brief, which would be moderated by Senator Warner. From 9:00 a.m. to 10:15 a.m., after a quick overview by Stan, the members would have the opportunity to ask questions—follow-ups on the "hows" and "whys." Let's not forget that Congress has immense control of the purse strings, so it was certainly in everybody's best interest that they had a thorough understanding of exactly how the taxpayers' hard-earned funds were being used to save lives and defeat the powers that were driven to destroy the "great Satan," as Saddam called us.

Following the seventy-five-minute session, the trio would gather their backup material and hightail it across the Capitol to the House side, then go down the stairs that led to the underground labyrinth of tunnels that connects the Capitol with the various House and Senate office buildings, as well as the Library of Congress. While all three would have preferred a fast-paced walk from the Capitol to the Rayburn House Office Building, timing dictated that on most days they hopped the underground train in order to arrive at Rayburn in time for the House briefing, which ran from 10:30 a.m. to 11:45 a.m. The small, open-air, single-car tram reminded me more of something you might see at Disneyland, but it sure was an efficient way to transit from one building to the next, particularly during Washington's often inclement weather.

After about a week into the sessions, I asked Stan how they were going. "You know, sir, it's a funny thing," he began without missing a beat. "These meetings are well-attended by members from both sides of the aisle. Most voted for the war, but a few of them against it. I never thought I'd see them all agree on anything." I wondered where he was going with this. "But to a person, we're getting only positive feedback. They appreciate the candor and the no-holds-barred forum seems to make them feel even more personally involved in the decision-making process." He cracked a slight grin and concluded, "Word on the street is that we've become the 'go to' event." One certainly couldn't ask for more than that.

PUBLIC AFFAIRS

Another area where Stan filled the void was in handling our public affairs; he became the face of the Pentagon on those days when the chairman or SECDEF were unable to tackle the daily press briefings. By the time one becomes a flag officer (a general or an admiral), most have had command positions that included speaking in front of large groups. We've been trained on what to say and how to say it. But saying a few words at a change-of-command ceremony is a far cry from walking into the Pentagon press room and facing a room packed with some of the most experienced—and respected—reporters in the world. Looking at those cameras—which are beaming live close-ups of you to a worldwide audience in the millions—even the least religious among us often utter a prayer that they don't inadvertently misspeak and come across as incompetent or a fool. Stan's a warrior, and I can guarantee you that he'd been much happier jumping out of airplanes than he was facing the Pentagon press corps. To quote him directly, "I wanted that role about as much as I wanted a root canal." But with the help and support of DoD communications experts Victoria "Torie" Clarke (assistant secretary of defense for public affairs) and Larry DiRita (special assistant to the secretary of defense), he did a yeoman's job and represented our military with an intelligence and competence that I had every confidence he would bring to the task.

Make no mistake about it, a carefully planned, well-executed public affairs campaign should be a key part of every commander's arsenal. While the term "public affairs" may be a relatively new one, leaders have been aware of its importance for generations. Do you really think nineteen million women would have packed factories and shipyards to make munitions and war supplies had it not been for "Rosie the Riveter" becoming such a cultural icon during World War II? And as patriotic a figure as one might find "Uncle Sam," it wasn't until J. M. Montgomery sketched him pointing directly at us and added the line, "I WANT YOU for the U.S. Army" that World War I recruiting went through the roof. These are just a few examples of tools that were created to capture the pub-lic's attention, engage them, and enlist their support. Even Abraham Lincoln was well aware how crucial it is to win the hearts and minds. "Public sentiment is everything," he said in August of 1858. "With public sentiment, nothing can fail; without it, nothing can succeed."

Our own military doctrine teaches us that the primary means of garnering positive public sentiment is through the proactive release of accurate informa-tion to both domestic and international audiences. Fostering a transparent, col-laborative partnership with the press—along with instituting a well-planned and intelligently orchestrated social media campaign—facilitates informed per-ceptions and undermines adversarial propaganda.

In 2014, President Obama reminded the graduating class of West Point cadets, "When we cannot explain our efforts clearly and publicly, we face ter-rorist propaganda and international suspicion, we erode our legitimacy with our partners and our people, and we reduce accountability in our own government."

For this to work, our message must be honest, timely, and consistent. With-out complete honesty, we lose credibility and support. The public understands why we must decline to answer certain questions when the answers might place our forces in harm's way. But they won't accept it if we lie to them. Whether it be the secretary of defense or the chairman, Stan McChrystal or me—having a credible spokesperson to serve as the "face of the Pentagon" is as important a piece of the battlefield as are airplanes and tanks and artillery shells.

I've always envied those to whom interplay with the fourth estate came so naturally. Don Rumsfeld was one of them. I don't know that he'd admit it, but I think he looked forward to bursting through the doors of the press room and storming up to the dais for a bit of verbal jousting. He took a lot of flak for some of his quips but I think it's because they just couldn't keep up with him; he was so pointed and quick that sometimes his responses flew right over their heads. But he always had a purpose for whatever he was saying. The most classic ex-ample occurred when Jim Miklaszewski (NBC's chief Pentagon correspondent at the time) brought up the fact that "there are reports that there is no evidence of a direct link between Baghdad and some of these terrorist organizations."

Rumsfeld looked him in the eye like a wise elder and started ruminating out loud, presenting a difficult-to-follow analysis that had the room full of educated journalists scratching their heads in wonder. "Reports that say that something hasn't happened are always interesting to me, because, as we know, there are known knowns; there are things we know we know. We also know that there are known unknowns. That is to say that we know there are some things we do not know. But there are also unknown unknowns, the ones we don't know we don't know. And if one looks throughout the history of our country and other countries, it is the latter category that tend to be the difficult ones."

"Uh, excuse me," the reporter interrupted, completely flummoxed, along with most of the others in the room. "But is this an unknown unknown? There are several unknowns, and I'm wondering if this one is an unknown unknown."

In a manner that only Rumsfeld could get away with, he gathered his material, stared down the reporter, and chuckled. "I'm not going to say which one it is." Of course the room erupted in laughter . . . but if they thought about it, he was right.

Another one who just seemed to "have it" was a familiar face to those of us who followed the first Gulf War, Army LTG Tom Kelly. As J-3 in the late '80s and early '90s, the big, blunt Irish tanker was instrumental in developing the battle plans for both Operation JUST CAUSE (the invasion of Panama) and DESERT STORM. Known for his wit and aggressive attacks against anyone he felt teetered too close to the line of operational security, his unique way of spinning a phrase combined with his gruff military bearing grew him quite an impressive following—so large that it landed him an appearance on Johnny Carson's *Tonight Show*. When asked about the progress of the war, he once said, "Iraq went from being the fourth-largest army in the world to the second-largest army in Iraq in one hundred hours."

So many in the press corps took his bellicose deportment as disdain for the media. But upon his retirement, he set the record straight with this eloquent and spot-on reflection on the importance of maintaining a free press:

Believe it or not, I've enjoyed this little interlude. Got a lot of letters from people who really don't understand the hurly-burly and give-and-take of a press briefing, and at no time were you ever impolite to me and at no time did I ever become offended. And as you know, I hold a lot of you in great respect . . . Having a free press has served the United States well for 215 years. It is a crucial element in our democracy. And if anybody needs a contrast, all they have to do is look at the country that didn't have a free press and see what happened there.

When Bob Gates became the secretary of defense, he reminded us that "the press is not the enemy, and to treat it as such is self-defeating."

Stan would soon be moving on to take over command of JSOC, and by the time that occurred, my workload was such that I was able to take over the spokesperson role myself. Even before he departed, there were instances when I'd throw myself into the fray and tackle the briefings.

My first briefing was on July 29, 2003—about a week after Uday and Qusay Hussein (Saddam's sons) were killed following a three-hour firefight in the city of Mosul, Iraq. It wouldn't be long before Larry DiRita would depart for Iraq to assist retired Army general Jay Garner in reconstruction and humanitarian affairs prior to the arrival of Ambassador Paul Bremer and the Coalition Provisional Authority, but on this, my maiden voyage, I was fortunate to have Larry at my "six." Clad in a dark blazer with a gray striped necktie and squared-off white pocket kerchief, his rapid patter was a contrast to my rather measured, deliberate style of speech. He had no problem interrupting me in the interest of clarity, or whenever he felt I was about to insert my size elevens into my mouth.

Although the Pentagon press room does have a "green room" less than twenty feet from the stage, I don't recall a single time that we used it. At the exact moment the briefing was scheduled to begin, Larry and I would stride into the room through a side door that opened directly into the E-ring corridor. As we approached the bright blue curtains that served as a backdrop, the murmur of the crowd would instantly fall as silent as if someone had just yanked out a speaker wire.

I stepped up onto the gray carpeted platform that extended beneath the rows of bright, hot TV lights mounted on the ceiling, placed my briefing notes onto the wooden lectern that bore the blue DoD seal, and with the U.S. flag behind one shoulder and the ubiquitous Pentagon logo behind the other did my best to honestly and concisely answer the questions that were often bellowed out simultaneously by representatives of all the top news-gathering outlets.

Standing directly to my left, Larry began by sating any curiosity there might have been as to the identity of this tall, lanky Air Force general standing beside him. I clasped my hands together as Larry began to speak, patiently awaiting my time to begin.

"We have with us today Lieutenant General Norty Schwartz. He's the director of operations for the Joint Staff. I'm not sure that he's had the great pleasure of being down here before. He's the guy who makes General McChrystal look so good on a day-to-day basis when he's down here. So I've asked General Schwartz to provide a little bit of context on the operations that have taken place since the major combat phase. And with that, I'll ask General Schwartz to take it away."

"Thank you, Mr. DiRita," I said clearly and deliberately, just before I felt a tickle in my throat. I cleared it, and it seemed to go away. "As he indicated, I'm Norty Schwartz, the director of operations for the Joint Staff, and I am happy to be with you here today." So far, so good.

I then went on to detail four effective operations, using graphics that had been prepared by the Joint Staff. Operation DESERT SCORPION—six raids and twenty-nine detainees. Operation SIDEWINDER—confiscation of small arms, heavy machine guns, RPGs, 60 mm mortar rounds, plus 282 detainees. Operation SODA MOUNTAIN—141 raids, 611 detainees, including sixty-two former regime leaders. More mortars, RPGs, plus various and sundry other weapons. Finally, IVY SERPENT, a sub-operation of SODA MOUNTAIN.

I continued for about another fifteen minutes, and I was already feeling a lot more comfortable up there. "We'll now take your questions, ladies and gentlemen," I offered, which prompted an immediate forest of hands to shoot up. "Yes, sir. Go ahead," I instructed a gentleman off to my left, ready to give a thorough and complete response.

"Larry, I have a question about the termination of the Policy Analysis Market," asked the man, looking right past me at DiRita, who answered the question with aplomb.

"I have a follow-up on that," piped in a voice from the back. Then another, and another. At that point my mind started to drift. Four questions, not one for me. A familiar face in the front row was about to make up for that, and the question she would pose was a doozy. Wearing khaki slacks and a pink blazer with her hair cropped much shorter than she wears it today, it was CNN's Barbara Starr. Alternating her glances between me and a small reporter's notebook she had resting on her lap, I could tell by her demeanor that she knew we'd find her question somewhat "controversial."

"General Schwartz, in the last hour we have noted that the New York Stock Exchange has taken a very significant swing, recovering from a ninety-eight-point deficit to bounce up eighty-five points in the last hour. And traders on the floor are very specifically saying that this swing . . . is due to rumors they are hearing on the floor of the stock exchange that the U.S. has captured Saddam Hussein. They are very specific on this."

She placed her pen atop the pad and stared at me through her black-framed eyeglasses, then launched her question as if firing off a poison-tipped spear. "Would you want to take this opportunity to either calm or excite the stock market and tell us . . . ?"

Let me be clear that there was no way that I was going to provide an answer in such a way as to intentionally impact the stock market, but it does serve as an excellent example of the profound impact our words can have—in this case on our economy. Had I answered in either the affirmative or the negative, fortunes could have been made or lost. Either way, Larry interceded long before Barbara completed her question. "He absolutely would *not* like to take this opportunity to calm or excite the stock market!" he exclaimed, prompting the whole room to erupt in laughter.

Barbara pushed back. "Do you have Saddam Hussein?"

"The short answer is I have no information on that. None," I emphatically stated.

"That's not a very clear answer, with great respect, sir." I felt like blurting out something like, *What's not clear about it? I just told you that I don't have any information on that one way or another!* But of course I would never do that. In this case, once again, DiRita didn't give me a chance to make a faux pas.

"There's just nothing more to report. We're not trying to be evasive, we're simply trying to state what we have at the moment, which is—"

Of course Starr wasn't about to leave it at that and now she cut in. "You have no information on Saddam—if you—you have no information on whether the U.S. government has Saddam Hussein?" she pressed.

"At this moment in time, that is an absolutely correct statement. I have no such information," I explained, thinking that one couldn't be any clearer than that.

Then others decided to hop onto the bandwagon. "Before you walked in here, was there any information to indicate that the U.S. was close to getting Saddam Hussein?" asked another familiar-looking reporter whom I couldn't place. "Is there any reason to believe at this point that the United States govern-ment—military—has Saddam Hussein in custody?"

"No, sir," I emphatically replied.

"Can we try it a different way, General?" someone else asked, prompting yet another outburst of guffaws. *WTF*, I thought. *Why are they not getting this?*

This went on and on until they finally seemed to understand that they could ask me a hundred more times and the answer would still be the same. We were actively hunting the man down, but so far we had not found him.

A week later I was back in there for another round. In a way, it kind of reminded me of my boxing days back at the Academy. I suppose sparring is sparring whether it's in the ring or in the press room. Instead of the status of Saddam, this time the issue was enemy casualties. "One of the things that's been kind of conspicuously absent since May first is reporting on enemy casualties . . . Have there been any Iraqi casualties during the course of operations since May first?" asked the frustrated journalist. What he was trying to say was that it had been over three months since he'd heard about any enemies that we'd killed, when every day they were hearing more and more about Coalition deaths.

Even though it's a pretty safe bet that you'll never see "stand-up comic" on my *curriculum vitae*, I did attempt to inject a little humor. I cracked a slight smile and responded, "Well, there's at least two, and that's Uday and Qusay." The room erupted as I had hoped they would.

Fortunately for me, I tend to be rather low-key, and, faithful to my pedigree in special operations—notwithstanding a few attempts at levity like the one I just mentioned—I did my best to be informative, believable, and accurate. I consider it an enormous privilege to have done my part to help our citizens to become engaged and gain a more thorough understanding of the sacrifices being made every day around the world, to protect our liberty.

LIBYAN NUCLEAR INTERCEPTION

It was an intricate plot worthy of the tightest Tom Clancy action thriller, but this was no fiction. Good intelligence allowed us to orchestrate the interception of a ship that contained components for the Libyan nuclear program—components that were sold on the black market by an international arms dealer who was the key scientist behind the development of Pakistan's nuclear bomb. In conjunction with international partners, the intelligence community tracked the shipment from Malaysia through the Suez Canal, and ultimately enlisted German aid to assist in diverting the vessel to a remote Italian port where our team inspected the ship and confiscated the illegal cache. In the end, the operation provided President Bush with leverage to force Gaddafi's hand to terminate his nuclear weapons program. Here's how it played out:

Earlier I shared how we generally used weekly meetings to secure the secretary's signature on deployments orders. In an ideal world, that's how they were handled. But we had our share of time-sensitive ops that warranted immediate, out-of-cycle action. This was one of them, and there was no way that it could wait until the weekly meeting.

For months, American and British intelligence had been tracking a shipment of advanced centrifuge parts manufactured at a Malaysian facility linked to an international black market nuclear development network. Using multiple reconnaissance assets, including U.S. Navy surface vessels, they followed the shipment to Dubai (an interim transshipment point) and watched as the cargo was transferred to the *BBC China*, a German-owned freighter. It was time to take action, and that's where we came in.

Upon receiving the intel, we used the full resources of the Joint Staff to expedite the formal authorization in the name of the secretary, including a range of options depending on how things went down, what forces would be required, rules of engagement, and so on. It was an extremely significant mission, and one that had the full attention (and direction) of the White House. We put it together faster than any other that I can recall. We were the tasking agency in the name of the SECDEF, and immediately upon his signing off on it, we used a secure electronic means to transmit it to Jim Jones (USMC general, then commander of European Command) so his teams could kick into gear and execute the mission in the Mediterranean, in close cooperation with the intelligence community. As the ship passed through the Suez Canal, the U.S. government officials contacted their German counterparts and requested that they contact the ship's owners and secure their cooperation in diverting the ship to the nearby Italian port of Taranto, where our agents were awaiting its arrival. When the vessel docked, the team made swift entry and located five forty-foot shipping containers bearing the logo "SCOPE"—the name of the Malaysian manufacturer that was suspected in the operation. The ship's manifest had had the crates documented as "used machine parts." Our team removed the questionable cargo and transported it to a nearby warehouse where it could be inspected. When they opened the crates, what they found was a far cry from the "used parts" listed on the manifest. Instead, they found thousands of aluminum components for assembling centrifuges—the equipment that enriches uranium and the enabler of Libya's nuclear weapon program—and the actual centrifuges that can be used to develop weapons-grade uranium for use in nuclear weapons. All told, the hardware was valued in the tens of millions of dollars.

All the while, U.S. and British officials had been attempting to get Libya to end its WMD programs, but it wasn't until they were confronted with the evidence gleaned from this operation that they agreed to do so.

The following February, President Bush put it all in context during a speech at the National Defense University (NDU), filling in the backstory on the black market network, and driving home how key a part this operation played in the cessation of Libya's nuclear proliferation program. Here's part of what he had to say:

A. Q. Khan is known throughout the world as the father of Pakistan's nuclear weapons program. What was not publicly known until recently is that he also led an extensive international network for the proliferation of nuclear technology and know-how. For decades, Mr. Khan remained on the Pakistani government payroll, earning a modest salary. Yet he and his associates financed lavish lifestyles through the sale of nuclear technologies and equipment to outlaw regimes stretching from North Africa to the Korean Peninsula. A. Q. Khan himself operated mostly out of Pakistan. He served as director of the network, making frequent trips to consult with his clients and to sell his expertise. He sold the blueprints for centrifuges to enrich uranium, as well as a nuclear design stolen from the Pakistani government. The network sold uranium hexafluoride, the gas that the centrifuge process can transform into enriched uranium for nuclear bombs. Khan and his associates provided Iran and Libya and North Korea with designs, components, and in some cases with complete centrifuges.

To increase their profits, Khan and his associates used a factory in Malaysia to manufacture key parts for centrifuges. Other necessary parts were purchased through network operatives based in Europe and the Middle East and Africa. These procurement agents saw the trade in nuclear technologies as a shortcut to personal wealth, and they set up front companies to deceive legitimate firms into selling them tightly controlled materials.

Khan's deputy, B. S. A. Tahir, ran a computer business in Dubai as a front for the proliferation activities of the A. Q. Khan network, and for his money-laundering operations. He used this company as cover for the movement of centrifuge parts to various clients. In this case—and others—Tahir directed the Malaysia facility to produce these parts based on Pakistani designs, and then ordered the facility to ship the components to Dubai.

For years, American and British intelligence operatives followed the network's transactions, shadowed members of the network (including Khan) around the world, and recorded their conversations—and doing so in very high-risk operations. [It was the work of these operations that led to the interdiction of the *BBC China*.] About two months ago Libya's leader voluntarily agreed to end his nuclear and chemical weapons programs, not to pursue biological weapons, and to permit thorough inspections by the International Atomic Energy Agency and the Organization for the Prohibition of Chemical Weapons.

On February 4, 2004, Khan appeared on Pakistan Television (PTV) and confessed to running the proliferation ring, and transferring technology to Iran, Libya, and to North Korea.

When I first raised my right hand and swore to support and defend the Constitution of the United States as a cadet in the United States Air Force Academy, Richard Nixon had recently been sworn in as our thirty-seventh president. As my journey wound down and I departed the Pentagon my final time as Chief of Staff, it was Barack Obama who wished me Godspeed. In the forty-three years in between, I faithfully served eight presidents—five of whom were Republicans, and three Democrats. I served each with equal intensity and dedication. There have been times when I've found a president's words to be so on point and so stirring that I found find myself stepping back and reflecting on how thankful I am to have chosen to dedicate my life's work to serving the greatest country on earth. That's how I felt upon hearing George Bush's stirring conclusion to his NDU speech:

> We will proceed as if the lives of our citizens depend on our vigilance because they do. Terrorists and terror states are in a race for weapons of mass murder, a race they must lose. Terrorists are resourceful. We're more resourceful. They're determined. We must be more determined. We will never lose focus or resolve. We'll be unrelenting in the defense of free nations and rise to the hard demands of dangerous times.

Gas centrifuges for uranium enrichment recovered from the BBC China *in Italy, en route to Libya, in 2003. They were later taken to the Y-12 Department of Energy National Security Complex in Oak Ridge, Tennessee, where this picture was taken (with a Y-12 guard also in the picture).* U.S. Department of Energy photo.

HAITI

2004 was a leap year. I know this for sure because it was well after midnight on the morning of Sunday, February 29, 2004, that the blast of the red switch phone's ringer alerted me to another crisis in need of attention.

A few hours earlier, Suzie and I had enjoyed a rare Saturday night out together—taco salads at a favorite local restaurant. It had been an eventful week, at home and abroad:

- Libya accepted responsibility for the Lockerbie bombing, and the United States responded by ending the travel ban to the nation that had been in place for twenty-three years.
- With less than a month before their presidential election, Russian president Vladimir Putin unexpectedly fired his prime minister along with his entire cabinet.
- A television containing eight pounds of TNT ripped apart the *Superferry 14* as it sailed through the waters off the coast of the Philippines, resulting in the deadliest terrorist attack at sea. One hundred and sixteen souls were lost in the attack by the Abu Sayyaf jihadist militant group. Haiti

was in a state of chaos, with rebels battling for control of the government. Execution-style killing were taking place on the streets, with bodies left as warnings of what was to come. Supporters of President Jean-Bertrand Aristide vowed to defend their leader even if it meant a fight to the death, as masses of resistance fighters were on the brink of invading Port-au-Prince. NBC News warned travelers of the dangers. "It's not a safe country. It is a lawless country," said NBC reporter Kerry Sanders.

Given the situation, while I wasn't expecting the call, it didn't particularly surprise me. "Sorry to wake you, sir," said the familiar voice on the other end. "Stan McChrystal here, and I need your help. It's Haiti."

It had been almost six months since Stan left the Pentagon to take over command of JSOC, where he was making great strides with his anti-terrorist initiatives, not to mention managing all manner of contingencies that the president and SECDEF deemed worthy of our nation's most elite special operations units.

"State needs our assistance in negotiating Aristide's departure from the country, as well as providing him with safe transport to a yet-to-be-determined location," he shared in a quick overview.

A *yet-to-be-determined location*, I thought. I could only imagine the frantic calls that State Department must be in the midst of making as they attempted to find a country that would agree to provide the president safe haven. Fortunately, that was not my business. Facilitating Stan's request was.

"I'll take care of obtaining the necessary verbal approvals," I assured him. "But you've got a fluid situation on the ground that requires you to move right now. In my mind, it's within your established mission authority to proceed as you see fit. I'll keep you abreast of what's going on on my end."

"Thank you, sir," he said. "I'm on it."

My first call was to the vice chairman, Pete Pace. "My recommendation is that you verbally authorize McChrystal's request," I told him.

"You got it," he replied without delay. That was all I needed to bump it up to the SECDEF, which I did via John Craddock, the SDMA (Secretary of Defense Military Advisor) who had replaced Ed Giambastiani. "This one's extremely time sensitive," I reminded him.

From that point on, Stan took the ball and ran with it—deftly orchestrating an extremely sensitive mission with virtually no advance notice. You hear so much about the battle between the military and the State Department, but here's a great example of the two of us working hand in hand—both with the common goal of doing whatever it takes to effectively execute the president's mission.

In this case, Stan's SEALs met Luis Moreno, the U.S. Embassy's second-ranking officer, at the Aristide residence and together they negotiated the president's departure. By the time the small convoy of heavily armed white Suburbans arrived at the airport, the unmarked white jet that Stan had secured was already waiting on the tarmac. Minutes later, the now ex-president was safely in the air, eventually to end up in the Central African Republic, where the plane would land at 1:00 a.m. (Sunday night, Monday morning).

DIRECTOR JOINT STAFF

So at this point we were coming up on two years in the job and the pace had not slowed down one iota. While we no longer had the official daily War Council meetings, my responsibility to keep our leadership fully informed had not diminished, and Iraq was still occupying the bulk of those discussions. On September 6, 2004, seven marines were killed outside Falluja when a car bomb exploded near a convoy of American and Iraqi soldiers. Less than a week later, nearly sixty people were killed by insurgent suicide bombers. Two days after that, another suicide bomber killed fifty men applying for jobs in Baghdad. On the final day of the month, as Iraqis celebrated the rebuilding of their infrastructure at the opening of a sewer plant, two car bombs exploded, killing forty-one people, including thirty-four children. Clearly, the nature of our Iraq mission had changed.

For the prior two years, I had felt comfortable that my areas of expertise dovetailed with the needs of the mission, which afforded me the opportunity to make valuable contributions. But at this point, those needs required more ground expertise than I was able to offer. There was no one better suited for this new mission than Lieutenant General Jim Conway, former commander of I MEF (pronounced "one MEF"—Marine Expeditionary Force) in Iraq. The big, burly Marine was well read, well respected, and the perfect choice to succeed me as J-3. In the course of the next two years he excelled—doing so well, in fact, that eventually he would receive his fourth star and be sworn in by fellow Marine Pete Pace as the thirty-fourth commandant of the Marine Corps.

Suzie and I were all set to pack up our boxes, finally get to spend some time together, and leave Washington for our next challenge, wherever that might be. I must say that by this point I considered myself to have a pretty decent strategic vision, but I certainly did not foresee things playing out the way they unfolded in Chairman Myers's office late one afternoon. "Norty," he began, with a grim countenance I'd come to recognize only preceded the very worst of news. "In spite of your best efforts to piss off the SECDEF, for some reason unbeknownst to me, he believes you'd make a superb DJS [Director of the Joint Staff], and I've been completely ineffective in talking him out of it."

Of course I knew that General Myers was my biggest advocate, and undoubtedly the one who approached Rumsfeld in the first place. The director is essentially the chairman's chief of staff, generally accepted to be a first among equals both in the joint world and among the three-stars. He or she orchestrates the activities of the directors of the Joint Staff including the J-1, J-2, J-3, J-4, J-5, J-6, J-7, and J-8. He or she is a gatekeeper in a sense—those things that the four-stars prefer not to deal with, the director does. He or she also is the closer. Four-stars certainly do the "setting up," but it's the director and his or her counterparts at the three-star level who are expected to close the deal. It's an important role, a great honor that I did not anticipate.

Just as the chairman is the senior member of the JCS (Joint Chiefs of Staff), the director is the senior member at the Ops Deps level of the system—the Ops Deps being the counterpart "threes" in each of the services. It's a parallel role to the chairman at one step lower down, where you try to resolve issues and settle things so that the four-stars can spend their time exclusively on the most consequential issues. You also are the interface with the deputies of the combatant commands—the fellow three-stars—working as the conduit between the chairman and the combatant commands.

What I found interesting was how well the four-stars knew the system, and they knew how things worked in the Tank, the chairman of the Joint Chiefs' private conference room, so if there were a particular top-level issue that a service chief or combatant commander did not want to take to the chairman or the vice chairman personally, they would call me and know that somehow I would get it done—or make sure that it got to the right person to get it done. I might get a call from Vern Clark or Mike Mullen (the two CNOs [Chief of Naval Operations] during my time as director) who would tell me, "Norty, the Navy's got a problem with a particular assignment for VADM 'X' or an unrealistic mission assignment, so let's try to work this out before it gets to the chairman." And on those issues that had secretarial, or White House, or congressional interest, then clearly the director would be involved because that was multidisciplinary, and one in which the chairman had an equity.

It was a great job that we thoroughly enjoyed, and it was far less stressful than the J-3 job. The icing on the cake was that instead of 4:45 a.m., I wouldn't have to get into the office until 5:45, so I was able to reestablish the rhythm and start running in the morning again.

The DJS position gave me a view of the larger defense enterprise and the larger combatant command architecture and insight into White House landscape, because I had White House access usually reserved for those at the four-star level. I was the only three-star to attend the annual White House combatant commander/chiefs conference the president hosted every year. It was not a trivial matter to have the opportunity to engage with the president at this level. We would meet in the Cabinet Room, and the president would begin by offering some introductory comments and insights, followed by brief comments from each of the military commanders, including the chairman and Joint Chiefs. Down the road when I attended as a four-star, I brought up the need for civilian leadership to articulate the enduring relevance of nuclear deterrence, a topic that immediately caught the president's attention and led to an extended discussion. This part of the conference was no social gathering; it was an opportunity for the commanders and Joint Chiefs to engage the chief executive directly on crucial issues surrounding national security, and for the president to do the same in the opposite direction.

Every afternoon around five or five thirty, Pete Pace (VCJCS) and I would join Chairman Myers in his office for a wrap-up session where they'd track through their day and then dump on me everything that needed to be acted upon—things like who should testify at a key congressional hearing or a combatant command task directly from the secretary. If it dealt with a particular operation, the three (J-3) might be included. If it were intelligence-related, most likely the two (J-2) would be called in. They'd give their two cents' worth and then be asked to leave, because the final half of our wrap-ups skinnied down to just the chairman, the vice, and myself. That's when the chairman fulfilled his statutory obligation to personally vet and approve joint assignments of the three- and four-star officers—assuring that people with joint service were promoted at rates similar to those without it. There's a whole process associated with flag officer management, and taking care of that for the chairman is the director's job. It was such an important one that it literally took a bite out of every day; but interestingly enough, it put me in the catbird seat to observe the process of every top-level promotion, and be a part of that process. I'd talk to the combatant commanders to make sure the chairman understood their preferences and their needs. I learned a lot about general officer management: how to build the bench, and how to do so in such a way that the long-term needs of our military were best served. Once specific individuals were identified as being best suited to meet those needs, I'd see how they'd subsequently be groomed for those potential positions. It was quite strategic, and a process that I found fascinating.

Ultimately the secretary of defense had to approve these selections, and at times he'd drop in and attend the meetings in person. On those occasions, once the topic of three-star assignments was about to be broached, I might be asked to leave the room; after all, being a three-star myself, it was feasible that my own selection might be a topic of their discussion. On the flip side, those times when it was only the chairman and the vice (which was usually the case), they didn't feel the need to exclude me from the discussion—even if I happened to be the topic of that discussion. They made no secret of the fact that I was a part of the larger plan that the secretary and the chairman had in mind, and that included Suzie and me being nominated for our fourth star. If confirmed, we would be one of only a dozen four-star generals in the entire Air Force.

In 2005 I pinned on my fourth star, and I had the incredible honor of being appointed a combatant commander—one of only nine in the entire United States armed forces at the time. But it was not to take over the command I had always hoped for. Rather than Special Operations Command, I was assigned to lead the US Transportation Command (TRANSCOM), which provides mobility support to all the service branches and defense agencies. In simple terms, I'd be leading an organization which ran the entire Department of Defense transportation network. Aircraft, ships, trucks, trains, you name it: if there was cargo or personnel to be moved for any of our military branches, it would be my responsibility (along with what I soon found to be one of the most driven, dedicated workforces one could ever imagine) to make sure that it arrived at the right time and in the right place.

Suzie and I loaded up our two cars and we headed west toward our new home at Scott Air Force Base, about twenty-five miles east of downtown St. Louis, just outside of Belleville, Illinois. As with the dozens of prior road trips we made together traveling from one assignment to the next, I was in the lead vehicle (in this case our red 1995 Ford Explorer), with Suzie following closely behind in our gold 2002 Explorer. No doubt we could have made the 850-mile trip in one very long day behind the wheel (over twelve hours of driving, plus stops), but instead of pushing it we decided to take our time and split it up, spending an uneventful night at the Holiday Inn in Louisville. I had picked up a pair of walkie-talkies so that Suzie and I had fairly decent comm for most of the way, and between the "How are you doing?" check-ins and the periodic requests for restroom breaks, I believe we got our money's worth out of them. Day two would be an easy hop with an anticipated arrival by early afternoon, certainly early enough that we wouldn't be driving directly into the setting sun. We were looking forward to taking in what friends had told us was a spectacular display of foliage as we drove through the Hoosier National Forest—with the hickories and oaks exploding into brilliant shades of autumn reds, browns, and yellows.

★ ★ ★

Suzie takes it from there: *Brilliant shades of reds and yellows? Hello! This was early September and it was over ninety degrees out there. Those trees had no intention of changing for at least another month! What we saw were shades of green. For miles and miles. Then cows. And more cows. And at one point, rows of these long buildings with huge fans mounted on their sides. Painted across the side of one of them in thick, red block letters was Southern Indiana Poultry. I reached across to the passenger seat and grabbed the compact gray walkie-talkie. "Hey Nort, did you see that?" I asked, knowing full well that his mind would be deeply preoccupied with something work-related and certainly not on sightseeing.*

Fortunately I had removed the unit from my ear or the loud blast of static that preceded his response might very well have punctured my eardrum. His voice crackled from the tiny speaker: "See what, Suz?" I could see through his rear window that he was searching to see what he had missed.

"We just passed a chicken farm," I said into the device. "Might be a good idea for you to turn around and leave them your 'egg sorting' resume, just in case this whole Air Force thing doesn't work out."

"You're always a step ahead of me, let's do it," he shot back in jest as we continued on our way.

Within an hour we passed over a river, then I spotted a green sign that said Welcome to Illinois, the Land of Lincoln. Thank God. At least we were in the right state. But boy, was it flat out there. And suddenly no more cows, or chicken farms, or anything else to speak of except for corn. Everywhere you looked, giant cornstalks blanketed the sprawling fields for as far as the eye could see. Norty described the crops as "robust," but I prefer the word . . . boring.

I so felt like picking up the walkie-talkie and mimicking the kid who whined to his parents every five minutes, "Are we there yet?" But good sense prevailed and I let it go.

In what felt like years later, the radio came alive with the great news: "This is it, next exit," Norty announced as he activated his right turn signal—a good half mile too early, but he was always very considerate of me in that way—just making sure to give me plenty of notice before any turn or change in course.

Once off the highway, he made a left turn at the bottom of the exit ramp, which took us under the highway overpass, then a right at the second stop sign. Still, all I could see was cornstalks. Wasn't this base supposed to be by St. Louis? I grabbed the radio and shared my enthusiasm. "My God, where are you taking me?" I moaned. "I'm not seeing any Gateway Friggin' Arch!"

"Stand by," was all he said as he crept along at a pace well under the posted speed limit. I could see through his rear windshield that he was looking down at a map or some sort of printed directions.

"Norty, this is ridiculous!" I complained. "How can you lose a whole air force base? Believe me, we didn't pass it. Obviously you got off the highway too soon!"

"I agree," screeched his unruffled voice as he signaled a turn that would take us back to Interstate 64. Ultimately we did find the base, and just as Norty was about to be faced with the challenges that come with coordinating the entire transportation needs of our Army, Navy, Air Force, and Marine Corps; our arrival was the embarkation of a new chapter in my life: I was about to learn that being the spouse of unified command's commander was light-years more challenging than anything I had been faced with to date.

★ ★ ★

We made it to the base in time to enjoy a nice dinner with the outgoing commander (and fellow Herc pilot), General John Handy and his wife Mickey, with a few days to spare before the change of command on September 7.

But first, just a little bit about the politics of how this was playing out: For more than ten years I had been a joint officer and while most of my contemporaries were supportive of my success, in the eyes of many, all these joint assignments meant that I'd become more distant from the Air Force. This was the lane that I had fallen into and I was proud to serve in each and every one of those joint assignments. And let's face it, in the process I was rising to the four-star level. And now, being combatant commander—it's ten times, a hundred thousand times more than anything that we ever expected. But what the naysayers didn't realize was that those ten years in joint positions gave me the opportunity to observe the Air Force from a unique vantage point; it gave me some insights into how people perceive the Air Force in a way that few other of my contemporaries enjoyed. Add to the mix the Special Ops fingerprints and you have a progression that's not what I would call typical for Air Force officers. But it got me noticed, and it gave me insights that allowed me to be far more effective in helping to guide our Air Force into the future. But none of this in any way diminished the affection that I've always had for my service. Every day of my career it was with a great deal of pride that I donned my Air Force blue uniform, and I could not be more grateful for where it eventually led.

The change-of-command ceremony was a great affair that took place on the parade field at Scott AFB on a sweltering Wednesday morning. As the U.S. Air Force (Midwest) band played at the center of the expansive grass field, I snuck a peep from behind the archway of a small, square brick edifice that would serve as our entryway. The main seating area consisted of white folding chairs perfectly aligned in rows on a permanent redbrick, riser type of structure, with each step leading up to the next level of seating. Every seat was filled, as were the temporary bleachers that were erected along both ends of the field. Immediately to the right of a simple wooden speaker's lectern was a row of plush, rich leather chairs where the VIPs were to sit; the way the tarmac was packed with white-over-light-blue U.S. Air Force EA (Executive Airlift) aircraft a mere thousand feet to the east, it felt like half of Washington had flown in to attend (and, in some cases, participate). I say that not as someone so important as to merit such a gathering, but rather as evidence of the magnitude of the position. Becoming a combatant commander was a big deal.

At the appointed time and with all the pomp and circumstance that one might expect, we entered through the brick archway in a sort of procession, first Secretary Rumsfeld, then General Myers, General Moseley (the newly sworn in Air Force chief of staff), General Handy, and me. One by one, we filed down the stairs, through a human passageway formed by two ranks of four Navy side boys (same term applies to both male and female sailors) facing each other, mirror images with their right hands held in perfect salute, their dress white uniforms so bright that I really could have used a pair of my aviator sunglasses. At the base of the steps, the red-brick flooring terminated in the center with an elaborate Air Force Star insignia that had been laid into the flooring, mosaic style, with custom colored bricks. As an homage to the base's first year of operation, the emblem was configured in the 1917 style consisting of a white five-pointed star inside a flag-blue circle, with a flag-red circle centered in the star. It was quite unique, and well known to be the focal point of the parade field.

We paraded past the guests and took our seats in those thick leather chairs. Suzie was already seated, as were Mickey Handy, Joyce Rumsfeld, Mary Jo Myers, and Jennie Moseley. It had only been five days since Air Force General "Buzz" Moseley had been sworn in as Chief of Staff, yet he was there along with the rest of them to lend his support. In the ultimate irony, in less than three years, General Moseley would be relieved by Rumsfeld's successor, Secretary Robert Gates, creating the void that I would fill to take his place as Chief.

In the manner prescribed by Air Force tradition and United States law, General Myers stood at attention and accepted the white, yellow-fringed TRANS-COM command flag from General Handy, then crisply rotated to face me and offered me the flag.

I grasped the lower portion of the thick, wooden mast with my left hand, and the top with my right, smiling at the chairman as I proudly accepted the flag, and with it formalized the change in leadership. I then turned and handed the flag to Air Mobility Command Chief Master Sgt. Michael Kerver, and took my seat beside Suzie.

Chairman Myers stepped up to the microphone and directed the following words to the impressive gathering of TRANSCOM workers assembled in the bleachers: "This struggle that we are engaged in depends on you. It depends on you to deploy, supply, and sustain the warfighters on the ground, refuel our defense in the air, and respond to humanitarian disasters around the world such as Hurricane Katrina—all the while enabling our armed forces to deter other potential threats while we're already at war."

With friends, family, and peers assembled behind me, and members of the command filling the parade field and bleachers in front, I stepped up to the microphone and began my first public speech as a combatant commander. I began by noting that TRANSCOM is "unique in an extraordinary time, a time when the nation is at war and we face the consequences of a daunting natural disaster at home . . ." I went on to share some of our challenges, and how exciting it would be to meet those challenges. Then I paused, looked at all who had assembled, and continued, "Let us honor those Americans who have given their lives in the cause of freedom and those who perished in last week's storm [with a death toll of at least 1,245 and property damage in excess of $108 billion, Hurricane Katrina was the costliest natural disaster in U.S. history]—and to a great public servant, the chief justice of the United States [Chief Justice William Rehnquist had died just a few days earlier]—by recommitting ourselves to the task of making it happen and getting it done. Together, we will serve our leadership and our nation's taxpayers well, efficiently, and, if need be, with courage, precision, and reliability."

This was all one big learning experience for me since when I started I didn't know a lot about commercial transportation, or even that much about the details of the supply chain, but I worked hard to soak it all in.

Addressing the component commanders and directors the following day, I uttered words that I hold very dear, and they actually became the command's motto: "A promise given is a promise kept." Those simple words expressed a philosophy that I expected to be followed in all our endeavors, with none more vital than the pledge I made to our geographic combatant commanders in the first few weeks after my arrival: I pledged to them that we would answer their call to provide deployment and distribution capabilities with the greatest speed and agility, the highest efficiency, and the most reliable level of trust and precision. It was all about relieving the combatant commanders—and particularly those that were in the middle of a fight—of any concern about their supply, of any concern about whether the system was going to perform at a level that would support their scheme of maneuver. It was all about making it happen for them.

We were in the midst of the surge in Iraq while at the same time sustaining Afghanistan; these were major undertakings that mandated efficient integration of air, land, and sea transportation resources to ensure there was no inadequacy or shortfall. The only way this was going to work was for me was to cultivate relationships both in government and on the commercial side. As an operator, my instinct was to focus on ops and performance management (such as ensuring the best possible support for CENTCOM in the movement of troops and supplies into Afghanistan), but Rumsfeld steered me in a different direction. "In the process of emphasizing performance, pay attention to *cost*. This is a $10 billion business in which you'll be working closely with the commercial side: FedEx, UPS, all the airlines, and maritime shipping companies with U.S. flags. By all means *run it like a business*." It was excellent guidance.

More than any position I had experienced to that point, this would focus on team building, both internal and external, and that team was one that consisted of less than 50 percent government resources. Well over half was performed on contract by commercial providers. We had a very extensive relationship and interaction with the cargo carriers and passenger carriers of the airline industry, a very close relationship with both the ship operators and the labor force associated with the maritime industry, and a not quite so close but still significant relationship with the trucking and rail industries. It's the rail folks who typically moved the armor and heavy loads from Army installations. We cultivated the teams with the CEOs and COOs of the top carriers, and tried to build the team with a focus on performance and cost, while ensuring that nobody experienced any inadequacy or shortfall.

One way or another, we had to ensure that at all times we had at the ready a mobilization base of long-range aircraft to support worldwide contingencies. The mechanism we had at our fingertips is called the CRAF activation—Civil Reserve Air Fleet. The CRAF is a voluntary contractual program where civil carriers (United, American, Delta, Southwest, JetBlue, FedEx, UPS, etc.), in exchange for being given preference in carrying commercial peacetime cargo and passengers for DoD (which is awarded according to a carrier's level of commitment in the CRAF program), agreed to augment military airlift capability during a crisis when requirements exceed DoD air mobility capability.

That was a preferable solution to one that could have been used: invoking our statutory authority to declare a national emergency and nationalizing the airlines. But the airlines are a major part of the American economy, so you do not want to interrupt their business except on the margins if there's any way to avoid that. Thus, the importance of having the CEOs offer their support completely voluntarily, and the importance of the CRAF contingency option. If needed during a large-scale contingency, airframes pledged to the CRAF could be activated in three progressive stages, with each stage providing additional airlift capacity:

- Stage I is for minor regional crises and humanitarian assistance/disaster relief efforts.
- Stage II is intended for major regional conflicts or major theater war.
- Stage III supports multiple theaters of war and national mobilization.

As of 2016, 453 (282 passenger and 171 cargo) aircraft were designated for potential activation.

As TRANSCOM commander, I was the activation authority for all three stages of CRAF, subject to the approval of the secretary of defense. In times of crisis when our own fleet was insufficient to handle the air transportation requirements, AMC (Air Mobility Command) would contact me and request that I activate the appropriate CRAF stage, which would obligate the preregistered participants to provide us with aircraft within forty-eight hours.

These activations not only allowed us to meet our service demands, but they also provided the airlines cover for any backlash or "failure to perform" contract violations they were forced to incur due to having a portion of their fleet committed to the activation. It gave them a measure of liability insurance they wouldn't otherwise have had, had they done this entirely voluntarily.

This is also true on the sealift side, with similar maritime contractual commitments.

We had routine meetings at the CEO level to talk about performance and cost—negotiating contracts and such. Those relationships sure came in handy during the 2007 holiday period when I made demands on the commercial airline passenger carriers during the surge. I needed airplanes and needed them fast, because the surge more than maxed out what we could handle with our military fleet.

I was placing a great demand at a time when there wasn't excess capacity. So we were actually pulling platforms out of commercial service to do charter work for the U.S. government. And some of the commercial carriers were easier to deal with than the others. I got it. They had commitments for a scheduled service that they were not going to interrupt. Fortunately, it never got to the point where they had to cancel scheduled flights, but we did call upon them to provide the airframes they held in reserve to fill gaps when an airplane broke down, so what we were really doing was zeroing out their contingency account. While these planes might not have been generating revenue, they were generating reliability across their fleet.

I needed the airlines' support and cooperation, and the only way I was going to get that was for me, as commander, to help their CEOs understand the importance of meeting the timelines of the surge, and understand how vital a part their cooperation was to make this happen. It had to be at this level because no one at any lower level was in the position to weaken the posture of their system during the holiday season. That had to come from the top. And it did. They reduced their reliability reserve in order to make airframes available for us to deploy troops.

Besides supporting the surge, we had a mandate from the secretary to move thirty-seven hundred MRAPs (mine-resistant armored protection vehicles) to Afghanistan and Iraq. These are the V-shaped hulled vehicles that were intended to improve survivability on the roads in Iraq and Afghanistan—specifically enhanced to withstand improvised explosive device (IED) attacks and ambushes. And they had to be moved by December of 2007. We worked our asses off with air, surface, and maritime means to make that happen—but we did it and in doing so we kept the promise and saved lives.

Operations ENDURING FREEDOM and IRAQI FREEDOM and humanitarian relief operations kept the command very busy. But there's another area where I believe that we at TRANSCOM were on the leading edge, and it's one that I believe every command, every department, and every company (whether military or civilian) should place in the highest priority. Arguably, it's even more relevant today than it was back then. Due to the nature of our mission we had abundant digital interaction with commercial industry—airlines, railroads, trucking companies, and such.

Long before the days of WikiLeaks and the big Sony Pictures hack, we discovered that there were others who were interested in our digital information—presumably because it would offer them tippers—indications of our intent and future movements. Inquiries to airlines or maritime companies might signal potential troop movement for deployment. We found that our unclassified systems were being surveilled. Certainly by the Chinese, but most likely by others as well. We immediately worked with NSA, DIA, and other intelligence organizations to institute precautions that put us well ahead of the pack in terms of trying to harden the unclassified side of our IT systems. We mandated a higher standard of security than the services required of their own organizations. Things that may sound mundane by today's standards—like prohibiting the use of thumb drives—hadn't even been thought of in those days, and we ended up encountering a great deal of friction on it—mostly from the services. For example, we were based at Scott AFB, and the base had an existing infrastructure that was provided by the Air Force—an infrastructure that was expected to operate at the same standard as all the other Air Force bases. But we were going to require a *higher* standard of security than was typical of the Air Force—for that matter, higher than the Army and Navy components.

It was an interesting period and it's one of those areas where I got to know Gordon England (twenty-fifth deputy secretary of defense, first deputy secretary of homeland security, seventy-second and seventy-third secretary of the Navy) quite well, because this was an issue that he championed. Same thing with Mike Hayden (past director of CIA and past director of NSA) and subsequently Keith Alexander at the NSA. Unlike other naysayers we came across, they were major advocates and supporters—big helpers in hardening our IT systems.

As an aside, it was also during this period that we had our first White House dinner. Earlier I mentioned that as director of the Joint Staff I was invited to the White House to attend the business portion of the president's annual Combatant Commanders' Conference (usually held in the Cabinet Room), but at the three-star level, I had to leave before the actual dinner. As combatant commander, there's no such prohibition; in fact, not only was I invited to the dinner, but Suzie was invited to accompany me.

We found it interesting that the Bushes hosted us upstairs in the Family Quarters, which was quite a compliment. Later on during the Obama years, we would dine with the president in one of the more formal areas of the State floor (although Mrs. Obama would host the wives upstairs while we conducted business), but the Bushes preferred the intimacy of the less traveled residence floor. While the men (at the time) had spent the bulk of the day in the Cabinet Room with the president, Suzie and the other spouses were already upstairs on the family floor—being graciously hosted by either Mrs. Bush or Mrs. Obama, depending on the year.

Once we concluded our business in the Cabinet Room, we'd be led by the president from the West Wing down the West Colonnade and enter the residence through the Palm Room on the lower level, then (in the case of the Bushes) through the Center Hall toward the Grand Stairway, where we'd climb two flights and meet our wives. Then each couple would get a personal picture taken with the president and first lady, usually in the upstairs center hallway in front of a beautiful white built-in bookcase, which was filled with books and White House memorabilia that one could easily become immersed in for days. Suzie stood to the president's left, looking resplendent in a violet and black skirt and matching lilac top set beneath a black high-waisted velvet jacket. Mrs. Bush, who stood between me and the president, looked elegant in a more casual style—wearing a black and white checked jacket over black slacks, with round diamond earrings that one couldn't help but notice.

From there we slipped into the Yellow Oval Room, which faces south and opens onto the Truman balcony, presenting a spectacular view of the Washington Monument. By this point I'd spent over thirty years proudly serving our great nation and you'd think that I'd take everything in stride, but that moment, having my best friend and the love of my life beside me to share a dinner with the president of the United States—in the very room that John Adams held his first presidential reception (even before the room was completed)—standing in the same place where, on December 7, 1941, FDR learned that the Japanese had invaded Pearl Harbor—Suzie and I just looked at each other and were totally humbled and overcome with emotion: pride, gratitude, deep appreciation, and an almost surreal "is this really happening?" disbelief.

I squeezed Suzie's hand, then we gave each other quick smiles and went our separate ways. What surprised us at first, but then we came to expect, was that typically Suzie and I were not assigned seats together. Instead, they would mix and match—not something I would have ever thought of, but it did lead to some interesting experiences!

★ ★ ★

Suzie elaborates: *The best example of this occurred back when Norty had just started as J-3, and it just might have been our very first party at this high level. I only bring it up now because it so perfectly illustrates the concept of this DC phenomenon of mix-and-match seating.*

Mary Jo Myers, Chairman Myers's wife, was a very good entertainer and she always came up with creative ways to handle the seating situation. This particular party was at Quarters Six—the beautiful official residence of the chairman of the Joint Chiefs. Perched high atop a hill directly across Grant Avenue from the Fort Myer parade field, the entire formal living room offered a spectacular view of the Washington Monument.

Nort had just started as J-3, and as I recall there were some other new Js who had recently been appointed to the Joint Staff, so in consideration of the fact that the whole group was about to embark upon a period of escalated stress in the ramp-up to the war, General Myers felt that a social gathering would be a great team-building exercise—an icebreaker of sorts—and a way for the group to get to know one another on a social level before being thrown together in the Tank.

Norty: You could call it sort of a "meet the Js" party.

Suzie: *I sure could, honey . . . but I won't. So before dinner during the initial reception part of the evening, Mrs. Myers handed each of us a small survey to fill out, asking all sorts of personal questions, things like "When was the last time you went to a movie?" and "When was the last time you read a good book that was not related to business?" and "When was the last time you ate out at a restaurant where the waiter's first question wasn't 'Would you like fries with your burger?'" There were about five questions like this. Once we were all finished, she collected them all and tallied the results. Those who'd recently done all five might have scored a "fifty," where those who'd only recently done a few of those things might only get a "twenty" or "twenty-five." And that's how our seating was determined; you sat with guest whose survey scores were similar to your own. She really only did it for fun and to be different, but there's probably some merit in the fact that the "fifties" would most likely enjoy discussing the books or movies or restaurants.*

Well, sure, for them it was fun. But how fun would that be for people like me who scored a zero? That's right, I scored a bagel. Bupkis. Zippo. Diddly squat. My assigned table was even labeled "Table Zero."

Norty: You know that's not true.

Suzie: *Well, it might as well have been. Norty headed off to his table and I slipped off in the other direction to mine. Then something struck me.*

Hey, wait a minute, Norty! How come you scored higher than me? The way you work, there's no way you did more of these things than me.

Norty:　I lied.

Suzie:　*Oh, OK. So I made my way over to my table and sat down. Thing is, adding insult to injury, I was the only one there! Not only was I a zero, but I was the only zero! OMG!*

Norty:　But you eventually had company.

Suzie:　*You can say that again. But not at first. I was just sitting there all alone and watching this mass of guests gathered around someone, when kind of like how the Red Sea parted for Moses to cross, the swarm stepped back just enough to allow the center of their attention to slip out and search for his table—which, by the way (thank God!), happened to be mine!*

　　Sporting a dark suit with a light-gray patterned tie, he was not at all what I would have expected. Sure, the craggy face, swept-back graying hair, and wire-framed glasses looked familiar, but instead of the anxious, sometimes cantankerous, self-assured man I'd seen on TV, Secretary Rumsfeld extended his hand with a sincere, warm smile and almost a twinkle in his gray-green eyes. "You didn't have to save them all for me," he said as he eyed the still-empty seats surrounding our round, six-top dinner table. "It's nice to have someone else to share the honor of winning Mrs. Myers's little personality exercise." Is this guy nuts? I thought. Then he continued: "You do know that the results proved us to be the most serious-minded and focused of this whole bunch. It's determination like that—unimpeded by distractions like movies and TV and such—that brings us success."

　　"Oh, no!" I quickly interjected while shaking my head. "You've got it all wrong. This is the losers' table, the table for the people who have no life, who don't know how to have fun!"

　　"Well, I'm a fun person!" he shot back defensively, seemingly annoyed that his entertaining and lighthearted reputation wasn't recognized by the hostess. I just stared at him in disbelief. Suddenly, he cast aside the feigned annoyance and broke into a great laugh. Truth is, he was fun! And charming.

　　By that time other "losers" had arrived to fill out the table, and in fairness to Mary Jo, she really wasn't trying to embarrass anyone; she just wanted us to understand that there's more to life than work—that it's every bit as important to take some time for yourself and let loose. Good advice, and we grew to become close friends.

Looking back, I remember being so nervous that whole dinner. I think I always come across so confident and sure of myself—and maybe now that's the case, but it sure wasn't back then. In my mind, suddenly I saw myself as Suzie Ptak, the schoolteacher from Arkansas. I couldn't help but wonder what my dad—a retired Air Force major—would have thought about his daughter hobnobbing with the head of our Department of Defense. I doubt if he would have been thrilled with what I was about to say: "So Mr. Secretary, I have to say that your recent decision to change the name of all the CINCs (Commanders in Chief) to 'combatant commander' is really stupid." He looked up from his linguini and kind of furrowed his brows; I suppose it had been a while since anyone called his decision "really stupid"—to his face, that is. I continued, "We all know that the commander in chief is the president. I mean, we're not idiots. So why can't we also have commanders in chief of the various commands?" He stared at me for a moment, then nodded with the realization that what I proposed was absolutely brilliant, and then right there on the spot, he agreed to rescind his order and revert to the old nomenclature.

No, that didn't happen. Except the part about him staring at me, that part's true, but it was with more of a "Who the hell is this woman?" kind of a look.

"I want you to know that I truly do respect your opinion," he said in a way that I took to mean I really couldn't care less what you think about this, but you've sure got chutzpah to have said it! "But you know that I'm not going to change it back, don't you?"

"Of course I do," I responded, wondering what just happened, but glad that I had the chance to speak my mind.

He stood, and I started to do the same, thinking that it was an indication that he was moving on to either go home or "work the room." But instead, he signaled me to stay seated. "Oh, I think you really need to meet my wife. You remind me a lot of her. Don't go anywhere, Suzie. I'm going to find her and bring her over. You two will get along just fine." He ran over to her table and did just that. And it was true. As soon as she opened her mouth I could tell—I could have been listening to myself.

Norty: That night driving home, Suzie was on a high. "Norty, you should have heard me; it was amazing . . . I was one-on-one with the friggin' *secretary of defense* and I told him how dumb a thing it was to change those titles!" Gulp.

"You mean the secretary of defense who just happens to be your husband's boss? At least he was before the party. I'll let you know if that's still the case when I get to work on Monday." She blanched, for a moment thinking that I was serious. But she knows me too well. I was—and still am—totally in awe of how she pulls off these things. I found it to be totally hilarious.

"Now that I think about it, why was I so nervous?" she continued in the car. "I was sitting there conversing with the secretary of defense, and he was listening to me. Who's to say that next time he won't act on my suggestion? Or maybe the next time won't even be him; it could be the president instead." Double gulp. That's Suzie, true to her promise that she would never be my puppy dog. But we did agree that it was wise for her to stop when she did. In the big picture, that event was an appropriate venue for her comments. It was supposed to be a team-building exercise and it was. And we grew to have great affection for both Joyce Rumsfeld and the secretary.

Suzie: *Right. And I decided that I would allow myself one zinger per social event and that's it. So if somebody tossed me a softball and I swung at it, that's it for the night. If they tossed me another, I had to let it go. Because I can get really caustic at times and as much as I might kid about it, at that level I just needed to be careful. I may come across as cavalier but I've always been in awe of what Norty has achieved, and nobody could be more respectful of the delicacy of some of those relationships. But that's never going to change the fact that I will always be the loud one and Norty will be the quiet one.*

Norty: Thank you for pointing that out to me.

★   ★   ★

TRANSCOM was a fascinating assignment. During my three years at TRANSCOM, we transported 2.5 million passengers, 3 million short tons of cargo, and 5,667 battle casualties in support of the wars in Afghanistan and Iraq. In addition to our support of the wars, we provided humanitarian relief operations for the 2005 earthquake in Pakistan; Hurricanes Rita and Wilma across the U.S. Gulf Coast; and in the summer of 2006 we evacuated over fifteen thousand people from Lebanon as Israeli and Hezbollah forces battled along the southern Lebanese border. In August 2008, the conflict between Russian and Georgian forces had ignited, prompting our delivery of vast quantities of humanitarian relief supplies for Georgian refugees and the immediate transport of all two thousand Georgian troops from Iraq back to Georgia when they were recalled to support the endeavor.

Perhaps the most important of all our missions is the movement of injured warfighters from the battlefield to medical treatment facilities. This is a complex process requiring close collaboration with doctors, hospitals, and evacuation crews. In 2007, we transported over 9,900 patients from the USCENTCOM AOR (Area of Responsibility) and over 16,000 patients globally.

Should the worst occur and a warfighter perish in the defense of our nation, we made it our business to ensure that they received the most dignified transport from the battlefield to final destination. During our time at TRANSCOM and with our commercial partners, we transported thousands of our fallen heroes to the airfield nearest the interment.

Suzie and I were relishing our time in St. Louis and were building lifelong friendships. I learned about industry and I learned a lot about supply chain and a lot about labor in both the maritime and airline areas. We were building a rock-solid reputation with the folks we supply. We had even become Cardinal fans, and the Redbirds were headed to the World Series. Life was good.

That's when I got the word that I had cancer.

★   ★   ★

Sometimes when you face a life-and-death situation, it just doesn't seem real at first. It's more like an out-of-body experience that you're observing—almost as if it were happening to somebody else. That's how it was for Suzie at first; it wasn't that she was in a state of shock; she was more . . . numb.

That changed in a heartbeat when I stepped onto the gurney and a single observation jarred her back to reality. I like to think of it as the "great equalizer." I may have walked into San Antonio's Wilford Hall Medical Center with four stars on my epaulets surrounded by a support staff including aides and security personnel, but in those final moments before being wheeled into the OR, I was wearing the same faded green cotton open-backed smock worn by every other patient in a similar pre-op situation, and of course there's nothing on under-neath. Apparently my butt was in full view, and that lone image drove home the reality for Suzie. This is not a dream.

In an instant, numbness became confusion. *What am I supposed to do now?* Then, as they wheeled me away, I saw a look I'd never seen before: fear. Who could blame her? It hadn't even been a week since we learned that I had cancer.

★ ★ ★

Suzie continues: *While it's true that I wear my emotions on my sleeve, I really do take everything in stride. But not this one; I was terrified. What made it even worse, this thing must have been so bad that nobody used the "c" word. When Norty first told me about it, he said, "It turned out to be malignant." Dr. Brennan said he was removing the "affected tissue." The nurses talked about "cases like this." Of course I was petrified when this "abnormality" was so scary that nobody could even say the word.*

Norty: I had been having a little discomfort on my tongue over a period of several months and I ultimately went to the doctor to have it checked out. They took a biopsy of it and determined that it was cancerous. I don't smoke and I don't chew tobacco, so this was pretty unusual.

"We're going to want to get that taken out as soon as possible, Norty," the doctor warned. "And I want Dr. Joe Brennan in San Antonio to take care of it. He's the very best head-and-neck surgeon in the Air Force."

"This Saturday [October 14, 2006] Suzie and I have a pretty big event to attend in Washington; it's the dedication of the new Air Force Memorial. All the generals are flying in for it, and President Bush will be there to officially accept the Memorial on behalf of the nation. That means we could fly to Texas as early as this Sunday, if time is really that much of a factor."

"Let me put it this way: I am not liking what I'm seeing. I want Dr. Brennan to give a second opinion, but the sooner we get that out, the greater the chances are that we can save your tongue. Every bit as important, I want it out before it has a chance to metastasize. My strong advice is for you to express your regrets and allow the president to accept the Memorial without you."

By Saturday we were at Wilfred Hall Medical Center in San Antonio with Col Dr. Joseph Brennan, unquestionably the Air Force's best otolaryngologist/ head-and-neck surgeon. With his experience, skills, and reputation, Joe Brennan could have gotten out and made millions in the private sector, undoubtedly becoming a famous surgeon. But instead, after 9/11, Joe decided to stay in the

Air Force and devote his life to treating the wounded. He spent the year before my surgery about fifty miles north of Baghdad in the Sunni Triangle at the Air Force Theater Hospital in Balad. That's one of about eight or nine deployments he's made to Iraq or Afghanistan.

During the Fallujah Offensive, he was treating over fifty patients a day—life-and-death cases where he had four to five minutes to clear the shrapnel from a patient's airway or that patient would die. We talked about some of his experiences:

It's essential that we be as close to the front as possible or by the time the patients get to us, it's too late. Most of the injuries we treat are a result of road-side bombs or other improvised explosive devices—deadly high velocity shrapnel that rips apart arteries and splays throughout the body; but they're so small, they often appear to be harmless little specks, like measles. Their devastation is indiscriminant, as are we. Allied personnel, Iraqi civilians, combatants—it doesn't matter; we treat them all equally.

Joe was excellent with me, he was superb with Suzie, and he is a real patriot who is motivated by passion instead of his pocketbook.

I felt confident as the anesthetic took effect; I knew that I was in expert hands.

Suzie: *There I was sitting in this tiny little waiting room, thumbing through a year-old issue of* Popular Mechanics *(the only other choices were* Car & Driver *and* Parents*) wondering if the procedure was almost over.*

Dr. Brennan had estimated four hours or so; surely it had been at least that long. I glanced at my watch. Five minutes had passed since the last time I checked, which meant that it had only been about a half hour since he left. It was going to be a long day. I put down the magazine and closed my eyes; surprisingly, I nodded off. Two seconds later, I was jarred awake by a loud, tinny rendition of the Air Force Song. Groggily I looked around for the source. It was my cellular ringtone.

I rummaged through my purse to find the phone and quickly glanced at the number. I didn't recognize it, and debated not even answering. "Holy mackerel, what if it's the doctor?" I suddenly thought, frantically hitting the "connect" button before they hung up.

"Hello," I bellowed into the device.

"Suzie, Pete Pace here. I'm calling to see how Norty's doing. Scratch that, I

know that he's doing fine. I'm really calling to see how you're doing."

I was floored. This man was chairman of the Joint Chiefs of Staff—the highest ranking officer in the entire U.S. military—who had the presence of mind and the thoughtfulness to call me during the surgery, and we had a war going on! That speaks volumes about his character and kindness.

"The truth is, General, it's very sad. To see him this morning in that hospital gown with his little butt sticking out, it was awful."

"I get it, Suzie. I totally understand," he said with compassion. "That would make me sad, too, if I had to look at his butt first thing in the morning!"

I cracked up. In the middle of all this, he actually got me to laugh. Momentarily, at least.

"The doctor said he's removing a third of Norty's tongue; maybe more if that's what it takes to get everything."

"He's not much of a talker anyway, so I wouldn't worry about that," he deadpanned in response.

Again, I laughed out loud. "Sir, I can't thank you enough for thinking of us."

"Hang in there, Suzie. Lynne sends her best, too."

This time he actually succeeded in calming me down. By the time I got off the phone, I didn't feel quite so doom and gloomy anymore.

It was well over four hours later that Dr. Brennan stepped into the waiting room, still wearing his surgical scrubs. "First of all, Norty's doing fine. He's still out and he will be for at least another hour, but he did just great. We ended up removing about a third of his tongue."

If Brennan ever decides to give up his ENT work, he really should teach a master's class in medical bedside manner. He demonstrated that perfect combination of compassion, sincerity, and a professional intimacy that made you feel like you had known him for many years. Combined with his informal demeanor, I felt both reassured and much less tense.

"So that means you got everything?" I asked.

"I have a good feeling about it, but it will be another hour before we get the official results back from pathology. What we do is go in and remove samples of all the surrounding tissue and . . ."

"Excuse me, Doctor," I interrupted. "I think you have me confused with someone who wants to hear the details. I don't want to see anything, I don't want to read about any of this online, I don't want to hear about tissue samples unless they're for my runny nose . . . I graduated from the 'Hear no evil, see no evil, *speak no evil' school of medicine. Just, please, come back and tell me that he'll be all right."*

About an hour later, that's exactly what he did. Thank God, it came back all clear.

Norty: I spent the night in the hospital but I was so medicated there's very little that I remember. I recall the wonderful protocol woman from Lackland AFB who took such special care of Suzie. On the flip side, my aide and security staff kept barging in—which was very attentive of them, but at times like these, I would think that common sense would dictate that one's privacy should be respected. On one of these intrusions, I remember trying to convince my aide to hook up my computer in the room so I could check my emails, but Suzie vetoed that one in no uncertain terms.

I'm told that Ron Keys called back to check on us. In fact, Suzie tells me that he called from the bus transporting all the generals back from the Air Force Memorial dedication, and Suzie held the phone up to my ear as every one of them took turns on the phone to send their best. It was very thoughtful of them, but it might as well have been Captain Kangaroo calling because I don't remember any of it.

It probably took a year to get full functionality back. As it turned out, speaking wasn't as much of a problem as control of saliva. I became a spitter. When I spoke, I frequently had to pause to swallow the moisture that had accumulated in my mouth. We don't even notice it, but our salivary glands are constantly secreting saliva that a fully functioning tongue involuntarily moves to the back of the mouth to be swallowed. The part of my tongue that handles that process had been removed. Eventually this took care of itself, but for the first twelve months, it took a conscious effort on my part to "drain the lake." Doing so was not always at the forefront of my mind, which at times led to some embarrassing situations.

The real cause for celebration occurred in October of 2011, when tests determined that I was still cancer-free; the rule of thumb being that if you are cancer-free for five years, the chance of recurrence is less than 5 percent. I will be forever indebted to Dr. Joe Brennan for granting me admission to that life-saving club.

Chapter Six

ALL IN

AUGUST 2008–AUGUST 2012

There had only been eighteen Air Force Chiefs of Staff in the entire history of the United States, and I never thought that I would be one of them. It didn't really sink in when the president announced my nomination, or even when the Secretary of the Air Force swore me in. But when Suzie and I walked into Air House (the Chief's official residence) and were welcomed by our aides, it suddenly became real. As you enter, there's a little foyer with a plaque on the wall that has the names of all the chiefs who lived in that house. Curtis LeMay is on there, Whiting is on there, Vandenberg is on there. All these legends. I looked at Suzie and just shook my head. Ironically, just over sixty years earlier, this had also been the residence of General Omar Bradley, the very general my dad had referenced when he doubted me.

The Chief is the highest ranking officer in the Air Force, a member of the Joint Chiefs of Staff, and military advisor to the president. Every prior Chief was chosen from either the fighter or bomber communities; I was the very first from Special Ops. Somehow that made it even more special for me. I was proud of my provenance at the tip of the spear, and with it came an escalated sense of responsibility to make every moment count. I knew my four years would fly by faster than a bullet—it truly felt like just yesterday that Dad dropped me off at the TWA terminal for that flight to the Academy—but when the day finally arrived that I would hang up that uniform for the very last time, I wanted it to be with a deep sense of satisfaction that only comes with the understanding that we had served the nation well and enhanced the lives of the airmen and their families.

But what was I walking into? We were a nation at war and the Air Force was in trouble. Our fleet of aircraft was aging, the nuclear enterprise had decayed, we were insufficiently committed to the war, and our greatest asset—the airmen and their families—were not getting the levels of care to which they were entitled. Between the war and the current state of the Air Force, I'd have to institute rigorous accountability and refocus our priorities in order to prove ourselves completely worthy of America's trust. I couldn't wait to begin. But first, there was that not insignificant matter of confirmation.

★ ★ ★

After thirty-four years I should have known better, but I failed to perform. Blindsided by a sucker punch. Instead of fighting back I became defensive, and losing this match would mean the end of my career. Mullen and Gates were in my corner, as was President Bush. The final hurdle was one that I had encountered many times before, the Senate Armed Services Committee, and word on the street placed them in my corner and supportive of my confirmation. I'd been given a heads-up on one potential challenge that might arise, but forewarned is forearmed, so I was fully prepared to meet the issue head-on.

Michigan Congressman Mike Rogers had called me to say that he believed I had misled him in 2003–2004 surrounding unsecured arms caches in Iraq. I remembered it well. It was during my time as J-3, so I wasn't even in the direct chain of command at the time; answering that question, if it were to be asked, would be easy. Besides that, I anticipated a few softballs tossed my way, but in the big picture I expected this session to be one of my easiest—and certainly most successful—testimonies before the committee. After all, they had already demonstrated their support by promoting me to four-star and backing my nomination to TRANSCOM commander. That's a far cry from how it would unfold on this blistering Tuesday morning, July 22, 2008, in room SR-325 of the Senate Russell Office Building—the recently named Kennedy Caucus Room.

I began my opening statement and thanked Suzie for being my best friend. Then I fielded questions from Senator Akaka about the long-range strike aircraft, and Senator Inhofe about our aging fleet. This went on for over two hours as I comfortably responded to queries from Senators Warner, Levin, Graham, and others.

As the main hearing began to wind down, I started to relax. Before these things begin, I have to get geared up for them; I have to will myself to become mentally engaged. Without this intentional focus, I tend to let my guard down, and that's exactly what happened. Bill Nelson from Florida brought up the 2003 testimony in which I declined to speculate as to the number of troops I believed would be required for Iraq, and questioned whether I had been candid with the committee. I indicated that back then I didn't feel qualified to make the assessment necessary to directly answer their question, so I didn't. It was not a great answer, but I was fading fast.

Then Senator Chambliss chimed in to inquire about the Rogers issue surrounding the unsecured munitions sites. I'd forgotten that they'd become close when both served in the House. "You became aware of the ammunition sites that were unsecured in Iraq during the course of [the early 2003] period of time. . . . What action did you take to ensure that the information relative to the fact that there were a number of sites that were unsecured were in fact going to be secured so that there could not be pilferage of the ammunition sites and the consequences of that being that insurgents would have the munitions with which to make IEDs which in fact they did?"

I explained that we did receive the information, we provided analytical resources to attempt to confirm the locations, then I passed the information along to my counterparts at CENTCOM and Combined Task Force 7.

He pushed. Did I follow up to ensure that they acted on that information?

I explained that I did my job by following up that the information was received and understood, but it really wasn't my place to get into what they did with the data. It was the truth, but I was less than eloquent in my presentation.

Senator Warner announced that they would continue this discussion in "executive session"—a follow-up closed hearing. It would take place immediately after this one in room SR-222, a secure room frequently used by the Armed Services Committee for their classified hearings. My hunch was that this was a setup and they had agreed to it ahead of time.

Downstairs we went. There were nine senators (of the original fifteen or so) and it was brutal. Bill Nelson pulled out a thick notebook and began to read from it—it was the transcript of that 2003 hearing. Nelson, Senator Levin, and others on the panel felt that I had been deliberately evasive. They were having second thoughts as to whether I would be candid with the committee as a service chief. I went on the defensive and tried to reiterate what the context of all this was, but I was not being impressive. I had lost my focus and I was unable to recover. I went from treading water to sinking fast. By the time I left the chamber I had very bad vibes as to the session's outcome, fairly certain that my lackluster performance had allowed this opportunity to slip away.

Suzie was waiting for me back upstairs.

Suzie: *When Norty told me what had happened in there, I was mad! I will never understand why he couldn't suck it up and be strong. How could he possibly lose focus and go down at a time like that? Because he got tired?! I told him that the next time he was in a situation like that, he had to bring Chief McQuiston, who was the Chief Master Sergeant (senior enlisted leader) at TRANSCOM. He's the most positive, inspirational person I know, and I wanted his face to be the last one Norty saw before he stepped into another situation like that.*

My confirmation was unraveling. The firestorm that would ensue played out in back-channel communications between Congress, the secretary of defense, the chairman, and even a retired service chief.

That night I got a call from Chairman Mike Mullen, who also saw this whole thing going south. He and Secretary Gates had worked this very hard. After I mishandled that closed hearing, even Senator Warner—usually an ally—called Gates and essentially asked, "Are you sure Schwartz is your man?" Gates called Mullen, who called me.

"Schwartz, you're going to have a *second* closed hearing," he said, making it crystal clear that if I wanted to salvage the confirmation I'd have to hit it out of the park. "Get your shit together this time."

Always maintain a reserve for the unexpected.

Before that second closed hearing, I went back to see Mike Rogers on this. Heather Wilson, a congresswoman from New Mexico, former Rhodes Scholar, and Air Force Academy graduate, heard about this situation from my friend and colleague, Bob Otto, who had quietly intervened on my behalf. Congresswoman Wilson knew Mike Rogers well and offered to facilitate a meeting.

When he and I met, I explained to him the situation surrounding the un-protected arms and I think he appreciated the explanation. I told him candidly, "Sir, we didn't blow you off. You had to appreciate that these were priorities chosen by folks on the ground. We don't command the folks on the ground from Washington." He got that, and it was a good meeting. I went on to explain that I was a young three-star at that time. "This is six years later; I am more mature than I was then. I think that I'm prepared to be a service chief in a way that he would respect." He let it go, and I assume he contacted Saxby to do the same, because I never heard any more about it.

Incidentally, years later as I was leaving the Chief's job, I went to see him again. I told him that I appreciated his accepting the explanation that was given during the confirmation process and that I hoped that my tenure had confirmed that his judgment to allow the confirmation to proceed was a good judgment and he concurred. He acknowledged that the commitments I made to him regarding faithful service had been fulfilled.

I wish the issue of "troop strength" could have been mollified in a similar manner. But that was not the case. Certain members were still very much on the fence.

Unbeknownst to me, an important private meeting was about to take place, one that I wouldn't hear about until years later. Senators Warner and Levin had reached out and met with General Eric Shinseki, who had long since retired as Army chief of staff. They essentially asked him for the "no shit" story on the numbers. Ric confirmed that the numbers were all over the place and there was really no way that I could have given them a definitive answer. I am told that Ric also expressed that "Schwartz is your man."

I went back for the second closed hearing.

Bill Nelson called me into a side office before the hearing started and we had a long talk. He indicated that if I reassured the members that I understood the necessity for candor with the committee, he would no longer hold the nomination, but would instead vote for my confirmation. He wanted to double down on the reason he had initiated this whole thing in the first place. I realized at that moment that the odds had swung back in my favor.

That whole episode reminded me that *it is not always about the facts; it's about influence and position.* Nelson is a senior senator. He's going to be around. Basically what he was saying was, "I can turn the committee for you. I'm the key."

True to her word, Suzie had contacted Chief Master Sergeant McQuiston, and she made sure that his would be the last face I saw before walking into that second closed hearing. He pulled me aside and whispered in my ear, "This is not about you and it's not about those politicians. It's about me and the other 600,000 members of our Air Force who *need you* to get us back on track! It's about the 300 million Americans who *rely* on you to keep them free! Now get in there and show them what General Norty Schwartz is made of! Go kick ass! You *are* going to be our Chief."

I nodded, stepped inside, and kicked ass. I was totally psyched and didn't care what they threw at me; I was going to smash it out of the park. I went on the offensive with the most eloquent, passionate, convincing four-minute soliloquy of my life.

Then something very interesting happened. They almost seemed to forget about my presence, and it turned into an internal discussion among themselves—and a real civics lesson for me. They started discussing that maybe one of the things they should do was to inquire of secretary of defense nominees about what kind of building they're going to run. There was this underlying notion that they liked the way Gates was running the building, but that certainly was less the case in the Rumsfeld days. So it turned into this larger discussion of the Rumsfeld versus the Gates Pentagon.

Suzie: *That's part of the whole dynamic of how this turned south in the first place. They saw Norty as the last vestige of the Rumsfeld era and they still felt blindsided by what played out during those days. The points they were attacking Norty on were from 2002 and 2003—the Rumsfeld years. And they needed to know if he was still going to have that sort of mindset. They're thinking, "The Rumsfeld era is gone; we're moving on. Are you coming with us?"*

Norty: Absolutely. They realized that the real issue was far more complex than what Norty Schwartz may or may not have done back in 2003. What happened at the end of the hearing is that I was able to observe the senior leadership having this wonderful discussion about whether they should be just as concerned about what kind of building a SECDEF nominee might run, as they were about his opinions on policy issues. Obviously, they felt that Gates was a better partner than Rumsfeld had been.

I almost felt like a real-life Frank Capra film was playing out right in front of me. All it needed was Jimmy Stewart up there. It really was a wonderful privilege to observe how—behind the scenes when the cameras were off—Democrats and Republicans and elders spoke about good governance. Bottom line, it was their way of concluding that management style matters.

We took a deep breath, returned home, and called Gates with an update. I could tell by his tone that this was not breaking news to him; I'm sure Warner had already called and said something like, "Don't worry, Schwartz is in. He did fine."

Two days later the confirmation was announced and we were off and running.

There were two big lessons in this for me.

Members of Congress have very long memories.

This is something to take very seriously because things you say and do years before will be quoted back to you, so you shouldn't be surprised when this happens.

Never relax prematurely.

From that moment on, I always psyched myself up and *stayed* up until it was absolutely clear that the hearing was over or the interview was done or the presser was complete. I dodged a bullet that time, but I never allowed myself to be in that position again.

Suzie: *And my lesson was that these things are just too much pressure for me. I never went to another hearing and I never watched them on TV. Norty can sit there and be attacked by them for hours on end and he's as cool as a cucumber— professional, respectful—I've never seen anything like it. I'd go ballistic and throw it right back in their faces. See no evil, hear no evil—works every time.*

NUKES

One of our first orders of business was cleaning up the nuclear debacle. It meant looking at both events (the unaccounted-for warheads and mistaken shipment to Taiwan) and the larger enterprise issues. Who was involved? What did they do? Where were they culpable? Did this warrant discipline? These were high-level people, commanders not fulfilling expectations. It was a defining moment for us because that kind of ineptitude could not be allowed to continue. We acted on that. We restored accountability and we put the nuclear business back into the organization of the Air Force. We did it with care, but resolutely.

The Air Force is responsible for two components of our nuclear triad, strategic bombers (now some B-52s and B-2s) and Minuteman intercontinental ballistic missiles (ICBMs), leaving the submarine-launched ballistic missile component under the supervision of the Navy. With the demise of Strategic Air Command in the early 1990s, the bomber business went to Tactical Air Command (now Air Combat Command), and it was its obligation to do both the *conventional* strike mission and the *nuclear* strike mission. Because of the wars and because of the actual orientation of Air Combat Command, the nuclear mission was not a particularly good fit for ACC.

And while there were synergies surrounding the ICBM missiles being in Air Force Space Command, those similarities were largely in the launch area. They were not in the space ops area. There again, the fit for the nuclear mission was not ideal for Space Command either.

From an enterprise perspective, having the strategic bomber mission and ICBM mission split between two organizations was not working well, nor was it effective that both of these organizations shared the nuclear operations with conventional endeavors.

The logical solution was to bring these two capabilities back together into a newly created single organization whose sole purpose was to maintain focus on the nuclear mission, under a culture that was more consistent with respect to the demands for precision required by this mission. To that end, we set up a three-star command called Air Force Global Strike Command that combined the nuclear-capable bomber mission and the Minuteman ICBM mission into a single organization at Barksdale Air Force Base, Louisiana.

That was a major undertaking that took several years to bring to full fruition. Lt Gen Frank Klotz (currently the Department of Energy's undersecretary for nuclear security and administrator for the National Nuclear Security Administration in a civilian capacity) was the first commander of Global Strike Command. The former Rhodes Scholar, former vice commander of Air Force Space Command, and former NSC director for nuclear policy and arms control was instrumental in getting it stood up as it should have been.

There was also a lack of focus in the sustainment of the weapons themselves as reflected by the Taiwan glitch. Our solution was to stand up the Nuclear

Weapons Center at Kirtland Air Force Base in Albuquerque. They are responsible for the acquisition, sustainment, and storage of nuclear missiles, weapons, and related components.

Considering the magnitude of the nuclear mission, one might ask how the focus and attention was allowed to wane without sending up red flags at the highest level. Good question, and it's one that we asked ourselves.

Over the years there had been staff divisions that focused on the nuclear business, but what once were divisions had withered down to a single action officer. Clearly the nuclear business and all of its dimensions needed much more focused attention than that. So the third thing we did was to create a Pentagon-based two-star director (subsequently elevated to three-star during the Welsh tenure) on the Air Staff who focused on nuclear matters—operational, resources, and policy. Called the A-10 (Deputy Chief of Staff for Strategic Deterrence and Nuclear Integration), they were my right hand with respect to the interaction that I would have with Joint Chiefs on the nuclear matters and internal headquarters supervision of the nuclear mission. For example, when the New Start treaty was being negotiated, it was this group of people who kept the secretary and me up to speed on the negotiations, on whether this was an acceptable distribution that sustained deterrence, and so forth. They not only maintained our focus on the mission area, but also worked the policy issues for which Washington is responsible.

The bottom line is *we put the nuclear business back into the organization of the Air Force.* These three initiatives were our way of reestablishing the relevance of deterrence as a mission within the Air Force, and of reestablishing the high standards that were required of that mission.

ALL IN

The secretary of defense had a perception that the Air Force wasn't fully committed to the fight in Iraq and Afghanistan. He had made the comment that it was like pulling teeth to get the Air Force to send more intelligence, surveillance, and reconnaissance (ISR) aircraft to Iraq—particularly Predator Remotely Piloted Aircraft (RPAs). My predecessor had complained about sending airmen to Iraq to guard prisoners and drive fuel trucks. He didn't believe those were appropriate jobs for Air Force personnel. I didn't disagree, but for me, we were a nation at war and people were dying, so we had to do whatever we could to make sure that America succeeded. This new philosophy reflected a change in the vector of the Air Force that we called "All In." It was our way of articulating that the United States Air Force was going to do whatever was needed, and we would pursue it willingly and with enthusiasm.

"All In" was about tilting the Air Force to be more visibly and culturally committed to the fight in every possible way, and that's exactly what we did.

F-22 RAPTOR AND LONG-RANGE STRIKE BOMBER

One of the more controversial decisions we made was to terminate the F-22 Raptor program at 187 airplanes. The F-22 is, unquestionably, the most capable fighter in history. While it's equipped to tackle ground attack and limited electronic warfare, it is primarily an air superiority fighter. And that plays into the controversy.

The F-22 is the most capable fighter in history.

The prior leadership (General Moseley, an F-15 pilot, and Secretary Wynne) viewed overwhelming air-to-air superiority as sacrosanct, so they refused to back down on their demand for at least 381 F-22s. This was despite clear resistance from Secretary Gates, who believed the 183 aircraft already approved for funding in December of 2004 would be sufficient to cover the risk of potential future wars against superpowers—the real adversaries we'd have to worry about in large-scale air-to-air engagements. Moseley never gave up in his principled attempts to get those 381 F-22s, and it remained an ongoing source of conflict between Moseley and Gates.

When I took over, Secretary Rumsfeld's advice kept replaying in my mind. "Put your emotions aside and run it like a business." Great advice at TRANS-COM, and just as essential here. Irrespective of my personal position on the fighter issue, I wanted an independent assessment to determine the minimum number of F-22 aircraft that we could live with—and what we came up with was a number of 243. Although this is not well known, Mike Donley and I fought hard for the 243, but in the end the secretary said no, even though we had shaved over 35 percent off the Moseley/Wynne demand for 381. Those additional sixty aircraft would still create an unfunded bill of $13 billion in a time that defense budgets were being tightened. It was his view that we needed to invest in other things like remotely piloted aircraft and MRAPs (to protect the ground forces from IED explosions) at the time.

The F-22 debate had consumed enough oxygen and it was time to move on. Secretary Donley and I wrote an op-ed in the *Washington Post* and made the argument for capping production at 187. We essentially conceded that this was an unwinnable debate. As we stated in our op-ed:

> Buying more F-22s means doing less of something else. In addition to air superiority, the Air Force provides a number of other capabilities critical to joint operations for which joint warfighters have increasing needs. These include intelligence, surveillance and reconnaissance, command and control, and related needs in the space and cyber domains. We are also repairing years of institutional neglect of our nuclear forces, rebuilding the acquisition workforce, and taking steps to improve Air Force capabilities for irregular warfare . . .

> Make no mistake: Air dominance remains an essential capability for joint warfighting. The F-22 is a vital tool in the military's arsenal and will remain in our inventory for decades to come. But the time has come to move on.

There were bigger stakes for the Air Force than continuing this fight either overtly or clandestinely, and Donley and I certainly were not going to go to the Hill behind Secretary Gates's back and lobby for more F-22s. That was never going to happen on our watch. Some people argue that that was too pristine a judgment and that in Washington anything is fair, but I say no. I had never been disloyal to a boss and I wasn't about to start then.

There was a method to our madness. We felt that the real coin of the realm was the replacement bomber, and convincing a very skeptical civilian leadership that it was a much smarter, in fact essential, thing to pursue. We had our work cut out for us.

About that same time, Secretary Gates also cancelled the Next-Generation Bomber (NGB), and he did it for rational reasons. The Next-Generation Bomber had grown too big; it had become something for everybody. For example, there was a requirement suggesting that it needed air-to-air missile capability for self-defense. Not completely nonsensical, but one can only envision such a thing where cost was no object, and that was not Bob Gates's view of the world. So he cancelled it.

But the necessity for long-range strike remained a valid need for the country and the Department of Defense. We felt it was our responsibility to convince Gates that a penetrating platform with long-range strike capability was an unquestioned requirement for a future secretary of defense or a future president—both for warfighting and deterrence purposes. And we had to convince him that we as an Air Force could field such a system with discipline and in such a way that would avoid the sort of elaboration and requirement "creep" that the original NGB program reflected.

We had to convince him that the B-52 and the B-1 were going to have to be replaced at some point in the not too distant future. The B-2 is still relevant in a much less benign or a standoff environment, but the reality was that the B-2 was twenty years old and the B-52 was fifty years old. The B-1 was sixty-plus airplanes and had become a good conventional platform but was not a penetrator.

We had to convince him that this undertaking was not going to repeat the B-2 experience of twenty airplanes. Originally, there were supposed to be 132 B-2s. We only ended up building twenty-one and then we lost one, and as result the cost of the B-2s were a billion dollars–plus each. He was not going to repeat that experience, and we had to make it clear that we were going to buy eighty to one hundred new bombers and not less. This was not going to be a niche fleet or boutique fleet like the B-2, but was going to be more like the B-52 model—meaning a hundred-airplane fleet that lasted for many decades.

The other aspect of it was the cost, and we settled on a cost in the 2010 time frame of about $550 million each. The notion was that the design imperative on this machine was cost. It's not performance, it's not advancing technology; the prime imperative was cost. So what that meant was not starting from scratch with new inventions when proven technologies could be used far more efficiently and cost-effectively. For example, by using engines that had already proven themselves—proven components that might entail some adaptation, but minimally so.

In addition, the airplane would not be a standalone platform. There would be other platforms that would feed this one in order to enable it to accomplish its missions; not every capability needed to be on the airplane itself. It had to be presented as part of a larger system of systems. We succeeded in getting the secretary's endorsement of that formula.

We had to convince him of all this, or like the Next-Generation Bomber, the long-range strike bomber would be dead in the water. We worked our asses off and we ultimately succeeded. We convinced Secretary Gates that it was an unquestioned requirement both for warfighting and deterrence purposes, and that we as an Air Force could field such a system with discipline. This one was well worth going all out; the F-22 was not.

One must choose carefully which battles to fight.

On October 27, 2015, the Long-Range Strike Bomber (LRS-B) contract was awarded to Northrup Grumman at an initial value of $21.4 billion. At the 2016 Air Warfare Symposium, Air Force Secretary Deborah Lee James announced that the aircraft was formally designated the B-21. It is expected to reach IOC (Initial Operational Capability) in 2025. *IOC reflects the time when a new weapon, item of equipment, or system is received by a unit or force that is adequately trained, equipped, and supported to sufficiently employ and maintain it.*

Mike Donley and I are proud that we succeeded in persuading Gates that the Air Force was going to exercise discipline like he had not seen, and so it's up to our successors to deliver on that promise. The Air Force has to, if it is going to bring this one home.

THE SURGE

On October 27, 2009, Sgt. Dale Griffin was killed by a roadside IED blast in Afghanistan's Arghandab River Valley. Well past midnight on the 29th, President

Obama and I were at Dover Air Force Base for Sgt. Griffin's somber, dignified transfer ceremony. We snapped to attention and saluted as six Army pallbearers carried his flag-draped transfer case from a C-17 into a white mortuary van. Sgt. Griffin was the last of eighteen fallen Americans we saw taken from the plane that night—one of fifty-eight killed in action in Afghanistan on the 27th.

The following day I was with the president again, this time inside the White House Situation Room. This was a very serious meeting that would lead up to the president's decision on the surge. How many more American troops would he order sent to Afghanistan? Although not present for the meeting (either in person or by VTC), General McChrystal requested forty thousand. Vice President Biden was seated directly to the right of the president, across from NSC Advisor Jim Jones. I was four seats down, directly across the table from Chief of Staff Rahm Emanuel, but I had no difficulty hearing the vice president's passionate presentation on why twenty thousand was a much more realistic number—with half to be used for counterterrorism, the other half for training Afghan forces.

The president went around the table to query each of the Joint Chiefs, along with the SECDEF, General Jones, and of course Chairman Mullen. The president was 100 percent locked in and demanded that each of us be completely candid, even though our opinions might not comport with what we believed his to be. "Norty, what's your view?"

I leaned forward so that I could have an unobstructed view of the chief executive past Army chief of staff George Casey, who was seated directly to my left. "Mr. President, the Afghan-Pakistan border area is the incubator of jihadism and we cannot allow that to metastasize. My advice is to go big."

The debate would go on for another month, with new questions raised in increasingly heated gatherings. Secretary Gates would propose what he called "Option 2A," which was thirty thousand troops from the United States and an expectation that NATO forces would provide an additional seven thousand. On November 29, the president announced that he would commit to the Gates proposal, and thirty thousand more young Americans would be sent to the war.

REDEMPTION

Long before President Bush first coined the phrase "War on Terror," we were well aware of the devastating threat posed by terrorism, working hard behind the scenes to combat that threat. We didn't talk about it and to this day the majority of our efforts (both failures and triumphs) remain classified, with details safely archived inside planning and operations cells in nondescript offices inside the Pentagon and at other locations throughout the country. In one way or another, counterterrorism remains a primary focus of our top-tier special operations units. From the catastrophe at Desert One through those times UBL slipped through our fingers, disappointment led to lessons learned and intensified resolve.

For years I'd worked closely with Homeland Security advisor Fran Townsend on counterterror issues related to the pursuit of bin Laden and other high-value targets. Now, as Chief, most of my time was spent tackling broader strategic issues more confined to the Air Force. Still, even then, there were times when I'd be asked to intervene. Perhaps the most noteworthy took place in early 2011.

"I need you to prepare sixteen nonmetallic weapons for use in a B-2" was all that Vice Chairman Hoss Cartwright said to me, but it was enough to start the ball rolling. I had known the well-respected Marine Corps general for years, and worked with him long enough to have built the solid level of trust required to facilitate his request. We had spent the past three years together as Joint Chiefs, and before that he was STRATCOM commander while I was commander at TRANSCOM. Lack of trust would not be an issue.

Basically, he was saying, "Norty, this is of the highest priority and I need you to make it happen with no questions asked. And by the way, there's no action order, no paperwork, and no other calls you'll get coming up the chain of command. Just take care of this one for me based on my word—and please don't ask for any details." Now you see why trust is so important.

At that point my responsibility was one of due diligence, getting his confirmation that it was an appropriate request—the implication being that it was either presidential or SECDEF direction. "Indeed, it is," he confirmed. I had a feeling it involved bin Laden, but I didn't ask.

I picked up the phone and made the appropriate contacts to ensure that he'd be given number one priority at the Ogden Air Logistics Center. Ogden was responsible for preparing the specific weapons; it's the Air Force weapons depot. Later on I would learn that they were being considered for use in a bombing of the bin Laden complex, one of three options that were under consideration. But in the end, it turned out they were not needed as we performed an Air Assault for Operation NEPTUNE SPEAR. That special night in Abbottabad felt like redemption for those of us who had been involved in so many of the challenges faced by the special operations community over the preceding thirty years.

DOVER / MISHAPS

Suzie: *In a high-risk business like ours, you're going to have some mishaps and you need to be prepared to deal with the crisis. When I first arrived, I wasn't. In the Air Force, when there's a crash and someone dies, the official term for the event is "mishap." To me, stepping on a shell at the beach and breaking a toenail is a mishap. Crashing a C-130 into the side of a mountain and killing all six crewmembers is no mishap, it's a catastrophe. Or a tragedy. It's certainly a heartbreak. But whatever you call it, I was ill-prepared to deal with it and I messed up. In my attempt to comfort a grieving spouse, I unintentionally put my foot in my mouth and said the wrong things, things that I thought would help, but just ended up causing her to burst into tears. That's one vision I will never forget. But as I watched that poor woman grieve, I vowed to learn how to do better—how to be part of the solution, not the problem.*

We had a freak situation where we lost an airman who was struck by lightning on the flight line. The storm was well beyond five miles off the coast, so he was out there working on an airplane and boom! It killed him. As if that's not horrible enough, the situation got even worse when his family arrived. They were totally dysfunctional, and the father decided to take it all out on Nort. While Nort believed that it was ours to accept if it would help the family deal with their grief, at that point I had yet to grasp that concept.

They wanted to see where it happened so we took them out to the flight line, but not only were they in mourning, but this family hated each other. They were so dysfunctional that they insisted on everyone driving separate cars. We had a caravan cutting across the runway to the spot where the incident occurred. The wife couldn't have been more than nineteen years old, probably even younger. She just lay on the ground and wailed at the top of her lungs, which kind of reverberated off the adjacent hangars. Then the father arrived and bolted out of the car in a beeline for Norty, screaming at him and berating him and getting in his face while accusing Nort of being responsible for the death. I just wanted to kill him because he was actually shoving my husband, and there was no one on this earth who was more heartbroken by these deaths than Norty! The chaplain came over and grabbed my hand, pulling me back a bit. He didn't say a thing, just squeezed my hand and pulled me back. When it was all over I went up to him and confided, "I wanted to kill that man. He was so unappreciative of Nort's kindness and attempts to help him."

And he said, "Suzie, the man has to do what he has to do." That grieving parent needed to vent and release the torment surrounding the loss of his son. Norty understood. It would take me a little longer. But this was a wonderful learning experience for me, and I did get better at it with time.

This became so important to us that Norty set up a course for all seventeen incoming squadron commanders that taught them how to handle mishaps. I put together a spouse panel on the topic, and I invited the spouse of another one of our mishap pilots to sit on the panel. She explained what she went through and what was good about how Hurlburt had handled it and what was not so good. She told us how she had felt comforted when Norty and I came by her home and spent time with her immediately after she got the news. She explained what's right to say at the time, and what not to say. Just being there for her and allowing her to talk about her husband made her feel better. But the one cardinal rule is to never say you understand . . . because the truth is, you don't (and can't).

About a year after the lightning mishap, we named the airman leadership school at Hurlburt after the young airman who had died. The family flew back for the ceremony, and I must admit that I was worried that the hot-tempered father would lose it again and use Norty as his punching bag. But this time, when the father approached Norty, it was to shake his hand and say "Thank you." At that moment I renewed my pledge to do whatever was in my power to care for the families of the fallen. Fourteen years later, I would have that opportunity.

In early April 2009, Secretary Gates changed the policy to allow families to welcome their fallen back at the dignified transfer ceremony—that's when the plane containing the fallen's remains arrives at Dover Air Force Base in Delaware. Norty and I made among the first trips up that April to greet the fallen returnee. There were three that night. We did our best to comfort the grieving families, but I was horrified by what I saw.

I held it all in until our flight back to Washington, then I exploded. "Can you believe that? They had those families crammed together in a hallway sitting on metal folding chairs!" This was not a suitable way to have the families grieve, and it was insulting for the United States of America to disrespect the memory of these heroes in such a way. There's a reason they call it the "ultimate sacrifice." We don't have a draft anymore, so they were not forced to serve. They chose to do it.

To sacrifice themselves to safeguard the freedoms of the greatest country on earth. Their families deserved far more than that country was providing for them that night.

I told Norty that we had to do something about this right away—and of course he agreed. I called in every chit I had and worked this like a pit bull in heat.

Less than six months later, we cut the ribbon on the Center for the Families of the Fallen—a lovely facility custom-designed to meet the needs of these families. There's a prayer and meditation room, private family sitting areas, and a kid's room where the little ones can go to watch videos. Some leave messages on the chalkboard for their daddy or mommy. Those are very moving and poignant; they'll just break your heart. Volunteers make sure there is always fresh coffee and cookies; diapers are available, as are books, CDs, makeup, and just about anything else they might need. To top it off, we opened up a Fisher House right next door. So not only do we have the Center, but the families can stay right there on the campus without having to find a hotel downtown.

★ ★ ★

This was not only the low point of my tenure as Chief of Staff—it was the low point of my entire career.

I first learned about it in May of 2010 when I received an Inspector General's report surrounding some questionable activity at the Dover Mortuary, an Air Force facility that processes the remains of the fallen from all branches of the military. It centered on specific instances where some of the workers felt the supervisors were not conducting business in accordance with state and national mortuary standards, particularly on issues concerning inventory of autopsied remains, and the ultimate disposition of some other remains. They declared whistleblower status in order to bring attention to this problem, which led to the intervention of the Office of Special Counsel, a watchdog group that protects them against reprisals. We'd been negotiating with the Office for many months. Finally, in November of 2011, we were advised that their findings of "gross mismanagement" were about to be released to the public.

We prepared for the release and we hoped that we had it contained. What we did not anticipate was that within a day it would snowball and explode into a public relations fiasco when reporters uncovered other incidents that occurred long before our tenure, some going all the way back to 9/11, including reports that between 2003 and 2008, the Air Force discarded the partial remains of up to 274 American troops into a Virginia landfill. You can imagine the sort of atmospherics of saying that the remains of a fallen soldier ended up in a waste dump. The truth is that most of these were particles on microscope slides that staff was trying to identify. As such, at that time, that was arguably the appropriate thing to do with these items. But the way it played out in the press, that was irrelevant. It became a public relations disaster.

Any way you look at it, it was terrible situation that was not worthy of the fallen or their families, one that took a tremendous toll on the leadership of the Air Force both emotionally and in terms of time. It tarnished the reputation of the Air Force externally—and, even more importantly, with our service brothers and sisters and their families who have to have confidence that if their son or daughter or father or mother die in a combat situation, when they come home they will be treated with the dignity and respect that one has every right to expect. It's an example of a bad story that never got better; one that consumed oxygen that we desperately wanted to use for other purposes. We dealt with both procedural and personnel internal issues and we reached out to the media and to those on Capitol Hill who had an intense interest; we did so with candor and full disclosure. But neither were satisfied.

Part of this issue started with a debate over a decision by a supervisor. A family had indicated a desire for the marine to be in uniform in the casket following his death from a roadside bomb in Afghanistan. But the marine's injury resulted in a disfigurement of his arm such that it could not fit into the uniform. So the supervisor directed the embalmers to remove a part of the arm bone so that it would fit into the uniform and be consistent with the family's wishes. The embalmer felt that this was an abuse of the dead and a violation of mortuary ethics, even though it was a result of an attempt to fulfill the family's request. There was a difference of opinion between the embalmer and the supervisor.

Other allegations were that workers at the mortuary misplaced a dead soldier's ankle, and that they permitted an Army hospital in Europe to ship fetal remains back to the United States in a cardboard box rather than the prescribed aluminum transfer case.

The Inspector General (IG) determined that there was not enough evidence to prove the supervisors had broken any regulations. These were not people who were acting frivolously; rather, their decisions were prompted by good faith desires to best meet family requests. Still, we took strong disciplinary action against the supervisors. That's not how it played out in the media, or in Congress, where some senators latched onto it as ammunition and an opportunity to grandstand. I think in part they were furious that anything but perfection would be permitted at the mortuary. They called our punishments inadequate.

Senator Jon Tester (D-Montana) fired off a letter to Secretary Donley, asking, "Why weren't they fired?" Senator Claire McCaskill (D-Missouri) issued her own missive, alleging that the Inspector General "may have acted to protect the Air Force at the expense of facts" in investigating the Dover scandal.

The following day I happened to be on the Hill testifying before the Senate Armed Services Committee, along with the other Joint Chiefs of Staff. The hearing had nothing to do with Dover. We were there to discuss whether the chief of the National Guard Bureau should be a member of the Joint Chiefs of Staff. I suppose I should have seen it coming, but even then, certain senators used it as an opportunity to get on the record and grill me about Dover.

The first was Senator Kelly Ayotte (R-New Hampshire), who leaned forward from her tall, black leather chair behind the long, curved wooden bench at the front of room G50 of the Dirksen Senate Office Building, a mass of photographers kneeling in the well that separated us from the row of senators. She read from a prepared statement, yet did her best to glance up from her paper and make eye contact as she solemnly stated her case and posed her question:

> General Schwartz, on a different topic . . . I'm deeply troubled by the reports about what's happened at the mortuary at the Dover Air Force Base, and I'm sure you would agree with me this is outrageous that remains of our soldiers would be put in a landfill and not treated with the appropriate dignity and honor, which they deserve. Can you tell me where we are with this and how we're going to ensure that this never happens again and, most importantly, those who have participated in this outrage are going to be held accountable?

I switched on the microphone, clasped my hands together, and thoughtfully looked up at the senator. I spoke slowly and deliberately:

Senator, first of all, let me clarify the allegation about putting remains in a landfill. These were portions, prior to 2008, which were sent away from the Dover mortuary to a funeral home for cremation, which is an authorized method of dealing with remains, particularly those that are separated from the larger portion of remains returned to the family. After that, the results of the cremation came back to the mortuary, then were sent to a medical-support company for incineration. So you had cremation, then incineration, and it was at that point that this medical-support organization placed the residuals from that effort into a landfill. In 2008, the Air Force came to the conclusion that that was not the best way to deal with those remains. And so it is now done in the traditional fashion of burial at sea. It has been that way since 2008. It will continue to be that way in the future.

At that point I started to get emotional, and it had to be clear that my words came straight from the heart:

And let me just conclude by saying the Secretary of the Air Force, Mike Donley, and I take personal responsibility for this. Our obligation is to treat our fallen with reverence and dignity and respect and to provide the best possible support and care for their families. That is our mission. The people who did not fulfill our expectations were disciplined, and there's no doubt what our expectations are today.

Later in the hearing, Senator McCaskill brought up her letter that questioned the IG's impartiality. She went on for over two minutes before finally posing her question to me:

I want to make sure that the Inspector Generals are not so busy looking after the institution that they fail to point out wrongdoing, which was not ever acknowledged, and that there is accountability for the people involved. And so I want you to address the special counsel's report as it relates to the Air Force investigation.

I did my best to put it into context:

Senator McCaskill, there clearly were unacceptable mistakes made. Whether they constitute wrongdoing is another matter entirely. And when you look at a situation like this, you look at the facts of the case, as an attorney might say. You look at the context in which the event or the mistakes occurred. And you also consider the demands that are placed on individuals and organizations. With respect to accountability, we also had an obligation to ensure that the statutory requirements for due process were followed. We did that precisely. And I can only speak for the case of the uniformed officer [there were two civilian employees who were not under my jurisdiction, but rather under the purview of Secretary Donley], but the uniformed officer received a letter of reprimand. We established an unfavorable information file. We removed him from the command list, and his anticipated job as a group commander at Shaw Air Force Base was redlined. This is not a trivial sanction. Of course, after the hearing, I was bombarded by questions from the press.

"There is nothing more sacred, there is nothing that is a more profound obligation than treating our fallen with reverence, dignity, and respect," I told them. "This was difficult work, and while their performance did not meet standards, this was not a deliberate act."

Ultimately, Defense Secretary Panetta called for a complete review of the mortuary operations. The reviewing panel was led by retired General John Abizaid. It included public-health and funeral-service experts. They released their report on February 28, 2012. It listed twenty recommendations intended to address problems with command, oversight, policy, operations, and workflow, identifying the command structure and lack of oversight as the main sources of the problem. As you can imagine, the report reopened the can of worms and reignited all the furor.

Secretary Donley and I stepped into the Pentagon press briefing room immediately upon the conclusion of General Abizaid's presentation. I stood off to the side and slightly behind Secretary Donley as he approached the wooden lectern beneath the row of bright TV lights mounted on the ceiling. He began with a prepared statement. Then the salvo of questions began. The secretary handled the first few, then they turned to me.

NBC correspondent Jim Miklaszewski asked for clarification on the issue of the command structure, immediately followed by a question from his associate, NBC national security producer Courtney Kube. She gestured with her small white reporter's steno pad as she spoke:

With all due respect, General Schwartz, General Abizaid called it dysfunctional, isolated and orphaned . . . Who should have been responsible during your tenure that there was this lack of oversight at Dover? I mean at a place where there should be monumental respect and attention paid to it. Who . . . Which . . . ?

I moved forward toward the podium and looked into her eyes. "You're looking at him. Me. I'm responsible."

She nodded and feverishly started scrawling onto the pad.

In the words of Harry Truman, "The buck stops here." I got up and made it clear that I was the accountable party. I took full responsibility. By doing so, it took the wind out of their sails and seemed to stem the tide. But it's a great example of a crisis that just detonates out of nowhere and you have to deal with it—quickly, effectively—and most importantly, honestly.

The following day I spoke at a breakfast meeting of the Defense Writers Group, fully prepared to share my thoughts on how we could most effectively deal with our shrinking Air Force budget in the years to come. But once again, just as I was about to begin my prepared remarks, the host made a preemptive strike. "Our guest this morning is General Norton Schwartz, Chief of Staff of the Air Force. Sir, thank you for joining us. The topic that's at the top of a lot of people's minds right now is the situation at Dover. Can you start off with some updates on . . . how to prevent the situation from occurring in the future?"

Fair question, and one that deserved my temporary deviation from the planned topic. I mention this now because—following a tracking of the facts and recommendations contained in the Abizaid report—I once again became a bit emotional as I opened up to the group:

Let me again just reiterate that I make no attempt, and couldn't even if I desired to, justify what happened prior to 2008, much less in 2002. We have endeavored since 2008 to ensure that we treat the fallen with the dignity and respect and in fact the reverence that they and their families deserve. This is a no-fail business. This is one of those areas where perfection is the only standard, and any deviation from that is not only a disappointment, it's an affront to the families of the fallen and our expectations of ourselves. So we have worked diligently over the last two years to implement changes which General Abizaid generally characterized as positive, and we'll certainly continue on that path.

Suzie took it all very personally. She continues: *It hurt my heart because we had personally done so much at Dover and there was really only goodness happening there by this time. But it broke on Norty's watch, so he was the one who stepped up and took full responsibility, even though it occurred long before his tenure as Chief.*

The sad thing is if you ever go to Dover, it is the most dignified place you've ever been to. Those remains have names the minute they get on that plane. There's a locker for each one of them and the people who are preparing for their arrival use their name. They are meticulous. Every uniform is correct and perfect because that uniform is going to lie in that casket. This is the most moving piece of this individual's journey for those families because when that plane opens up and those cases are revealed, it is the moment that that family knows that it's real. Their knees will buckle and they will fall to the ground if someone's not there holding them. Many of them are absolutely wailing and sobbing, as Americans do. They are beside themselves. The people inside the mortuary are so respectful and every transfer is incredibly stressful for them.

The way the story unfolded was just a devastating, debilitating thing to go through, and Norty was in a no-win situation. If there was any "winner," it would have to have been ESPN, because that was the beginning of my watching Mike & Mike *on ESPN every morning instead of the news. From that day on, I could never look at any newspaper, I could never watch any broadcast news report and I could never surf any news-related websites. It was just too painful.*

FORCE SIZE

In an era of fewer resources being appropriated for defense, a smaller, more focused Air Force is the only rational approach. But getting there is easier said than done, and my attempts at working through this turned into a bloodbath.

The main issue is that if the Air Force gets smaller, which of our three components gets smaller and by how much? Is it the active duty that gets smaller, or is it the reserves? And if both get smaller, who gets smaller than the other? And what about the National Guard? Then there's the raging debate about costs. And availability. Can you depend on a reserve unit on very little notice? And how about the Guard's responsibility to their respective states? We ended up with at least three conflicting camps that were questioning each other's motivations, more if you throw in Congress and the governors.

This is all highly contested and highly controversial, and the goal needs to be to have these discussions without it becoming profoundly divisive. I failed at this, and instead, we beat each other up. It took place on my watch and I feel largely responsible for it. It was bad for the Air Force and we ended up with a black eye on Capitol Hill. So much for my belief that we should be one Air Force. The reality is that that's not the way it is and I don't believe it ever will be that way.

AIR FORCE STANDARDS

It's been called "one of the capstone acts of my thirty-nine-year career," and it just might be the most lasting contribution of my tenure. It's a single paragraph on page nineteen of a tiny blue booklet I had written and distributed to over 600,000 airmen just before I retired; every member of the Air Force would receive their own personal copy. The paragraph is entitled "Government Neutrality Regarding Religion" and it's still being debated today:

> Leaders at all levels must balance constitutional protections for an individual's free exercise of religion or other personal beliefs and the constitutional prohibition against governmental establishment of religion. For example, they must avoid the actual or apparent use of their position to promote their personal religious beliefs to their subordinates or to extend preferential treatment for any religion. Commanders or supervisors who engage in such behavior may cause members to doubt their impartiality and objectivity. The potential result is a degradation of the unit's morale, good order, and discipline. Airmen, especially commanders and supervisors, must ensure that in exercising their right of religious free expression, they do not degrade morale, good order, and discipline in the Air Force or degrade the trust and confidence that the public has in the United States Air Force.

When it was published, it prompted a barrage of accusations against the Air Force, and against me personally. But I see it very differently. This is not about limiting people's capacity to believe or practice whatever faith they want to practice. This is about reinforcing the notion that *commanders cannot suggest or even give the impression that they're making choices based on what their subordinates believe.*

In May of 2014—almost two years after I distributed the booklet—Virginia Congressman Randy Forbes was still on the warpath to somehow void this instruction. He wrote to General Mark Welsh asking him to revise the language. Forbes also called on Mark to revoke a memo I distributed to commanders in September 2011. The memo merely reminded those leaders that they must avoid even the appearance of using their position to proselytize.

This is the same Forbes who confronted me about this in the middle of my testimony before the House Armed Services Committee—a hearing that was on an entirely different subject. Later on he had a member of his staff relay to me what I call a non-apology apology. "The congressman did not want things to unfold that way," I was told. But to me, it was the substance we should have been focusing on, not the forum in which it played out. Both my memo to the commanders and the passage in the "blue book" were bona fide efforts to fulfill my obligation to be a secular commander of the armed forces, and I would argue that that's a requirement for effective leadership in the diverse American armed forces.

Command of America's sons and daughters requires impartiality and inclusiveness.

I asked my spokesman, Sam Highley, to issue the following response:

> We have seen instances where well-meaning commanders and senior non-commissioned officers appeared to advance a particular religious view among their subordinates, calling into question their impartiality and objectivity. We can learn from these instances.

DEPARTMENT OF THE AIR FORCE
OFFICE OF THE CHIEF OF STAFF
UNITED STATES AIR FORCE
WASHINGTON DC 20330

SEP 1 2011

MEMORANDUM FOR ALMAJCOM-FOA-DRU/CC

FROM: HQ USAF/CC
1670 Air Force Pentagon
Washington, DC 20330-1670

SUBJECT: Maintaining Government Neutrality Regarding Religion

Leaders at all levels must balance Constitutional protections for an individual's free exercise of religion or other personal beliefs and its prohibition against governmental establishment of religion. For example, they must avoid the actual or apparent use of their position to promote their personal religious beliefs to their subordinates or to extend preferential treatment for any religion. Commanders or supervisors who engage in such behavior may cause members to doubt their impartiality and objectivity. The potential result is a degradation of the unit's morale, good order, and discipline.

Chaplain Corps programs, including activities such as religious studies, faith sharing, and prayer meetings, are vital to commanders' support of individual Airmen's needs and provide opportunities for the free exercise of religion. Although commanders are responsible for these programs, they must refrain from appearing to officially endorse religion generally or any particular religion. Therefore, I expect chaplains, not commanders, to notify Airmen of Chaplain Corps programs.

Our chaplains are trained to provide advice to leadership on matters related to the free exercise of religion and to help commanders care for all of their people, regardless of their beliefs. If you have concerns involving the preservation of government neutrality regarding religious beliefs, consult with your chaplain and staff judge advocate before you act.

NORTON A. SCHWARTZ
General, USAF
Chief of Staff

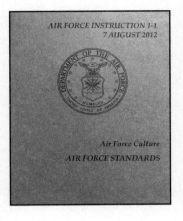

AIR FORCE INSTRUCTION 1-1
7 AUGUST 2012

Air Force Culture
AIR FORCE STANDARDS

2.11. Government Neutrality Regarding Religion. Leaders at all levels must balance constitutional protections for an individual's free exercise of religion or other personal beliefs and the constitutional prohibition against governmental establishment of religion. For example, they must avoid the actual or apparent use of their position to promote their personal religious beliefs to their subordinates or to extend preferential treatment for any religion. Commanders or supervisors who engage in such behavior may cause members to doubt their impartiality and objectivity. The potential result is a degradation of the unit's morale, good order, and discipline. Airmen, especially commanders and supervisors, must ensure that in exercising their right of religious free expression, they do not degrade morale, good order, and discipline in the Air Force or degrade the trust and confidence that the public has in the United States Air Force.

Air Force Instruction 1-1, 7 August 2012, Air Force Standards

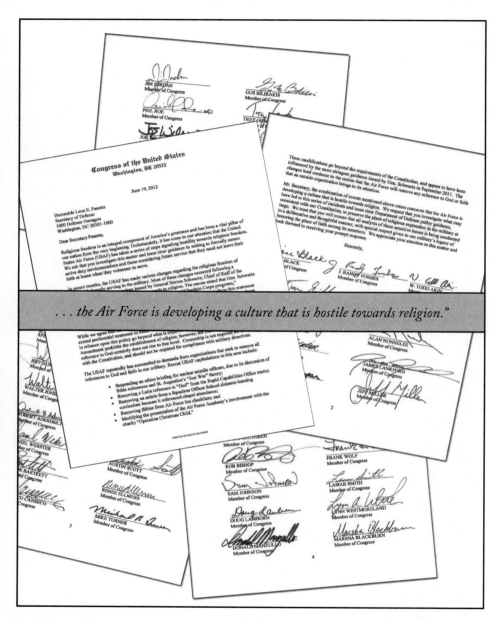

Congressman Todd Akin (R–Missouri), along with Congressman Diane Black and Congressman Randy Forbes, sent a letter signed by sixty-six members of Congress urging Secretary of Defense Leon Panetta to investigate a pattern of hostility toward faith in the United States Air Force.

REFLECTIONS

There are so many reasons why I love this country, and why we decided early on to dedicate our lives to her service. You've heard me vent about those times when I was challenged on the Hill or in the press room by inquisitors who, at the time, I may have felt pushed harder than was appropriate—demanding answers to questions that were accusatory rather than exploratory. But much more frequently, you've heard about the honor I've felt at every juncture along the way—learning from leaders who set high standards and demanded that they be met or, even better, exceeded. They took me under their wings and asked nothing in return beyond the satisfaction of rejoicing in my success. When *Wide World of Sports* talks about the thrill of victory and the agony of defeat, it often seems like they're encapsulating how the past thirty-nine years have felt to me.

Throughout it all there remained an unwavering constant—that's the awe I felt for the brilliance of our founding fathers, battling among themselves to forge a document so powerful and enduring, it lives and breathes today. Within that document they entrenched a phenomenon that was totally unique at the time: the peaceful transfer of power.

The concept of this peaceful transition is something every American military leader experiences from his or her first squadron (or company) change of command and then all the way up the ladder. Effective leaders exult in their successor's triumphs, and do everything in their power to enable it.

The first time I walked down the Pentagon's Arnold Corridor as Chief, my mind was flooded with a plethora of bold new concepts I was excited to institute—substantive ideas that would remedy some glitches I'd experienced along the way, and others that would bolster our capabilities in ways we'd never imagined.

In the last few weeks before I turned over the reins to my worthy successor, I was proud of what we had accomplished, yet disappointed at the times we missed the mark. Even worse, I was astonished by how many of those bold new concepts were still floating around in my mind because I allowed the day-to-day demands of the job to snatch priceless hours that could have been used for these more strategic endeavors. *If I only knew then what I knew now*, I told myself. But in life there are no do-overs, and the best I could do was to share those insights with Mark Welsh.

I sat down at my computer and drafted a no-holds-barred document—a completely candid analysis of those areas where I could have done better. Then

I went back to that list and offered tangible recommendations on how he might learn from my experiences.

In my thirty-nine years of service, I've had the honor of assuming many commands—from venerated leaders whom I hold in the highest regard. Yet not once had any of them provided me with a document like the one I was about to give Mark.

I leaned back in my chair and reviewed what I had written: a six-page analysis for the incoming Chief. Then I put myself in his position. Would he view this as an inability on my part to let go and let him run the show? I went back and added one more paragraph:

> *I realize that your reaction to much of this will be: if you felt this way, why didn't you do something about it? It's a fair point and I hope what I've offered here might help you avoid some regrets with the things I know I should have addressed, and I regret I simply didn't.*

Here are the key issues I presented to Mark, in the hopes they would highlight areas where greater awareness might serve him well early in his tenure—followed by a copy of the complete memo.

Acquisition: The structure of the Headquarters Air Staff with SAF/AQ under the secretary does not lend itself to him getting the fidelity of information needed to monitor and provide oversight for Air Force acquisition programs. We experienced several major problems despite our focus on this area.

Recommendations: Acquisition oversight cannot be outsourced to AQ or AFMC or ACC—it remains an area virtually guaranteed to generate major problems.

Nuclear Enterprise: The nuclear enterprise, for all its recovery, remains fragile and constantly hovers on the edge of scandal and atrophy. It must be subjected not only to brisk inspection and accountability, but also to senior leader intervention in the budget process to maintain its credibility and viability.

Recommendations: I strongly urged him to retain the Nuclear Oversight Board, but refresh its energy, and to keep the A-10 close—it's easy to lose that relationship in the day-to-day workings of the staff because the A-10 is a two-star. Visit nuclear bases early and often.

Strategy: When I came to this office, I was not as comfortable as I needed to be with strategic issues or the future security environment. I found myself struggling in the Tank, sometimes failing to weigh in on strategic issues in the presence of experienced, seemingly better prepared Joint Chiefs. I found it very difficult to cultivate an ethos among the four-stars that we as a collective body are the Air Force's strategic leaders.

Recommendations: I recommended that he set aside one CORONA (the senior Air Force leadership conference) as the primary strategy anchor for the year, and then address institutional strategy at every CORONA, both in open and executive session. The leadership must be personally involved in the formulation and presentation of options and perspectives, and should be challenged to make real decisions.

USAFA: The Air Force Academy proved to be a source of significant problems that did not see many solutions on my watch. We had a difficult time with the senior leadership.

Recommendations: I suggested that he reiterate the contents of the March letter to the Superintendent, tell the current leader that he expected him (or her) to deliver on the requests in the letter, and ask for better communication with Mark and the secretary during the remainder of his tenure.

Institutional Innovation: The day-to-day exigencies of the job can be overwhelming, leaving little time or energy to deal with more abstract issues like strategy or innovation. I regret not attending more to cultivation of a general sense of innovation in the Air Force and hoped he could give some attention to its reinvigoration. If you provide the problems, [airmen] will produce solutions.

Recommendations: If he leads the charge in laying out the problems he wants to see fixed, airmen will solve them, and he and other senior leaders can incentivize

DEPARTMENT OF THE AIR FORCE
OFFICE OF THE CHIEF OF STAFF
UNITED STATES AIR FORCE
WASHINGTON DC 20330

AUG   6 2012

MEMORANDUM FOR GEN MARK A. WELSH III   Mark

FROM: HQ USAF/CC
1670 Air Force Pentagon
Washington, DC 20330-1250

SUBJECT: CSAF Transition Issues

After four years as Chief of Staff, I have learned much about our Air Force and about this job.
Most of it strongly reinforces what both of us know—that this is the greatest Air Force on earth,
that Airmen make it so, and that we have an indispensable and increasingly important role to
play in national security.

However, I have also learned some hard lessons that I want to pass along as you assume
responsibility for the future of our Air Force, in the hope that you will be better able than I was
to address these issues during your tenure. This can be a lonely job, and the isolation does not
lend itself to attaining the organizational awareness you require. Everyone wants to tell you the
good news, and you will be routinely sheltered from critical challenges that require your focus.
The following issues are ones I present in the hope they will highlight areas where greater
awareness may serve you well, early in your tenure.

Acquisition. I came to the job under the pressure of several serious institutional challenges; one
being the enduring problem of Air Force acquisition, exacerbated by the still-lingering aftermath
of Druyun scandal. The structure of the Headquarters Air Staff with SAF/AQ under the Secretary
does not lend itself to you getting the fidelity of information needed to monitor and provide
oversight for Air Force acquisition programs. We experienced several major problems despite
our focus on this area, including the improper passing of KC-46 competitive information to
contractors at the worst possible time, and the AFG Light Attack contract protest, among others.

Primary among the acquisition issues and the one with the greatest impact on the Air Force,
however, has been the performance of Lockheed Martin and the Joint Program Office on the F-
35 program. I found over time, as did the CNO and Commandant, that we had to become
intimately and personally involved in that program in a way that exceeded others. The acting AQ
(Dave Van Buren) did not help in that process—he routinely briefed the Secretary on that and
other programs, and I was often kept out of the loop. This may not have been deliberate, as I did
not assert myself initially, but I should have. Yet, even the Secretary was unaware of major
negative program developments. Program costs and metrics are lost in a difficult to penetrate fog

and are very hard to assess. OSD CAPE, AT&L, and DOT&E play a huge role, and our dealings with them tend to be weak. We had to take an officer out of NDU and put him in CAPE TACAIR because we did not have the needed aviation experience in that office. As a result of continued surprises in that program, we asked Phil Breedlove to be the F-35 "czar," essentially taking over some of the AQ's oversight and information roles, and hiring direct support for him in that role (currently Colonel Dawn Dunlap). Our Special Assistants, Terry Marlow and Tom Ehrhard, found themselves having to painstakingly research and analyze JPO briefings to the senior leadership and present us with key issues in the program because the staff largely failed to do so. The same dynamics on a smaller scale existed for the KC-46 and programs like LRS-B run by the Rapid Capabilities Office (RCO); we did not need to micromanage those programs, yet I often found myself blind-sided by the acquisition community and was generally left to hear bad news from outside sources.

Additionally, things got fairly adversarial between the USAF and contractors and remain so in attempting to close on LRIP 5. I probably could have facilitated a closer relationship with senior contractor officials to better gauge their approach. In the case of Lockheed Martin, both of us have bet our institutions on the F-35 program, and it probably requires more time with certain CEOs before crises erupt so that we can better deal with them. Although we need to be a demanding customer for all our programs, especially with the F-35 JPO and Lockheed Martin, I think senior relationships could use some more attention from the uniformed military.

Several key decisions await you on big acquisition programs. ACC will be forced to make a call on F-35 IOC, and that will be one of your first contentious decisions. Because the program has continued to slip even after it came under the spotlight, you will either continue to use the criteria ACC proposed initially and announce a "late" date, or you will relax those criteria to bring the date back to an earlier one—and perhaps suffer congressional criticism for lowering the bar. Also, when you investigate F-35 O&S cost estimates, you will likely discover that the aircraft is almost too expensive to fly and our efforts to rein those costs over the past year have proven largely marginal. Other overlooked issues include production rate (the contractor wants to build more than we are likely to ever use), and the number of the total buy (1,763) which looks increasingly untenable.

Other programs loom large as well. You are charged with keeping LRS-B alive and moving ahead, and it requires very intrusive oversight to keep the program from inflating requirements that if allowed to proliferate, will surely kill that program as we come under further budgetary pressure. The same goes for KC-46 development costs and schedule. Only with good, intrusive information sources and analysis can you assess these programs and determine which levers you might pull to help them. That information is hard to get and you'll need your acquisition know-how to uncover the essentials.

Recommendations: Acquisition oversight cannot be outsourced to AQ or AFMC or ACC—it remains an area virtually guaranteed to generate major problems. Thus, high-quality, balanced, well-analyzed information is key. I recommend you take a much more active role in the F-35,

2

LRS-B, and KC-46 programs, demand that the program offices deliver briefings well ahead of their formal presentation, that your staff do a very thorough scrub of the briefing and prepare you to engage on problem areas with a critical eye. You may consider instituting an Acquisition Oversight Board modeled on the Nuclear Oversight Board, which has proven effective in bringing senior leadership focus and attention on that critical area. I recommend you retain the F-35 "czar" role with the CV and his assistants, and take the time to engage with key CEOs and OSD officials on a regular basis to help facilitate understanding and personal relationships. On both F-35 and LRS-B, our senior leadership also needs a high-quality low observable advocacy briefing that helps all of us better advocate for those systems in both external and internal venues—we continue to run into resistance from the Navy and AT&L in an area that most of our senior leadership is unprepared to counter. We are very good at LO technically, but weak from an institutional advocacy perspective.

Nuclear Enterprise. As with acquisition, the nuclear enterprise required resuscitation when Secretary Donley and I arrived. Although I believe we made substantial progress in this area, you get few kudos for improvement, only attention when something bad happens. The lingering institutional attitude about the nuclear enterprise is that it is now fixed. I disagree. We instituted the Nuclear Oversight Board, which acted as our single most effective senior oversight institution in addressing everything from career field issues to inspections to funding. The A10, while small, proved effective in both fighting for funding and dealing with various OSD nuclear issues concerning treaty compliance and the structure of the nuclear triad.

Your challenge in dealing with the nuclear enterprise will be different from mine; and in many ways more compelling. The nuclear enterprise, for all its recovery, remains fragile and constantly hovers on the edge of scandal and atrophy. It cannot be left to the nuclear priesthood for oversight, but must be subjected not only to brisk inspection and accountability, but also to senior leader intervention in the budget process to maintain its credibility and viability. Nuclear will never be "fixed." Again, like acquisition, it requires consistent Chief-level words and action to keep it in smooth air.

Recommendations: I strongly urge that you retain the Nuclear Oversight Board, but refresh its energy. Your speeches must refer to it, talk about how it will receive your attention, and you should retain a healthy skepticism about how the staff more broadly treats this vital mission area. Keep the A10 close—it's easy to lose that relationship in the day-to-day workings of the staff because he is a two-star. Visit nuclear bases early and often to communicate your personal dedication to the well-being of these Airmen. It is too easy to overlook this area and allow it to atrophy to set in yet again—with predictable results.

Strategy. When I came to this office, I was not as comfortable as I needed to be with strategic issues or the future security environment. I found myself struggling in the Tank, sometimes failing to weigh in on strategic issues in the presence of experienced, seemingly better-prepared Joint Chiefs. Yet, strategy is about the future, and only you are responsible for the future of our Air Force and its strategic relevance. For that reason, I needed help; and my guess is you will,

3

too. Early-on we attempted to get the other four-stars engaged in the strategic direction of the Air Force, and found great reluctance to discuss larger issues—a major 12-hour series of discussions resulted in four-stars critiquing slides rather than confronting real institutional issues; with few substantive outcomes.

Strategy is the purview of the senior leadership. It is not the responsibility of the staff to come up with brilliant strategic formulations and the four-stars to critique them. You will find many on the staff who want to change the staff structure in hopes that it will better provide strategic focus—but I think that would be short-sighted. The staff cannot tell us what the strategy should be, but should be providing us support in coming up with collective senior leadership strategic vision. I found it very difficult to cultivate an ethos among the four-stars that we as a collective body are the Air Force's strategic leaders. We, not just our staffs, need to assess and debate our views about the future security environment; set priorities and make clear, tough decisions about our institution's role and relevancy in that environment; and then communicate and act on those priorities and decisions. Those decisions and actions should refer not only to national strategy, but to very sensitive issues about our institutional strategy for regaining the initiative in defense policy and national security circles inside and outside the Pentagon. To help that problem, I produced a yearly "CSAF Vector" to communicate some strategic vision for the Air Force, but never saw it really achieve much traction in the institution other than in the nuclear enterprise.

Recommendations: I recommend you set aside one CORONA as the primary strategy anchor for the year, and then address institutional strategy at every CORONA, both in open and executive session. The leadership must be personally involved in the formulation and presentation of options and perspectives, and should be challenged to make real decisions. Subsequent CORONAs and executive meetings should have time set aside for real information about the status of those decisions and how budgets and policies are contributing to movement. I also recommend you consider putting out a yearly document like Jon Greenert produced—a chief's "way ahead" that lays out your vision and priorities; and then make sure your direction is followed up at each CORONA to give it traction. Your Strategic Studies Group has prepared a summary of relevant examples that could serve as models if you choose to go this route.

USAFA. The Air Force Academy proved to be a source of significant problems that did not see many solutions on my watch. We had a difficult time with the senior leadership—our candidate for superintendant decided to retire, we had few viable alternatives, and we chose to continue the Mike Gould for another year—that will be an important decision for you. I will provide a copy of the co-signed SecAF-CSAF letter in March 2012 that we presented to Mike Gould which outlined our dissatisfaction with several elements of the USAFA mission and our requests for him to provide information over the next few months. In short, I am concerned about the deficit of a broader (Air Force) institutional perspective at the Academy—they have become insular and self-referential. The Dean has too much power and is inclined to allow the atrophy of STEM concentration as well as the dilution of the core curriculum in favor of greater student choice. USAFA is not Princeton, in my view, and we should not avoid contrasting ourselves with other

4

institutions. There exists a very dysfunctional relationship between the Chief Diversity Officer (CDO) and the entire institution, but rather than deal with the problem directly, Mike has chosen to "manage" the situation. Finally, his relationship with the Director of Athletics and football team is viewed by some as the Superintendant being a cheerleader for the team rather than the Superintendant. They will continue to lobby for entry into the Big East or other major conference for the purposes of gaining millions in revenue—another decision you and the Secretary will likely face in the coming year.

Recommendations: I suggest you reiterate the contents of the March letter, tell Mike that you expect him to deliver on the requests in the letter, and ask for better communication with you and the Secretary during the remainder of his tenure.

Institutional Innovation: The day-to-day exigencies of the job can be overwhelming, leaving little time or energy to deal with more abstract issues like strategy or innovation. Yet, our Air Force depends on them as part of our history and culture, and for its very livelihood. I regret not attending more to cultivating a general sense of innovation in the Air Force and hope you can give some attention to its reinvigoration. Innovation starts with a problem to be solved. If you prioritize those problems in your speeches and "way ahead," and demand innovative solutions, Airmen will without doubt provide them. Several problems are sitting on the table that cry out for Air Force solutions; for example the Defense Strategic Guidance discussed that rather than maintain a two major war force, we must swing forces or move to deter a second conflict. To date, nobody has provided an operational concept or force-sizing construct to do that—and only the Air Force can or will. Likewise, Air-Sea Battle still lacks a true operational concept because it has remained entrenched in the Pentagon rather than being pushed out to various places in the Air Force for innovative ways to integrate Navy and Air Force capabilities and solve emerging A2/AD problems. If you open that aperture, my sense is ideas will flow. How can we optimize ISR orbits rather than simply assign them to ground units? It's a key problem that so far lacks Air Force solutions. If you provide the problems, they will produce solutions—and each four-star in the Air Force should be pursuing, and competing for, primacy for your chosen problems with innovations from their respective organizations.

Recommendations: Innovation isn't something the Chief can mandate. It also doesn't always involve Facebook or TEDS or some other trendy thing. But, if you lead the charge in laying out the problems you want to see fixed, Airmen will solve them, and you and other senior leaders can incentivize those solutions by how you highlight them in speeches, appearances and recognition. Additionally, if you give a few trusted two or three-stars the license to come up with new ideas, Plan B's and C's to Air Staff plans, and do discreet Red Teaming of "consensus" Air Force ideas, you will pave the way for some successes that can enable others to open up. I didn't do this well and hope you can recover a sense of urgency for imagination and innovation.

CORONA: I started out and remain critical of CORONA—the process and the event itself. We have a golden opportunity for Air Force executives to provide strategic direction that underperforms. First of all, each CORONA as it stands now is essentially a tactical exercise—

5

briefings are just "submitted" and "vetted" rather than having a year-long conception of what CORONA meetings should accomplish or cover—in short there's no strategic approach. Then, CORONA briefings are either not sufficiently actionable or have inadequate information for senior decision. You might consider some of the following to improve the positive strategic impact of CORONA on the institution:

- **CORONA briefing ROE.** Briefings should be limited to either TRUE decision briefings or executive education briefings. Five-panel slides are not that useful, especially in the "other views" panel which mostly either lists those who agree. Hardly anyone reads the other four panels—they are eye charts in most cases. Decision briefings should present genuinely different and difficult options. Finally, when a decision is made (such as the definition of airpower sometime back) it should not be revisited again and again.
- **CORONA scheduling.** Certain issues should be reviewed every year—decide which CORONA will do that and execute that plan. Then, the CVA should put together a proposed CORONA schedule and it should be discussed by the four-stars well before the event, perhaps at a regularly scheduled DCO. Every CORONA should involve some very senior government official speaking to the group—it's a highly leveraged moment that should be exploited to the fullest. Every CORONA should have an institutional strategy discussion with data. Why is the Air Force at the lowest budget share of any service since the National Security Act of 1947? Why do the other services and OSD have more say over our budget than others have over the other three service's budgets? Why can't we get the $30B NIP separated from our budget so it shows our real share? Is the current and looming procurement holiday going to sacrifice the future of the Air Force? How do we best balance modernization, readiness, and force structure in this down-turn?

I realize that your reaction to much of this will be: if you felt this way, why didn't you do something about it? It's a fair point and I hope what I've offered here might help you avoid some regrets with the things I know I should have addressed, and I regret I simply didn't.

V/r

Norty

NORTON A. SCHWARTZ
General, USAF
Chief of Staff

6

those solutions by how he highlights them in speeches, appearances and recognition.

CORONA: I started out and remain critical of CORONA. CORONA briefings are either not sufficiently actionable or have inadequate information for senior decision.

- **CORONA briefing ROE.** Briefings should be limited to either *true* decision briefings or executive education briefings. Decision briefings should present genuinely different and difficult options.
- **CORONA scheduling.** Every CORONA should involve some very senior government official speaking to the group—it's a highly leveraged moment that should be exploited to the fullest. Every CORONA should have an institutional strategy discussion with data.

Chapter Seven

I DON'T CARE ABOUT
YOUR GODDAMN AIRPLANES

While Suzie is a vital part of everything I do, her contributions to our Air Force and to our country are so extraordinary—this book would be grossly incomplete without a chapter dedicated to her unique accomplishments, told by her from her perspective. She is the staunchest, most passionate and supportive advocate for airmen and their families above all others.

Here are a few samples, in her own words:

If there's one word I would use to describe myself it would be passionate. I have nowhere near the calmness that Norty has. While he carefully considers the pros and cons before giving his opinion, I speak first and think later—sometimes way later. People who are quiet often don't know what to make of me. I think I scare some of them, really, but that's never been my intention. It's worked for me over time because people have learned that's who I am, and since I always speak my mind, they will always know exactly where I stand in open and honest terms. It's part of what makes the two of us such a great team. For most of Norty's career I was fortunate to follow a spouse who did little, which played to my advantage because whatever I did was better than doing nothing.

Our personalities couldn't be any more different, and I truly believe that's been one of our strengths. He was always perceived as a strong and decisive leader, but particularly in the early years I don't believe he was viewed as the most energetic, outgoing, or vocal individual. His nature was to sit at the computer instead of getting out with the team. Over the years, I would almost beat him over the head with a stick trying to get him to get out of his office. "Have you walked the halls today?" I would ask, because he had his routine and getting out to interact with people was not within his comfort zone. I've always felt that a leader needs to do more than just stay on task and push paper across the desk. People respond to enthusiasm, and that word was not a part of his vocabulary in the early days. I used to tell him that the Army ate him up and spit him out: "Honey, the Army does not respect the quiet, professional Air Force officer. Kick some ass in there!"

Don't get me wrong: He was always highly regarded intellectually and his competency was never questioned, it's just that fostering personal human connections was not his forte. He's as happy as a clam to be sitting in a corner by himself, while more than thirty seconds of that would drive me crazy. So we balance each other out and function as the perfect team.

AIR CONDITIONERS

I was very active when Nort was wing commander at Hurlburt, and I ran every day. I'd begin at our house, then round the corner and continue up a little street that had a mix of both enlisted and young junior officers. They'd be walking their dogs and picking up their newspapers, so I'd stop and chat; eventually I got to know a lot of families. One young spouse I had befriended had seemed a bit dejected—no surprise since she was trying to raise her three little ones (all under five) completely by herself while her husband was deployed overseas.

I had just been given a gift certificate for a free haircut, color, and highlight, and I had a feeling this would be just the ticket to cheer her up. When I rang her doorbell, she lit up and invited me in. It felt like I had walked into a blast furnace. "Honey, why is it so hot in here?" I asked. "It's always like this now," she explained. "Ever since they put in the new air conditioner units last month, it only blows hot air. They came out to check it but said there was nothing they could do."

My blood started to boil (as if it weren't already boiling from the heat in there). I had a pretty good idea about what had been done and I wasn't going to stand for it. I got right in my car (of course without either thinking it through or giving myself time to calm down) and raced directly to the civil engineering squadron commander's building, screeching to a stop in the loading zone beside the front door. Racing through the maze of cubicles, I flew past his secretary and walked right in to his office. "Hi ma'am. What can I do for you? Would you like to take a seat?" he said. "No, I don't want to have a seat but I think you might want to." I could almost see a big white "thought bubble" appear over his head—the *kind you see in comics: "Now what's her #%*@ problem?" it read.*

I told him the story. "Either you guys put in some totally inadequate new 'energy efficient' system or it's just plain junk. Either way, this is Florida in the summer and she's got a baby crying nonstop because it's so damn hot in there." He listened intently and promised to take care of it, which he did beginning that very afternoon. They discovered that the entire section of thirty homes had been given air conditioner units intended for much smaller homes—they were useless. But he replaced them all.

Norty has always encouraged me to do whatever I think is right, as long as it was never for us. And it was Nort who suggested I start at the top. "Don't start with the master sergeant because you put the squadron commander in a bad situation. You go directly to him and give him every opportunity to succeed—to do the right thing because he wants to." As the years went on, "starting at the top" entailed higher starting points. By the time Nort became Chief of Staff, I'd be calling the three-stars on the Air Staff. They'd always take my calls, but I'm sure when they hung up they would roll their eyes, just like the squadron commander must have done when I barged into his office.

SPOUSES NEVER FORGET

As spouses, we view everything as personal—everything. And that's not the case with the active service member or politician. Some of these senators could rip you a new one and then ten minutes later they're perfectly happy having cocktails with you. But we spouses don't get over it and we never forget. Norty talked about the unwarranted attacks by Florida Senator Bill Nelson in the course of his confirmation hearings. I still get form emails from Nelson since we used to vote in Florida, but I never open any of them; they go straight to trash, which is exactly where they belong. On the flip side, Norty—and other military members—see this interaction as routine business. They don't see it as personal. They see it as a cost of doing business or something.

Another one who is right up there with Nelson is Missouri Senator Claire McCaskill. I will never forget how she waltzed into the Senate committee room in the middle of Norty's confirmation hearing and went off on Air Force General and then AMC commander Duncan McNabb on issues of fraud, waste, and abuse on the C-17 executive support packages. She was just flat-out wrong. She had no idea what had been said before her arrival, then she launched into a soliloquy *and waltzed right out. It was all just an excuse to be on camera yet contribute nothing of substance.*

I am very much behind the people who are sincere in their beliefs and passionate in their presentation, as long as they are respectful. But this woman sees herself as the savior of humanity whose goal in life seems to be making it into the Guinness Book of World Records for needless TV appearances. Chances are that I'll catch flack for being so blunt, but that's never stopped me before, so it's not going to stop me now.

Norty is more tactful by calling her "prickly," but I say she's just an awful human being. I think "Who are you to question these honorable officers with such arrogance and disrespect?" These military members have sworn an oath to uphold and defend the Constitution and have given over thirty-five years of their life to this country. These are strong decent men and women you are attacking and some of these politicians come in like they are deities and give two years—you're kidding me!

If I sound upset, it's because we spouses never forget!

INTO THE WAR ZONE

We flew into Afghanistan and about thirty minutes out they had me put on a helmet and full body armor, which in itself was kind of an out-of-body experience since we were coming in on the G5 (the Gulfstream G5 is a small, plush business jet) and not some military transport plane. Suddenly I started crying. Chief McQuiston, the same one that I brought in to psych up Norty for his confirmation hearing, saw me and came up to the front, where I was sitting. He placed his hand on my shoulder and tried to calm me down.

"Suzie, there's really nothing to be scared about. We just have to wear these as a precaution."

"This is not about being scared," I said. "This is thinking about all those soldiers and airmen down there who have to wear ten times more than I am wearing, in 120-degree heat and in their case it is about dodging IEDs and what not . . . Every American should have to put on something like this and walk around for a day to appreciate what they go through."

On my second day in Afghanistan I was flown back to Bagram to meet with a group of Afghan women who had gone through extraordinary security to be allowed to meet with me at the Bagram Air Base—some to the point of endangering their own lives if word of their presence were to leak out. This was no ordinary meet and greet. These courageous women didn't put their lives on the line for a free lunch and photo op.

It was a wide range of women with diverse backgrounds: business owners, educators, government leaders, multimedia, and nongovernmental organization representatives from Kabul, Kapisa, and Parwan provinces. They were respectful but pulled no punches. They asked tough questions and they expected honest answers. "We know you can fight the war but where are all these other things you promised for our country after the fighting? You promised security but we have none. Where there's no security, there is no education, no health, and no employment. The Afghan women are used by politicians to get foreign aid money, but our conditions have not improved." It was eye-opening and I took detailed notes. I promised to pass along their concerns (which I did), but I also made it clear that I was not in a position to promise anything as far as results were concerned. Still, they seemed appreciative to have been heard, and they could tell that I was sincere in my pledge to relay their apprehensions. I was honored to be afforded the opportunity to participate in this and other similar discussions in countries all across the globe.

Later, after Norty became Chief, the requests for my participation were almost overwhelming. There'd be parties and dinners at Air House—the official home to the Air Force Chief of Staff—and I'd be the one responsible for supervising menus, themes, decorations, and all that comes with pulling off social events like these; events that routinely included all manner of dignitaries, both foreign and domestic. I loved this, and had a blast with every one.

I would accompany Norty on trips all around the world, meeting presidents, kings, and princes. Each one was special in its own way. But if I had to pick the one thing that touched me the most (with the exception of my interaction with the families of our fallen), I think it would have to be that day with those valiant young women, struggling to turn the tide on women's oppression left in the wake of the Taliban.

They were not overstating the deadly risk these women assumed in order to meet with me. Just after we departed, the security situation deteriorated. On April 27, insurgents with automatic weapons and rocket-propelled grenades opened fire on a military parade celebrating the 1992 victory of the Mujahideen *over the People's Democratic Party of Afghanistan communist government. Their target was Afghan President Hamid Karzai. An intense firefight lasted for about fifteen minutes, leaving three dead and more than ten wounded. Karzai was safe, but until years later, no longer would U.S. military spouses be allowed to enter Afghanistan. I was the very last American military spouse allowed in-country in an official capacity.*

WELCOME TO SAUDI ARABIA

While in Saudi Arabia on official business, I decided to visit the hotel gym while Norty was out conferring with his Saudi counterpart. I'd been briefed on the need to remain completely covered while in public, so I took great care to push the button for the "Women's Gym" floor when I entered the elevator in my U.S. Air Force gym shorts and tank top. Unfortunately, I had left the room without my keycard, and the only place the elevator would take me without it was the lobby. My pounding the "stop" button was fruitless, as was pushing the "15" that would take me back to my floor. The elevator jolted to a stop and the doors slid open. There I stood in my skimpy workout attire, much to the dismay of the six fully robed individuals I walked past on my stroll to the front desk to pick up a new keycard. I was so mortified I wanted to stay inside the room the rest of the trip. It was probably just in my head, but from that point on I felt that everyone was staring at me whenever I passed, kind of snickering to one another behind my back, like "That's her, the elevator lady!"

SHE KEPT HER WORD

Traditionally when a Democrat comes into office, I've found the military is not their top priority. So it had particular impact on me when Mrs. Obama announced that caring for military families was an area to which she pledged to devote significant time and energy. And the best part is that she has lived up to her word on this. What she and Dr. Biden have achieved through the "Joining Forces" initiative on spouse employment, wellness, and education has been humongous.

On November 10, 2011, Norty and I attended an event at the beautiful Chamber of Commerce building. We were the only service chief and spouse in attendance. I forced him to attend. I remember sitting in the front when Mrs.

Obama began to speak. "Today, America's businesses have stepped forward with pledges to hire a hundred thousand veterans and military spouses by 2014," she announced. "That's right, a hundred thousand jobs. a hundred thousand veterans and spouses who will have the security of a paycheck and a good career. That's thousands of families that can rest just a little bit easier every night."

The audience erupted in applause, and Norty leaned over and squeezed my hand. That's when I burst into tears. I cried because it hit me how far we had come from the early days of me trying so hard to get a job, and now, thanks to the hard work of Mrs. Obama and Dr. Biden, eighty major companies were there supporting spouse employment, and they continue to support it across the country.

Norty adds: This is yet another area where Suzie's success was palpable. Last year, the First Lady and Dr. Biden announced that *all fifty states have taken action* to make it easier for military spouses to overcome employment barriers by streamlining the employment-related licensing and credentialing process. The very issue that Suzie was so enthusiastically advocating has become a reality, and military spouses who were previously hampered by certain states not recognizing the credentials of another—can now continue working no matter their location.

Once Suzie made the choice to devote herself to this career path rather than the one where she could have been heroically successful, she attained rock star status. I'm not just referring to her individual achievements—which were epic—I'm referring to her role in what we accomplished together. From Tulum to Timbuktu and everywhere in between, every one of the relationships that we cultivated over time were principally her doing. I'm not the most engaging person, and personal human connections have never been my strong suit.

Suzie: *You can say that again.*

Norty: In spite of my personal deficits in that area, I'm fully aware that without solid, honest, trusting relationships, it's impossible for anyone to make it to the top. Our closest friends on the civilian side—the Ellsworths, the Bordons, and the Pews—all Suzie's doing.

In many ways it was Suzie who maintained connectivity with my own friends, as well: the Munsons and the Lauderdales. She maintained the relationships with our colleagues and our contemporaries. I'm not a letter writer, but somehow Suzie finds the time—and the means—to maintain contact and keep us engaged.

Our close relationship with the Myerses (General Richard Myers, past chairman of the Joint Chiefs of Staff) is mostly from Suzie's contact with Mary Jo. The same applies to our close relationship with the Paces (General Peter Pace, past chairman of the Joint Chiefs of Staff)—mostly due to Suzie's friendship with Lynne.

What ended up happening was that I had professional relationships with people and they were strong and in many ways intimate—but they were rarely *personal*. Suzie consistently compensated for that. She makes friends easily and these were good people to be friends with—and I'm not saying that from a career path or advancement point of view. These are just lovely, worthwhile people that we're honored to call our friends.

Chapter Eight

A NEW PLAYING FIELD

The state of modern warfare has changed since Barry Goldwater handed me my diploma—the *world* has changed. Air raid sirens warning of impending Russian nuclear attack have been replaced by text messages announcing shooters on campus. From Vietnam to *Charlie Hebdo* to the Istanbul Ataturk Airport attack, and everything in between. Ho Chi Minh has been replaced by UBL and ISIS. Now, so much is focused on terrorism. Special operations have expanded exponentially and today, in most cases, are the first "go-to" element the president calls upon.

When I first donned the uniform, special operations was in its decline. Through failed missions as much as successes, we learned. We grew. Those early operators—daring innovators with unbridled passion for the mission—became even greater leaders and mentors and inspirations for those of us who followed in their giant footsteps. Scholtes, Potter, Downing, Schoomaker, Hobson . . . these are the ones to whom we owe our gratitude for creating the greatest special operations force in the world.

Islamic fundamentalists still pose a genuine threat to the American population in the homeland and will continue to require our efforts to neutralize that threat. My own view is that we're better off neutralizing the threat at a distance rather than at our borders or inside our borders. ISIL is a prime example of how clearly this will be a continuing theme until this generation of jihadists gets gray hair and gets tired. This requires a combined arms approach with sufficient ground presence to generate target intelligence and stiffen friendly forces. We have such assets on the ground and we are striking concentrations of ISIL by both air and ground assault, as well as interdicting logistics and financial resources.

But as we are now largely out of Iraq and have a much reduced footprint in Afghanistan, it's time to shift the focus of our attention from a 90 percent–plus concentration in the Persian Gulf area to something a bit more balanced. Our strategic interests call for more attention in the Asia-Pacific and the Indo-Pacific than was the case when we were completely consumed by the ground wars in Iraq and Afghanistan. Korea, China, Japan, Indonesia, Malaysia, India, Thailand, Vietnam—they are all worthy of our attention.

NORTH KOREA

More missiles (now intercontinental in range); potential nuclear buildup; unstable leader. Not long ago, an American student was convicted and sentenced to fifteen years hard labor; shortly thereafter he was returned to the United States in such bad condition he died a few days later. While isolated, it's clear we intend to impose additional sanctions. To the extent they affect the North Korean elites, that is appropriate. We are also reinforcing the resolve and patience of our South Korean ally and leaning on the Chinese to influence Kim Jong Un due to significant China-Korea dependencies. But we are now in an era when we must also defend. Thus, missile defense rises in importance for us and our Japanese and South Korean allies. Deterrence alone is insufficient.

CHINA INCURSIONS INTO SOUTH CHINA SEA

It is worrisome. The Chinese are changing the geography and asserting sovereignty well beyond their immediate borders. We have to enlist the support of regional allies to resist this attempt at fait accompli politically, economically, and militarily. What we have to do in order to combat these and other threats is to improve the "full spectrum" readiness and the wherewithal of our forces for continuing counterterror campaigns as well as deterring near-peer adversaries.

AIR-SEA BATTLE DOCTRINE

In recognizing the unique challenges of the Western-Pacific arena, Gary Roughead (chief of naval operations) and I initiated the Air-Sea Battle concept, an institutional partnership of the Air Force and Navy in the areas of acquisition, tactics, and procedures. A collaboration of this scope was unprecedented. The ultimate goal of Air-Sea Battle is interoperable air and naval forces that can execute networked, integrated attacks-in-depth to disrupt, destroy, and defeat an adversary's anti-access/area denial capabilities, in turn sustaining the deployment of U.S. Joint forces. There are a number of joint Air Force/Navy initiatives that were funded as a result of this initiative. One resulted in a test where an F-22 actually retargeted a Tomahawk cruise missile launched by a submarine—a perfect example of how two stealth vehicles from two different service branches (Air Force F-22 and Navy sub) collaborated to achieve tactical success. More such opportunities will become apparent . . . and essential to our military posture.

TECHNOLOGY

Technology is offering us means and avenues of engaging the enemy that change the state of play in nontrivial ways. Midair refueling was one of these game-changers; having the ability to refuel aircraft of all types en route to their destinations really allows us to project power. GPS and integrated avionics were also right up there. But in my mind, the remotely piloted aircraft, or RPA (often referred to as "drone"), is the single most significant advance since radar. This goes back centuries to the bow and arrow. The spear, artillery, aircraft—there's been a momentum to extend the distance between combatants from the very earliest days. The difference is that now we have the ability to fly lethal aircraft without risk of physical danger to the pilot. It's monumental.

It's quite likely that I will be remembered for my aggressive advocacy for the expansion of RPAs. In my last year as chief, we trained 350 RPA pilots as compared to 250 fighter and bomber pilots. I believe that by 2028, at least 50 percent of all Air Force pilots will be flying RPAs from many miles away. But they are not a be-all and end-all. On the positive side, they offer constant surveillance: hours, days, weeks of observation; high-confidence targeting; very accurate delivery of low-collateral damage munitions. On the flip side, there are perceptions of remote targeting, absence of physical risk, and the potential for global proliferation of the capability due to relatively low barriers to entry.

For years we had been referring to these platforms as "drones" or "unmanned aerial vehicles" (UAVs), but there's a reason that I worked hard to phase out that nomenclature in favor of "remotely piloted aircraft" (RPA). These systems are hardly unmanned. It takes at least 168 people to operate, maintain, and support these missions, so we didn't want to maintain the misperception that they are "unmanned."

Long before I arrived, Secretary Gates had his eye on the ball and recognized that having timely, accurate, and actionable operational intelligence was essential to support the battlefield decision-making process. We were a nation at war and American casualties were mounting. Gates understood the urgent need to provide his commanders with every possible resource to defeat the enemy, and he was miffed when those around him took a business-as-usual approach. As he shares in his own his own autobiography, *Duty: Memoirs of a Secretary at War*, his impatience with the "damnable peacetime mindset inside the Pentagon" was boiling over, fueled in great part by the difficulty he was having in meeting his field commanders' insatiable need for intelligence, surveillance, and reconnaissance (ISR) capabilities: "a mix of unmanned drones, propeller-driven reconnaissance aircraft, analysts, linguists, and data fusion capabilities that collected and fed critical battlefield information—including intercepted phone calls of terrorist leaders and live video transmission of insurgents planting IEDs . . ."

RPAs are one of many means of collecting data—data that when processed, analyzed, and integrated becomes the fuel that feeds our global integrated ISR process. It provides us with a capability that is absolutely vital at all levels of conflict—strategic, operational, and tactical, where the difficult guesswork on what hostile forces are around the corner, on the roof, or over the wall is substantially reduced for our ground forces. To Secretary Gates— just like the downrange commanders who were clamoring for these tools—it was a no-brainer: *ISR saves lives.* His frustration was palpable, but those at the top levels of the Air Force did more to exacerbate his apprehension than assuage it. It seemed that very little had changed since 1992, when, as CIA director, Gates pushed hard to convince the Air Force to partner with him in developing technologically advanced drones to provide continuous photographic and intercepted signals intelligence coverage. "The Air Force wasn't interested," Gates recalls, the rationale being that "people join the Air Force to fly airplanes, and drones had no pilots."

In the summer of 2007, Secretary Gates directed the Air Force to present him with a plan to increase its RPA capacity posthaste, but the drawn-out implementation timetable the Air Force proposed demonstrated that the Service failed to grasp the urgent need for downrange ISR. Instead, the Air Force proposed ending all funding for the revered U-2 spy plane, which was still providing remarkable intelligence. "I thought proposing to ground it at this juncture was just plain crazy," Gates laments. "Further, nearly every time Moseley and Air Force Secretary Mike Wynne came to see me, it was about a new bomber or more F-22s. Both were important capabilities for the future, but neither would play any part in the wars we were already in." Once again, the traditional "fighter/bomber" culture seemed to cloud the leaders' abilities to consider new paradigms. Gates rightfully recognized that success on the twenty-first-century battlefield demanded outside-the-box innovations. He felt like he was butting heads with a service whose culture seemed to impede his objectives—in this case the rapid expansion of RPAs.

Between his twenty-six years in the CIA and four years as president of Texas A&M University—two institutions with rock-solid cultures—Secretary Gates knew that it would take fortitude to overcome the perceived antipathy to pressing battlefield needs. Yet without Service support, a swift expansion of our airborne ISR assets would be unlikely. He convened an ISR task force in hopes of finding viable options, and turned to a "strong supporter and valuable ally"—Chairman Mike Mullen. About the same time, the nuclear debacle ignited and became the straw that broke the camel's back.

Strolling down the Arnold Corridor of the Pentagon, Gates glanced up at the long row of ornately framed oil portraits lining the wall, and thought about the men who had led his Air Force since its inception in 1947. (Gates was an Air Force 2nd Lieutenant assigned to the Strategic Air Command as an intelligence officer.) General Carl Spaatz, fighter pilot. Hoyt Vanderberg, fighter pilot. Curtis LeMay, bomber pilot. Bomber, bomber, fighter . . . each of the eighteen prior chiefs had been either a fighter or bomber pilot. It was time for a fresh perspective.

There's one segment of the Air Force that duplicates many aspects of the fighter/bomber culture, and that's where the secretary turned for the solution: special operations. I have little doubt that my background as an operator played a huge role in his placing his trust in me to be Chief. Do I respect the fighter/

bomber communities? Absolutely. But I share that respect with every other American service man or woman who lays their life on the line to protect our liberty.

I've shared a lot about how much of my good fortune I owe to my Army mentors, but I've also enjoyed significant collaboration with my Navy partners. The SEAL Creed includes a clause that reads "We expect innovation." Perhaps that's a concept that should be added to the Airman's Creed. It certainly encompasses what the secretary had in mind in his call for expanded ISR and RPAs, and I pledged to him that I shared his vision and would do everything in my power to expedite its implementation.

During my tenure, the three primary RPAs were the MQ-1 Predator, the MQ-9 Reaper, and the RQ-4 Global Hawk. The Reaper and Predator are AC/DC; they can do either kinetic (offensive lethal strike) or non-kinetic (ISR) missions, or both, and it's one of their distinct advantages. They see the target and they can strike the target, with very little delay.

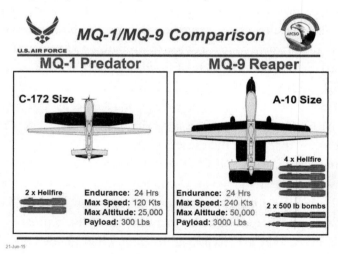

The **MQ-1 Predator** is an armed, multi-mission, single-engine, propeller-driven remotely piloted aircraft that operates over the horizon at medium altitude (25,000-foot ceiling) for long endurance and provides real-time intelligence (including full-motion video), surveillance, reconnaissance, target acquisition, and strike capability. Given its significant loiter time, wide-range sensors, and precision weapons, it provides a unique capability of performing strike, coordination, and reconnaissance (SCAR) against high-value, fleeting, and time-sensitive targets. Special Operations Command (SOCOM) divested the MQ-1 in FY 2015, and the Air Force is in the process of divesting the MQ-1 and replacing all aircraft with MQ-9s.

The **MQ-9 Reaper** is an armed, multi-mission, single-engine, turboprop, remotely piloted aircraft that is employed primarily against high-value, fleeting, dynamic, time-critical targets, and secondarily as an intelligence collection asset. About four times heavier than the Predator, the Reaper can fly twice as fast, go twice as high, and carry significantly more weapons than the MQ-1. The MQ-9 carries a robust suite of visual sensors for targeting, as well as a laser range finder/designator, which precisely designates targets for employment of laser-guided munitions, including its GBU-12 Paveway II Laser-Guided Bombs. The Reaper is also equipped with a synthetic aperture radar to enable GBU-38 Joint Direct Attack Munitions targeting. The MQ-9 can also employ four laser-guided Air-to-Ground Missile (AGM)-114 Hellfire missiles, which provide highly accurate, low-collateral damage, anti-armor, and anti-personnel engagement capabilities. The full-motion video from each of the imaging sensors (infrared, color/monochrome daylight TV, and image-intensified TV) can be viewed as separate video streams or fused.

USAF photo

The **RQ-4 Global Hawk** is a high-altitude (60,000-foot ceiling), jet-powered, long-endurance (thirty-plus hours) remotely piloted aircraft with an integrated sensor suite that provides a persistent, near-real-time broad spectrum of global, all-weather, day or night intelligence, surveillance and reconnaissance using imagery intelligence (IMINT), signals intelligence (SIGINT), and moving target indicator (MTI) sensors. With its long loiter times over target areas, Global Hawk can survey as much as 40,000 square miles (100,000 km²) of terrain a day.

Global Hawk is a big airplane used for surveillance only. USAF photo

RQ-170 SENTINEL

The Lockheed Martin RQ-170 is a low-observable RPA that got a lot of attention in December of 2011 when the Iranian government announced that they had brought one down near the city of Kashmar in northeast Iran. Just a few months earlier, Marc Ambinder of the *National Journal* tweeted that an RQ-170 was overhead on May 2 during Operation NEPTUNE SPEAR, the JSOC raid on the bin Laden compound in Abbottabad, Pakistan. The *Washington Post* identified the bat-winged stealth RPAs as providing the real-time imagery that President Obama and his national security team were watching during the raid.

RPAs are also equipped to eavesdrop on electronic transmissions, enabling U.S. officials to monitor the Pakistani response, according to the *Post*, which went on to quote retired Air Force Lt Gen David Deptula, who served as head of intelligence and surveillance for the Air Force. "It's a difficult challenge trying to secure information about any area or object of interest that is in a location where access is denied. The challenge is multiplied when the surveillance needs to be continuous, which makes non-stealthy slow-speed aircraft easier to detect." The RQ-170 is an ISR platform that meets that challenge.

When I got back to Washington in 2008 we had between eight and fourteen orbits of remotely piloted aircraft surveillance capability. That's the level that Secretary Gates publicly dismissed as an indication of the Air Force's half-hearted commitment to the effort. Each orbit, or CAP (Combat Air Patrol), provides twenty-four-hour coverage, 365 days a year. To do so, each CAP optimally requires four aircraft and ten crews, including the pilot and sensor operator, seated side by side in their "cockpit," a high-tech cubicle in a secured building often thousands of miles away from the aircraft they are piloting.

From the moment I stepped in, I felt a great responsibility to live up to the SECDEF's guidance. So, in part in response to that, but more importantly in response to the battlefield demand signal, we set out to grow the remotely piloted aircraft capability as rapidly as we could. We compressed the OPTEMPO to provide the same coverage with only 2.5 aircraft and seven crews—an effective means of accelerating the escalation in capability, but at the expense of stressing the people and equipment. These metrics would never hold up in the long haul. It became a matter of how quickly we could train our air crews and maintainers and intelligence experts—an operation that comprises far more than just a pilot and a sensor operator.

For the MQ-1 Predator or MQ-9 Reaper, some 168 personnel are required to maintain each CAP, and that's just for the airplane piece. In addition, there's a whole backside for processing the collected data—dozens of people—imagery and signals analysts, intelligence advisors, mission controllers, senior commanders, military lawyers—all participating in the operations from twenty-seven networked and linked centers scattered around the world, exploiting and disseminating the data in real time over secure radio, satellite, and chat rooms. It is a global enterprise we call the Distributed Common Ground System (DCGS), also known as the AN/CSQ-272 SENTINEL weapon system.

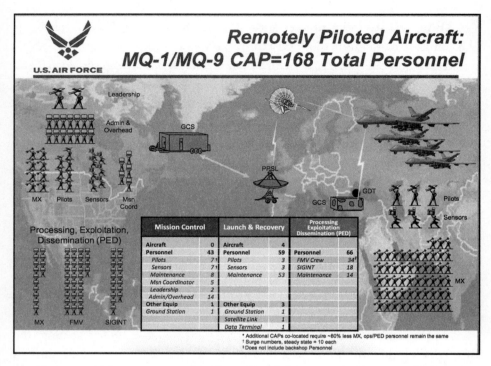

From its early inception, Air Force DCGS has evolved into an ISR operation capable of providing worldwide, near-real-time simultaneous intelligence to multiple theaters of operation. These centers (called distributed ground stations, or DGSs) consist of people and computers and communications that bring in the collected data and allow analysts to look at it, digest it, and turn it around to send it back out as finished intelligence. It's a vast network that can support multiple ISR platforms in multiple theaters of operation simultaneously, from centers that may be located many thousands of miles away. This reduced forward footprint puts fewer airmen in harm's way with no sacrifice in operational capability. While each DGS operates independently, the interconnectivity enables robust communication, data sharing, and resilience. If one DGS workload exceeds capacity, another DGS can assist in real time, providing seamless and uninterrupted mission execution. DCGS crews also rely on the expertise of partner distributed mission site crews normally collocated at National Security Agency locations—once again, fully networked and in real time.

This same level of partnership extends to the downrange teams that fly the aircraft. Whether it be the high-altitude manned U-2 Dragon Lady, the unmanned RQ-4 Global Hawk, or the multirole, medium-altitude MQ-1 Predator and MQ-9 Reaper, the flight crews are integrated into the DCGS framework regardless of physical location.

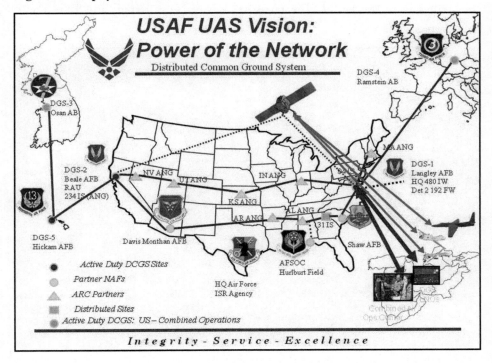

In one particular instance, the DGS-4 DART (Distributed Common Ground System Analysis and Reporting Team), in communication with a forward deployed analytical team, received a tip from a reliable source that a terrorist cell was preparing to take action against blue forces. The DART knew their DGS crews would be executing missions in that area later that day and also knew a fellow Air National Guard DGS site was presently operating there. Via encrypted chat and other secure communications, the DART analyst pushed the intelligence tip to the respective DGS crews as well as the CAOC (Combined Air Operations Center) that was tasking these missions. Located in the Air Force Central theater of operations, the CAOC provides the command and control of airpower throughout Iraq, Afghanistan, and eighteen other nations. The Predator was subsequently redirected to the suspected terrorist assembly area where unusual activity was observed. As this was reported back to the ground elements, planning was under way to conduct operations against the terrorists. After operations were completed, the CAOC passed requests to the

DGS-4 crew to get U-2 battle damage assessment imagery. DGS-4 imagery analysts were able to provide an immediate assessment and confirmation that the strikes were successful. The terrorist cell was eliminated, and Blue Force lives were saved.

Each day more than fifty ISR sorties are exploited, over 1,200 hours of full-motion imagery reviewed, over 3,000 signals intelligence (SIGINT) reports produced, 1,250 still images exploited, and twenty terabytes of data managed.

Strides were being made and lives were being saved. That's a testament to the immense value of effective, actionable ISR, and to Secretary Gates for having the dogged determination and persistence to go to the mat to ensure that his commanders were provided with every possible resource to defeat our adversaries.

We continued to grow, and if anything, our pace actually accelerated. We supplemented our active duty elements with Guard and reserves. Our colossal locomotive was steaming faster and faster down the tracks. But as hard as we worked to hasten an already burgeoning expansion, the demand signal from the commanders was growing even faster. And it would grow infinitely if we let it. It culminated in a great debate: how much is enough? Between the SECDEF, his key staff, the Air Force, combatant commanders and their staffs, planners, and analysts—it seemed like everyone had a different opinion. The debate was lively as everyone lobbied passionately to advance their positions, both financial and operational. It embodied everything for which I'd been trained throughout my career, going all the way back to my time in the Plans Directorate—learning from Generals Gabriel, O'Malley, and Dekok. I relished the process and felt fortunate to have been afforded the opportunity to make such a substantial contribution to this new generation of warfare. Exciting times.

We collectively came to the conclusion that sixty-five orbits was a realistic goal, and that's the number that the secretary directed us to meet—each providing 24/7 aerial coverage.

CENTCOM would still have first call, but our presumption was that if we built to sixty-five orbits (which would require around three hundred airplanes), that would allow prudent use of this capacity by other commanders at the same time; our supposition was that there had been lots of suppressed demand in other parts of the world where the commanders knew that if they asked, they would have been denied because of CENTCOM's position of first priority.

When I arrived, there were between eight and fourteen orbits of a platform that was modestly backed by Air Force leadership. By the time I left, we had grown exponentially in terms of capacity and machines and personnel, and the technology had become a vital component of our Air Force arsenal, one that promises to play an even larger role in the decades to come.

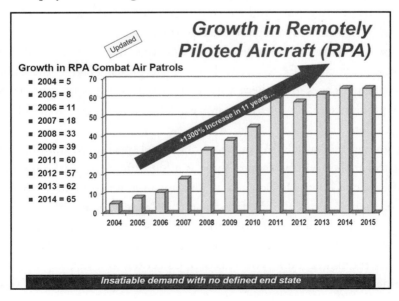

Growth in Remotely Piloted Aircraft (RPA)

Updated

Growth in RPA Combat Air Patrols

- 2004 = 5
- 2005 = 8
- 2006 = 11
- 2007 = 18
- 2008 = 33
- 2009 = 39
- 2011 = 60
- 2012 = 57
- 2013 = 62
- 2014 = 65

+1300% Increase in 11 years...

Insatiable demand with no defined end state

The other aspect of the RPA story is that in instituting our "All In" commitment to meet this accelerated battlefield demand, we ended up freezing people in these crew and maintenance jobs for five years or more, and some people suffered as a result of this. For some, staying at Creech Air Force Base for years longer than they might otherwise had impaired potential career advancement. In addition, initially we had to take traditionally trained pilots from other weapons systems and reassign them to the RPA program. It was all coming to a head and we needed to make a fundamental decision: were we going to continue to operate remotely piloted aircraft with traditionally rated pilots, or was there some kind of tailored training program that was more appropriate to the remote pilot?

RPA pilots still have to have basic airmanship skills, and still need to understand aircraft performance, aviation geometry, and airspace. They need to understand interaction with air traffic control, command and control, and the air-ground interface. But there are other aspects of traditional military aviation that are not necessary in the remote piloting context—things like formation flight (at least for now) and aerial combat maneuvers.

We came to the conclusion that a six-month program specifically dedicated to training remote pilots seemed like a viable curriculum that made far more sense than borrowing pilots who had completed eleven months of traditional flight training. We cut back on topics wherever prudent and maintained those that were tactically sound, and we stood up a dedicated training program for remotely piloted airmen to replace the traditional cockpit scenario.

Upon completion of the course, pilots were not only RPA certified, but they also became officially FAA-certified as private pilots. Having these piloting skills and experiences gives them a sense of airmanship, airspace geometry, and conflict avoidance that is integral to every aviation platform. It makes them better RPA pilots.

Following the basic RPA course, pilots attend specialized training in whatever platform they will be flying. There is a big difference in training requirements between Global Hawk—a large airplane used for surveillance only—and the more tactical birds, the Predators and the Reapers. Much like a traditional fighter pilot, Predator and Reaper pilots must become proficient in delivering weapons, understanding the weapon dynamics in terms of lethal ranges, approaching the target (taking into account direction, altitude, angle of attack), mastering how to ensure that the blast radius or ellipse occurs in a way that minimizes unnecessary loss of life and other collateral damage, and coordinating with ground elements to preclude the possibility of firing on friendlies.

It was a recognition that RPAs were not just a temporary feature of our Air Force, but rather an enduring new weapons system. Taking it a step further, we needed to have a bench of remote aviators who could grow up to be colonels and supervisors and planners who would know their weapons systems just like the fixed-wing and the rotary-wing conventional pilots do today. To that end, we created an entirely new career path focused entirely on RPAs.

It was a combat platform no different than fighters or gunships or U-2s, and it was going to be a lasting part of our Air Force. The notion was that this was not going to be a leper colony because the pilots were operating from locations out of harm's way. They were combat aviators whose actions could be every bit as lethal and calibrated as their counterparts in the manned cockpits. To signal this, we approved remote pilot wings—just like traditional pilot wings, but with their own insignia.

We did everything we could to instill a sense of community that was akin to our other weapons systems. Part of that was coming up with a means of recognizing accomplishments that went considerably above and beyond, something that acknowledged remote operators for their impact on the battlefield. We came up with the Distinguished Warfare Medal, the DWM.

By this time Secretary Panetta had replaced Gates, and he was the one who would have to approve the new medal. I had gotten to know Panetta pretty well, especially after working so closely with him on the F-22 oxygen issue. If there were ever any doubt as to his compassion and respect for the men and women of our military (and there were no doubts), the way he handled that engagement would have laid them to rest.

Before I ever broached the subject with the SECDEF, we had in-depth discussions with Chairman Marty Dempsey and the rest of the Joint Chiefs. They got it, and ultimately suggested expanding it to include cyber warfare specialists who had an extraordinary impact on combat operations, even though—like the RPA aviators—often they were not physically present in the combat zone. It was an appropriate addition in keeping with the evolution of combat. Once we obtained the buy-in (reluctant in some cases) of the Joint Chiefs, I met with the civilian policy personnel; they'd be ones to work out all the details should it be approved, and raise any red flags if there were reasons why it should not be implemented. They had none.

Armed with all the data, I felt prepared to present to Panetta. The meeting was set for a blistering afternoon in early summer of 2012. In fact, that July was the second hottest month in the history of the District.

Upon entering his huge inner office, I was warmly greeted by his affable companion, whose thick auburn tresses dangled from his belly as he enthusiastically sniffed, then licked my extended hand.

"Bravo, get over here and leave the general alone!" commanded the SECDEF, motioning for his gorgeous golden retriever to join him in the sitting area where we were about to meet. Bravo's presence was not uncommon—at the Pentagon or at CIA, where the secretary proudly shared how the companion sat in on many of the briefings for the May 2011 bin Laden raid.

"So what do you have for me, Norty?" the Secretary asked as we settled in.

I pulled out some backup material and began. "Sir, we are entering a new era that has operators in new disciplines that are creating effects on the battlefield that need to be recognized," I told him. "While they do not entail physical risk, nonetheless they provide the kind of outcomes that have a profound effect on the battlefield situation. It's true for our RPA crews and it's also true for cyber. The question is, how do we recognize their excellence? I contend that a medal is the appropriate recognition."

I handed him a rendering of one of six proposed designs. "The Distinguished Warfare Medal."

"Did you know that it's been more than seventy years since the last combat medal was introduced?" Panetta asked, scratching the canine's head as he reviewed the sketches.

"I did, sir," I answered. "Seems like we're overdue."

Secretary Panetta announced the award on February 13, 2013, just a few days before he left office, five months after I had retired. It was his final press conference from the Pentagon briefing room. "This award recognizes the reality of the kind of technological warfare we are engaged in in the twenty-first century," he said. "Our military reserves its highest decorations, obviously, for those who display gallantry and valor in actions when their lives are on the line and we will continue to do so. But we should also have the ability to honor the extraordinary actions that make a true difference in combat operations. The contribution they make does contribute to the success of combat operations, particularly when they remove the enemy from the field of battle, even if those actions are physically removed from the fight."

He retired with the satisfaction of knowing that these dedicated airmen would be appropriately acknowledged and rewarded. The new medal would be ranked as the eighth highest individual award behind the Medal of Honor, which would put it ahead of the Bronze Star and the Purple Heart.

Now, I wish I could say that the story ended there, but that's not the case. Chuck Hagel had barely been sworn in as SECDEF when the complaints starting coming in. First the Veterans of Foreign Wars criticized the medal's order of precedence. Then the Military Order of the Purple Heart. Alumni asked, "How can you recognize someone who wasn't even close to the battlefield and value that service more than someone who was wounded?" Congress picked up on it and chimed in, with three military veteran congressmen (Duncan D. Hunter, Tom Rooney, and Tim Murphy) introducing legislation to reduce the precedence of the medal to somewhere below the Purple Heart. The bill gained 124 cosponsors, while a corresponding bill introduced in the Senate had gained thirty-one cosponsors. Other veterans' groups and lawmakers lobbied the Pentagon and President Obama to downgrade the medal's status. They weren't suggesting that the medal be cancelled, just that it be lowered in rank.

On April 15, Secretary Hagel announced what was expected to be a concession to adjust the medal's rank. Instead, he opined that the medal was "unnecessary," and he killed it completely.

It was ultimately decided that rather than awarding a medal, they would issue a "device"—in this case a quarter-inch bronze "R" (for "remote")—that the recipient would pin to an existing noncombat medal to recognize direct contributions to specific combat events by those not physically in the battle. This was not what we had hoped to achieve, which was to provide a venue to recognize remote warriors that was roughly equivalent, recognizing the differences in physical risk.

In hindsight, I probably should have seen the writing on the wall as soon as the medal's precedence was announced, and dealt with it head-on at the time. Likewise, it was a mistake not to have involved Congress from the start. After thirty-nine years in the Air Force, I should have known better.

The big takeaway from all this is that coming to terms with new modes of combat is very difficult on many levels, many of them unanticipated. Doing so in the midst of insatiable demands from battlefield commanders in multiple war zones escalates the challenge—and the stakes—to off-the-chart levels. We stepped into a triage situation (a.k.a. "the surge") that was impossible to be adequately and effectively served by our insufficient number of skilled aviators who had been trained for that platform—dedicated men and women, to be sure—but ones without a career path, many of whom were driving two hours each way to their secure location in the middle of the Nevada desert. Crews were overworked in inadequate conditions, and many suffered damage to their careers since they were unable to find time to pursue career advancement opportunities. Throw in a lack of family time and you have an acute problem with morale that presaged an exodus from the Air Force.

But lives were being lost and you can't help but ask yourself how many can be saved by adding just one more CAP, or five more, or ten more. So we borrowed pilots from other platforms, and even trainers from the schools—which of course exacerbated the problem because fewer trainers meant fewer new pilots to solve the problem—a catch-22.

In spite of all this, and in no small part due to the great vision, drive, support, and inspiration of my bosses—Secretary Gates and Secretary Panetta—we did what it took to meet current demands and chart a path to the future. In 2007, the Air Force was providing eight Predator CAPS. When I retired, we were providing fifty-six. It was a good start; we laid a solid foundation.

But the truth is that when I left, our Air Force was still going through growing pains as we tried to come to terms with this new mode of combat. Secretary Gates had called for sixty-five CAPs. That was met in 2015, then reduced to sixty in late 2015 to allow the community to stabilize and rebuild—a very smart move.

RPA operator and maintenance manning is the result of accessions, the training pipeline, and retention of more experienced personnel. But on the retention side, other needed adjustments are necessary, including diversifying the locations where these personnel serve. If the only active duty locations are Creech AFB (Indian Springs, Nevada) and Holloman (outside of Alamogordo, New Mexico), that is not the strongest incentive for members and families to continue to support that mission. There are other "environmentals" as well as institutional issues the Air Force must address: promotion rates, school selection rates for officers, family support capabilities, local advanced degree programs, and workload.

My successors instituted other measures to stabilize the mission area:

- The Air Force is currently in the midst of hiring civilian contractors to fly and maintain government-owned RPAs, ground stations, and equipment for ten combat air patrols per day in addition to the sixty flown by the Air Force. It's an effective solution for surveillance missions only. While we used this concept for training, our successor leadership elected to expand contractor support for non-kinetic (ISR) RPA operations.

- Enlisted airmen are now authorized to fly the RQ-4 Global Hawk on ISR missions—the first time our Air Force has had enlisted pilots since World War II.
- $35,000/year retention bonuses are being offered to RPA pilots who agree to renew their active duty service commitment for an additional five years, for a total of $175,000 in bonus pay over the five years.

The expectation is that these modifications will allow the system to stabilize to the point that by 2019, we can safely and efficiently support seventy CAPs, sixty using Air Force personnel plus the ten staffed by the civilian contract suppliers.

FUTURE TECH

As I look to the future, I envision an Air Force that effectively controls and exploits air and space, and eventually cyberspace, in ways that provide even greater margins for global stability and economic vitality. We anticipate significant challenges in gaining access to the commons as our adversaries pursue asymmetric methods for thwarting our use of air, space, and cyberspace.

The proliferation of precision means that state and non-state actors will continue to build sophisticated air defenses, long-range missiles, and even short-range precision systems that will threaten our bases, our deployed forces, and, if one throws readily available and easily modified low-cost drones into the mix, our homeland.

Surely there will be greatly increased demand for space- and aircraft-based intelligence, surveillance, and reconnaissance capabilities so that our military forces and national leadership retain unprecedented understanding of the global operational environment. The ability to perceive and anticipate an adversary's actions and intent offers a decisive advantage in warfare and in maintaining the peace. As the demand for RPAs continues to expand, new platforms will evolve, and new systems will be developed to broaden and enhance the platform's capability.

Unmanned aircraft systems (UAS) and the effects they provide have emerged as one of the most in-demand capabilities the USAF provides the Joint Force. The attributes of persistence, endurance, efficiency, and connectivity are proven force multipliers across the spectrum of global joint military operations.

Secretary Donley, Lt Gen Dave Deptula, and I created an actionable plan entitled "Unmanned Aircraft Systems Flight Plan" that takes us all the way out to 2047. A few years later it was updated by the "RPA Vector" report. Between the two of them, we can get a pretty good feel for what we envision for the future of RPA warfare.

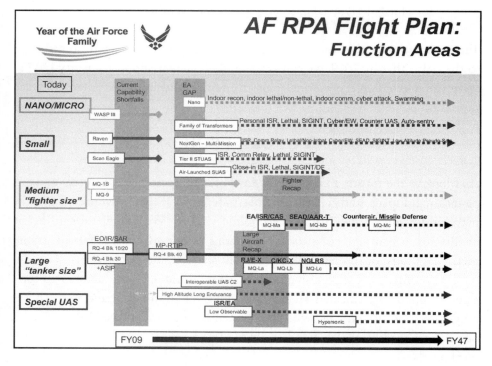

The USAF UAS Flight Plan describes a family of unmanned aircraft consisting of small man-portable vehicles, including micro- and nano-sized vehicles, medium "fighter-sized" vehicles, large "tanker-sized" vehicles, and special vehicles with unique capabilities, all capable of performing autonomous operations. The concept is to build a common set of airframes within a family of systems with interoperable, modular "plug and play" payloads that can be tailored to fit the mission—weapons and sensors that plug right in. There will always be fiscal restraints, and modularity provides a way to upgrade, augment, and replace technologies while preserving the bulk of the airframe investment and keeping costs down.

We are currently developing the MQ-X, a stealthy RPA capable of surviving in heavily defended, contested airspace and performing a wide variety of ISR and strike missions. It will use modularity for rapid reconfiguration to serve any of a number of widely divergent missions. It must accommodate autonomous intelligence, surveillance, and reconnaissance operations, since it is possible that an enemy will be able to interrupt the links between the operator and the aircraft.

The next-generation RPA must project power and have the ability to strike quickly from over the horizon in contested and anti-access/area denial (A2/AD) environments—where enemies operate advanced radar systems and other advanced air defenses, fifth-generation stealth fighter jets, and long-range precision-guided weapons that make physical access very difficult. But peer- and near-peer actors also have the ability to disrupt transmissions in the electromagnetic spectrum, creating contested communications environments that must be overcome. RPAs will eventually be robust man-on-the-loop autonomous systems that can adapt on their own to operate effectively in hostile environments despite disturbances. They will have the capability to assess, recover, learn, and adapt from adverse events, and in doing so successfully complete their mission objectives with minimal impact.

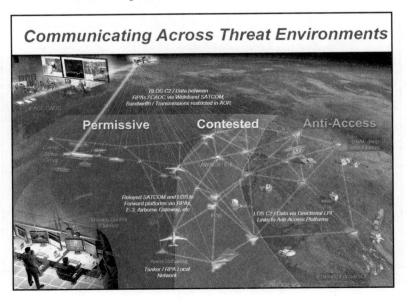

In the near term, automation (versus full autonomy) will be implemented to decrease operator workload. This will initially include auto takeoff and landing operations, plus full integration with other vehicles and personnel on the ground during launch and recovery to include auto taxi. It differs from full autonomy in that the system will follow preprogrammed decision logic. Eventually this will mature to the point of full man-on-the-loop autonomous flight operations. While people maintain control of the overall mission, the moment-to-moment decisions are made by the aircraft's automated systems, subject to human intervention.

In a further evolution of what Gary Roughead and I tried to achieve with the Air-Sea Battle initiative, the NextGen systems must take joint operations to the next level and further enable cross-domain synergies between all land, sea, air, space, and cyberspace domains. They must be multi-mission capable, adverse weather capable, net-centric, interoperable, and must employ appropriate levels of autonomy.

As the technology advances, using multi-aircraft control (MAC) will provide a mechanism for substantial savings in manpower. Multi-aircraft control allows one pilot to simultaneously control multiple aircraft, resulting in a reduction in the number of pilots required to execute high volume CAPs.

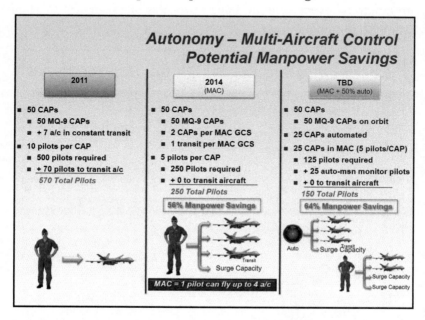

Advances in miniaturization of sensors and power supplies will yield smaller and smaller RPAs. The Defense Advanced Research Projects Agency (DARPA) is exploring a new class of algorithms for high-speed navigation in cluttered environments. Their hope is to develop small autonomous RPAs that will navigate high-clutter environments at speeds of up to forty-five miles per hour—independent of communication with outside personnel and without reliance on GPS. DARPA program manager Mark Micire has said the intent is for the small RPAs to exhibit the same kinds of capabilities as birds of prey and flying insects. "Goshawks, for example, can fly very fast through a dense forest without smacking into a tree. Many insects, too, can dart and hover with incredible speed and precision." Applications for such a vehicle could include cyber-attack, indoor reconnaissance and communications relay, and signals intelligence (SIGINT), as well as lethal and nonlethal attacks.

Many other RPAs will use enhanced sense-and-avoid systems that enable unmanned aircraft to sense its surroundings and avoid obstacles and other vehicles. In fact, it's a key element in any autonomous or semi-autonomous flight system.

On the flip side, we foresee large, tanker-sized RPAs that could serve as communications nodes while simultaneously providing air refueling and ground moving target indicator (GMTI) missions with onboard radars. The key concept will be multipurpose, achievable through interchangeable modularity. Single use aircraft for single purpose missions will become ancient history.

WAMI (Wide Area Motion Imagery) and WAAS (Wide Area Airborne Surveillance)

Certain RPAs can be fitted with a pod set capable of scanning a small city and broadcasting multiple simultaneous discrete video feeds to coalition forces.

The Air Force is also working to broadly expand the capability of its GMTI airborne surveillance platform, which allows RPAs to detect and track moving targets on the ground. With each sweep of the radar, thousands of vehicles can simultaneously be detected and tracked.

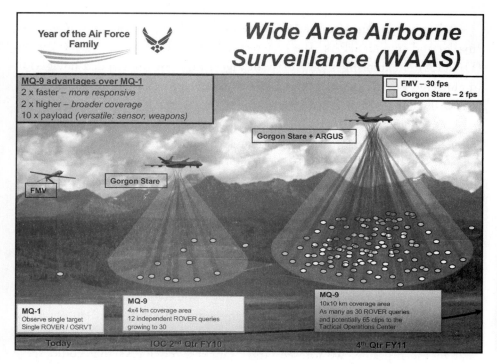

Loyal Wingman

An electronic "brain" is inserted into a fourth-generation F-16 fighter jet to allow an autonomous flying wingman to operate in tandem with manned F-35s in the battlefield of the future. Air Force Research Lab is well into the algorithms that will control the autonomous jets, and is doing so with an eye toward modular interchangeability that will enable the "brain" to be rapidly transferred from aircraft to aircraft, much like SIM cards are easily transferred from one mobile phone to another.

Hypersonic speeds greater than Mach 5.5 may be in the future, but developing the propulsion technology and materials that can withstand the extreme heat is most likely twenty years or more down the road. The Air Force Research Laboratory and Boeing have been working on an emerging hypersonic test platform called the X-51A WaveRider. Once success is realized, the technology promises to be a next-generation game-changer.

Perdix mini-drone

Attacks through cyberspace and evolving electronic warfare technologies threaten to neutralize some of the advantages of our strike platforms, our command and control systems, and our ISR networks. To meet these challenges, our military will need to work with the scientific community and our industry partners so that we may have the capability to secure and protect the commons. It's that model that led the Department of Defense Strategic Capabilities Office to work with MIT on a unique semi-autonomous mini-drone that functions within a swarm of fellow mini-drones in an embryonic approach that might usher in the next generation of ISR RPAs. Think of a swarm of tiny electronic honeybees, independent, yet navigating in a perfectly synchronized choreography—each transmitting its observations back to the hive in real time, or collectively jamming or overwhelming an enemy radar station.

In January 2017, *60 Minutes* profiled the autonomous "Perdix mini-drone," a swarming UAV capable of low-altitude ISR and other missions. Originally developed at MIT with a 3D-printed airframe, the DoD Strategic Capabilities Office successfully upgraded the foot-long aircraft using all-commercial components. The Department of Defense details the technology:

> In one of the most significant tests of autonomous systems under development by the Department of Defense, the Strategic Capabilities Office, partnering with Naval Air Systems Command, successfully demonstrated one of the world's largest micro-drone swarms at China Lake, California. The test, conducted in October 2016, consisted of 103 Perdix drones launched from three F/A-18 Super Hornets. The micro-drones demonstrated advanced swarm behaviors such as collective decision-making, adaptive formation flying, and self-healing.
>
> "Due to the complex nature of combat, Perdix are not pre-programmed synchronized individuals, they are a collective organism, sharing one distributed brain for decision-making and adapting to each other like swarms in nature," said SCO Director William Roper. "Because every Perdix communicates and collaborates with every other Perdix, the swarm has no leader and can gracefully adapt to drones entering or exiting the team."

The demonstration is one of the first examples of the Pentagon using teams of small, inexpensive, essentially autonomous systems to perform missions once achieved only by larger, more expensive ones. Roper stressed the department's conception of the future battle network is one where humans will always be in (or at minimum "on") the loop. Machines and the autonomous systems being developed by the DoD, such as the micro-drones, will empower humans to make force application decisions faster.

Our Air Force maintains the world's most advanced systems for detecting, identifying, and targeting an adversary. We are currently the sole provider of the worldwide communications and precision navigation and timing capabilities that are increasingly required to conduct operations in all domains. Our challenge extends far beyond merely maintaining this edge, as new adversaries emerge with unique and often unforeseen threats to our security. All across the Air Force, committed partners like the five-thousand-plus men and women of the Air Force Research Laboratory work in tandem with NASA, Department of Energy National Labs, DARPA, and other DoD research organizations to discover, develop, and integrate inventive and affordable air and space warfighting technologies that promise to ensure that our air, space, and cyberspace forces have the tools they need to stay well ahead of the curve. Inside these walls, success is fueled by imagination and dreams, and the most rewarding journey propels flights of fancy into the bold systems and trailblazing technologies that will keep our adversaries at bay and safeguard our freedom.

The proliferation of weapons of mass destruction will require that we increase our ability to monitor and detect technology transfer and weapon movements, while at the same time ensuring that our own weapons retain their dominance over those of our adversaries.

B61-12

Since the late 60s, various versions of the B61 nuclear bomb have been a staple of the United States' thermonuclear arsenal. The variable yield bomb is designed to withstand the rigors of high-speed aircraft carriage in both strategic and tactical nuclear weapon scenarios. Until now, the B61 has been an unguided weapon that required at least an intermediate yield to ensure an effective strike. The Mod 12 replaces the tail section with a new guided tail kit (the Tail Subassembly or TSA) that converts it to a smart weapon, improving accuracy and potentially lowering its nuclear yield—two desired military capabilities. A lower yield means potentially less collateral damage and less radioactive fallout that civilians might encounter, with no sacrifice to target accuracy.

It will all fall into place in Europe, once the F-35A stealth fighter bombers replace the F-16s and Tornado PA-200s assigned to NATO and U.S.

nuclear-capable bombers, providing platforms modified to handle the first guided nuclear bombs deployed by the United States in Europe.

We are pursuing the means to rapidly place our nation's satellites into operational orbits essentially on call so that we can detect the threats and provide warning necessary to protect our nation and our allies from ballistic missile and rocket attacks and from other hard-to-attribute threats in the commons. Our ability to operate in air, space, and cyberspace gives our nation a clear advantage in speed, range, and flexibility.

X-37B Orbital Test Vehicle

The Air Force Rapid Capabilities Office is taking the RPA concept into the realm of low Earth orbit with the Boeing X-37B Orbital Test Vehicle (OTV). A reusable space plane that looks like a miniature space shuttle, at twenty-nine feet in length with a wingspan of fifteen feet, it's about a quarter the size of the shuttle. All four OTV missions flown to date began with vertical launches from Cape Canaveral atop Atlas V rockets. After a total of 1,367 days in orbit, the first three successfully concluded with autonomous horizontal landings onto the landing strip at Vandenberg Air Force Base, and the fourth mission landed on May 7, 2017, surpassing OTV-3's 674 days in orbit.

Order	Launch date	Mission	Duration
OTV-1	April 22, 2010	USA-212	224 days
OTV-2	March 5, 2011	USA-226	468 days
OTV-3	December 11, 2012	USA-240	674 days
OTV-4	May 20, 2015	USA-261	700+ days

These capabilities are what makes the United States Air Force vital to our national security. No other institution on earth provides the range of capabilities in the air, in space, or the global command and control to integrate their use. This is our unique and enduring contribution to the joint team, and yes, it was my calling.

Common to our heritage is the relationship between the aviator and the machine. Alone together in the vastness of sky or space, the relationship is etched into our very psyche. It is so powerful an idea that it has attracted the best and the brightest that the world has to offer to our nation's service. It is these people who made us the service of technological innovation. But today the evolution of the machine is beginning to outpace the capability of the people we put in them. We now must reconsider the relationship of man and woman, machine and sky. We must ask and ultimately answer if we will perform manned or unmanned combat. While there is legitimate concern about autonomy in military systems, sensationalized by Hollywood among others, there's one overriding principle that will never change: *airmen will always perform the essential role of consenting to the application of lethal force, and lethal authority will never be delegated or relinquished.* That's exactly how it should be.

For the next thirty years or so, I believe there will continue to be a combination of both—a mix of manned tactical aviation and remotely piloted aircraft required to achieve air dominance. The expectation is that by 2022, paired warplanes will be capable of conducting ground strikes in hostile, well-defended environments, while pilotless cargo helicopters deliver supplies to troops on the battlefield. We must continue to evolve and embrace the culture of technological innovation that has been our hallmark. We have always used and will continue to use this technological innovation to provide for the security of our nation. Technology will allow us to better execute defense when in the past only offense was truly viable.

CONTROVERSY

On August 10, 2012, I stepped down after four years as Air Force Chief of Staff. That morning, I was on NPR's *Morning Edition* speaking with Pentagon reporter Tom Bowman about my tenure. Tom talked about how I got the job after my predecessor was relieved for—among other things—clashing with the SECDEF over how many fighter jets the military needs. Then he went on to posit that I am most likely to be remembered for my staunch advocacy for the use of drones. Notwithstanding his choice of the word "drone," I couldn't disagree with him. Nine times out of ten, it's the first topic that is raised when I am interviewed, or answering questions at a post-lecture Q & A. Depending on the audience, I can often predict the question:

"Do you think that's a fair way to fight? Killing people by pressing a button from thousands of miles away?" *There's far more involved than merely "pressing a button," but yes, I believe it's an excellent way to take out a terrorist before he takes more innocent lives.*

"Do you have any idea of how many innocent civilians you're killing when you try to sterilize it with terms like 'collateral damage'? You murder entire families, sometimes entire huge wedding parties—just to get one supposed terrorist. Are you not bothered by that?" *The best information we have is that there is one civilian casualty for every seven legitimate combatants in the Afghan theater. In Yemen, the ratio was one to five. This is according to one of the best sources,* Long War Journal. *I would argue that any civilian loss of life is not what uniformed personnel strive for. They strive mightily to avoid that outcome.*

The fact is remotely piloted aircraft, or drones, permit more considered, more accurate, and more proportionate application of lethal force than any other comparable weapon system. Because they can spend longer time over the target than equivalent manned aircraft, they give their operators the time to maximize the certainty that they are engaging the right enemy combatants, and they have the time and the means to confirm whether there are noncombatants in the vicinity of the intended target.

It is the ability of remote systems to maintain target area surveillance—long enough for their remote operators to carefully and deliberately evaluate potential targets against the criteria that allow them to shoot—that makes this system so discriminating and effective.

Soldiers and airmen under fire on the ground are far more likely to shoot back at the sources of fire aimed against them, possibly causing much greater danger to noncombatants, than are remote operators whose safety and lives are not at immediate risk.

There were about 150,000 Air Force flights during the surge period in Afghanistan in 2011. Sadly, about three thousand of those flights were medical evacuation sorties of our wounded and our dead. Compare that total to 25,000 close air support sorties and support of ground forces, of which 1,400 had at least one weapon release. So what this means is that out of 25,000 sorties, 1,400 actually released a weapon. There were many sorties that flew with no weapon release at all. That's what a professional Air Force does. Ready, finger on the trigger, but extremely careful and deliberate about applying lethal force in practice and in principle.

Less than a quarter—333—of those 1,400 weapon releases were by remote systems, with the other 1,067—three-fourths—from manned aircraft. Were those 1,067 weapon releases from manned aircraft somehow more practical, less immoral, less unfair than those 333 that were released by unmanned aircraft? I think not.

The bottom line is this is all about discipline. Are mistakes made from time to time? Yes, but that is not the policy, nor is it the training, nor is it the ethos or supervision of the personnel who perform the demanding missions.

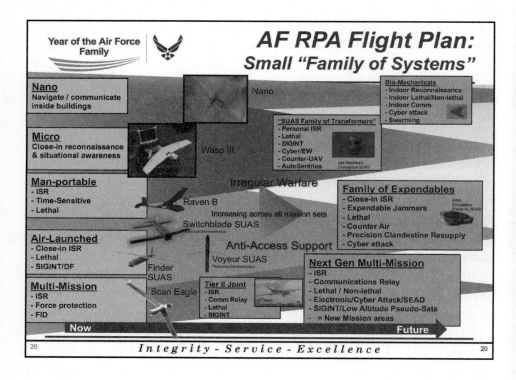

★ ★ ★

Today, my meetings take place in corporate conference rooms instead of the Cabinet Room, but I've tried my best to make the time I spend in the private sector as worthwhile as my years in the military. Subsequent to my Air Force retirement, I became president and CEO of Business Executives for National Security (BENS), a fiercely nonpartisan and nonprofit entity that supports the U.S. government by bringing best business practices and business expertise to bear on the problems that government faces, specifically in the national security sector. We try to elevate the performance of our government and its efficiency and effectiveness.

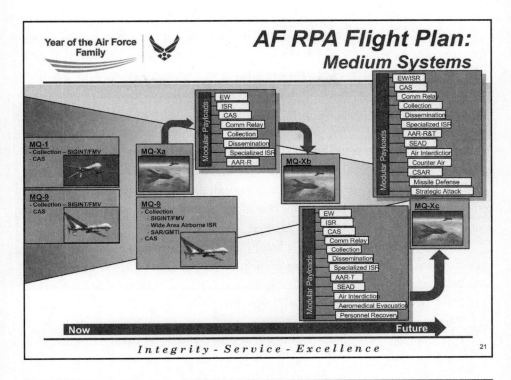

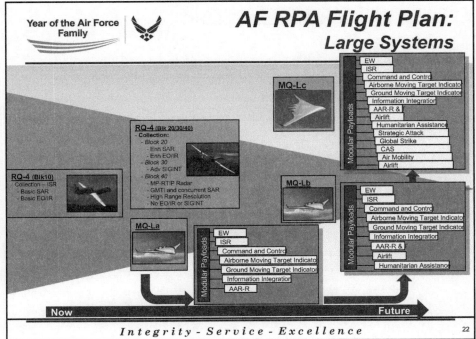

Founded in 1982 by business executive and entrepreneur Stanley A. Weiss, we currently have about 450 members, and these are all accomplished people who want to give back. The real purpose is to connect government need for business-driven problem solving with the capabilities of our members who have the time, the passion, and the particular skill required to deliver an effective solution. We don't take direct corporate contributions and we are very scrupulous about conflict of interest. All of our resources are from individual donations, and all of our members' work is pro bono. For those reasons, as well as many years of working together, we're trusted by government partners that know we won't embarrass them. It is a good fit for Suzie and me and it's about giving back—a continuation of a career of public service.

It has also provided me with a forum to share some of my thoughts on various national security issues as they continue to evolve:

How To Boost Domestic Intelligence and Privacy To Prevent the Next Terrorist Attack
By Norton A. Schwartz
April 14, 2015

January's attacks in Paris sparked debates about our civil liberties, freedom of speech and freedom of the press, but also discussions about the use of intelligence to combat the terrorist threat at home and our expectation of privacy. In February, the Senate Intelligence Committee marked its first open hearing since June that provided the public insight on how the United States collects and disseminates intelligence data. Given recent events and debates, it should come to no surprise that the focus of the hearing was the National Counterterrorism Center, the clearinghouse for our country's terrorism information.

Our nation views intelligence collection with apprehension and the sentiment is understandable. An Associated Press-GfK poll in January noted almost 60 percent of respondents disapproved of the Obama administration's handling of intelligence surveillance policies, and 61 percent favor protecting civil liberties over keeping the country safe from terrorist attacks.

There appears to be a perceived dichotomy between counterterrorism activities and civil liberties—a belief that intelligence efforts and civil liberties stand in opposition to one another. Support one and you run afoul of the other.

Like most things, the issue is not black and white nor is it zero-sum, but the perception exists nonetheless. It is therefore incumbent upon our policy makers and the intelligence community to be transparent in the activities we are pursuing and to better articulate how those efforts are in line with our civil liberties and Constitutional principles. Indeed, bolstering our intelligence community and strengthening civil liberties can go hand and hand, and the former can sustain the latter.

In a recent report that I co-signed with eighteen other security and intelligence leaders, Business Executives for National Security, or BENS, embraced the importance of our civil liberties and transparency within the intelligence apparatus. And we specifically recommend steps that ensure protections are in place.

The report, "Domestic Security: Confronting a Changing Threat to Ensure Public Safety and Civil Liberties," makes several recommendations that include calling for the establishment of better integrated fusion centers in high-threat areas within the U.S. Fusion centers serve as coordination mechanisms for federal, state, and local authorities, and are meant to provide efficient sharing of threat-related data. Better integrated, fusion centers would maximize the quality of information shared and the speed with which we can respond to threats. But also, importantly, they centralize oversight. This step helps us, as citizens, to have greater confidence that counterterrorism efforts are consistent with our laws and expectations.

We also recommend standardizing rules for domestic intelligence analysts that would make it clear what type of information is appropriate to collect, review, and disseminate. Currently, the level of training among analysts in different departments and agencies is uneven, weakening our civil protections and allowing for potential, albeit unintended, mistakes.

We also call for strengthening the coordination and oversight of our law enforcement and public safety agencies, while empowering the 800,000 eyes and ears of state and local law enforcement professionals in a manner that reinforces our civil liberties. The terrorist threat to our nation is evolving and is increasingly characterized by homegrown and self-radicalized individuals like the ones that attacked in Paris. As the threat evolves, so too must our country's efforts to counter and manage such threats.

Sen. Richard Burr, R-N.C., the intelligence committee's chairman, is making strides to gain public confidence in our intelligence policies by holding open hearings. The Obama administration is furthering the effort with the Office of the Director of National Intelligence's release of principles to provide transparency in intelligence, and by declassifying thousands of documents pertaining to secret intelligence programs.

Further steps like the ones outlined in BENS' report should also be taken. Our intelligence efforts and civil liberties are intertwined. We cannot pursue one without the other. Bolster one and you bolster the other.

By Norton A. Schwartz // Gen. Norton A. Schwartz, ret., is president and CEO of Business Executives for National Security. He was the 19th chief of staff of the U.S. Air Force.

Enlisting the Private Sector
AUGUST 26, 2015 | GENERAL NORTON SCHWARTZ

The whole of the warring nations are engaged, not only soldiers, but the entire population, men, women and children. The fronts are everywhere . . . the front line runs through the factories.

—Prime Minister Winston Churchill (1940)

Addressing the House of Commons in 1940, Prime Minister Winston Churchill observed that in the new age of total warfare, Great Britain's civil society and businesses were no longer removed from the warfront, but that instead "the front line runs through the factories." In making this observation, the Prime Minister's message was clear: confronted by a new and significant challenge, responsibility for ensuring their nation's security was vested with all Britons, and that only by synchronizing the efforts of the public, civil, and business sectors was victory attainable. Powerful as these words were at the time, they remain equally prescient today.

Today the United States is confronted by an increasingly complex and shifting array of national security challenges, ranging from an assertive Russia to the spread of violent extremism and persistent cyber threats. Many of these challenges are too complex for the U.S. government to address alone, requiring our nation's public and private sectors to confront them together and work collaboratively in support of our national security.

Indeed, as the owner and operator of over 85 percent of our critical national infrastructure, the private sector can play a significant role in confronting these challenges. For example, American companies have helped to sustain economic sanctions against Russia and Iran by refraining from doing business with specific entities. The result in part: Iran's oil exports have been reduced by half to just 1 million barrels per day and this week the Russian ruble closed at record lows against the dollar.

Technology and social media companies are also key partners in preventing the spread of violent extremist ideology. In February, representatives from Twitter, Facebook, and Google all attended a White House–sponsored summit on countering violent extremism, and in recent months Twitter has suspended as many as two thousand extremist accounts. As groups such as the so-called Islamic State continue to use social media to spread their virulent ideology, it will be important to collaborate with technology companies to identify extremist users and constrain their ability to incite violence.

Increasingly, the private sector must also confront national security challenges in a more direct manner; namely, as the primary target of state and non-state actors. Nowhere is this truer than in cyberspace, where over 60% of all targeted cyber-attacks affected small and medium-sized companies last year.

In 2014 the average annual cost of cybercrime to a U.S. company was estimated to be $12.7 million. However, what is less quantifiable is the damage a successful cyber-attack can have on a company's reputation, competitiveness, and ability to innovate. A North Korean attack on Sony Corporation may also portend a worrisome new trend in which private companies are viewed as acceptable targets for nation states to coerce and vent political grievances.

It is here, in cyberspace, where close collaboration between the public and private sectors is essential, and it is also where encouraging progress is being made. Already, private companies are working with the Department of Homeland Security, Federal Bureau of Investigation, and U.S. Secret Service— among other federal agencies—to share cyber threat information and respond to cyber intrusions. Other entities, such as private sector Information Sharing and Analysis Centers (ISACs), afford an alternative, if imperfect, method of sharing information among industry sectors. In fact, American Express has called the financial services ISAC "one of the best tools any company can have when it comes to cyber protection."

Recently, Defense Secretary Ash Carter announced a series of new initiatives aimed at leveraging the combined expertise of the public and private sectors to manage cyber threats. As Secretary Carter stated, "In addition to dangers, there are also really great opportunities to be seized through a new level of partnership between the Pentagon and Silicon Valley—opportunities that we can only realize together."

Encouragingly, the private sector understands this as well. John Donahoe, President and CEO of eBay Inc., recently stated, "When you step back and look at the role of a company versus the role of a government, clearly if we're going to provide the safest possible experience in aggregate, government and companies need to work together."

Indeed, as the United States navigates the complex threat environment before it, close collaboration with the private sector will be critical. This collaboration will require private sector leaders to appreciate their potential for helping to ensure our national security, and government leaders to effectively leverage and complement the unique capabilities of our private sector.

Seventy-five years ago Winston Churchill proclaimed that "the fronts are everywhere." Although the scale of the challenges confronting us today are much less grave, threats such as violent extremism and cyber have blurred the distinction among national security and the private sector. And yet, while the scale has changed, the prescription for confronting them remains the same: determined collaboration between all segments of our society.

Chapter Nine

FLIGHT PLAN

You can't imagine how many people have asked what I consider to be the "secret to my success," as if there's some undisclosed formula that if followed would guarantee a seat at the chairman's table in the Tank. Did I plot my way to the top? Step on others along the way? Do politics play a role? Well, the answers are "there's some element of that," "absolutely not," and "it's clearly a backdrop." Let me explain.

I would be disingenuous to say that I didn't have ambition. I did. But I would not characterize it as the unbridled ambition that some people have. I had goals, but they were incremental, never some grand scheme that I believed would speed me to the top. My first ambition was to be a pilot, then an instructor pilot, then a flight examiner. This continued through the squadron and wing commander levels and on up the ranks, yet I was always flexible enough to deviate from my plan as alternative opportunities arose along the way. I was fully aware of which jobs were key, and I did what I could to be the most qualified candidate for those jobs. I wanted to be as competitive as I could be, and by that I don't mean on a one-on-one basis, but rather to have credentials that would place me in favor with hiring authorities. I am an avid student of the bureaucracy and that's a major part of the flag officer assignment process. But none of that is what drove us. What really lit the fire was a sense of obligation and a love of this culture and community that both Suzie and I came to know. One of the most rewarding things about becoming Chief was having the opportunity to make a substantial, long-term impact on those issues about which we were passionate.

**Ambition properly calibrated is a positive attribute;
unbridled ambition rarely leads to success.**

As for the politics, it's a backdrop, clearly. Hiring authorities have discretion so there are human factors involved in those kinds of decisions: whether you're respected, whether there is some relationship there. The truth is:

Politics do matter. Proximity matters more.

A person who is known and trusted has a much better chance of being hired than someone who's a stranger. My hunch is, the fact that I was a little bit of an outsider actually worked to my advantage. By an outsider I mean that I had been in the *joint* world for ten years. I wasn't part of one of the major mainstream "tribes" of the Air Force. I think that caught Secretary Gates's attention, so maybe that turned out to be an asset rather than a liability.

I also think it's important that neither Suzie nor I walked up anybody's back along the way. There were people who did not agree with certain calls I made, but I don't know of anyone that I would characterize as an enemy or an adversary. This was never a political ploy, it's just who I am and how I was raised. I believe there were others who were more inclined to do that sort of thing than I think I was. Certain things seem fairly obvious to me. This falls into that category, and it's one of the standard admonitions I included in every one of my initial command briefs; for both its obvious and more subtle implications:

Keep your zipper zipped. It's the right thing to do, and I assure you it will make everyone's life a lot easier.

I tried to avoid self-promotion, and Suzie would probably argue that I went overboard with this. But I think that's a big difference between me and others like Wes Clark, who clearly were self-promoters. That could be another reason why we didn't have many enemies.

Leave it to others to toot your horn.

From the moment we recite the Air Force Oath of Office, we begin the lifelong process of shaping our reputation. There will always be temptations—it's how we handle them that makes or breaks us. For me, it's been pretty easy to do the right thing and make the right choices. A lot of that has to do with the values that were instilled in me long before I ever thought about donning Air Force blue. For others, it may not come quite as easily. Benjamin Franklin reminds us that "it takes many good deeds to build a good reputation, and only one bad one to lose it." Warren Buffett has a slightly different observation: "It takes twenty years to build a reputation and five minutes to ruin it. If you think about that, you'll do things differently." He's right. So, think about it.

Reputations are hard to earn and easy to lose.

In the words of Don Rumsfeld, "Don't do or say things you would not like to see on the front page of *The Washington Post*."

WORKING WITH BOSSES

I had the honor of directly working for two presidents, three secretaries of defense, and four chairmen, and they all had very different styles, which is not a trivial thing.

Personality and style counts.

PRESIDENTS

I found President Bush to be more approachable and easier to talk to than President Obama, so I felt a little more comfortable in President Bush's presence. Bush was warmer, less formal, and more gregarious, where President Obama was more reserved and cerebral. Both were keenly interested in our views but it was more official with President Obama. They both really got to know their chiefs, and they got to know Suzie, as well.

SECRETARIES OF DEFENSE

Rumsfeld, Gates, and Panetta. One was a businessman, one was a defense professional, and one was a politician. Each of them was successful despite their different managerial styles. Rummy was very demanding, but never cruel. He didn't suffer fools and required both exquisite knowledge and performance by people who worked for him. He could definitely poke, but only if you gave him an opening. If you showed any weakness or a lack of knowledge, Katie bar the door. You courted disaster if you were not fully prepared when you walked into the room with Don Rumsfeld, and in my view that's fair. At this level, that's exactly how it should be.

Bob Gates was equally demanding but less accessible. He played things a little closer to the vest, rarely making a decision at the table or in a more public session. He would take the presentation, make sure that he understood the options, and then typically make a decision separately. No question that he was decisive, but he was much more discreet, which isn't a big surprise considering his background as an intelligence professional. He was not as open—at least not with me.

Panetta was someone I worried about because he really didn't have a strong defense background, but he turned out to be a magnificent team builder. Whereas Secretary Gates was the captain of the ship, Leon Panetta was the chief of the boat. He emphasized teamwork and collaboration to a degree that neither Rumsfeld nor Gates had ever done, and with a much greater level of participation and involvement on the part of the senior military *and* civilian leadership than was ever the case under Secretaries Rumsfeld or Gates—much more open and gregarious, but extremely effective.

There is no cookie cutter for a successful president, secretary of defense, or any leader—that's the basic theme. There are multiple styles that will work . . . if *we* make the necessary midcourse corrections to accommodate those styles. It's highly doubtful that Bob Gates would suddenly start sharing everything with me just because I told him that I functioned better that way, and can you imagine how President Obama would react if I'd ask him to "lighten up"? My point is that they are not the ones who are going to be doing the changing. It's largely how *we* deal with the divergent styles that will determine whether we can work together as an effective team.

From my perspective, I enjoyed working for each of them. Each of them was brilliant, had great instincts, was good at staying ahead of the wave—and every one of them worked their ass off. I felt challenged by them, and I have the utmost of respect and affection for all three, without reservation.

CHAIRMEN

Dick Myers and Pete Pace were a great team as chairman and vice chairman of the Joint Chiefs of Staff. They were interchangeable, they were mutually supportive, and both of them were excellent bosses. Obviously, Dick and Pete had the special challenge of the immediate aftermath of 9/11 and the work-up for OIF—Operation IRAQI FREEDOM and continuation of ENDURING FREEDOM. I think that Dick Myers hasn't gotten enough credit for managing that very demanding and stressful time. It was 24/7 work, and he handled it masterfully. Dick and Mary Jo were the quintessential senior couple.

Mike Mullen and Hoss Cartwright were not a great team. They operated in somewhat different spheres, so there wasn't the same sense of cohesion and interchangeability between the two of them. They would have somewhat different angles on things. It was a little bit more difficult both as a service chief and as a member of the Joint Chiefs to deal with them because they were not nearly as well aligned as were Pace and Myers.

Mike Mullen and I, and Suzie and Deborah, got along great. I think that the Mullens believe that we did what we said we would do when they hired us, which was to bring the Air Force back and reestablish its reputation both inside the DoD and outside. I think that Admiral Mullen was a little bit more difficult to deal with than Dick Myers had been on general officer matters. I felt that Myers had a broader, more joint perspective of the flag officer management than Mike Mullen. Mike was a little bit tilted toward the Navy. Myers didn't tilt very much at all. That was one difference that we had to deal with. But both took us into their confidence. Both were instantaneously accessible. Both had challenging moments: for Myers, the buildup to the war; for Mullen, the surge and the friction within the White House over the surge. Those were very demanding times for both of them respectively.

Marty Dempsey came on in the fall of 2011, and we were together for about six months. Marty was dealing with the backside of the conflicts. I think Marty was most likely given guidance from the secretary or even the president that they wanted the chairman to be a little bit less visible and take a somewhat lower profile than Mullen had, and he did that. Marty was a little bit more of an inside person than Mullen was. Mullen also tended to act more independently, which was his privilege. Again, a difference in style. But he was less a representative of the Joint Chiefs than he was his own man. I think Marty reset that and was more representative of the Joint Chiefs and a little bit less his own man.

THE BACKBONE OF THE AIR FORCE—NCOs

You have all kinds of issues when you're a cadet, many surrounding your own personal identity. I was no different. In the early '70s, many of us at the Academy tried to make a statement by pushing the limit on the length of our sideburns, and I did too. It was an NCO who turned things around for me, and it was the first of so many times that a noncommissioned officer proved the adage that "NCOs are the backbone of the Air Force." It's NCOs who mold and develop young officers.

But it wasn't always that way at the Academy. It was a relatively new initiative during our time to have an NCO presence. The reason the Air Force chose to do that was, in large measure, to give cadets exposure to the crème de la crème of the NCO corps so that they would be better prepared to interact with professional NCOs when they got into the Air Force. To a man, these were very, very solid NCOs who reminded cadets that there was a bigger team out there. They commanded respect and, as a result, produced more well-rounded cadets and lieutenants.

I'll never forget the time Senior Master Sergeant Gene Reinartz came up to me and stared at my sideburns, which were considerably longer than Air Force regulations allowed. He was a Security Forces cop. Well over six feet tall, with an imposing physical presence made even more intimidating by an imposing personality; there were a lot of strips on those XXL sleeves. He was one of the tough, gruff NCOs of yesteryear. He did not mince words and he was no politician, and that's the way it should be.

He looked at my sideburns as he pulled me aside and asked, "Do you want to lead or follow?"

"Clearly I want to lead," I replied.

"Then you ought to not push your sideburns so much." That interchange was instrumental in changing my perspective on what it meant to lead instead of following the pack. I got it completely.

The beauty is that we have stayed in touch over the years, and he felt so proud that one of his "babies" became the Chief of Staff of the Air Force. He played a big part in that, particularly in those early years. He's in his late eighties now.

Those traditional Vietnam-era noncommissioned officers were quite tough and damn good at what they did. In recent years some of that toughness has waned, and that's not for the better. Today's NCO corps has become more sophisticated and less bare-knuckle. While that's politically correct, I'm not sure it's progress. We need NCOs who run a tight ship and who know how to kick ass when nonperforming asses need to be kicked. It's now increasingly about taking care of airmen and less about pushing them and holding them accountable, and there's got to be a healthy balance between the two. I equate the role of the Air Force NCO to that of middle management in the private sector.

The people that actually do the work need to do it well. They need encouragement and you need supervision that provides that encouragement. Sometimes it's positive encouragement, but when that fails to do the trick, somebody has to step in and squeeze. That's the role of the NCO.

Performance remains the product of the professional NCO.

Sammy Knag was the best C-130 crew chief I ever met. He could do more with a roll of duct tape and a screwdriver than most could do with a four-hundred-piece aviation tool set. Sammy was with me on the around-the-world Night March mission I mentioned earlier. What I did not mention before was that early on, one of the welds on the parabolic radar dish cracked so we were without functioning radar—a real problem on multiple fronts. We needed the low-level terrain-following element for tactical reasons, and we needed the weather portion to make it back safely.

Getting repair parts while flying twenty thousand feet over the Indian Ocean on a black mission was obviously impossible; if they weren't already on the airplane (and they weren't), we weren't going to get them. But Sammy rummaged through the plane and found an old bungee cord. Somehow he used it to stabilize the dish in such a way that we were able to complete the mission and make it safely back to Europe. Did I mention that there were a hundred thousand volts flowing through that dish? Sammy's not even a radar specialist. He's just an airplane general mechanic who had great instincts, and he didn't blink when it came down to risking his own life to save all of ours. Sammy is exceptional, but he's not unique. What I mean by that is there are so many exceptional NCOs who, day in, day out, use their experience, creativity, and ingenuity to bail us out of precarious situations like that one. Subsequently, we worked together on a number of different things through the years, but here was an example of a magnificently committed aircraft maintainer.

Ultimately, Sammy went off into the top tier areas of special operations that were—not surprisingly—high-risk endeavors, because he was so good and he was so dependable. The beauty of it was that he cultivated a younger generation of maintainers that were just like him.

When it comes to combat controllers, you're not going to find any better than Wayne Norrad. Wayne had been a tactical team leader on one of the original six special mission units after Desert One, when then Major John "Coach"

Carney assembled his "Det 1 MACOS" Special Tactics Unit in 1980. Norrad is well known within the CCT (Combat Control Team) community as one of the early pioneers of combat control and pararescue. He, along with just a small handful of others, was personally responsible for helping mold the joint special operations special tactics team into what it is today.

Wayne was team chief on a training mission that I piloted, one of many that we had flown together. We took off from Charleston Air Force Base in South Carolina and the late-night skies were clear for the entire route to the intended drop zone, so I can't use bad weather as an excuse for what I was about to do. As we approached what I thought was the designated DZ, we activated the green light signal and they made the jump, somehow landing a significant distance from the intended target—so far off that they landed in an adjacent state (yes, state). They were eventually able to convince a farmer to provide them with transportation back to the base, but understandably, they were not happy about it. It was approaching dawn by the time Wayne found me, and he wasted no time in getting right up in my face. "Don't ever do that again," he said, both exhausted and perturbed. This was a real wake-up call for me. I learned that *even though at times I may engage the aircraft's autopilot, I can never engage my own.* Wayne gave me the ammunition; what I did with it was my own choice.

Never sleep through your wake-up calls.

These are the major game-changers in life. Internalize them!

We have to remember that *these are human beings.* These great airmen, or soldiers, or SEALS that jump from the airplane, are precious American fighting men and women. Not very many folks can do this for a living and do it well. Wayne's point was "Come on now, you're better than this." He knew we were a premier crew and there was no excuse for me failing to perform like that by dropping them in the middle of nowhere, so many miles from our target. We had failed him, failed his crew, and failed ourselves. The long-term message was that this is a hazardous enough business; don't make it more hazardous than it needs to be. To this day I don't know why I dropped the ball, but thanks to Wayne's "in my face" wake-up call, you better believe it never happened again. (And for the next thirty years, Wayne never let me forget it.)

Senior Master Sergeant Mort Freedman was a hard-nosed, battle experienced combat controller. Mort had earned the Silver Star when he and his team were left behind at an airfield in a place called Kham Duc, Vietnam, on Mother's Day in 1968. A force of six thousand enemy troops had invaded the tiny town southwest of Da Nang and were doing their best to take down all the U.S. and South Vietnamese forces still there. Eight U.S. planes were shot down that day, but eventually one made it through and was able to evacuate the final contingent still remaining on the ground. Or so they thought. Turns out that Mort and two team members were still there, trapped and hiding from the masses of enemy fighters. Lieutenant Colonel Joe Jackson answered the call by flying his C-123 through intense rocket and tracer bombardment, all intent on blasting him out of the sky. Somehow he landed, pulled Mort and the team out of there, and escaped in one piece. Seven months later, President Lyndon Johnson awarded Lt Col Jackson the Medal of Honor in the East Room of the White House. Mort earned the Silver Star.

By the time I met him, Mort was Noncommissioned Officer in Charge of the USAF Academy Sport Parachute Team and later chief of the combat control team at Clark Air Base in the Philippines. But he also was the sport parachuting safety officer when I was president of the sport parachuting club at Clark. We did a fair amount of jumping together, and we became extremely close—eventually to the point of him unofficially adopting me. When it came time for me to check out for my civilian jumpmaster certification, it was Mort's job to evaluate my performance.

Back then we had automatic opening devices installed on the reserve chutes to ensure that the chute would open once it passed through a predesignated altitude, even if the jumper neglected to pull the rip cord. We might set it for three thousand feet, for example, so once the device sensed that it was at three thousand feet or lower, it would deploy. The problem was that the sensor had no way of knowing if it was passing through three thousand feet (or whatever the designated altitude) on the way up or on the way down. So one of my jobs as jumpmaster—and this was just one of many things Mort was testing me on that day—was to ensure that the sensors were deactivated prior to takeoff, and not activated until we were well above the designated altitude, at which time I would safely activate each one on all of the jumpers.

We boarded the aircraft and I went through the preparatory steps as the aircraft climbed to our jump altitude, at which time I activated the sensors. So far, so good. Then something happened—I don't recall what—but we had to abort the jump and return to base. As the plane started descending, I went around to each jumper and deactivated the devices one by one as Mort looked on, carefully checking to make sure that I did everything according to regulation. By now we were down to about four thousand feet, still descending, and while of course I'm disappointed that we had to abort the jump, I felt that I had handled the situation properly—and, most importantly from Mort's perspective, safely. Suddenly he shot me a look. He didn't say a word, just stared at me, clearly displeased. *What did I do?* I wondered. He swiveled with purpose to jumper number three and flipped off the auto-opening device. Somehow—I have no idea how—I had missed that one. Had Mort not caught it, within minutes that chute could have opened inside the aircraft, with potentially devastating consequences. I was in a daze. Making a mistake of that magnitude was so unlike me, and doing so in front of Mort was unfathomable.

We had our post-flight debrief and he busted me on the spot. I failed, and he was not happy about it. Nor was I. It was a clean kill, and it was a very big deal. But there's a lesson in there, and it's one that stays with me to this day: for Mort Freedman, it didn't matter who you were or who you might become, you performed up to standard or you didn't. I never forgot it, and that lesson was very consequential in how I matured and who I ultimately became. Everyone who served with him knew this and respected him for it. He would die for you in a second, no question. But in training, you had to meet his standard, and "Mort's standard" was legendary in the community.

Those standards kept people alive in tough spots all through Vietnam and propelled the combat control community to a level of competence that was exceedingly well respected. Ultimately it was Mort's babies that were involved in Desert One. Mort was well known as one of the greats of the Vietnam generation and he had an enormous influence on me; in fact, I'd say that he was one of the most important people in my life.

For Mort Freedman, you performed to standard or you didn't. That lesson has stayed with me to this day.
Freedman personal collection

On March 27, 2014, the world lost one of the good ones. Mort, who cheated death on so many occasions on the battlefields of Southeast Asia, succumbed to adrenal cancer. Six close friends from all over the world flew to Cagayan De Oro, Philippines, where on May 14, 2014, they put his ashes to rest in the warm blue waters of the Bohol Sea, not far from where he lived.

Chief Master Sergeant Jimmy Lebit was one of the senior maintainers at Hurlburt over many years. We first worked together when I was a captain, then again when I came back as a colonel. Jimmy was an old-school chief, technically competent and a marvelous line leader. I learned a lot from Jimmy on how to operate in the field, how to deploy, and how to work airplanes in austere environments. In the early '90s, Jimmy was president of the Hurlburt Chief's Group and I was the ops group commander at that time.

One evening Jimmy walked into my office and said that he and his colleagues had chosen to make me an honorary chief, with the ceremony to take place at the next month's Chief's meeting. A commander being honored by his NCOs in that manner was heart-stopping.

Schwartz personal collection

Here we are over thirty years later, and that framed certificate still hangs in my office. It's one that means a great deal to me.

CONGRESS

I spent a lot of time on Capitol Hill. Sometimes it was on a specific issue related to a particular state delegation; often it was on broader matters that applied to the Air Force or the entire military. Testimonies before both House and Senate Armed Services Committees were frequent. Interacting with members was enlightening. What really made it fun was the wide range of personalities.

My experience with Michigan Senator Carl Levin was representative. Of course, Levin had been the ranking member of my problematic confirmation hearing, and that was only one of many times we locked horns in the committee room. As the debate over our efforts to downsize—including some Michigan-based assets—became more controversial, he asked Mike Donley and me to drop by his office so we could try to iron out our differences behind closed doors. I was prepared for the meeting to play out much like our prior encounters, which had for the most part been in front of the cameras in the course of our Armed Services Committee testimonies. He was frequently on offense, probing, seeking clarity. While this was a no-bullshit, serious conversation, he was respectful and left the grandstanding for the Senate floor. I was impressed by the depth of his understanding and in this case his genuine desire to comprehend the data.

The Florida delegation kept me busy as we worked the issues related to the F-22s at Tyndall Air Force Base in Panama City. There were questions about the sustainability of the base, particularly with fewer F-15s and production curtailed on the F-22. So we had to do some missionary work to persuade them that we had a viable plan they could support. Congressman Allen Boyd Jr. worked it hard on behalf of the base. He understood the military—he had been an Army infantry officer in Vietnam. Secretary Donley and I accepted his invitation to tour the 325th Fighter Wing with him in June 2009, where we were briefed by representatives from the Bay County community, who had impressive presentations about the important role Tyndall plays in our national defense. Clearly they were concerned after we had just announced the accelerated retirement of all forty-eight F-15s assigned to the base. He was a passionate advocate on behalf of his constituency.

Understandably, the Delaware delegation needed a lot of engagement as a result of the Dover Port Mortuary issues. This was an explosive matter that dealt with one of their installations and we did not want them to be blindsided when the shit hit the fan, and they never were. We kept Senators Tom Carper and Chris Coons in the loop throughout the Port Mortuary ordeal, but that took a good deal of our time.

Earlier I mentioned my challenges with showboating by some of the members, and the disrespect shown by Forbes, McCaskill, Nelson, and others. On the flip side, one of my greatest honors was meeting with Hawaii Senator Daniel Inouye, rest his soul. Senator Inouye was a remarkable man, a recipient of both the Medal of Honor and the Presidential Medal of Freedom.

I needed his help in getting a general officer confirmed, because Senator Mark Begich of Alaska—a freshman senator who had succeeded Ted Stevens, the longest-serving Republican member of the Senate of all time—was making it difficult for this confirmation to proceed. With his status as an elder and senior statesman, and chair of the Senate Appropriations Subcommittee on Defense, I looked to Senator Inouye to sort of nudge the junior senator in the right direction. I had never done this before, but this was a difficult enough issue that I felt it necessary to see if Senator Inouye would at least discuss the matter with Begich. He was supportive, gracious, and a true gentleman in every sense of the word. Here's a man who was the president pro tempore of the United States Senate—making him the highest ranking Asian American politician in U.S. history—who actually took the time to pick up the phone and call me with an update following his conversation with Begich. This was not something I had ever expected, and it's just another indication of how extraordinary a man he was.

In the end, the issue worked itself out, but even after his dialogue with Senator Inouye, it would take weeks before Begich would agree to go along with this very worthy confirmation.

BUILDING THE BENCH

General Larry Welch (12th Chief of Staff of the Air Force) once told me that if a Chief doesn't spend 25 percent of his time on general officer management, he (or she) is not doing his job. I had a lot of experience with building the bench from my time as director of the Joint Staff, where at the end of each day I would work with Chairman Dick Myers on flag officer management. It's a long-term process, and not an easy one. Once you've identified the prime contenders, you have to groom them and challenge them and stretch them so that when they get to more senior positions, they have the depth and credibility to succeed.

Even early on it was pretty obvious that the flag officer ranks tended to be white and male. Mike Donley and I worked hard to make it more diverse, and eventually minority officers started having a shift in opportunities. There were more rising to senior positions of trust, not because they were minorities or female but because they were spectacularly good officers. We worked hard to create four-star capable officers, and we had some success at that.

Shortly before I retired, General Janet C. Wolfenbarger became the first woman to achieve the rank of four-star general in the Air Force. We had been grooming her for this for many years, and it was well deserved. Starting as an administrative clerk, Airman Larry Spencer put in more than forty-four years of distinguished service before he retired as four-star General Larry Spencer. He's currently president of the Air Force Association and publisher of *Air Force*

Magazine. In 2012, Secretary Donley and I made it clear to the president and the U.S. Senate that Larry was the ideal choice to become the next vice chief.

The Air Force now has two diverse four-stars and others at the three-star and two-star rank. Youngsters need role models to look up to, and these are all exemplary role models. It was a significant effort to get it right, but I'm proud of the substantial strides we made.

GIVING BACK

We celebrated excellence in any number of ways, to say thank you and to encourage continued high performance. You highlight success and you reward excellence—not monetarily, but through taking care of the kids, whether recognizing them through a decoration, or Officer of the Month, or NCO of the Year, or making sure that they get a job that keeps them on the development glide path. Witnessing success and witnessing excellence was one of the high points of all my positions.

One time when I was chief, Suzie and I went to an event at McChord. There were eight people in the special tactics community that were getting awards that day. We awarded three Silver Stars and five Bronze Stars. It was a remarkable moment.

On another occasion, I vividly remember being there as Secretary Donley awarded the Air Force Cross, the second highest award, to Staff Sgt. Zachary Rhyner, a young combat controller based at Pope AFB, North Carolina. There have probably been less than a dozen Air Force Crosses earned in the last twenty-five years. I also presented him with a Purple Heart that day. What a glorious privilege to have a chance to do so. This went to a young airman who went back to Afghanistan and was wounded on the second trip. He was quite a trooper. Despite injuries he sustained as the result of persistent insurgent fire, Sergeant Rhyner coordinated more than fifty aerial attacks to continuously repel the enemy during the beleaguering battle that occurred during his first deployment. According to the decoration citation, he provided suppressive fire with his M-4 rifle against the enemy while fellow teammates were extracted from the line of fire.

We try our best to hold everything together at all times, but I became particularly emotional with this one. "The team survived this hellish scene . . . not by chance, not by luck, and not by the failings of a weak or timid foe," I said before hundreds of Zach's friends, family, and coworkers in attendance that day, a fifty-foot American flag quite appropriately mounted as our backdrop on the wall behind me. "A grateful nation could not be more proud for what you do and no doubt what you will do," I said, looking him in the eye.

As fortunate as I was to have one Air Force Cross on my watch, three years later I was privileged to have another. Captain Barry Crawford was awarded his for his heroic actions calling in airstrikes during a 2010 battle in Afghanistan, which allowed his special operations team to get out of the kill zone and ultimately saved the lives of his American comrades and allowed for the safe return of all U.S. forces, the evacuation of two Afghan commandos killed in action, and the rescue of three other wounded Afghan commandos. As I said that day in our Pentagon's Hall of Heroes, "Captain Crawford repeatedly and conspicuously disregarded his own safety to assist his United States and Afghan teammates. It is not hard to be utterly impressed by his bravery and inspired by his selflessness."

MENTORS

Suzie and I certainly could not have gotten this far without the magnanimous mentors who have shown us the way. We tried our best to do the same—to try, as best we could—to be an excellent couple ourselves—to work hard, to be good role models, to recognize excellence, and to celebrate it openly and joyfully. It seemed to work well for us over the years.

We see it in the number of babies that Suzie talks about in the squadron; we did our best to encourage them along the way, and have stayed connected to them over the years. Bob and Chris Otto are good examples of this. Bob has recently retired as a three-star deputy chief of staff for intelligence, surveillance, and reconnaissance.

Then there's Cheryl and Darryl Roberson, now an Air Force three-star and commander of Air Education and Training Command. Darryl was a squadron commander at Elmendorf in the 90th Squadron. Bob Otto was my ops group commander. And of course they were all there during 9/11.

Then there is Loren Reno. We were lieutenants at Clark together in the very, very beginning. He retired as a three-star deputy chief of staff for logistics, installations, and mission support. My hunch is that he would probably tell you that that we were mentors to him and Karen.

So there were both senior people and younger folks that we continued to encourage. It was great fun for us, and we hope, both valuable and fun for them.

Chapter Ten

TO THE VERY END

There are some things worth fighting for, and the country needs good people to do that work. There's no great joy in combat, to be sure. But there is great joy in serving with people who place service above self, who understand that integrity is a profound attribute, and who every day actually do try to serve better than the day before. The fact that Suzie and I ended up as the first couple of the Air Force truly was an extraordinary privilege.

I believe the armed forces of the United States remain a meritocracy in which even a young man from a small town in south Jersey, whose father sold manual typewriters for a living, could grow up to be a chief of service—the highest ranking officer in that branch of the armed forces. And it's not because I'm a particular hot rod and it sure isn't because I'm a natural pilot—it's because with hard work and good fortune, anything is still possible in this country. It's not true in the UK, it's not true in the French armed forces, and it isn't true in the Asian militaries. There still are opportunities here for leading, for having a very productive public service career in the armed forces, no matter who your parents were. You don't need to have a judge or a politician or a doctor or extraordinary wealth or anything else. Just passion for the country, conviction about hard work and character, and good fortune. The United States Air Force gave a youngster from a small town in New Jersey a home for forty years, and for that I will be forever grateful.

**Public service is a noble endeavor, and
America needs good people to do such work.**

In the fall of 2011, the new two-star list came out and there were twenty-two new Air Force two-stars on the list. I knew just seven of them well. At that moment, I had an epiphany. It occurred to me that being the last man standing—which I was of my year group—had its downside. The leadership of our services is to some degree a generational occupation, and it's not a good thing when a chief of service knows fewer than a third of his or her new two-stars. It was clear that it was time to move on. Intellectually I understood this. Emotionally it was a little tougher to grasp, for both Suzie and me.

Just a few months earlier, Suzie and I had attended a stirring dedication ceremony at Hurlburt Field. To commemorate the completion of her forty-seven-year journey, the MC-130E Combat Talon #64-0567 was unveiled as a static display in the Air Park. And what a storied journey it had been: she took fire in Vietnam, then returned to make history with Brenci, Meller, Uttaro, and Thigpen sharing pilot duties in the first fixed-wing airland flight using NVGs—a technology that was employed in her participation in Operation EAGLE CLAW, the attempted rescue of Americans held hostage in Iran. She led the airland assault into Rio Hato AB for Operation JUST CAUSE in Panama, then departed the country with an equally crucial mission: transporting Manuel Noriega, the captured Panamanian dictator, to Miami to stand trial for drug trafficking. In 2003—still a vital resource—she was one of the first MC-130Es to fly missions to Afghanistan in support of Operation ENDURING FREEDOM.

Most of the airmen in attendance wore either ABUs (camouflage airman battle uniforms), like Chief Master Sgt. of the Air Force Jim Roy, who was seated on Suzie's right, or blue service dress, like Chief Master Sgt. Dale Berryhill, who was up-front sharing stories about the eccentricities of flying the Combat Talon. For me, somehow the only uniform that felt appropriate was my sage-green flight suit.

Front and center behind the speaker's podium, the guest of honor looked magnificent—brand-new, in fact—with a fresh "Blackbird" camouflage paint scheme and the V-shaped Fulton STARS skyhook still secured to her nose. Hard to imagine that she logged over 21,000 flight hours. Suzie looked up at me and smiled when CMSgt Berryhill said, "Each [aircraft] has a unique attitude and often quirky personality. There's a good reason she's nicknamed Wild Thing."

Suzie knew me well enough to recognize that this was hitting me very close to home. From my first introduction to the special operations community through my initial command as a general officer, this "Wild Thing" was so much a part of my personal journey. I'd spent so many hours inside that cockpit with Uttaro and Hobson, learning new techniques and improving those I thought I knew. But more than that, I was learning what it meant to be a leader, and how character and integrity and one's word and transparency are every bit as important to inspire and motivate one's crew as is a proficient mastery of the flight controls.

"64-0567 has served its crews and nation proudly," the chief concluded. But he might as well have been echoing the pride that Suzie and I felt when we recognized that it was time to move on. We had devoted ourselves to trying to lead our Air Force in an honorable way, so we left without regret and believing that we did our best. We ran hard and we had given it every ounce of our beings and our passions—and so it was time to pass the torch and we did so to a very, very good couple . . . the Welshes.

We're still privileged to receive congressional invitations to testify on various issues upon which they believe I may shed some light. On November 10, 2015, Arizona Senator John McCain announced, at a hearing of the Senate Armed Services Committee, the beginning of a new effort to "reconsider, and possibly update" the Goldwater–Nichols legislation of 1986. I was invited to share some thoughts and recommendations with the committee, and I did so on December 10, 2015.

It felt wonderful to be back inside the huge Senate Armed Services Committee hearing room, SD-G50 in the Dirksen Senate Office Building. It was perhaps unusual that I was not confronted by Senator McCain when he commenced with his interrogation. Please don't misunderstand—it's not that he actually cracked a smile, but it was certainly a more cordial interplay than I had experienced in the past. Of significance is that they sought out input from some of us who have swapped our dress blues for business suits, and we were honored to provide that input.

As for Suzie, although I never thought it possible, I believe she's even busier now than she was during our active service years—and that time is 100 percent devoted to her worthwhile causes: She continues to support Sesame Workshop for military families, Operation Homefront, the Armed Services YMCA, Tragedy Assistance Program for Survivors, the Fisher House Foundation, the National Military Family Association—and that's all on top of her endeavors as president of the Military Spouse Programs for Victory Media, the publisher of *Military Spouse* magazine.

★ ★ ★

Complex situations during tough times can unleash greater creativity and innovation, aiming us toward novel solutions. The catalyst for all this is leadership, the kind that harnesses individual brilliance into collective genius and leverages individual efforts into team achievements. If there is a legacy from our service, Suzie and I hope in the end it is this: family and teamwork. That was the signature of our tenure.

As for the opportunity to write this book, I'm admittedly a modest voice compared to others, but a very thankful one nonetheless.

Suzie's Letter

Want to send a question to Suzie Schwartz? E-mail: editorial@milspouse.com

Air Force Chief of Staff Gen. Norton Schwartz (Ret.) and Suzie, congratulate members of the Powers family following the presentation of the Silver Star posthumously in the Pentagon.

(Photo by U.S. Air Force photo/Scott M. Ash)

At the Ready

You are closer than you think...

BY SUZIE SCHWARTZ, Air Force Spouse (Ret.)
Vice President, Military Spouse Programs

PEOPLE USED TO ASK ME ALL THE TIME:

"How do you prepare to be the Chief's wife? I couldn't do what you do." Or they'd ask how I could possibly know about all the things they'd hear me talk about. They would say that there is no way they could have that much information just in their head or even at their fingertips.

The answer? You are more prepared and more able and more ready to step to the next level than you believe.

Why? Because each step you take, each move, helps you prepare for the next challenge. Every experience, every...

Suzie Schwartz
@MrsSuzieSchwartz

Home | **About** | Photos | Likes | More ▾

About Suzie Schwartz

Page Info

PAGE INFO

Short Description — Advocate for military families, passionate about connecting people and organizations to support our military community. Avid crafter and hostess.

Relationship Status — Married to General Norton Schwartz.

[all volunteer force]

WASHINGTON, D.C. ★ BY SUZIE SCHWARTZ

Building Spouse Leadership

In the summer of 2008, Norty and I were at Scott Air Force Base, Illinois, getting ready for retirement.

The paperwork was in and we thought U.S. Transportation Command would be the last stop in a wonderful military career. But as is often the case for military families, our plans were suddenly changed when we received new orders—this time to Washington, D.C.

Being asked to serve the Air Force—and the nation—for more years was a joyous surprise. I was excited about the prospect of using all the things I had learned along the way to help shape the lives and experiences of Air Force families. This was an opportunity I never dreamed would present itself to me.

I married my husband [recently retired Air Force General Norton Schwartz] when he was a Lieutenant and moved soon after to Hurlburt Field, Florida. I left my job, my apartment and my family, and...

Colonel Linda Lawrence, left, the 31st Medical Group commander at Aviano Air Base, Italy, briefs Suzie Schwartz, wife of the Air Force Chief of Staff General Norton Schwartz, on medical services at Aviano on July 11, 2011. Air Force photo by Airman Briana N. Jones

...ty for Military Children are helping to make military family moves easier for both spouses and children.

Many spouses might not realize it, but as they work through such challenges and experience the esprit de corps that is a part of military service, they are strengthening their own leadership abilities along the way. I admit that as a young military spouse, I never saw myself as a leader. But as Norty and I moved from one base to another, I was honing my own leadership skill by watching other spouses. Even though this was not formal training, I now understand I was mentored by fabulously strong and resilient spouses at every step of this journey.

Such experiences help prepare military spouses to lead in many different ways. On the most personal level, spouses are leaders in their families—a role that is especially important during the long deployments our military men and women often face. At our Air Force installations, they also lead through initiatives like the Key Spouse Program, in which military spouses support the local base mission through mentorship and communication with families.

When Norty assumed the duties of Air Force Chief of Staff, I was given the opportunity to lead on a much larger scale.

As I struggled to find the best way to communicate with our airmen and their families spread out all across the globe, I met Senior Airman Michael Malarsie. While deployed as a Tactical Air Control Party Member in Kandahar, Afghanistan, Michael found himself in an intense battle that cost him his eyesight. During his recovery in the United States, he used social media as a way to share with others his experiences and his indomitable spirit. He inspired me to use these new tools to better connect with our Air Force, and I'm now able to quickly communicate with thousands of military men and women and their families through my Facebook page. The use of such innovations to better con-

...employment Partnership and the Military Compact on Educational Opportuni...

...nect with our military families, as well as the amazing support our service members receive from the American public, make me optimistic about the future of our Air Force and our joint team. Today's military spouses may be different than the ones I encountered in my earlier years with Norty, but they are no less involved. I know the younger spouses I had the opportunity to mentor will continue to find new and better ways to support their families and the joint team.

As Norty and I prepare to enjoy life after this career of service, we feel privileged to have been members of the outstanding U.S. armed forces team, and I will always be proud to consider myself a military spouse. ★

—Suzie Schwartz is the wife of General Norman Schwartz who recently retired as the Air Force Chief of Staff.

Suzie is engaging and always authentic.

PROMOTIONS

	Second Lieutenant, June 6, 1973
	First Lieutenant, June 6, 1975
	Captain, June 6, 1977
	Major, November 1, 1982
	Lieutenant Colonel, March 1, 1985
	Colonel, February 1, 1991
	Brigadier General, January 1, 1996
	Major General, March 4, 1999
	Lieutenant General, January 18, 2000
	General, October 1, 2005

* Chart denotes effective dates of promotion.

GLOSSARY

1st Lt—First lieutenant

2d Lt—Second lieutenant

ABU—Airman battle uniform

A1C—Airman First Class

AC-130—Spectre four-engine turboprop gunship

ADM—Admiral

AFA—U.S. Air Force Academy

AFA—Air Force Association

AFB—Air Force base

AFSOC—U.S. Air Force Special Operations Command

AF/XO—Air Force Deputy Chief of Staff for Plans and Operations

Amn—Airman

AH-64—Apache helicopter gunship

Airman—Enlisted rank

Airman—any member of the Air Force (military or civilian, male or female)

AO—Action Officer

AOC—Air Officers Commanding

ASTRA—Air Staff Training Program

AWACS—Airborne Warning and Control System

B-1—Lancer strategic bomber

B-2—Stealth bomber

B-52—Stratofortress strategic bomber

BDU—Battle dress uniform

BFM—Basic Fighter Maneuvers

BG—Brigadier general (Army)

Brig Gen—Brigadier general (Air Force)

Black Hawk—UH-60 utility helicopter

C-130—Hercules four-engine turboprop transport aircraft

C-5—Galaxy jet transport aircraft

C-17—Globemaster jet transport aircraft

CAT—Crisis Action Team

CCM—Command Chief Master Sergeant (Air Force)

CENTAF—Central Command, Air Force Component

CENTCOM—Central Command; one of America's Unified/Joint Commands

CG—Commanding General (Army)

CG—Coast Guard

CH-47—Chinook helicopter

CIA—Central Intelligence Agency

CINC USCENTCOM—Commander in Chief, Central Command

CINC—Commander in Chief

CINC—President of the United States

CJCS—Chairman Joint Chiefs of Staff

CMSAF—Chief Master Sergeant of the Air Force

CMSgt—Chief Master Sergeant

Col—Colonel (Air Force)

COL—Colonel (Army)

CONUS—Continental United States

CP—Command post

CPL—Corporal (Army)

Capt—Captain (Air Force)

CNO—Chief of Naval Operations

CPT– Captain (Army)

CSA—Chief of Staff of the Army

CSAF—Chief of Staff of the Air Force

CSAR—Combat search and rescue

CT—Combat Talon (I and II); MC-130 Hercules Special Operations aircraft

DAIG—Department of the Army Inspector General

D-Day—Beginning of hostilities

DDO—Deputy Director of Operations

DEPORD—Deployment order

DIA—Defense Intelligence Agency

DJS—Director of the Joint Staff

DoD—Department of Defense

DOV—Chief of Standardization and Evaluation

DZ—Drop zone

EAC—Emergency action cell

F-15—Eagle fighter jet

F-16—Falcon fighter bomber

F/A-18—Naval/Marine fighter bomber

F-22—Raptor fighter jet

F-35—Lightning fighter jet

F-117—Night Hawk stealth bomber

FAC—Forward air controller

FBI—Federal Bureau of Investigation

FLIR—Forward-looking infrared

FOB—Forward operating base

FRAGORD—Fragmentary order

GCCS—Global Command Control System

G-Day—Beginning of ground phase of a campaign

Gen—General (Air Force)

GEN—General (Army)

GOMO—General Officer Management Office

GPS—Global Positioning System

Hellfire—Laser-guided antitank missile

H-Hour—The specific hour at which a particular operation commences

HQ—Headquarters

HUMINT—Human intelligence (as opposed to electronic or signals intelligence)

Humvee—High-mobility, multipurpose wheeled vehicle

IADS—Integrated Air Defense System

ICAF—Industrial College of the Armed Forces

ICBM—Intercontinental ballistic missile

IED—Improvised explosive device

IFR—Instrument flight rules

IG—Inspector General

J-1—Personnel staff officer/section, joint headquarters

J-2—Intelligence staff officer/section, joint headquarters

J-3—Operations staff officer/section, joint headquarters

J-4—Logistics staff officer/section, joint headquarters

J-5—Strategic plans and policy staff officer/section, joint headquarters

J-6—Communications staff officer/section, joint headquarters

KC-10—Aerial refueling jet aircraft

KC-135—Aerial refueling jet aircraft

JATO—Jet-assisted take-off

JCS—Joint Chiefs of Staff

JDAM—Joint direct attack munition

JIC—Joint Intelligence Center

JOC—Joint Operations Center

JRSC—Jam-resistant secure communications

JSOC—Joint Special Operations Command

JSOTF—Joint Special Operations Task Force

JSTARS—Joint Surveillance Target Attack Radar System

JTF—Joint Task Force

LAPES—Low-Altitude Parachute Extraction System

LG—Lieutenant general (Army)

LLDB—Vietnamese Special Forces

LNO—Liaison officer

Lt—Lieutenant (Air Force)

LT—Lieutenant (Army)

Lt Col—Lieutenant Colonel (Air Force)

LTC—Lieutenant Colonel (Army abbreviation)

Lt Gen—Lieutenant General (Air Force)

LZ—Landing zone

M1A1—Abrams tank

MAC—Military Airlift Command

MACV—(U.S.) Military Assistance Command, Vietnam

Maj—Major (Air Force)

MAJ—Major (Army)

Maj Gen—Major General (Air Force)

MC-130—Special Operations variant of Hercules four-engine turboprop aircraft

MEDEVAC—Medical evacuation helicopter

MEUSOCs—Marine Expeditionary Forces, Special Operations Capable

MG—Major General (Army)

MH-47—Chinook helicopter (Special Operations)

MH-53—Pave Low helicopter ("Super Jolly Green Giant") (Special Operations)

MH-60—Black Hawk helicopter (Special Operations)

MI—Military intelligence

MOS—Military occupation specialty

MQ-1—Predator armed remotely piloted aircraft

MQ-9—Reaper armed remotely
   piloted aircraft
MRE—Meals, ready to eat
MSG—Master Sergeant (Army)
MSgt—Master Sergeant (Air Force)
NATO—North Atlantic Treaty
   Organization
NBC—Nuclear, biological, chemical
NCO—Noncommissioned officer
NEO—Noncombatant evacuation
   operations
NGO—Nongovernmental
   organization
NMCC—National Military
   Command Center
NORAD—North American
   Aerospace Defense Command
NSA—National Security Agency
NSC—National Security Council
NTC—National Training Center,
   Fort Irwin, California
NVA—North Vietnamese Army
OPLAN—Operation plan
OPORDS—Operation orders
PDB—President's Daily Brief
POW—Prisoner of war
Predator—MQ-1 armed remotely
   piloted aircraft
PSYOPS—Psychological operations
PT—Physical training
PVT—Private (Army)
RADM—Rear admiral (upper half)
RDML—Rear admiral (lower half)
ROK—Republic of Korea
ROTC—Reserve Officer Training
   Corps

RPG—Rocket-propelled grenade
RPA—Remotely piloted aircraft
RPV—Remotely piloted vehicle
RQ-4—Global Hawk remotely
   piloted aircraft
RQ-170—Sentinel remotely piloted
   aircraft
SATCOM—Satellite
   communications
SCIF—Sensitive Compartmented
   Information Facility
Scud—Soviet-design ballistic missile
SECDEF—Secretary of Defense
SF—Special Forces
SFC—Sergeant First Class (Army)
SGM—Sergeant Major (Army)
SGT—Sergeant (Army)
SIGINT—Signals intelligence
SMU—Special Mission Unit
SMSgt—Senior Master Sergeant
SOCCENT—Special Operations
   Command, Central Command
SOCEUR—Special Operations
   Command Europe
SOCOM—Special Operations
   Command
SOF—Special Operations Forces
SOG—Special Operations Group
SOS—Special Operations
   Squadron
SOS—Squadron Officers School
SOW—Special Operations Wing
Spectre—AC-130 aircraft
SrA—Senior Airman
SSgt—Staff Sergeant (Air Force)
SSG—Staff Sergeant (Army)

STARS—Fulton surface-to-air recovery system

STRATCOM—U.S. Strategic Command

T-37—Tweet jet trainer aircraft

T-38—Talon jet trainer aircraft

T-41—Mescalero propeller trainer aircraft

TAC—Tactical Air Command

TACON—Tactical Control

TF—Task Force

TLAM—Tomahawk land-attack missile (cruise missile)

TOC—Tactical operations center

TOT—Time on target

TOW—Tube-launched, optically tracked, wire-guided antitank missile

TRANSCOM—United States Transportation Command (USTRANSCOM)

TSgt—Technical Sergeant

UAE—United Arab Emirates

UAV—Unmanned aerial vehicle; remotely piloted aircraft (RPA)

UBL—Usama bin Laden (spelling used by most U.S. government organizations)

UDT—Underwater demolition team

UK—United Kingdom

UN—United Nations

UPT—Undergraduate pilot training

USAF—United States Air Force

USAFA—United States Air Force Academy

USAFE—United States Air Force Europe

USAFR—United States Air Force Reserves

USSOCOM—United States Special Operations Command

USTRANSCOM—United States Transportation Command

VADM—Vice Admiral

VC—Vietcong

VFR—Visual flight rules

VTC—Video teleconference

WMD—Weapon(s) of mass destruction

WO—Warrant Officer

WWMCCS—Worldwide Military Command and Control System

XO—Executive Officer

XO—Air Force Deputy Chief of Staff for Plans and Operations

GENERAL NORTON SCHWARTZ, U.S. AIR FORCE (RET.)

General Schwartz served as the nineteenth chief of staff of the U.S. Air Force, retiring from military service in October 2012. As Chief, he served as the senior uniformed Air Force officer responsible for the organization, training, and equipping of 680,000 active duty, Guard, Reserve, and civilian forces. As a member of the Joint Chiefs of Staff, the general functioned as military advisor to the secretary of defense, National Security Council, and the president.

General Schwartz has served as Commander of the Special Operations Command-Pacific, as well as Alaskan Command, Alaskan North American Aerospace Defense Command Region, and the 11th Air Force. He was also commander, U.S. Transportation Command, where he served as the single manager for global air, land, and sea transportation for the Department of Defense.

He is a command pilot with more than 4,400 flying hours in a variety of aircraft. He participated as a crewmember in the 1975 airlift evacuation of Saigon, and in 1991 served as chief of staff of the Joint Special Operations Task Force for Northern Iraq in Operations DESERT SHIELD and DESERT STORM. In 1997, he led the joint task force that prepared for the noncombatant evacuation of U.S. citizens in Cambodia.

General Schwartz graduated from the U.S. Air Force Academy with a bachelor's degree in political science and international affairs, and from Central Michigan University with a master's degree in Business Administration. He is an alumnus of the Armed Forces Staff College and the National War College, a member of the Council on Foreign Relations, and a 1994 Fellow of MIT's Seminar XXI.

He and his wife Suzie reside in McLean, Virginia.

RONALD LEVINSON, COAUTHOR

A veteran film and television producer, director, writer, and studio executive, Ron coauthored *Without Hesitation: The Odyssey of an American Warrior*, the autobiography of General Hugh Shelton, fourteenth chairman of the Joint Chiefs of Staff, which was published by St. Martin's Press in hardcover, paperback, e-book, and audio versions. A past board member of the U.S. Air Force Public Advisory Council, Ron is a graduate of the University of Southern California, member of the Academy of Television Arts and Sciences, Blue Ribbon Emmy Awards judge, and member of the Writers Guild of Canada (recognized by the Writers Guild of America).

INDEX